EMILY DICKINSON

A Collection of Critical Essays

Edited by
Judith Farr

Eau Claire District Library

Prentice Hall, Upper Saddle River, New Jersey 07458

Library of Congress Cataloging-in-Publication Data

Dickinson, Emily, 1830–1886.
   [Essays. Selections]
   Emily Dickinson : a collection of critical essays / edited by
Judith Farr
      p.   cm.—(New century views)
   Includes bibliographical references (p.).
   ISBN 0–13–033524–X
   1. Dickinson, Emily, 1830–1886—Criticism and interpretation.
I. Farr, Judith. II. Title. III. Series.
PS1541.A6 1996
811'.4—dc20
                                 94–48010
                                     CIP

This book is dedicated with affectionate esteem to Richard B. Sewall, author of *The Life of Emily Dickinson* and editor of *Twentieth Century Views of Emily Dickinson* (Prentice Hall, 1963). In the poet's words, his "Crusade's Achieving" and his "Journey" have enabled my own.

Acquisitions editor: Tony English
Editorial/production supervision and
   interior design: Mary McDonald
Copy editor: Alice Manning
Cover design: Karen Salzbach
Buyer: Mary Ann Gloriande

 © 1996 by Prentice-Hall, Inc.
Simon & Schuster / A Viacom Company
Upper Saddle River, New Jersey 07458

Printed in the United States of America
10 9 8 7 6 5 4 3 2 1

ISBN 0-13-033524-X

Prentice-Hall International (UK) Limited, *London*
Prentice-Hall of Australia Pty. Limited, *Sydney*
Prentice-Hall Canada Inc., *Toronto*
Prentice-Hall Hispanoamericana, S.A., *Mexico*
Prentice-Hall of India Private Limited, *New Delhi*
Prentice-Hall of Japan, Inc., *Tokyo*
Simon & Schuster Asia Pte. Ltd., *Singapore*
Editora Prentice-Hall do Brazil, Ltda., *Rio de Janeiro*

Contents

The essays in this volume are reproduced in their original formats, without stan-dardization. The "Chronology of Important Dates" at the rear has been designed to describe both the significant events of Emily Dickinson's life and those that affected the publication of her poems. Since her life was largely conducted off the public stage, the "events" that befell her were frequently of a private nature—for example, the departure, death, or estrangement of a friend—although they coincide with, or may have been complicated by, such external happenings or general crises as the Civil War. It has been interesting to me to note the number of events I found it nec-essary to list, even in this partial chronology of Dickinson's supposedly quiet life.

I am indebted to the community of Dickinson scholars for insights that helped prompt the selections I have made here.

Introduction

Judith Farr

Emily Dickinson's name was known during her lifetime only to her family, her friends, and a few residents of the country town of Amherst, Massachusetts, where she lived from her birth in 1830 until her death in 1886. But today, hers is a famous name. Generally considered first among women poets, she is on the short list of celebrated Americans, and—although many of her personal characteristics and artistic practices continue to be hotly debated and disagreed about— she has become a cult figure in the United States and abroad. Now it is usual to meet her name not only on bookshelves, but on pillows and rainwear, recipe sheets and T-shirts, tote bags and stationery. The single known image made of her while alive, the daguerreotype of a shy seventeen-year-old pupil at Mary Lyon's seminary at Mount Holyoke, has been taken as a symbol of both artistry and integrity. As such, it was publicized in a commemorative stamp by the United States Post Office (1971) and employed by the National Endowment for the Arts (1991) in an ad to promote free speech. Only a few writers like "dear Dickens,"[1] as Dickinson called him, or Shakespeare, who (she said) kept literature firm, have so distinctly captured the public imagination as well as the feverish attention of professional scholars.

This may be true for several reasons. The nearly two thousand poems and hundreds of letters now officially in the Emily Dickinson canon exhibit a spacious humanity that fills a role classically attributed to artists: to see more deeply and richly than is ordinary. Dickinson's brief, acute forms and her apparently homespun though strangely magical and special diction both disarm and intrigue. The common reader has found them less daunting than more elaborate forms like the epic or ode, and most who meet her verse recognize that it presents great themes with originality and a kind of shrewd but radiant understanding. Her wisdom seeks an expression whose economies please the sophisticate by their cunning and the less canny reader by their daring. The poetic intelligence that produced such epigrams as "To multiply the Harbors does not reduce the Sea" or "Emerging from an Abyss, and reentering it—that is Life" (L, 386, 1024) seems possessed of a clarity of vision that comes from broad sympathies and fully felt experience. Enchanting with a singular intensity of image and cadence, it often voices itself in aphorisms, riddles, conundrums, and proverbs: literary formulations that have their roots in

[1]*The Letters of Emily Dickinson*, ed. Thomas H. Johnson and Theodora Ward (Cambridge, Mass.: Harvard University Press, 1958), #809. Future references within text.

folklore as in high art. Generations of readers have treasured them against the pain or perplexity life's randomness may produce.

What most interests Emily Dickinson is of interest to us all: the complex fate of human beings in this tragic yet beautiful world and the possible fortunes of the human spirit in a subsequent life. Scholars and poets praise her. But as with Dickens and Shakespeare, a smitten public created Emily Dickinson's fame, responding not only to her words upon the page but to the artistic personality that these admirers imagined. After intermittent periods of neglect—perhaps attributable to the mangled texts produced by Dickinson's friends and family—which were the only ones available until the 1950s—and to the legends about her conduct that made her seem a mere eccentric, not a genius—that fame is now worldwide.

She herself deemed fame "a fickle food / Upon a shifting plate,"[2] declaring fatalistically that, while she would not court it by seeking to "print,"[3] if fame were hers, she could not escape it. Evidence suggests that in the late 1850s and early 1860s, as she was entering scores of poems into the sewn packets that are now called "fascicles," Emily Dickinson hoped to make her already aristocratic family prouder by achieving the honorable name *poet*. (Indeed, she wrote so to her brother Austin and to her best friend Susan Gilbert, his wife.[4]) Several factors, however, seem ultimately to have discouraged her from publishing. One was probably the maddeningly imperfect understanding of her poetic methods shown by intimate editor-friends like Thomas Wentworth Higginson, who counseled her to change them. Another, perhaps, was her acceptance of upper-class Victorian notions that a true lady does not exhibit herself. In her poem "Publication—is the Auction / Of the Mind of Man—" (*P*, 709), she declares publishing "foul" with fastidious and spirited hauteur. Even Susan Dickinson, whose collaboration in her poetic career she early counted upon, had ambivalent feelings about well-born women broadcasting their sentiments in the fashion of women scribblers (as Hawthorne contemptuously called them) like Lydia Sigourney or Harriet Beecher Stowe. On the few occasions when Dickinson's poems appeared in a newspaper or anthology during her lifetime, it was not with her consent. Indeed, after "A narrow fellow in the grass" came out in the *Springfield Republican* (1866), she sent a rather anguished note to Higginson. Its last line implies her fear of seeming both unladylike and conceited: "Lest you meet my Snake and suppose I deceive [by claiming not to publish] it was robbed of me—defeated too of the third line by the punctuation. The third and fourth were one—I had told you I did not print—I feared you might think me ostensible" (316).

---

[2]*The Poems of Emily Dickinson*, ed. Thomas H. Johnson (Cambridge, Mass.: Harvard University Press, 1955), 1659. Future references within text.

[3]Her usual word for "publish." See letter 316 to T. W. Higginson. "Print" was the accepted synonym for "publish" in the nineteenth century; thus, a reviewer of Dickinson's *Poems* (1890) comments that the poet "was singularly averse to print" (cf. Willis J. Buckingham, *Emily Dickinson's Reception in the 1890s*, [Pittsburgh: University of Pittsburgh Press, 1989], 34). But some recent textual scholars interpret the word as an allusion to "print[ing]," a proof of her awareness that the idiosyncratic visual configuration of her poems would resist the printing conventions of her time. Thus, they reason, Dickinson chose private forms of "publication."

[4]See letter 238 of summer 1861.

Today, scholars are deeply interested in Dickinson's lineation—that is, her arrangement of lines and line lengths in the fascicles, which is frequently different from that in the posthumously printed texts. Her concern for the visual/verbal effect of her poem and her dismay at its alteration are now seen as aesthetically based. Engagingly, when the third and fourth lines of her "Snake" lyric are, as she intended, unpunctuated, they clarify the action she describes. She writes:

A narrow Fellow in the Grass
Occasionally rides—
You may have met Him—did you not
His notice sudden is—(*P*, 986)

That is: If you haven't met and do not know snakes, they nevertheless instantly notice you. By omitting punctuation after "not," Dickinson describes the breathless immediacy of this experience.[5] (She may also have wanted close rhyme on the related sounds of "not[e]" and "notice," a habit of wordplay evident in other poems.) The *Republican's* editors, however, rendered her lines more commonplace, by using a comma: "You may have met him—did you not, / His notice sudden is."

For almost thirty years, Dickinson was a hard-working poet. She was especially prolific between 1860 and 1865. During this period of keen creativity, probably stimulated by personal anguish, she copied around three hundred poems into the notebooks each year. At some point, she renounced publication and "published," instead, in the fascicles she hid in her room and in many letters to friends that enclosed poems. Thus she concealed her formidable poetic gifts and yet revealed them in the guises permitted mid-Victorian women: private expression and social communication. That unlike the Brontës, George Sand, or George Eliot (whose works she admired), Emily Dickinson never wrote under a male pseudonym illustrates her sensibility. Her genuine reticence and her fierce sense of personal integrity would not, I think, have permitted her to mask and then advertise herself. Moreover, her poems—unlike their works, which were chiefly novels—were composed increasingly to please her own taste and no one else's, with an ever-developing conviction that "Glory" such as comes to famous women "is a bright [but] tragic thing" (1660).

Significantly, however, she gave no instructions that the forty notebooks and loose poems lying in a locked box in her bedroom be destroyed. The story of how her sister Lavinia opened the box after Emily's funeral, discovered more poems than she ever supposed her sister had written, and determined to see them into print is one of the great episodes of American literary history. To the Dickinson family, exacerbated by feuds and by Austin Dickinson's adultery with Mabel Loomis Todd, fell the task of presenting or suppressing the poet's life work. Their own passions—weirdly suggestive of the powerful feelings that animate the Dickinson poems—were to divide the family for decades and separate the poems into rival caches: Those sponsored by Susan Dickinson's daughter, Martha

---

[5]Cf. Kamilla Denman's discussion of these lines in her essay in this volume.

Dickinson Bianchi, and those edited by Mabel Todd and her daughter, Millicent Todd Bingham. Because Lavinia Dickinson did not believe with Emily that "literature [like love] is its [own] exceeding great reward" (*L*, 410), she wanted her sister's accomplishments publicly acknowledged. Disappointed by Sue, to whom she first appealed, she persuaded Mabel Todd, assisted by T. W. Higginson, to edit the poems and approach Roberts Brothers of Boston about printing them. Fearful of sending into a mannerly, late-Tennysonian climate such seemingly irreverent witticisms as "to note the fashions—of the Cross" (from the boldly introspective "I measure every Grief I meet" [*P*, 561), and rightly aware that Dickinson's singular punctuation and metrics would provoke rebuke, they began the process of modifying the poet's work.

To this day, no printed text, with the exception of R. W. Franklin's facsimile edition of *The Manuscript Books*, presents all the poems of Emily Dickinson just as she copied them into her fascicles. (Franklin is now preparing a new, much-needed variorum edition of the poems that will address such problems as her lineation.) The Todd-Higginson-Dickinson *Poems* (1890) became a best-seller, although many of the poems were shorn of some of the poet's lines, supplied with inappropriate but fashionable titles, and weakened by forced rhymes and substituted words. Subsequent editions, like *The Complete Poems of Emily Dickinson*, first brought out in 1914 by Martha Dickinson Bianchi and still extant, also tampered with the poems. It was not until 1955, with the publication of Thomas H. Johnson's *Poems of Emily Dickinson* taken from her manuscripts, that her public learned of stanzas in Dickinson's verse with which they were wholly unacquainted, words that they had never seen. They also met a highly idiosyncratic Emily Dickinson, who took special pleasure in dashes, capitals, and irregular orthography.

Johnson's restorations often revealed the accuracy and power of the poet's diction. So, for example, Dickinson's line "Cornice—in the Ground" in "Because I could not stop for Death—" had been changed by Todd and Higginson to "The cornice but a mound," suggesting that she regarded a *cornice* or horizontal molding as a dirt pile. (What she describes in that great surreal poem about dying, of course, is the sinking of the headstone of a grave after many years. Not only is Dickinson almost invariably precise for precision's sake; she had an interest in architecture and enjoyed rendering shapes meticulously.) Because of crucial restorations such as this one to poem 712, Johnson's text was adopted as foundational.

But Johnson also arranged the Dickinson poems in traditional metric forms such as the quatrain or triplet, which, contemporary critics like Susan Howe (or Jerome McGann in this volume) argue, cannot always be confidently discerned from the handwritten texts. Johnson assumed that lines flush left in Dickinson's fascicles were turnover lines (for example, that "A narrow Fellow in the Grass," with "the Grass" set out as a separate entry against the left margin, is one line) and that Dickinson adopted this traditional device for continuing a line from lack of writing space—an assumption which the appearance of her handwritten text does, in this case, justify. For current textual critics, however, the first stanza of the fascicle poem of "A narrow Fellow" has, indubitably, six *lines*, and the line that Dickinson calls her third (in her letter to Higginson) should properly be called her fourth and fifth. Quite simply though controversially, they insist that the way her words appear reveals intent. Moreover, for these critics, the fascicles take precedence even over other transcriptions made by the poet herself, for the fascicles, in their view, are Dickinson's private and therefore most genuine poetic documents, her public transcriptions being possible compromises in accord with mid-Victorian taste.

To objections that the poet herself might not have intended her poems to be viewed as experiments in form, some argue (as her editors have from the first) that Dickinson's intentions either are unimportant or cannot be known.[6] An additional complication is that Dickinson may form a poem differently in different contexts. The poem "Take all away from me, but leave me Ecstasy" (1640) is recorded in a note to Helen Hunt Jackson (976) as a quatrain, but in a letter to Samuel Bowles the younger (1014) as prose. In fact, her occasional indifference to maintaining classic spatial distinctions between her "poetry" and her "prose" has even encouraged the appearance of a collection of lines from her letters as *New Poems of Emily Dickinson.*[7]

Yet the immediacy of Dickinson's voice survives. In all extant versions, its meditations on such lasting themes as "Life," "Love," "Nature," and "Time and Eternity"—Higginson's cosmic categories for *Poems* (1890)—have somehow triumphed over the editorial hand. Today, we would complicate those early categories to show that her subjects include the sexual roles of men and women, both within and without the marriage covenant; the burden of being female; the responsibilities, fears, and blessings afforded by an artist's life; the problem of religious doubt. But however its subject matter is described, the voice of Emily Dickinson has influenced her listeners from the first. Ever since 1890, the fame for which she expressed both desire and distaste has become—and remains increasingly—hers.

---

[6]In *Black Riders* (Princeton, N.J.: Princeton University Press, 1993), Jerome McGann writes, "it does no good to argue . . . that [Dickinson's] odd lineations are unintentional. . . . Besides, certain textual moments reveal such a dramatic use of page space as to put the question of intentionality beyond consideration" (28). F. O. Matthiessen anticipated the judgment that Dickinson's variants—which McGann sees as creative parts, sometimes conclusions, of her poems (*op. cit.*, 38)—should be noted as intrinsic to them. He wrote in 1945 in "The Private Poet," "even several of the best known [poems] must be printed ultimately as private poems still, with the variants noted [on] the page." He also engaged the current textual debate on the same footing, saying "If we are to enter into the full nature of what it meant to be a poet in [Emily Dickinson's] circumstances, we must print each manuscript *in toto* as the special case it is." (See *The Recognition of Emily Dickinson*, ed. Caesar R. Blake and Carlton F. Wells, [Ann Arbor: University of Michigan Press, 1964], 231.)

[7]Edited by William H. Shurr et al. (Chapel Hill: University of North Carolina Press, 1993). Among the "poems" this book presents are lines or groups of lines that Dickinson on no occasion indicated that she thought of as finished poems; thus, for example, "To him to whom Events and Omens / are at last the same," a line from letter 1006, becomes Shurr's "new poem" 436.

2

Though we know much more about Emily Dickinson than about many famous writers, the historical personage who bore that name (variously transmuting it to "Emilie," "Miss Emily E. Dickinson," "Uncle Emily," or just "Dickinson") continues to be viewed as mysterious. The dates of her birth and death, the facts of her schooling, her background and parentage, and the few places she saw besides Amherst—namely, Boston, Cambridge, Monson, and East Hadley, Massachusetts; Philadelphia; and Washington—are easy enough to isolate. But there are different accounts of her temperament and multiple interpretations of the cardinal traits of her behavior.

To choose an obvious and instructive example, there is the question of her reclusion. From about 1860, she ceased to visit people's houses. (A letter of autumn 1869, in which she says to Susan Dickinson, "I humbly try to fill your place at the Minister's" [333], shows her still abroad socially, but such occasions had become rare.) As a "belle of Amherst" (*L*, 6), she had once enjoyed buggy rides, dancing, parlor games, and other forms of merriment. Then, for reasons that are not clear, she became a semirecluse; over time, even old friends were turned from her door. Before she died, she had taken to having others address her envelopes, as if even her handwriting must be kept from view. This is the cracked if amiable poetess who appears in novels and plays, poised at her second-story window, ready to reel down gingerbread to the local children in her little basket. Was she an agoraphobe, a *poseuse* (as her brother claimed), a nun self-dedicated to Art, the Elizabeth Barrett–like victim of a repressive father's claims on her; or was she an actress in a drama she invented to amuse and call attention to herself? Did she withdraw from the larger world (she sent a carriage to fetch chosen ones to see her until the end) out of disappointed love?[8]

Some Dickinson critics have advised setting aside all such questions. But it is unlikely that that will happen. Lyric poetry, in particular, has substantial investment in a poet's life—if not from actual deeds, then from thinking and dreaming.

---

[8]See in order: for agoraphobia, Martha Dickinson Bianchi, *Life and Letters* (Boston and New York: Houghton Mifflin, 1924); for Dickinson's adoption of the mid-Victorian emblem/mask of the nun, see Judith Farr, *The Passion of Emily Dickinson* (Cambridge, Mass.: Harvard University Press, 1992); for self-dramatization, Sandra Gilbert and Susan Gubar, *The Madwoman in the Attic* (New Haven, Conn.: Yale University Press, 1979); for Edward Dickinson's influence, Vivian R. Pollock, *Dickinson* (Ithaca, N.Y.: Cornell University Press, 1984); for neurotic effects induced by the Dickinson household, John Cody, *After Great Pain* (Cambridge, Mass.: Harvard University Press, 1921) and Cynthia Griffin Wolff, *Emily Dickinson* (New York: Alfred A. Knopf, 1986). Jane Eberwein in *Dickinson, Strategies of Limitation* (Amherst, Mass.: The University of Massachusetts Press, 1985) discusses the usefulness of reclusion and a reputation for eccentricity to a woman poet. Most contemporary critics treat some impediment to a fulfilled love relationship as a possible catalyst in Dickinson's semiretirement. Few regard the latter (in the fashion of earlier biographers) as the exact result of a "love disaster." See Richard Sewall, *The Life of Emily Dickinson* (New York: Farrar, Straus, Giroux, 1974), especially pp. 152–56, for an account of the disastrous love myth. Sewall's view (154) that Dickinson's life "is not to be explained by any one 'love disaster' " and his emphasis on the gradualness of her retirement—he entertains (though does not fully believe) Lavinia's explanation that it was "just a happen"—have been important in modifying earlier, more dramatic accounts of Dickinson's behavior.

And this particular lyric poet writes, and puns on, "I" and "eye" hundreds of times. Many other lyrics—for example, the large group of poems written to "Signor," "Sir," and "Master"—seem to reflect a confessional intensity harrowing to their readers. One wants to compare their searing self-inquiry and anecdotal specificity to works of Keats or Byron appreciated by Emily Dickinson, though her tone, unlike theirs, is typically charged with reticence and her verbal structures and techniques differ.

Lyrics like the Master poems[9] invent a substantial narrative whose emblematic metaphors draw life from chosen texts and paintings of Dickinson's day. Although the unattainable Master is characterized as her lover for all eternity, her language with its (as I think) pointed allusions to current artifacts also places him in the "now." A reader encountering poems that describe the poet's "Lifetime folding up" under the spell of an absolute commitment that makes her "A Member of the Cloud" (*P*, 273), a reader aware that the poet indeed became a semihermit after age thirty, is likely to ask questions.

The Dickinson family—upon being questioned—named a number of different men for whom Emily gave up the world. Yet the Master in the poems seems not only human, with specific characteristics, but godlike. Is "Master" a kind of Christian Muse but historic personage[10] whose beautiful and forbidden face (she dwells on that face repeatedly) inspires her sense of destiny as a poet? Did she think it a destiny that, since nineteenth-century America enjoined social obligations on women, forced her to choose retirement and even eccentricity as the means of being free to write? Emily Dickinson was a known sceptic, one of the few girls at Mary Lyon's Seminary who never professed Christ, yet she was a close reader of Thomas à Kempis' *The Imitation of Christ* and described herself as Christ's "Bride" (817). Was hers a mystical union with the Master who transcends masters? Was "Master," despite the masculine figure and language she assigns to him, really a woman: either Kate Scott Anthon or Susan Dickinson?[11] Was

---

[9]As I have suggested in my book *The Passion of Emily Dickinson* (178–244).

[10]The chief candidates for a real Master are the minister Charles Wadsworth (see, for example, Wolff, op. cit., Sherwood, *Circumference and Circumstance: Stages in the Mind and Art of Emily Dickinson* (New York: Columbia University Press, 1968), and Pollak, op cit.) and the editor Samuel Bowles (see Sewall, op. cit., Higgins, *Portrait of Emily Dickinson: The Poet and Her Prose* (New Brunswick, N.J.: Rutgers University Press, 1967), and Farr, op. cit.).

[11]Rebecca Patterson's *The Riddle of Emily Dickinson* (Boston: Houghton Mifflin, 1951) identified Dickinson's forbidden, not-quite-requiting lover as a beautiful widow, Mrs. Anthon, a friend of both Emily and Sue. She was derisively treated for introducing the possibility that Dickinson had lesbian proclivities. But Patterson is now regarded as both prophet and forerunner by apologists for Dickinson-as-lesbian: see, for example, Paula Bennett, *Emily Dickinson, Woman Poet* (Iowa City: University of Iowa Press, 1991), ix. A growing number of writers, including myself, identify Susan Gilbert Dickinson as the person Dickinson chiefly loved, but there is disagreement about whether the poet (always or only sometimes) consciously saw herself as a lesbian in the contemporary carnal sense of the word, or whether hers was an exalted romantic attachment such as Lillian Faderman or Carroll Smith-Rosenberg describe in their respective books, *Surpassing the Love of Men: Romantic Friendship and Love between Women from the Renaissance to the Present* (New York: William Morrow, 1981) and *Disorderly Conduct: Visions of Gender in Victorian America* (New York, 1985). Some writers in this debate, which has prompted partisan feeling, speak of critics who "privilege" the Master materials as belonging to a

Dickinson a neurotic spinster, afraid in her mature years of venturing into society, who embroidered a trope of blighted passion to excuse and protect herself? (As Barton Levi St. Armand explains in *Emily Dickinson and Her Culture: The Soul's Society* (Cambridge: Cambridge University Press, 1984), such tropes were endemic to mid-Victorian literature.) Are all these interpretations true, in whole or in part? Such questions keep Dickinson scholarship lively as well as thorny.

Just as it is essential to consult a dictionary regularly in reading Emily Dickinson—she preferred to use words in more than their primary meaning—one profits from an appeal to the poet herself in weighing biographical matters. Her letters, read in the context of sociological data collected in a logbook like Jay Leyda's *Years and Hours of Emily Dickinson* (New Haven, Conn.: Yale University Press, 1960), provide great insight into such issues as her hermeticism. True, we must recall that her letters themselves are, from about 1858 on, conscious and conscientious works of art. They are artistic documents that reflect a heightened self-conception and an ardor for arresting language that results in aphorisms ("The crucifix requires no glove"[*L*, 539]). Furthermore, they may record different kinds of "evidence" at different times. But they still reveal.

Thus she tells Austin at age twenty-three, "I ran home . . . for fear somebody would see me" (*L*, 254). She complains in middle age of her "Cowardice of Strangers" (*L*, 716). Writing to the urbane Judge Otis Lord, wooing her when she is fifty-two, she asks pardon for her provincial awkwardness and "rustic love" (*L*, 750). To Susan Dickinson,[12] she writes that she is ill at ease at Sue's soirées, "a sorry figure in a drawingroom"; she is "from the fields," best at home "with the Dandelion" or with Sue alone. Higginson complained after he visited her in the Dickinson mansion that she "drained [his] nerve power"; he was "glad not to live near her" [*L*, 342a]. Samuel Bowles, however, found her funny, charming, and sociable. When she was twenty-four, Edward Dickinson had to persuade her to visit him in Washington, where guests at the Willard Hotel recalled how amusing she was. But by age thirty-six, Emily uses him as an excuse to Higginson for not leaving the house: "[Father] likes me to travel with him but objects that I visit" (*L*, 319). Austin Dickinson recalled that his sister's letters could be too "high up,"[13] too absorbed by introspective rapture, to provide news. Then there is a line written by the young Emily at Mary Lyon's. She has been left alone for a day and records, "I enjoyed the solitude finely" (*L*, 16).

"heterosexual tradition" (Bennett, 210). Martha Nell Smith in *Rowing in Eden: Rereading Emily Dickinson* (Austin: University of Texas Press, 1992) finds Dickinson specifically alluding in the poems and letters to lesbian intercourse, joins others in regarding the Dickinson/Sue relationship as "powerfully sensual" (129), and seeks the final solution to problems of the "Master" by identifying a transvestite Sue as that figure. In my own view, the Master and Sue are different persons who inspire different responses, different poems. But one must, I believe, acknowledge Sue's absolute importance in the poet's life. For theirs was the longest of Dickinson's ardent relationships, lasting almost forty years, and it permanently fulfilled itself in numerous letters and letter-poems of profound and complex feeling. No one has yet claimed any indisputable evidence for the sexual consummation of this romance of the heart, just as there is no evidence for any other consummation(s).

[12]In a letter acquired in 1992 by Amherst College.

[13]See *Leyda, Years and Hours of Emily Dickinson*, I, 203.

Dickinson scholars sift all these materials for interpretation. What many have glimpsed is the image of a complicated, intense woman whose ultimate avoidance of social excitements may have been induced by no one cause. She was not unlike other New England writers—Emerson or Hawthorne or Thoreau—in her avoidance of most company. Certainly she seems to have experienced an acute, ever-developing shyness, but it served as support for a burning need to write. Early Dickinson scholarship has sometimes divorced Emily Dickinson from her place in time, whereas remembering that placement is essential to understanding her, both as a person and as a writer. In the matter of her reclusion, for example, one should recall that mid-Victorian America often associated the achievement of high art with the reclusion of the artist. *The Atlantic Monthly*, read ravenously by Emily Dickinson, recommended in January 1860, at the height of her creativity, that anyone who wanted to be an "artist" "must be lifted away and isolated from worldly surroundings [and] must be alone." The word *artist* would strongly have commended itself to her, for the prestige of the Hudson River and Pre-Raphaelite painters was very great—not only in her culture but in her own family.[14] Indeed, not only did the painting traditions of the nineteenth century encourage her choice of subject matter, they gave her symbolic motifs, defined visual images of which she made emblems, and probably influenced the lineal arrangements of her poems.[15] Painting was the art form she consistently chose to describe her writing; the name of Thomas Cole, founder of American landscape painting, the pseudonym she amusedly adopted for herself as a writer-draftsman (*L, 214*).[16] Like the art journals collected by Austin and Sue, the *Atlantic* often described the activities of contemporary painters such as Thomas Cole, Frederic Edwin Church, and Sanford Gifford. These men were famed for their periodic reclusiveness, disappearing for months or even years when engaged in a project. As a secluded artist, Dickinson might have seen herself belonging spiritually to their company.

That the artist's life, always excepting the novelist's or theatre person's, ought to be solitary was a Romantic notion that survived into the mid-Victorian age and beyond. The New England Impressionist painter John H. Twachtman wrote his fellow painter Alden Weir in 1891, "To be isolated is a fine thing and we are then nearer to nature."[17] Joined with the concept of an exalted love as both selective and renunciatory—the grieving widow, Queen Victoria, speaking from behind half-open doors or refusing company was a familiar image to Emily Dickinson—this notion would suggest that an artist in love with the muse could rewardingly sequester herself. And for a woman artist, such sequestration

[14]The Austin Dickinson family collected Hudson River and American Pre-Raphaelite paintings. See St. Armand, op. cit., 250–55.

[15]The intensely personal importance of painting for Dickinson and her poetry is treated at length in Farr, op. cit. passim.

[16]In her essay in this volume, Martha Nell Smith discusses Dickinson's drawing in relation to her "comic power."

[17]Quoted in H. Barbara Weinberg, Doreen Bolger, and David Park Curry, *American Impressionism and Realism, The Painting of Modern Life, 1885–1915* (New York: Harry N. Abrams, Inc., 1994), 61.

allowed the abrogation of societal demands. This may have been incitement, comfort, or both to her after 1860. Of course, the tradition of the poet in the tower is espoused only by a person who likes towers. Dickinson's "tower," at the top of her house, she called her "northwest passage": that is, the passage to the orient, *Orient* being one of her synonyms for art.

To see Emily Dickinson whole requires reviewing a multitude of considerations. In all biographical matters, a reader will profitably recall her "*My* business is to love" and "My Business is Circumference" (*L*, 269, 268). *Circumference* was her Emersonian term for poetry, the sum of meaning. Her real business, she claimed, was writing poetry. But human love was intrinsic to poetry, she thought, and not necessarily displaced by it. Though in many of her poetic techniques she seems so modern, she was not *ars gratia artis* in her sympathies; she never ruthlessly canonized art above life, as some modern poetry does. ("Art's inner Summer," she wrote, was "never Treason to Nature's" [*L*, 1004].) Indeed, in "Circumference, thou bride" (*L*, 898), one of her finest poems on the artistic process, she explains writing in the language of, and as an act of, passion. If we are to trust what Dickinson writes in letters as in poems, she was much experienced in loving. But she compares love to a book whose "chapter . . . in the night" (*L*, 645), or sexual fulfillment, she never experienced.

Her writings suggest that she did not wholly wish to. Using her frequent equation of sexual love with food, she told Otis Lord when she was forty-eight that "it is Anguish I long conceal from you to let you leave me, hungry, but you ask the divine Crust and that would doom the Bread" (*L*, 562). That is, she must let them both remain "hungry"—the word applies to both "me" and "you"—for, although she suffers in saying so, she cannot marry him. To marry, or give him her "divine Crust," would destroy her essential nature, the "Bread"—her life, as bread is the "staff of life." Her phrase is finely paradoxical, for crusts, often discarded, are a common image for what is dispensable, but in reality they protect the bread. By yielding up her privacy and name in marriage, she would lose her self. One remembers that a central trope of her poetry is having by *not* having, satisfaction in renunciation. So central is it, indeed, that I have included in this collection three essays—by Richard Wilbur, Vivian R. Pollak, and Joan Burbick—which approach it with different insights and strategies. Certainly, for Dickinson, "Water, is taught by thirst" and the "light," to which she likens passion, by darkness (*P*, 135, 611).

One of Emily Dickinson's poems, written around 1861, seems both an answer to the question of her retired life and an apologia for it. It is a description of sublime entertainments:

Alone, I cannot be—
For Hosts—do visit me—
Recordless Company
Who baffle Key—

They have no Robes, nor Names—
No Almanacs—nor Climes—
But general Homes
Like Gnomes—

Their Coming, may be known
By Couriers within—
Their going—is not—
For they're never gone—
                    (298)

The speaker of this poem is never solitary; she is visited by the angels of Art. Since Dickinson's frame of reference here is Christian, Puritan, and Transcendental, and since her Bible was one of the three texts essential to her (the others being Shakespeare's complete works and Webster's dictionary [1847]), she makes her muses the "Hosts" of Scripture. She might sign herself to Higginson "Your Gnome" (*L*, 280), *gnomes* being, in folklore, ageless, deformed dwarfs who live in the earth and guard buried treasure. This was her way of conceding that her verse had the cryptic peculiarities he censured as odd or metrically deformed, like the verse of the Victorian "Spasmodics." Calling herself a gnome playfully acknowledged her withdrawal from society. And yet, dramatically, it was her sign that she possessed the profoundly fundamental responses to experience that true creators need. In her poem, her *Hosts* are gnomic; they transcend sex, time, and place ("Robes," "Names," "Almanacs," "Climes"). They come to her, but she also sends for them, since "known / By Couriers within" may be interpreted as either external communication recognized by the speaker or a thrill of rapture—she sometimes calls it "Transport" (*P*, 167)—that animates the speaker herself. Emily Dickinson told T. W. Higginson, "I find ecstasy in living" (*L*, 342a), an enigmatic claim, it might seem, for an *isolata*. Yet her poem explains it. Alone, she is forever in the presence of the transcendent.

3

From 1890 until about 1974, debate flourished about whether Emily Dickinson is a major poet. In his *Life* (1974), Richard Sewall still found it necessary to answer the question often asked of him: "Just how good is she?" (706); therefore, I take that date as marginally ultimate. Few, I think, would pose such a question now. New questions arise, however, as to how or where Dickinson's writing should be placed in the literary tradition; and to traditional or old answers, new ones are being added.

In "Emily Dickinson among the Victorians" (1947),[18] George F. Whicher echoed a judgment made immediately subsequent to the appearance of *Poems* (1890). Mindful of the deficient understanding of her art characteristic of such editors as Higginson, and faced with the verse itself (its dazzlingly willful intricacies, its frequent avoidance of superficial regularity—in metrics, in tonality, even in spelling or what we would now call the look of the text), Whicher declared, "Emily Dickinson revolted from the literary standards to which her

[18]A lecture delivered at Johns Hopkins, afterwards included in his *Poetry and Civilization* (Ithaca: Cornell University Press, 1955), 41–62.

age paid deference." He then went on to propose the two alternative traditions to which her art has been most frequently assigned: She had a "temperamental affinity with the metaphysical poets" and "she stands as a precursor of the modern mind."

This viewpoint is predictable. Dickinson's metaphysical qualities are almost everywhere evident, easily emblematized in such a line as "the numerals of Eden" (*L*, 664), in which the word *Eden* (much used in her day as a metaphor for consummate sensual delight) is linked—as Donne links himself, his wife, and a compass—to arithmetic.[19] That her poetry has informed modern poetry we learn from modern poets themselves. From the first, some of her best critics have been themselves distinguished poets. Anthony Hecht and Richard Wilbur, in this volume, bring to the study of her verse an imaginative empathy and a technical knowledge that emerges from their own mastery of the craft. Hecht names Theodore Roethke, e. e. cummings, Richard Wilbur, Robert Frost, and W. H. Auden as men whose verse pays her the tribute of imitation; I would add the names of T. S. Eliot, William Carlos Williams, Hart Crane, and Robert Bly (who once imagined death as crossing a distance by night to the "chapel" of Dickinson's grave[20]). To a whole line of women writers from Marianne Moore and Louise Bogan to Elizabeth Bishop and Adrienne Rich, she has been, in feminist parlance, a "foremother." Calling Dickinson "modern" or "crypto-modern" is a facile generalization from qualities that she does indeed project: her religious skepticism, her pleasure in forms that dodge perfect closure, her habit of pitting against the tetrameter superstructure associated with hymns (thus with the order that faith enables) fidgety and even violent rhythmic currents that suggest doubt. And there is the often bleak intellectuality that David Porter analyzes in this book. Still, the question lingers: Does either "modern" or "metaphysical" quite catch the character of Dickinson's writing?

She has, of course, been compared to and distinguished from the Romantics.[21] That Puritanism contributed to her complex formation as child and woman is incontestable. Yet, as Richard Wilbur reminds us, her Puritan roots were often challenged by her vocabulary. Indeed, Allen Tate, although conceding her Puritan qualities, added, "Cotton Mather would have burnt her for a witch."[22] Even characteristics common to medieval verse have been located in the art of Emily

---

[19]So metaphysical has she always seemed that Mabel Loomis Todd designated a stanza of George Herbert's "Matins," copied (and altered) by Emily Dickinson, as a Dickinson poem. Dickinson's pencil markings of certain metaphysical poems may be seen in the Houghton Library collection of her books. As I inferred in 1961 (in "Compound Manner" [reprinted in Edwin H. Cady and Louis J. Budd, eds., *On Dickinson*, {Durham, N.C.: Duke University Press, 1990}]), the markings suggest her own interest in these poets.

[20]In "Visiting Emily's Dickinson's Grave with Robert Francis" in *Man in the Black Coat Turns* (1981).

[21]See, for example, Joanne Feit Diehl, *Dickinson and the Romantic Imagination* (Princeton, N.J.: Princeton University Press, 1981).

[22]In "New England Culture and Emily Dickinson," reprinted in Blake and Wells, eds., *The Recognition of Emily Dickinson*, 167.

Dickinson[23]; and, I suppose, the chief theme of her love poems—adoration, carnal and spiritual, with no hope of consummation—might be said to constitute a special continuance of the courtly love tradition. Yet among those listed so far, "medieval" seems the category least appropriate to her poetry.

For years, if and when Dickinson was taught in the graduate schools, she was presented as a "Transcendentalist" in the company of Emerson, whose *Poems* (1850) was one of her favorite texts. For her, it is true, the natural world was of transcendental significance, this world holding the possible implication of a world unseen. Her great preoccupation is not love, not death, but the question of eternal life, of consciousness beyond the grave. So a large number of her poems devote themselves to the moment of translation from earth to a variously imagined "heaven." But, as Suzanne Juhasz's essay shows here, she had a relentlessly measuring mind that confronts and details and inspects. It finally deflates the airy elevation of the Transcendental mode.

In what tradition might Emily Dickinson have placed herself? In some poems like "I would not paint—a picture—," she seems (modestly? deviously? puckishly?) not to include herself among poets at all. Rather, she muses:

What would the Dower be,
Had I the Art to stun myself
With Bolts of Melody!
(505)

To be stunned, to be surprised: This was, to her, writing or hearing poetry. Her metaphysical play on *bolts*, or shafts (like arrows), and thunder*bolts* harmonizes with her vision of an art founded in nature, especially in its most acute and expressive forms. Her lines might suggest to us an aesthetic not particularly manifest in lyric poetry of the 1860s, with a few exceptions like that of a favorite, Robert Browning. Yet when she wrote Higginson to ask him if her verse was "alive" (*L*, 260), she did not prepare him to regard it as either experimental or retrogressive. As a group, the writers she told him she had taken as teachers were Victorian: John Ruskin (the importance of *Modern Painters* to her is fundamental) and both Brownings.[24] Elizabeth Barrett Browning was, she wrote, the "Foreign Lady" who converted her mind, sanctified her soul, and taught her the magic that was poetry (*P*, 593). With Tennyson as poet laureate of the age—once rare, then disappointing, but still absorbing even in his sexist mode of *The Princess*—she was (with conflicting emotions) so engaged as to see him in dreams. The pictures of Carlyle, George Eliot, and George Sand hung on her wall.

There is hypothetical evidence that Dickinson regretted the cost to her of divergences between her own style and what was popular. That she put an X in her copy of Emerson's *Poems* next to "Woodnotes," for instance, has always seemed to

[23]See William Robert Sherwood, *Circumference and Circumstance: Stages in the Mind and Art of Emily Dickinson* (1968), passim.
[24]See Letter 261, 25 April 1861.

me poignant, for this poem by Emerson laments, "hard / Is the fortune of the bard, / Born out of time." Nevertheless, Emily Dickinson was—indisputably—a mid-Victorian. The word *Victorian*, of course, is tainted for some. It is infected by implications of sentimentality (to which Dickinson could occasionally be given), synonymous with inert, empty forms and pompous rhetoric. To associate the word *Victorian* with Dickinson, to place her in her own era, may provoke outrage and even moral censure. To do so, one critic claims,[25] is to be "ungrateful" to Emily Dickinson, whose art strove "to exist on a different plane altogether." Dickinson's poetry, like that of the Victorian Gerard Manley Hopkins, to which it is often compared, does live on a singular plane of its own. Indeed, the qualifying characteristic of all great lyric verse is that it transcends its place in time. But because she took and translated so much—subjects, themes, topical diction, a Ruskinian aesthetic—from the art and culture of her day, it is useful, even imperative, to recognize Emily Dickinson as she was: a remarkable—or, if one likes, an exceptional—mid-Victorian.

4

In the last twenty-five years, a further classification has been proposed for Dickinson's poetry; that is, as one of the most distinguished examples of a tradition of "women's writing." Certain characteristics of Emily Dickinson's style—for example, her multiplicity of attitudes, her verbal indirection, what is regarded as her generalized antagonism, and (a touchstone of today's criticism) her subversion of inherited or traditional stances toward experience—make her, it is argued, a gender-conscious (if not gender-defined) poet and the archetypical practitioner of "woman's language."[26] Underlying this premise is the supposition that, as Julia Kristeva argues, there is such a thing as *écriture féminine* that is basically negative and distinct from mainstream literature (that being, by definition, masculine and positive, as befits men's superior political and social power).[27] Supporting the concept of "woman's language" is also Sandra M. Gilbert and Susan Gubar's premise in *The Madwoman in the Attic* that historically when women wrote, they did so under sociological constraints that wholly affected their reception and translation of experience. Some feminist critics see a woman writer like Dickinson as the citizen of a separate country from male writers. One critic insists that men and women think and read differently, and that they therefore write differently.[28]

---

[25]Helen Vendler, "The Unsociable Soul," *The New Republic*, August 3, 1992, 37.

[26]Cristanne Miller, *Emily Dickinson, A Poet's Grammar*, (Cambridge, Mass.: Harvard University Press, 1987), 161, 162. Miller's final chapter, "The Consent of Language and the Woman Poet," is one of the ablest overviews of feminist interpretations of Emily Dickinson, and I am indebted to it in my own summary.

[27]See *Desire in Language: A Semiotic Approach to Literature and Art*, trans. Leon S. Roudiez, Alice Jardine, and Thomas Gora (New York: Columbia University Press, 1982), passim.

[28]See Margaret Homans, *Women Writers and Poetic Identity: Dorothy Wordsworth, Emily Bronte, and Emily Dickinson* (Princeton, N.J.: Princeton University Press, 1980).

Arguments like this last are reminiscent of folklore, popular psychology, vaudeville jokes, and cartoon literature, but they are also articulated in some of the more thoughtful works of such writers as Virginia Woolf. They are efforts to explain and justify Dickinson's fondness for obliquity and syntactical disruption as opposed to what is deemed "linear," and thus "male," verbal arrangement.

Emily Dickinson's poems seem both to fit and to escape such stylistic categories. On one hand, for example, her pleasure in ellipsis, in exquisite subtleties, in private Dickinson-language (as in words like "purple" or "Etruscan") might seem "feminine" according to the rubric established by feminist critics. But the poems of Yeats, with their highly distinctive vocabulary and metaphysic, have similar characteristics. Hélène Cixous characterizes feminine texts as "volcanic,"[29] and not only does Dickinson write often about volcanoes, she contrives—as Kamilla Denman shows in discussing her punctuation in this book—a visually kinetic poetry. (So does e. e. cummings in a related way.) Feminist readers argue for the operative presence of anger in the art of Emily Dickinson and attribute it to her displacement from the tradition of male writing. (Male anger, so volcanic in Byron, Pope, and Swift, is presumably kindled by other causes.) A poet who could write "I had been hungry, all the Years—" or "Mine Enemy is growing old— / I have at last Revenge—" (*P*, 579, 1509) distinctly understands anger; to say she is thereby in the tradition of feminine writing is regarded as a useful way of explaining it.

On the other hand, Dickinson is a poet who likes to begin poems with theses that remind us that her father and brother were lawyers—"This was a Poet—It is That"; "Prayer is the little implement" (*P*, 448, 437)—and who characteristically develops her lyrics with an internal logic that inexorably follows the laws of premise, development, conclusion. If logic is linear and masculine, "Uncle Emily," her *nom de lettre* in notes to nephew Ned, nevertheless adopted it. Our vision of Emily Dickinson is inevitably enriched by taking account of her gender, a womanhood that she did not always relish, for she was brilliant and ambitious in a culture that praised women for compliance and self-effacement. Certainly her sex had an effect on her subject matter, especially her ironic view of marriage. Still, one recalls the indignant remark of Georgia O'Keeffe, "I am not a *woman* artist, I am an Artist." True art, as Dickinson herself suggests in her poem above about the visitation of the "Hosts," finally escapes categories: national, temporal, sexual.

What will her readers be concerned about in the twenty-first century? From current trends, we may deduce at least two issues. First, there is the nature of her fascicles. Should they be regarded as a collection of individually discrete poems, as a collection that intermingles themes for varying purposes of emphasis or signification, or—like Whitman's *Leaves of Grass*—as one long poem? This volume includes Sharon Cameron's essay from *Choosing not Choosing*, which argues that

---

[29]In "The Laugh of the Medusa," trans. Keith Cohen and Paula Cohen, reprinted in *The Signs Reader: Women, Gender and Scholarship*, ed. Elizabeth Abel and Emily K. Abel (Chicago: University of Chicago Press, 1983), 292.

Dickinson's variant words in the fascicles connect apparently separate poems. A growing number of scholars report themselves concerned with the complexion of the fascicles as it affects the editing issues noted earlier. Second, how Dickinson should be "printed" (again, her own word) will undoubtedly fuse with the question of how her poems should be read and in what construction, with both matters acquiring increasing importance. The historical topics respecting Dickinson's poetry—the problems of biography, the importance of her reading (Richard Sewall probes in this book the often overlooked significance to her of just three works), the question of her aesthetic, her adoption of various literary modes such as the Romantic Grotesque (as Cynthia Griffin Wolff's essay shows)—these will, all signs indicate, remain imperishable.

Finally, because it is my particular sphere of interest and not fully represented here, I should like to conclude by discussing the significance of Dickinson's attraction to the visual arts. In "The Art of Peace" in this volume, Barton Levi St. Armand eloquently reveals how Dickinson's nature poetry reflects her reading of Ruskin and her knowledge of Hudson River painting. I would propose deeper study along these lines for evidence that techniques of painting and even the conceits of specific paintings are sometimes manifest in her poetry. An improved understanding of her uses of symbolism and of her verbal arrangements results from it. To illustrate how this is so, I will appeal to poem 317 in Johnson's *Complete Poems*. But in order to suggest how new approaches to her lineation and the composition of the fascicles may be warranted by the appearance of her texts, I will present the poem as it appears in R. W. Franklin's *The Manuscript Books of Emily Dickinson* (p. 214).

The poem is preceded on the fascicle page by the last line of poem 240 ("Ah, Moon—and Star!"), and it is separated from 240 by Dickinson's division line that "frames" it partly:

So I can never go!

Just so—Christ—raps—
He—doesn't weary—
First at the knocker—
And then—at the Bell—
Then—on Divinest tiptoe
Standing—
Might he but spy the
hiding soul!

When he—retires—
Chilled—or weary—
It will be ample time
for me—
Patient—upon the steps
until then—
Heart—I am knocking
low
At thee!

This poem was addressed and sent to Susan Gilbert Dickinson about 1862. Its subtext is almost certainly the Pre-Raphaelite painter William Holman Hunt's *The Light of the World*, the most famous of all English mid-Victorian religious paintings.[30] Ruskin wrote an exegesis of the painting in Dickinson's favorite *Modern Painters* (3, 67), which was reprinted in the *Knickerbocker* magazine (January 1858), familiar to connoisseurs like the Dickinsons. The Boston press featured descriptions and cartoons of it in winter 1857 and spring 1858 as a Pre-Raphaelite show that included the painting toured New York and New England. *The Light of the World*—so popular as to be copied twice by Hunt—became an emblem of Christ's persistent love for an obdurate humanity. As Dorothy Huff Oberhaus shows in this collection, Emily Dickinson had respectful, even affectionate feelings for Christ the Savior by comparison with God the Father. And in "Just so—Christ—raps!" she exercises them wittily, substituting herself for Hunt's Christ, who (in the painting) stands knocking on a closed door that represents the human soul. Hers is a love poem, I take it, to Sue; and it is her speaker, not Christ, who stands at the door of the listener's heart. In place of Hunt's red-haired Christ in his white robe, the cognizant Sue is asked to see Emily Dickinson, whose hair was red and whose dresses by 1862 were white.

The poem's painterly subtext shows that its author was not isolated from the artistic life of her time, and shows, further, the intensity of her emblematic transformations. It provides another way of understanding her use of visual materials, and helps a reader who acknowledges them to "see" her better. The words as they appear in the fascicle are inscribed by a bold hand that makes loose letters (particularly *A*, *W*, *g*, and *y*) not far from brushstrokes. As a word-picture, preceded and followed by lines that encase it, the whole wears a look of tension and yet embellishment. That the words "standing," "hiding soul," "for me," and "low" are set off as independent entries seems important here. It invites their being read together as a contrapuntal development of the central theme. Since the standing speaker begs the hiding soul for love, *me* and *low* become one, while *hiding* and *standing* represent the two persons divided in the poem. The isolation of the word *low* on the fascicle page describes the speaker's humbling by the "Heart" she loves and thus her humility, not merely the low sound (hence secrecy or timidity or respectfulness?) of her knocking. Finally, Dickinson's entry of this poem immediately following the last line of poem 240 must interest anyone concerned with the comprehensive design of the fascicles. For the last line of 240 is "So I can never go!" which may serve as the proviso of "Just so—Christ—raps!" and, perhaps, as an integral part of it. Was Dickinson intending all this? We work with what we see and the words we read.

And it is Dickinson's language, her words, that must always hold the center of any study. She claimed that "A Word that breathes distinctly / Has not the power to die" (*P*, 1653). What distinguishes her as a poet are the sharp intensity, the vivid (or living) distinctness, the essential justice and rich frugality of her language. About 1884 she wrote:

[30] A more extended discussion of this painting appears in Farr, op. cit., 267–69.

Talk not to me of Summer Trees
The foliage of the mind
A Tabernacle is for Birds
Of no corporeal kind
And winds do go that way at noon
To their Ethereal Homes
Whose Bugles call the least of us
To undepicted Realms

(1634)

Her subject here is the intellect or imagination that is a sacred home or "tabernacle" for all images and ideas. Her first line imperiously waves away the concept of (and perhaps the long tradition of poems about) nature's seductive loveliness, which is seen at its best in summer's leafy trees. There is, she says, a superior "foliage": the brain, which houses incorporeal "birds," or thoughts, akin to the supernatural "Hosts" of poem 298. This tabernacle of intellect even accommodates the vision of an ethereal future, a life and a place that it has never seen, but that is real, and "Realm" enough, since death calls "the least of us" to it. Our respect for the verbal authority of this poem can be complete, even without enhancements provided by history, linguistic theory, or biography.

In November 1890, the then-famous American writer Louise Chandler Moulton reacted with delight to the "adorable"[31] book of a new poet. Among the poems she most admired was one that the author's editors had named "Prelude." It begins in Franklin's text:

This is my letter to the World
That never wrote to Me—
The simple News that Nature told—
With tender Majesty

Mrs. Chandler Moulton did not read that precise poem but a regularized version of it. Nor could she see the curious little flourish in Dickinson's second stanza, as it appears in fascicle 24 (page 548 of *The Manuscript Books*). There, the poet writes to her future readers:

Her Message is committed
To Hands I cannot see—
For love of Her—Sweet—country—
men—
Judge tenderly—of me

Here, Dickinson has made a five-liner, not a quatrain; and she sets "men" out alone. She did not need to do so for spatial reasons. The effects of this poem for today's readers are as provocative as one could expect, or wish, from the woman her neighbors called "the Myth." In addition, they illustrate this poet's wide appeal. Thus, the gender critic may note that she speaks of the letter as "Her,"

---

[31]Cf. Buckingham, op. cit., 37.

while the addressees are (if we understand that the poet is seriously/mischievously playing on the word) "men." Biographers and textual critics may be gratified by the poet's description of her poem as a letter, thus combining those forms into one for our speculation. Novelists, playwrights, and poets working with the Dickinson legend may respond to an appealing persona who calls to us from an imagined time, a fabled loneliness. (Martha Graham entitled her white ballet on Emily Dickinson's solitude "Letter to the World.") Finally, the general public that— yes—loves Emily Dickinson is usually moved by the lyric's direct appeal, its apparent humility and simplicity, its linkage of the speaker and nature. And this is but a minor poem, not among the one hundred or so much-anthologized, vibrant, tough, and rare great pieces, like "Because I could not stop for Death—" or "After great pain, a formal feeling comes—" or "Wild Nights—Wild Nights!" or "Behind Me—dips Eternity—."

International conferences on the poetry and its translation into such languages as Japanese, Bulgarian, and Greek; the annual Walk to Emily Dickinson's Grave in Amherst; the scores of publications that come out yearly; the plays, novels, song settings,[32] and the other tributes, great and small, to her achievement as a poet— all attest to the fact that Dickinson has reached "the World." In a typically dismissive (yet fascinated) line she once spoke of Fame's "siteless Citadel" (*L*, PF 98, p. 926). That is, she said paradoxically, fame is a fortress that is not founded in any place. This was perhaps another of her observations on its ephemerality. But the fame of Emily Dickinson is now universal. A true citadel, it is well founded, and as the new century draws on, it is likely to assume even more stature and influence.

---

[32]Carlton Lowenberg's *Musicians Wrestle Everywhere: Emily Dickinson and Music* (Berkeley, Calif.: Fallen Leaf Press, 1992) records over 1600 musical settings of the Dickinson poems by 276 composers from 1896 to the present.

The Wayward Nun
beneath the Hill

Emily Dickinson and the Mysteries
of Womanhood

Sandra M. Gilbert

Young Mabel Loomis Todd had been living for two months in Amherst, Massachusetts, where her husband, David, had just been appointed Director of the Amherst College Observatory, when on November 6, 1881, she wrote her parents an enthusiastic letter about one of the town's most fascinating citizens:

> I must tell you about the *character* of Amherst. It is a lady whom the people call the *Myth*. She is a sister of Mr. Dickinson, & seems to be the climax of all the family oddity. She has not been outside of her own house in fifteen years, except once to see a new church, when she crept out at night, & viewed it by moonlight. No one who calls upon her mother & sister ever see her, but she allows little children once in a great while, & one at a time, to come in, when she gives them cake or candy, or some nicety, for she is very fond of little ones. But more often she lets down the sweetmeat by a string, out of a window, to them. She dresses wholly in white, & her mind is said to be perfectly wonderful. She writes finely, but no one *ever* sees her. Her sister, who was at Mrs. Dickinson's party, invited me to come & sing to her mother sometime. . . . People tell me the *myth* will hear every note—she will be near, but unseen. . . . Isn't that like a book? So interesting.[1]

By now that letter has become almost as famous as the Mythic Miss Dickinson herself, largely because it seems to have contributed to a process of mystification and fictionalization that surrounded one of America's greatest writers with what Thomas Wentworth Higginson once called a "fiery mist."[2]

Reprinted from *Feminist Critics Read Emily Dickinson* (1983) by permission of Indiana University Press.

[1]Jay Leyda, *The Years and Hours of Emily Dickinson*, 2 vols. (New Haven: Yale University Press, 1960), vol. 2, p. 357.

[2]See T. W. Higginson to ED, in *The Letters of Emily Dickinson*, 3 vols., ed. Thomas H. Johnson (Cambridge: Harvard University Press, 1958), vol. 2, p. 461: "I have the greatest desire to see you, always feeling that perhaps if I could once take you by the hand I might be something to you; but till then you only enshroud yourself in this fiery mist & I cannot reach you, but only rejoice in the rare sparkles of light."

Higginson himself also, of course, contributed to this process that transformed a reclusive poet-cook into a New England Nun of Love-and-Art.[3] More than a decade before Mabel Todd recorded the rumours she had heard about "the rare mysterious Emily,"[4] he visited his self-styled "Scholar" in her Amherst home, and though his notes on the meeting are not as gothic as the stories Mrs. Todd reported to her parents, they add both fire and mist to the mythic portrait, with their description of how there was "a step like a pattering child's in entry" and "a little plain woman . . . in a very plain & exquisitely clean white pique . . . came to me with two day lilies, which she put in a sort of childlike way into my hand & said, 'These are my introduction' in a soft frightened breathless childlike voice. . . ."[5] Interestingly enough, moreover, even the "little plain woman's" most prosaic remarks seemed to enhance the evolving Myth with just the dash of paradox needed to give a glimmer of irony to the dramatic halo around her: "She makes all the bread," Higginson observed, "for her father only likes hers & says, '& people must have puddings,' this *very* dreamily, as if they were comets—so she makes them."[6]

After her death, in fact, a number of Dickinson's admirers like to dwell on that ineffable glimmer of irony. "Even though her mind might be occupied with 'all mysteries and all knowledge,' including meteors and comets, her hands were often busy in most humble household ways," wrote her cousin Helen Knight Wyman in a 1905 article for the *Boston Cooking School Magazine* on "Emily Dickinson as Cook and Poetess."[7] She "wrote indefatigably, as some women cook or knit," added R. P. Blackmur in 1937.[8] As the Myth grew and glowed, drama, domesticity, and Dickinson seem to have become inseparable. It is no wonder, then—given this unlikely, often absurdly literary image of an obsessively childlike, gothic yet domestic spinster—that recent readers of Dickinson's verse have struggled to deconstruct the "Myth of Amherst" and discover instead the aesthetic technician, the intellectual, and the visionary, whose lineaments would seem to have been blurred or obliterated in the "fiery mist" generated not by the poet herself but by her friends and admirers.

I want to argue here, however, that though their fictionalizations may sometimes have been crude or melodramatic, Mabel Loomis Todd, Thomas Wentworth Higginson, and many others were not in fact projecting their own fantasies

---

[3]For a newspaper story about a real "New England Nun" whose career would have been known to Dickinson, see Leyda, vol. 1, p. 148. For a fictionalized account of a "New England Nun" that mythologizes female domesticity in a way partly (though not wholly) comparable to Dickinson's own, see Mary E. Wilkins Freeman, "A New England Nun," in *A New England Nun and Other Stories* (New York: Harper & Row, 1891).

[4]Leyda, vol. 2, p. 376.

[5]Ibid., p. 151.

[6]Ibid.

[7]*The Boston Cooking-School Magazine*, June–July 1906.

[8]Quoted by James Reeves in an *Introduction to the Selected Poems of Emily Dickinson* reprinted in *Emily Dickinson: A Collection of Critical Essays*, ed. Richard B. Sewall (Englewood Cliffs, N.J.: Prentice-Hall, 1963), p. 119.

onto the comparatively neutral (if enigmatic) figure of Emily Dickinson. Rather, as I will suggest, all these observers were responding to a process of self-mythologizing that led Dickinson herself to use all the materials of daily reality, and most especially the details of domesticity, as if they were not facts but metaphors, in order to recreate herself-and-her-life as a single, emblematic text, and often, indeed, as a sort of religious text—the ironic hagiography, say, of a New England Nun. More specifically, I want to suggest that Dickinson structured this life/text around a series of "mysteries" that were distinctively female, deliberately exploring and exploiting the characteristics, even the constraints, of nineteenth-century womanhood so as to transform and transcend them.

Finally, I want to argue that such a provisional and analytic acceptance of the Dickinson Myth may serve the reality of Dickinson's art better than the contemptuous rejection of legend that has lately become fashionable. For by deciphering rather than deconstructing the intricate text of this poet's life, we may come closer to understanding the methods and materials of her actual, literary texts. Throughout this essay, therefore, I will try to "read" biographical mysteries, and I will use the word "mystery" in almost all the current as well as a few of the archaic senses given by the *OED*. These include "a religious truth known only from divine revelation"; "a mystical presence"; a "religious . . . rite, especially a sacramental rite of the Christian religion"; "an incident in the life of [Christ] regarded . . . as having a mystical significance"; "a hidden or secret thing . . . a riddle or enigma"; "a 'secret' or highly technical operation in a trade or art"; a secret rite; a "miracle-play"; "a service, occupation; office, ministry"; "a handicraft, craft, art, trade, profession, or calling"; and finally "a kind of plum cake." All these senses of "mystery"—even, or perhaps especially, the plum cake—have some application to both the Myth and the mythmaking of Emily Dickinson.

For like her Romantic precursor John Keats, one of the poets to whom she turned most often for sustenance, Dickinson understood that a "life of any worth is a continual allegory."[9] Thus she ambitiously undertook to live (and to create) "a life like the scriptures, figurative—which [some] people can no more make out than they can the hebrew Bible." Such a life, as Keats observed, need not be theatrical; one might be both public and melodramatic without achieving true significance. "Lord Byron cuts a figure—but he is not figurative—," Keats commented wryly, and Dickinson would have seen such a remark as offering her permission to dramatize the private "trivia" of domesticity, rather than public turmoil, permission even to conflate puddings and comets. For again, like Keats, she would have perceived the essential reciprocity of the life/text and the literary text. About Shakespeare, for instance, Keats famously observed that he "led a life of Allegory: his works are the comments on it."[10] But as I hope to show, the same striking statement can be made about the mysteries Dickinson enacted and allegorized.

---

[9]John Keats, to George and Georgiana Keats, Friday, Feb. 18, 1819.
[10]Ibid.

Dickinson's impulse to enact mysteries can be traced almost to her childhood. Two episodes from her year at Mount Holyoke, for instance, seem to have signalled what was on the way. The first is one that Mabel Todd claimed to have heard about from the poet's sister Vinnie. The seventeen-year-old Emily, wrote Mrs. Todd, "was never floored. When the Euclid examination came and she had never studied it, she went to the blackboard and gave such a glib exposition of imaginary figures that the dazed teacher passed her with the highest mark."[11] The second episode is more famous and has been widely discussed, even by biographers and critics who dislike the "Myth of Amherst." Throughout Dickinson's time at Mount Holyoke, the school was in the throes of an evangelical revival eagerly encouraged by Mary Lyon, the school's founder and principal. According to Clara Newman Turner, there was an occasion when "Miss Lyon . . . asked all those who wanted to be Christians to rise. The wording of the request was not such as Emily could honestly accede to and she remained seated—the only one who did not rise."[12]

In these two episodes, we can discern the seeds of personal and religious mysteries that Dickinson was to develop and dramatize throughout both her life/text and her literary texts. Moreover, these two episodes suggest that we can reduce the major Dickinsonian mysteries to two categories: mystery as puzzle (secret, riddle, enigma, or blackboard battle with imaginary figures), and mystery as miracle (mystic transformation, inexplicable sacrament, or private parallel to traditional Christian professions of faith). If we bear these two categories in mind as we meditate on Dickinson's "life as Allegory," we find that, on the one hand, at the center of this poet's self-mythologizing mystery-as-puzzle we confront a kind of absence or blank, the enigmatic wound that many biographers have treated as if it were the subject of a romantic detective novel called "The Mystery of the Missing Lover." At the center of the Dickinson mystery-as-miracle, on the other hand, we encounter a presence or power, the "white heat" (365) of Dickinson's art, whose story we might label "The Mystery of the Muse." Yet these two mysteries—we might also call them the mysteries of Life and Art—are of course connected. For, even more than most other writers, Emily Dickinson the poet mysteriously transformed the pain associated with the puzzle at the center of her life into the miracle of her art; through that transformation, indeed, she became the "Myth of Amherst."

To speak of puzzles and miracles, however—or even to speak of all the finely distinguished definitions of "mystery" that the *OED* offers—is still to speak in generalities. When one becomes more specific, however, the puzzle of Dickinson's life is, at least on the surface, vulgarly and easily defined: who *was* "he"? Were there several of "him"? And was it because of "him" (or "them") that this brilliant woman more or less completely withdrew from the world? When she declared, at the age of thirty-eight, that "I do not cross my Father's ground to any House or

---

[11]Leyda, vol. 1, p. 131.
[12]Ibid., p. 135.

town,"[13] was she secretly anticipating "his" return? By now, a century and a half
since Emily Dickinson was born, it seems fairly certain that we will never know
"his" (or "their") identity. But that the "Myth of Amherst" spent part of her poetic
lifetime nurturing romantic feelings about someone, whether real or imaginary, is
quite certain: we know, for instance, from her so-called Master letters and from
the later letters to Judge Lord, that this puzzling poet was a dazzling writer of love
letters, better than Charlotte Brontë and at least as good as John Keats. In addition, she produced a series of elegant and often sensual verses memorializing
romance, real or imaginary—poems that range from the suave and courtly "The
Daisy follows soft the Sun—" (106) to the subtly voluptuous "Wild Nights—Wild
Nights!" (249)

It is clear, too, that Dickinson's relationship with her real or imaginary lover
(or lovers) gave her "great pain" that must have had something to do with her
renunciation of him and/or the world. Her heartbroken and heartbreaking
"Master" letters suggest this, and impassioned poems like "Why make it doubt—
it hurts it so—" (462) and "My life closed twice before its close—" (1732) would
be hard to understand otherwise. Poem 462, for instance, is obviously tormented
and almost certainly autobiographical:

> Why make it doubt—it hurts it so—
> So sick—to guess—
> So strong—to know—
> So brave—upon its little Bed
> To tell the very last They said
> Unto Itself—and smile—And shake—
> For that dear—distant—dangerous—Sake—
> But—the Instead—the Pinching fear
> That Something—it did do—or dare—
> Offend the Vision—and it flee—
> And They no more remember me—
> Nor ever turn to tell me why—
> Oh, Master, This is Misery—

Mysteriously, the poet/speaker transforms herself here into an "it"—a mere lump
of suffering flesh—but the identity of the Master whose favor she begs is more
mysterious. Still, even the stumblings and hesitations, the advances and retreats in
this work authenticate the pain it expresses. Gasping and elliptical, it seems like a
speech spun out of delirium; reading it, we become witnesses to a crisis in love's
fever, watchers by the sickbed of romance.

It is difficult, though, to ignore the curiously theatrical language evoked by
Dickinson's odd combination of speech and silence, frankness and mystery. In the
sentence before last I used the words *seems, fever, romance*. These words do, of
course, refer to states of being that are somehow "true," but their truth is more
likely the truth of art, of metaphor, than the truth of "reality." As we watch this
puzzling enactment of "a woman's life," we may begin to feel rather like a dazed

---

[13]*Letters*, vol. 2, p. 460.

audience watching a brilliant schoolgirl solve entirely imaginary problems in geometry. Significantly, indeed, the more vivid the mystery-as-puzzle of Dickinson's life becomes, the more it melts into the mystery-as-miracle of Dickinson's art. For if the mysteries of this poet's life are often riddles of absence or silence, then the mysteries of her art are marvels of transformation, "conversions of the mind" (593) in which we see a great performer turning defeat into triumph like a magician changing water into wine.

Dickinson wrote a number of verses that not only enact but also describe and analyze such marvelous transformations. In these works, her Master/lover has stopped being an ordinary man—if he ever was one—and becomes a miraculous and sacramental being, on at least one occasion a god in the garden of love, and, more frequently, a muse in the heaven of invention. In poem 322, "There came a day at Summer's Full / Entirely for me," for example, the speaker's lover is a "Sealed Church" with whom she is "Permitted to commune" on this one transfigured occasion. When the two part, she declares that "Each bound the Other's Crucifix— / We gave no other Bond—." But that, she adds, is "Sufficient troth, that we shall rise— / Deposed—at length, the Grave— / To that new Marriage, / Justified—through Calvaries of Love—." Most striking here is Dickinson's deft fusion of the language of love with the vocabulary of Christianity, a poetic gesture that goes back at least to the medieval romance—for instance to the "Cave of Love" inhabited by Tristan and Isolde—but that this self-mythologizing New England nun makes distinctively her own. For as she transforms her real or imaginary lover/Master into a suffering god of love and herself into his "Empress of Calvary," Dickinson performs a complementary conversion. Defining herself and her lover as "Sealed churches" and their erotic communion as a sacrament, she converts the Christianity she had begun to reject as a seventeen-year-old Mount Holyoke student into a complex theology of secular love.

In "I have a King, who does not speak—" (103) and "My Life had stood—a Loaded Gun—" (754) she performs equally skillful but slightly different acts of poetic prestidigitation, converting the mysterious figure she romanticizes from a lover into a male muse. Significantly, moreover, though the male muse in both these poems is given an impressive title—in one he is a King, in the other a Master—he is strangely passive and silent in both works; indeed, it is his passivity and silence that apparently empower the poet's triumphant speech. The enigmatic "King who does not speak," for instance, enables Dickinson, like a modern priestess of Delphi, to "peep" at night, "thro' a dream" into "parlors shut by day."

> And if I do—[she declares] when morning comes—
> It is as if a hundred drums
> Did round my pillow roll,
> And shouts fill all my Childish sky,
> And Bells keep saying "Victory"
> From steeples in my soul!

Similarly, when the poet imagines herself as a "Loaded Gun" she arranges for her owner and Master to carry her into "Sovereign Woods" where "everytime I speak for Him— / The Mountains straight reply—"

And do I smile [she adds ironically], such cordial light
Upon the Valley glow—
It is as a Vesuvian face
Had let its pleasure through—

Plainly, no matter what Dickinson meant by the famous riddle that ends this mysterious work,[14] the central mystery-as-miracle the poem records is the woman writer's appropriation of her Master/owner's power. Though he has identified her, seized her, carried her away, it is finally she who, in a kind of prototypical role reversal, guards him with her deadly energy. "None stir the second time—" / she boasts, "On whom I lay a yellow Eye— / Or an emphatic Thumb."

The mysteries of Dickinson's art accomplished some transformations of experience, however, that were even more remarkable than those recorded in "I have a King" and "My Life had stood." There, the poet had made the Master/lover who evidently humbled her into a figure who paradoxically strengthened her. But in other poems, she converted "great pain" itself—the humiliating vicissitudes of romance, for instance, along with all the other terrors of her life—into an extraordinary source of energy. "A *Wounded* Deer—leaps highest," she insists quite early in her poetic career (165, written in 1860), and in the same poem she also points out the power of "The *Smitten* Rock that gushes! / The *trampled* Steel that springs!"—eerie transformations of anguish into energy. A year or two later (1861), in poem 281, one of her many mortuary poems, she exclaims that the sight of death is "so appalling—it exhilarates— / So over Horror, it half Captivates—." Brooding by someone's deathbed, she remarks that here "Terror's free— / Gay, Ghastly, Holiday"—an even eerier transformation of agony into energy. In a number of poems about volcanoes, moreover, she speculates

If the stillness is Volcanic
In the human face
When upon a pain Titanic
Features keep their place—

and wonders

If at length the smouldering anguish
Will not overcome—
And the palpitating Vineyard
In the dust be thrown?
[175]

Finally, in a poem that is both searingly sincere and a triumph of irony, Dickinson describes the way she herself has been transformed through the sufferings of love into a paradoxical being, an *Empress* of *Calvary*, a Queen of Pain.

---

[14]"Though I than He—may longer live / He longer must—than I— / For I have but the power to kill / Without—the power to die—"

Title divine—is mine!
The Wife—without the Sign!
Acute Degree—conferred on me—
Empress of Calvary!

[1072]

Surely this poem's central image is almost the apotheosis of anguish converted into energy, what Dickinson elsewhere called the "ecstasy of death." Transforming the puzzles of life into the paradoxes of art, the poet/speaker is on a kind of "gay, ghastly, Holiday," reminding us that she is the same woman who once told Thomas Wentworth Higginson that "I had a terror . . . I could tell to none—and so I sing, as the Boy does by the Burying Ground—because I am afraid—."[15]

It is significant, however, that the "gay, ghastly, Holiday" into which Dickinson so often converts her "great pain" is *not* a weekend in "Domingo" or a passage to India. On the contrary, though she characterizes herself as an Empress of Calvary, this poet is always scrupulously careful to explain that she "never saw a moor . . . never saw the sea" (1052). Her muse-like "King who does not speak" maintains his inspiring silence in a *parlor*, after all, and even the Master who owns the "Loaded Gun" of her art sleeps on an "Eider-Duck's / Deep Pillow" that sounds as homely as any bedding nineteenth-century New England had to offer. Dickinson loved exotic place-names—admiring, for instance, the "mail from Tunis" that the hummingbird brought to the bushes on her father's ground (1463)—but nevertheless the news of those distances came to her at home, in her parlor, her kitchen, her garden. For her,

Eden is that old-fashioned House
We dwell in every day
Without suspecting our abode
Until we drive away.

[1657]

Moreover, as Adrienne Rich has reminded us in one of the best recent essays on Emily Dickinson's cloistered art,[16] Dickinson felt that although

Volcanoes be in Sicily
And South America
I judge from my Geography—
Volcanoes nearer here
A Lava step at any time
Am I inclined to climb—
A Crater I may contemplate
Vesuvius at Home.

[1705]

---

[15]*Letters*, vol. 2, p. 404.

[16]Adrienne Rich, "Vesuvius at Home: The Power of Emily Dickinson," in *Shakespeare's Sisters: Feminist Essays on Women Poets*, ed. Sandra M. Gilbert and Susan Gubar (Bloomington: Indiana University Press, 1979).

For as a mistress of the mysteries of transformation, Dickinson was not just an extravagant miracle-worker, an Empress of Calvary; she was a magician of the ordinary, and hers was a Myth of *Amherst*, a Myth, that is, of the daily and the domestic, a Myth of what could be seen "New Englandly."[17] In this commitment to dailiness, moreover, even more than in her conversions of an unidentified figure into a muse and agony into energy, she defines and enacts distinctive mysteries of womanhood that have great importance not only for her own art but also for the female poetic tradition of which she is a grandmother.

Many male poets, of course, have also performed miracles of literary transformation. Some, for instance, have metamorphosed beloved women into muses (one thinks of Keats's "La Belle Dame sans Merci"). Others have transformed agony into energy (Donne's Holy Sonnets). Still others have even converted the ordinary into the emblematic, the secular or domestic into the sacred (Wordsworth, Stevens, George Herbert). What is notable about Dickinson, however, is (first) that in poems and letters she performs all these kinds of transformations, sometimes simultaneously, and (second) that the images into which she transforms ideas and events are so often uniquely "female"; that is, they are associated with women's literature and women depicted in literature, or else they are associated with woman's life and woman's place. Specifically, the womanly mysteries-as-miracles of Emily Dickinson's life/text fall into five major groups: the mystery of romance (a woman's literary genre); the mystery of renunciation (a woman's duty); the mystery of domesticity (a woman's sphere); the mystery of nature (figuratively speaking, a woman's analog or likeness); and the mystery of *woman's* nature.

As we have already seen, the first two of these groups include poems in which Dickinson describes and discusses her transformations of her mysterious master into an empowering muse as well as her conversion of agony into energy—both metamorphoses accomplished with the aid of imagery drawn from "female gothic" novels like *Jane Eyre* and *Wuthering Heights* or with the help of ideas drawn from the works of a woman artist of renunciation like George Eliot. With astonishing frequency, however, this poet's transformative processes are facilitated not just by literary models but by anti-literary female activities. More often than not, indeed, she negotiates the difficult passage from life to art through the transformation of objects and images drawn from her "ordinary" daily domestic experience. In fact, she uses such objects not only as key symbols in an elaborate mythology of the household, but also as props in her poetry's parallel mysteries of romance and renunciation.

No doubt the most striking and ubiquitous of Dickinson's domestic symbols is her white dress. As I have argued elsewhere, that extraordinary costume is in one sense a kind of ghostly blank, an empty page on which in invisible ink this theatri-

---

[17]See poem 285: ". . . Without the Snow's Tableau / Winter, were lie—to me— / Because I see— New Englandly. . . ."

cal poet quite consciously wrote a letter to the world that never wrote to her.[18] But to begin with, of course, Dickinson's radiantly symbolic garment was "just" a dress, an "ordinary" "everyday" item of clothing not unlike the morning dresses many Victorian young ladies wore. At the Dickinson Homestead in Amherst, indeed, it is still possible to see a white cotton dress said to have been the poet's. Enshrouded in a very prosaic and very modern plastic bag, its carefully protected tucks and ruffles remind the viewer that such a costume would have had to be maintained— laundered, ironed, mended—with intense dedication. And Dickinson was as conscious of that requirement as her descendants are, not only conscious that her white dress made special demands on her life but conscious that the idea of her dress made special demands on her art. In a fairly early poem she confessed this most dramatically.

> A solemn thing—it was—I said—
> A woman—white—to be—
> And wear—if God should count me fit—
> Her blameless mystery—
>
> A hallowed thing—to drop a life
> Into the purple well—
> Too plummetless—that it return—
> Eternity—until—
>
> I pondered how the bliss would look—
> And would it feel as big—
> When I could take it in my hand—
> As hovering—seen—through fog—
>
> And then—the size of this "small" life—
> The Sages—call it small—
> Swelled—like Horizons—in my vest—
> And I sneered—softly—"small"!
>
> [271]

Though it is in some ways obscure—what exactly is "the purple well," for instance?—this poem is particularly clear about one point: Dickinson's white dress is the emblem of a "blameless *mystery*," a kind of miraculous transformation that rejoices and empowers her. Dropping her life into that puzzling purple well, she renounces triviality and ordinariness in order to "wear"—that is, to *enact*—solemnity, dedication, vocation. In return, she will receive an indefinable bliss associated with the transformative power of "Eternity." But—and this is just as important— even as she dedicates her self and her life to becoming "a woman—white," she realizes the intrinsic significance of that self and life. "The Sages—call it small—": to conventionally "wise" men her female works and days may seem tiny, trivial; but

---

[18]See Sandra M. Gilbert and Susan Gubar, *The Madwoman in the Attic: The Woman Writer and the Nineteenth-Century Literary Imagination* (New Haven: Yale University Press, 1979), pp. 613–21.

as she meditates upon her own transformative powers, she feels this apparently "small" life swell "like Horizons—in my vest—" and, sneering "softly—'small'!", she utters the arrogance to which, as an artist of the ordinary, she has a right.

If the mysteries of romance and renunciation that Dickinson enacted in life and recorded in her poetry both parallel and complement the mystery of domesticity she also explored, all three quasi-religious concerns are particularly well served by her transformation of an ordinary white dress into the solemn habit of a New England nun. Apparently (or so she often hints) some event connected with the secret drama of her relationship with a muse-like Master (or a masterful Muse) affected her so deeply that it forced the very idea of whiteness across the shadow line that usually separates the metaphorical from the literal. Most people, after all, are capable of imagining themselves in what Dickinson calls "uniforms of snow." Even most poets, however, don't make the passage from the mental pretense implied in the metaphorical to the physical pretense of a theatrical enactment. Yet this is the extraordinary passage that Dickinson did make. What she also called her "white election" (528), therefore, suggests not only that she transformed her life into art more readily than most other writers but also that, more than most, she used her "small" life itself as an instrument of her great art: even the most ordinary materials of her life, that is, became a set of encoded gestures meant both to supply imagery for, *and* to supplement, the encoded statements of her verse.

In one of her most famous self-explanations, Dickinson once assured Higginson that "When I state myself, as the Representative of the Verse—it does not mean me—but a supposed person."[19] The remark may seem a reasonable confession to those who have grown accustomed to New Critical theories about the "extinction" of personality in poetry, but if one meditates long enough on the central mysteries of this artist's "life of Allegory," it is impossible not to conclude that even in making such an apparently straightforward remark she was performing one of her most cunning acts of transformation. For after all, the point her white dress most definitively makes is that she herself, the "real" Emily Dickinson, was as much a "supposed person" as the so-called "Representative of the Verse." Clad in her white costume, she was, in literal fact, the "Myth of Amherst," and this precisely because she was the mystery—both the puzzle and the miracle—of Amherst.

Into what sort of extraordinary "supposed person" did this transfiguration of a white dress convert her, however? As I have suggested elsewhere, Dickinson as a "woman—white" was a relative of Wilkie Collins's notorious *Woman in White*, of many a gothic ghost and pallid nun, of Elizabeth Barrett Browning's Aurora Leigh (who wears a "clean white morning gown"), of the redeemed spirits in the Biblical book of *Revelation* (who go in shining white raiment), and of Hawthorne's "Snow Maiden" (who wears, of course, a "uniform of snow").[20] In addition, as Mabel Todd noticed, she is related to Charles Dickens's Miss Havisham (who flaunts a tattered, decades-old wedding dress to assert, as Dickinson also did, that she is "the Wife

[19]*Letters*, vol. 2, p. 412.
[20]See Gilbert and Gubar, *The Madwoman*, pp. 613–21.

without the Sign").[21] Like Hawthorne's Hester Prynne, moreover, the "Myth of Amherst" uses an item of apparel to signify both tribulation and redemption, while like Melville's Moby Dick she embodies the contradictory mystery of her identity in a color that is no color, a color that is an absence of color. At the same time, however, the line that probably tells us most about the allegorical (rather than allusive) "meaning" of her white dress is the one that promises the least: "Big my secret but it's *bandaged*."

Appearing in poem 1737, which seems devoted to some of the more painful (and melodramatic) aspects of Dickinson's romance, this sentence tells us simply that the speaker's secret is a bandaged *wound*, but we cannot doubt that the mysterious hurt is bandaged in white—bandaged, that is, in this poet's central metaphor for aesthetic redemption born of pain, bandaged in myth born of mystery—and therefore, as she also tells us, "It will never get away." Earlier in the poem, however, though Dickinson does not actually tell us her "secret" she gives us a useful clue about its function in her life. The work begins by describing the constancy of anguish that sustains this wounding hidden love.

> Rearrange a "Wife's" affection!
> When they dislocate my Brain!
> Amputate my freckled Bosom!
> Make me bearded like a man!
>
> Blush, my spirit, in thy Fastness—
> Blush, my unacknowledged clay—
> Seven years of troth have taught thee
> More than Wifehood ever may!
>
> Love that never leaped its socket—
> Trust entrenched in narrow pain—
> Constancy thro' fire—awarded—
> Anguish—bare of anodyne!
> [1737]

In particular, however, the poet insists that her secret incurable "anguish" is a

> Burden—borne so far triumphant—
> None suspect me of the crown,
> For I wear the "Thorns" till *Sunset*—
> Then—my Diadem put on.
> [1737]

A crown of thorns converted into a glittering diadem: without presuming to speculate about the "facts" Dickinson may or may not be describing through this secularized crucifixion imagery, it is possible to see that her fictionalizing of those "facts" tells us something crucial about the transformative energy her white dress

---

[21]For Mabel Todd on Dickinson's similarity to "Miss Haversham" [sic], see Leyda, vol. 2, p. 377.

represents. For as the garment of a mythic or supposed person who is the Empress of Calvary, that dress is once again a paradoxical image of agony transformed into energy; in itself, in fact, it is a paradoxical, even an oxymoronic, costume—as oxymoronic as the "fiery mist" with which Higginson complained that she surrounded herself. Through this artful bandage, this cloth that both shrouds and staunches, conceals and reveals, the mysterious poet of transformation converts absence into presence, silence into speech, in the same way that Christ, through *his* mysteries, converted thorns into jewels, bread and wine into flesh and blood, death into life.

At first, of course, it may seen that in her dependency on Christian imagery, as in her allusions to male-created female characters from Hester Prynne to Miss Havisham, Dickinson was enacting and examining traditional masculine mysteries rather than distinctively feminine ones. Not only is her Christianity notably heterodox, however; the real white dress on which she founded her drama of supposition was significantly different from the white garments she would have encountered in most male-authored sources. For the white dresses imagined by the nineteenth-century male writers who seem to have been most interesting to Dickinson are invariably exotic or supernatural. Wilkie Collins's woman in white is a madwoman attired in the uniform of her derangement. Hawthorne's snow maiden is an eerily romantic being dressed for a fairy tale. Dickens's Miss Havisham wears a gown designed for a most unusual occasion—a wedding that has been indefinitely postponed. Even Melville's metaphysical whale is a freak of nature who represents the freakishness of Nature. Only a female-created character, Elizabeth Barrett Browning's Aurora Leigh, wears an *ordinary* dress—a "clean white morning gown" transformed by art into an extraordinary costume.[22]

But of course, like Aurora, another "supposed person" whose life as a woman was inseparable from her defiantly female poetry, Emily Dickinson wore such a dress,[23] an ordinary dress made extraordinary by neither circumference nor circumstance but only by the white heat of her creative energy. And indeed, she tells us in one of her most direct poems, this transformation of the ordinary into the extraordinary is a bewitching female art she actually learned from Elizabeth Barrett Browning.

> I think I was enchanted
> When first a sombre Girl—
> I read that Foreign Lady—
> The Dark—felt beautiful—

[22]See Elizabeth Barrett Browning, *Aurora Leigh,* in *The Poetical Works of Elizabeth Barrett Browning* (New York: Crowell, 1891), pp. 21, 28, 149.

[23]Nancy Rexford, costume curator at the Northampton Historical Society, has assured me that the white Dickinson dress at the Amherst Homestead is a comparatively "ordinary" cotton day dress—what we would now, perhaps, call a "house dress" or at least a dress designed for casual wear—fashioned in the style of the 70s or 80s, the period when Dickinson would have worn it regularly. She also notes, however, that it was not at that time at all "ordinary" for such a garment to be made in *white* unless it was a child's dress or a summer costume designed for wearing at the seaside (which Dickinson's plainly was not).

she begins, describing her first encounter with Barrett Browning's "witch-craft." Then she goes on to list a series of witty transformations through which the common became the uncommon, the daily the divine.

> The Bees—became as Butterflies—
> The Butterflies—as Swans—
> Approached—and spurned the narrow grass—
> And just the meanest Tunes
>
> That Nature murmured to herself
> To keep herself in Cheer—
> I took for Giants—practising
> Titanic Opera—
>
> The Days—to Mighty Metres stept—
> The Homeliest—adorned
> As if unto a Jubilee
> 'Twere suddenly confirmed—. . .
>
> [593]

It is not insignificant, surely, that these metamorphoses, like so many others Dickinson explores in her life/text, not only depend upon the patriarchal Christian mysteries of transformation, they parody and subvert them. For ultimately, Dickinson's symbolic use of her white dress in life and art is only one example of what is not only a striking mythology of domesticity but also an extraordinary theology of the ordinary, the homely, the domestic, a theology that constitutes a uniquely female version of the philosophy Thomas Carlyle called "natural supernaturalism."[24] Like many of her male contemporaries, including Carlyle himself, this woman who had even as a schoolgirl rejected Christianity grew up doubting traditional Christian pieties. But where Carlyle substituted a belief in the grandest sacraments of nature for his lost faith in the established Church, Dickinson celebrated mysteries that such Victorian sages would have thought "smaller"—the sacraments of the household, the hearth, the garden. And where in his famous *Sartor Resartus* (*The Tailor Retailored*) Carlyle saw all the natural world as the metaphorical clothing of a mysterious God's cosmic energy, Dickinson in both life and art transformed her own clothing into a metaphor for the energy that moved her own, female mysteries. Thus, although she never yielded to Miss Lyon's evangelical fervor, although she was never born again as a "hopeful" Christian, this skeptical poet was converted, and by a woman teacher, to a religion that parodied and paralled patriarchal Christianity.

An alternate version of the last stanza of Dickinson's tribute to Barrett Browning (593) tells us that when she first "read that Foreign Lady"

---

[24]See Carlyle, *Sartor Resartus*, book 2, chapter 8, "Natural Supernaturalism." Carlyle's picture, incidentally, was one of three portraits that hung on ED's bedroom wall. The other two were of Eliot and Barrett Browning.

The Days—to Mighty Metres stept—
The Homeliest—adorned
As if unto a *Sacrament*
'Twere suddenly confirmed—

and then the poet goes on to explain her own transformation further:

I could not have defined the change—
Conversion of the Mind
Like Sanctifying in the Soul—
Is witnessed—not explained—

Learning from Barrett Browning how to see the sacramental radiance of the ordinary world around her—the "small" world of the household and the garden—this onetime dissenter seems to have been born again as a "wayward nun" dedicated to celebrations that her Father and her minister might find mysterious indeed. " 'Twas a Divine Insanity—" she goes on to say, describing her introduction to Barrett Browning, and adds that she means to keep herself "mad" (since such madness is of course "divinest sense"):

The Danger to be Sane
Should I again experience—
'Tis Antidote to turn—

To Tomes of solid Witchcraft—
Magicians be asleep—
But Magic—hath an Element
Like Deity—to keep—

Converted to this new religion, she finds that the life that the "Sages" called "small" really has "swelled like Horizons" in her breast, and her days transformed by "Magic," are stepping to "Mighty Metres."

In fact, I would argue that once she had learned the female mysteries of "solid Witchcraft" from Elizabeth Barrett Browning's powerful example, Emily Dickinson became a "wayward nun" (722) who regularly spoke—in life as well as in art—through an elaborate code of domestic objects, a language of flowers and glasses of wine, of pieces of cake and bread and pudding—and of a white dress, a point her Amherst neighbors intuited quite early. If we return to Mabel Todd's description of the "Myth of Amherst," moreover, we can see, now, that Mrs. Todd's observations emphasize not only the mystery and magic but even the *textuality* of the behavior that characterized Dickinson's "life of Allegory." Indeed, beginning with two observations that subtly contradict each other ("She dresses wholly in white, . . . but no one *ever* sees her") the fascinated Mrs. Todd goes on to report gestures that sound more like those of a goddess or a priestess than those of a New England spinster. "Her sister . . . invited me to come & sing . . . & if the performance pleases her, a servant will enter with wine for me, or a flower . . . but just probably the token of approval will not come then, but a few days after, some dainty present will appear for me at twilight. People tell me that the *myth* will hear every note—she will be near, but unseen. . . . *Isn't that like a book?*" [italics mine]. That the "myth" will be near but unseen recalls the schoolgirl working her magic on imaginary figures, transforming an ordinary blackboard into a setting for epic prestidigitation. But the code of wine and flowers or wine and cake suggests the rituals of a strange yet oddly familiar religion. Put together, moreover, these puzzles and miracles that haunted even the more prosaic souls of Amherst are indeed "like a book." In fact, they are part of the book of poems that a supposed person named Emily Dickinson actually wrote.

It should not be surprising, of course, that a woman poet transformed the minutiae of her life into the mysteries of her art. That is, after all, what countless male poets do, though with very different material. More to the point, celebrations of domesticity streamed from the pens of almost all the female novelists and poets who were Dickinson's contemporaries, as Nina Baym shows in her study of nineteenth-century American "Woman's Fiction."[25] Even more than most of these writers, moreover—many of whom were tough, independent professionals and some of whom seem to have propagandized for domesticity without transforming its details into significant metaphors or myths—Dickinson was actually immersed in the transformative mysteries of the household [cooking and baking]. . . .

Like Austen, who claimed that hers was an art of the miniature, an art that engraved domestic details on a "little bit (two Inches wide) of Ivory,"[26] Dickinson created out of what the "Sages" might call "small" details a mystery-play that questioned the very concept of size. Like Woolf, whose Mrs. Dalloway and Mrs. Ramsay transform the "humdrum" acts of party-giving, stew-making, knitting, and sewing into rich aesthetic rituals, Dickinson invented a religion of domesticity, a mystery cult in which she herself was a kind of blasphemously female "Word made Flesh" (1651) and the servings of cake and wine she sent to chosen friends were sacramental offerings.[27] But even more than Austen or Woolf the self-consciously female "Myth of Amherst" had a vision of what Muriel Rukeyser has called a "world split open"—a world transformed through the transformation of vision itself.[28] In this, interestingly, she was a prototypical modernist-surrealist as well as a prototypical modern woman poet who followed her great mother Elizabeth Barrett Browning in creating a new way of seeing for all the poetic daughters who have come after her. Another anecdote recounted by one of Dickinson's bemused relatives will help

[25]Nina Baym, *Women's Fiction* (Ithaca: Cornell University Press, 1978).

[26]*Jane Austen's Letters to Her Sister Cassandra and Others*, ed. R. W. Chapman, 2nd ed. (London: Oxford University Press, 1952), pp. 468–69.

[27]For a related, but differently designed, discussion of "A Word made Flesh" and its implications for Dickinson's own sense of herself as somehow divine, see Margaret Homans, *Women Writers and Poetic Identity* (Princeton: Princeton University Press, 1980), pp. 212–14.

[28]See Muriel Rukeyser, "Käthe Kollwitz" ("What would happen if one woman told the truth about her life? / The world would split open") in Rukeyser, *The Speed of Darkness* (New York: Random House, 1968).

illustrate the kind of distinctively female, proto-modernist surrealism that marked this writer's transformed and transformative vision of domestic details. The poet's "little nephew [Ned]," wrote her cousin Clara Newman Turner in 1900,

> boylike had a way of leaving anything superfluous to his immediate needs at Grandma's. After one of these little "Sins of Omission," over came his high-top rubber boots, standing erect and spotless on a silver tray, their tops running over with Emily's flowers. At another time the little overcoat was returned with each velvet pocket pinned down, and a card with "Come in" on one, and "Knock" on the other. The "Come in" proved to be raisins; the "Knock," cracked nuts.[29]

Besides telling us, again, about Dickinson's wit and charm, this story tells us something about her ability to see, "New Englandly," of course, through the ordinariness of things to the seeds of the extraordinary, the roots of difference concealed behind appearance. For if boots can hold flowers and pockets can hide raisins, then it is no wonder that the flesh may be a word and words may be "esoteric sips / Of the communion Wine" (1452)—sacramental signals of mysterious power and energy. It is no wonder, either, that such power is not to be found by questing through distances but instead is lodged "at home," in an ordinary bedroom; no wonder that the priestess of this power once took her niece up to that room and, mimicking locking herself in, "thumb and forefinger closed on an imaginary key," said "with a quick turn of her wrist, 'It's just a turn—and freedom, Matty!' "[30] Going *in* to the ordinary, *in* to the seed, *in* to the flower in the boot, *in* to the flesh in the word and the word in the wine was the central maneuver of all Dickinson's mysteries of transformation, a point that should go far in explaining not only the sometimes puzzling imagery of her life/text but also her sometimes puzzling dislocations of language.

Such dislocations, after all, are really other kinds of transformations, and they come about because as she enters and splits open the commonplace Dickinson also necessarily cracks open ordinary usages, revising and reinventing the vocabulary she has inherited from a society that does not share her piercing visions. "They shut me up in Prose," Dickinson tells us punningly in poem 613,

> As when a little Girl
> They put me in the Closet—
> Because they liked me "still"—

But "Still!" she boasts, "Could themself have peeped—"

> And seen my Brain—go round—
> They might as wise have lodged a Bird
> For Treason—in the Pound—
>
> Himself has but to will
> And easy as a Star
> Abolish his Captivity—
> And laugh—No more have I—

[29]Leyda, vol. 2, p. 481.
[30]Ibid., p. 483.

To this wayward nun, as to all winged things, walls and fences pose no problems: she frets not at the convent walls of language because she knows she can leap over them any time she pleases, or perhaps, more accurately, she can transform them into windows whenever she wants. A number of phrases from the poems quoted in these pages exemplify such linguistic metamorphoses: "hovering seen through fog," "the Instead—the Pinching fear," even "They shut me up in Prose." All these transformations of vocabulary abolish the "Captivity" implicit in ordinary usage, and—importantly—they do this by expanding, rather than annihilating, meaning.[31]

Ultimately, moreover, such expansions of meaning, together with the transformations of vision that energized them, must have led Dickinson from an exploration and enactment of the mysteries of domesticity to related celebrations of the mysteries of nature and of woman's nature. This priestess of the daily, after all, continually meditated upon the extraordinary possibilities implicit in the ordinary flowerings of the natural world. In her "real" life as the "Myth of Amherst," she created a conservatory and a herbarium; in the supposed life of her poetry, she saw through surfaces to the "white foot" (392) of the lily, to the "mystic green" (24) where "Nicodemus' Mystery / Receives its annual reply" (140), to the time of "Ecstasy—and Dell" (392) and to the time when "the Landscape listens" (258). In one of her most astonishing visions of transformation, too, she recorded the moment when "the Eggs fly off in Music / From the Maple Keep" (956). For hers was a world of processes in which everything was always turning into everything else, a world in which her own, and Nature's, "cocoon" continually tightened, and colors "teased," and, awakening into metamorphosis, she struggled to take "the clue Divine" (1099).

That this vision of nature-in-process, together with her transformative visions of domesticity, eventually brought Dickinson back to a complementary vision of the mystical powers in woman's nature seems inevitable. It is in the female human body, after all, that the primary transformations of human nature happen: egg and sperm into embryo, embryo into baby, blood into milk. (And it is the female bird who produces and nurtures those musical eggs.) As anthropologists observe, moreover, and as a poet of domesticity like Dickinson knew perfectly well, it is women who perform the primary transformations of culture: raw into cooked, clay into pot, reed into basket, fiber into thread, thread into cloth, cloth into dress, lawless baby into law-abiding child.[32] And it is because of such natural and cultural transformations, Erich Neumann tells us, that the Great Mother was worshipped throughout the matriarchal ages he postulates.[33]

---

[31]Homans, analyzing this phenomenon, argues differently (but to the same end) that Dickinson deliberately exploits language's potential for ambiguity, duplicity, and fictiveness (*Woman Writers and Poetic Identity*, pp. 165–214 passim).

[32]See, for instance, Sherry Ortner, "Is Female to Male as Nature Is to Culture?" in *Woman, Culture, and Society*, ed. Michelle Zimbalist Rosaldo and Louise Lamphère (Stanford: Stanford University Press, 1974).

[33]Erich Neumann, *The Great Mother* (Princeton: Princeton University Press, 1955).

Though Dickinson may not have consciously worshipped such a goddess, some glimmering consciousness of that deity's powers must always have been with her, presiding over *all* the mysteries she served. Two poems tell us this, the poem from which I take my title and one other. Both are quite clearly matriarchal prayers, but they emphasize different aspects of Dickinson's distinctively female answer to traditional Christianity. In the first, she tells us quite frankly both who she worships and who she is:

Sweet Mountains—Ye tell Me no lie—
Never deny Me—Never fly—
Those same unvarying Eyes
Turn on Me—when I fail—or feign,
Or take the Royal names in vain—
Their far—slow—Violet Gaze—

My Strong Madonnas—Cherish still—
The Wayward Nun—beneath the Hill—
Whose service—is to You—
Her latest Worship—when the Day
Fades from the Firmament away—
To lift Her Brows on you—
                                        [722]

In the second, interestingly enough, Dickinson tells us what she will not tell us—as if to remind us that her mysteries are both miracles and puzzles:

Only a Shrine, but Mine—
I made the Taper shine—
Madonna dim, to whom all Feet may come,
Regard a Nun—

Thou knowest every Woe—
Needless to tell thee—so—
But can'st thou do
The Grace next to it—heal?
That looks a harder skill to us—
Still—just as easy, if it be thy Will
To thee—Grant me—
Thou knowest, though, so, Why tell thee?
                                        [918]

With this last poem, of course, we come full circle back to where we began; we confront once more the mystery of absence, the gap that haunts Dickinson's own account of her life, as well as everybody else's story of it. Now, however, we may be able to see how richly and powerfully this wayward nun transformed that apparent emptiness into a fullness, how the hollow rubber boot bloomed with flowers and the flowers had white feet and the silent eggs suddenly began to sing. Now, too, it may be clear that most of the *OED*'s senses of the word "mystery" have some application to this artist's "life of Allegory." Certainly her fivefold transformations—of romance, renunciation, domesticity, nature, and woman's nature—tell us truths about her own religion while hinting at paradoxical enigmas and riddles; certainly, too, her poetic "witchcraft" involves both esoteric and ordinary arts—the secrets of the poet as well as the skills of the housewife. As she mythologizes her self, moreover, she even transforms her own life into a kind of "miracle-play," a mysterious existence in which, as the Empress of Calvary, she enacts mysteries that parallel those that marked the life of Christ. And didn't she, finally, speak to her communicants both literally and figuratively through "a kind of plum cake"? Sending her famous black cake to her friend Nellie Sweetser in 1883, she wrote "Your sweet beneficence of Bulbs I return as Flowers, with a bit of the swarthy Cake baked only in Domingo."[34] But of course by "Domingo" she meant her own kitchen, where her mysteries of culinary and literary transformation took place side by side.

[34]*Letters*, vol. 3, p. 783.

Emily Dickinson's Books and Reading

Richard B. Sewall

The conditions of [Emily Dickinson's] life, and her temperament, made her especially dependent on books. . . . She could hardly have lived without them. If, using a legal term she must have heard around the house a good deal, she called her friends her "estate," more often than not she used metaphors of eating and drinking—life-sustaining processes—to describe what books meant to her. As a girl she came home from Mount Holyoke to "a feast in the reading line." Thirty years later, she began her most famous poem about books, "He ate and drank the precious Words— / His Spirit grew robust—." In the letter to Lyman (the most sustained statement we have from her about books), the metaphors are mostly vitalistic. When the doctor forbade reading, "He might as well have said, 'Eyes be blind', 'heart be still.' " Her "blood bounded" when the restriction was finally removed. "Shakespear was the first. . . . Give me ever to drink of this wine." She "devoured the luscious passages. I thought I should tear the leaves out as I turned them." Few poets have ever confessed so voracious a passion.

As the source studies of her poetry add to our knowledge of her reading, both what and how she read, several truths emerge. She can no longer be regarded, for all her withdrawn ways, as working in grand isolation, all uniqueness and originality. She saw herself as a poet in the company of the Poets—and, functioning as she did mostly on her own, read them (among other reasons) for company. In another series of metaphors, they become people. They are "the dearest ones of time, the strongest friends of the soul," her "Kinsmen of the Shelf," her "enthralling friends, the immortalities." In a poem of about 1862 she takes a "venerable Hand" and finds it warming her own:

A passage back—or two—to make—
To Times when he—was young—

His quaint opinions—to inspect—
His thought to ascertain
On Themes concern our mutual mind—
The Literature of Man—

Reprinted from *The Life of Emily Dickinson* (1974, 1994) by permission of the author and Farrar, Straus and Giroux.

What interested Scholars—most—
What Competitions ran—
When Plato—was a Certainty—
And Sophocles—a Man—
(#371)

She chatted, or argued, or agreed with these friends, it seems, quite as she did with those of flesh and blood. Many of her poems appear to be her end of conversations struck up with what she found on printed pages. . . .

We have seen her work Beecher's "earthquake in the South" into a poem and sum up Hitchcock's proof of immortality in her poem about "the Chemical conviction"—to show, perhaps, what a poet could do with an orator's phrase and a scientist's attempt at theology. Her response to Higginson's "Decoration" is the most famous of these conversation poems only because its nature is in no need of proof. Scholars have recently been pointing out her similar use of passages from such disparate sources as Hawthorne's stories, Ik Marvel's *Reveries*, Thoreau, Mrs. Browning's *Aurora Leigh*, Emerson's essays, Quarles's *Emblems*, and the endless string of fugitive verses in the periodicals (the *Republican*, the *Hampshire and Franklin Express*, the *Atlantic, Harper's*, and *Scribner's* were among those that came to her door).[1] The process can go on indefinitely as we explore the range of that prehensile mind and burrlike memory. In the obituary Sue wrote for Emily in the *Republican*, she spoke of her as turning more and more, as she grew older "to her own large wealth of individual resources for companionship, sitting thenceforth, as some one said of her, 'in the light of her own fire.' " The metaphor is a good one. Much of the fuel for that fire came from her reading.

She read hungrily, uncritically, and with her whole being. In her recorded remarks about things she read, one of the few adverse comments we find is on Harriet Prescott [Spofford]'s "Circumstance," a story that appeared in the *Atlantic* in May 1860. She wrote Higginson that "it followed me, in the Dark—so I avoided her—" and that, in its way, was a compliment. Her capacity for absorbing what we would consider banalities was apparently lifelong, not just an aberration of youth. At twenty-one, when she should have been outgrowing some of her girlish sentimentalities, she wrote Susan Gilbert about some books that were not sentimental enough for her:

---

[1]Since the decade of the 1950s, which produced workable texts of the poems and the letters, source and "affinity" studies have multiplied. . . . Although I still agree with Whicher that "Emily Dickinson's poetry is not derivable from her reading" (p. 224) and with Henry Wells (*Introduction to Emily Dickinson*, 1947, p. 278) that "her library, however important, was always secondary to her practice," the value of such probing into sources, parallels, and affinities is indisputable. She appears in ever-widening perspective, and her stature grows. She comes to us increasingly as the summation of a culture, not (as she was long regarded) a minor and freakish offshoot. [George Frisbie Whicher's *This Was a Poet* (New York: Charles Scribner, 1938) is the first critical biography of Emily Dickinson that places her firmly in the tradition of English and American literature.—Ed.]

I have just read three little books, not great, not thrilling—but sweet and true. "The Light in the Valley," "Only," and A "House upon a Rock"—I know you would love them all—yet they dont *bewitch* me any. There are no walks in the wood—no low and earnest voices, no moonlight, nor stolen love, but pure little lives, loving God, and their parents, and obeying the laws of the land; yet read, if you meet them, Susie, for they will do one good.

It is reassuring to find "Alton Lock" and "Bleak House" ("it is like him who wrote it—that is all I can say") mentioned in the next paragraph; but what she liked next year in the poems of Alexander Smith, the young Scottish writer who was making such a stir, was his "exquisite frensy" and "some wonderful figures, as ever I met in my life."[2] While she could say of Whitman (in 1862), "I never read his Book—but was told that he was disgraceful," and of Poe (in 1879), "I know too little to think," she thought enough of John Pierpont's "very sweet" elegy on his son to copy its ten anguished stanzas for her friend Mary Warner in 1856, and of George Parson Lathrop's very similar elegy, "The Child's Wish Granted," to tell Francis Norcross in 1881 that it was "piteously sweet."

The truth seems to be that what is banal to us was lifeblood to the "advanced" young people of Amherst, who vibrated sympathetically to Ik Marvel's *Reveries*, or Longfellow's *Kavanagh*, or the tearful effusions of the sub-poets. Perhaps they found compensation for the earnest, overly pious culture of their community and the rigors of their "real life" homes. Although Emily's reading sobered considerably as time went on (the allusions to sub-literature diminish rapidly after the mid-1860s), she never lost her taste for sentiment. Her very last letter (to the Norcross cousins) is, *in toto*, the title of Hugh Conway's *Called Back* (1883), a novel in the sentimental-melodramatic mode at its worst. And yet she found it "a haunting story, and as loved Mr. Bowles used to say, 'greatly impressive to me.'"

One aspect of her early, and perhaps later, reading deserves comment, since it illuminates certain aspects of her poetry, its subjects and form. She read, not just to pick up conversations with her authors or to quench her burning thirst at the Pierian spring, but competitively. This streak was apparent from the first. As a girl, she wanted her letters to be the brightest and best. She joshed Austin about his poetic pretensions, with a hint about the competition he'd meet in the family. She said that one day she hoped to make Austin and Sue proud of her. One way to

---

[2]A copy of Alexander Smith's *Poems* (1853) is in the Dickinson Collection at Harvard. The opening soliloquy of Walter, the poet hero, will give a notion of the "wonderful figures" (and perhaps the theme) that attracted ED.

As a wild maiden, with love-drinking eyes,
Sees in sweet dreams a beaming Youth of Glory,
And wakes to weep, and ever after sighs
For that bright vision till her hair is hoary;
Ev'n so, alas! is my life's passion story.
For Poesy my heart and pulses beat,
For Poesy my blood runs red and fleet.
As Moses' serpent the Egyptians' swallow'd,
One passion eats the rest. . . .

begin was to do what other poets had done, only do it better. In this she had ample precedent in the custom of the day among the Minnie Myrtles and Grace Greenwoods, whose verses on birds and buttercups, sunsets and cemeteries, dotted the poetry departments of the journals and newspapers. The would-be poetesses (the vogue was notably female) were frankly imitative, which meant, we can assume, competitive. A theme or subject would go the rounds—frustrated love, early death, the seasons, the "little things" in nature—and the point would be to see who could do it best. There seems a hint of this in Emily's attitude when she said of Mrs. Spofford's "The Amber Gods": "It is the only thing I ever read in my life that I didn't think I could have imagined myself!" There surely is a suggestion of competitiveness when she sent Higginson her reaction of his "Decoration," or in her refusal to embarrass Wordsworth about his "Light that never was, on sea or land": "Myself could arrest it but we'll not chagrin Him. . . ."

If Emily read competitively and for companionship, she also read for inspiration—but inspiration in her own special sense. In one phase of her reading, she seems constantly to have been on the lookout for the nugget, the germ, some striking word or phrase that would set her mind going. Such at least seems the gist of a passage in the letter to Joseph Lyman about words and their effect on her. She speaks of literature here in terms not of wholes—the philosophy, or the moral, or the message embodied in the total work—but of parts, the single, glowing words:

> We used to think, Joseph, when I was an unsifted girl and you so scholarly that words were cheap & weak. Now, I dont know of anything so mighty. There are [those] to which I lift my hat when I see them sitting princelike among their peers on the page. Sometimes I write one, and look at his outlines till he glows as no sapphire.

"In the beginning was the Word" has been said of her, and rightly. When she was fifteen she wrote Abiah Root, thanking her for a letter, "At every word I read I seemed to feel new strength." Many statements and certainly the practice of her later years indicate that the particularizing of "every word" was not casual. "A Word is inundation, when it comes from the Sea." "You need the balsam word," she wrote to her bereaved cousins. "How lovely are the wiles of Words!" she exclaimed to Mrs. Holland. Some such enthusiasm was surely the meaning behind her remark that for several years in the late 1850s her "Lexicon" was her only companion. As late as 1883, thanking Mrs. Holland for her "full sweetness, to which as to a Reservoir the smaller Waters go," she paused to say, "What a beautiful Word 'Waters' is!" She rejoiced in the sheer thrill of words wonderfully put together. She wrote Joseph Lyman, after the doctor said she could read again, that

> Shakespear was the first; Antony & Cleopatra where Enobarbus laments the amorous lapse of his master. Here is the ring of it.

> "heart that in the scuffles of
> great fights hath burst the
> buck[l]e on his breast"

—a passage expressive of her own sense of liberation, surely, but the thrill seems to have come mainly from "the ring of it."

At least three poems deal explicitly (and many more implicitly) with the power of words for evil as well as good.

> A word is dead
> When it is said,
> Some say.
> I say it just
> Begins to live
> That day.
> (#1212, about 1872?)

Words can be dangerous. A syllable "can make to quake like jostled tree":

> Could mortal lip divine
> The undeveloped Freight
> Of a delivered syllable
> 'Twould crumble with the weight.
> (#1409, about 1877)

A careless word can kill:

> A Word dropped careless on a Page
> May stimulate an eye
> When folded in perpetual seam
> The Wrinkled Maker lie
>
> Infection in the sentence breeds
> We may inhale Despair
> At distances of Centuries
> From the Malaria—
> (#1261, about 1873)

Her manuscripts, sometimes with half a dozen variants for a single word, show how carefully she chose. She once begged off seeing a caller because, she said, "My own Words so chill and burn me."

Her feeling for words went far beyond the aesthetic response—"lovely" or "beautiful" or "ringing." In her sense of their power to heal or kill, we again come close to what she read for and how she used what she read. She could be said to have been in the tradition of Shelley's vitalism, when he implored the west wind to scatter his poems abroad to "quicken a new birth"; but the immediate, intimate power of the word, of the "jostling" syllable or the malarial sentence, is different from the nineteenth-century notion of winged words, message-bearing verses. There is something in her of Emerson's idea of each word as once a stroke of genius, a poem, but much more of the idea of the Incarnation as she transferred it from theology to poetics. She made two statements of it, one in prose and one in a poem. Both are undated.

The import of that Paragraph "The Word made Flesh" Had he the faintest intimation Who broached it Yesterday! "Made Flesh and dwelt among us."

In the poem she describes the experience of partaking the Word as a kind of communion. Of the first fourteen verses of the opening chapter of the Gospel according to St. John, she ignored the reiterated metaphor of the "light" that "shineth in darkness" and chose only the most explicit statement of the Incarnation.

A Word made Flesh is seldom
And tremblingly partook
Nor then perhaps reported
But have I not mistook
Each one of us has tasted
With ecstasies of stealth
The very food debated
To our specific strength—

A Word that breathes distinctly
Has not the power to die
Cohesive as the Spirit
It may expire if He—
"Made Flesh and dwelt among us["]
Could condescension be
Like this consent of Language
This loved Philology

(#1651)

It is the poet, of course, who brings about this mystical transmutation of word into flesh. She knew that the achievement was rare. "Sometimes," she wrote Lyman, "I write one." This is why, in her first letter to Higginson, she was eager to know if her verse was "alive," whether it "breathed"—that is, whether she had achieved the miracle of Incarnation. It is not surprising that Higginson, schooled in the Victorian virtues of form and message, did not understand what she meant. He was not ready, nor was nineteenth-century America, for so intensely sacramental a poet.

Her method was just that: the intensification, or concentration, of meaning in words until they glowed "as no sapphire"—until, that is, they became, in mutually supportive combination, the Word, a poem that could "dwell among us," alive, a corporate fusion of meaning and (like human life) mystery. This sense of life is the most difficult of all things to create—and she knew that, too. This is one reason, surely, why many of her poems seem cryptic, incomplete, barely reducible to coherent statement, as if she was conscious of an element of the ineffable, even in usual things, like hummingbirds or sunsets. Or perhaps it was the sheer magnitude of meaning that defied communication. This seems to be the gist of her remark to Mrs. Holland, "There is not so much Life as *talk* of Life, as a general thing. Had we the first intimation of the Definition of Life, the calmest of us would be Lunatics!" She read and heard plenty of talk about Life—the Victorian mode was not famous for its succinctness—and, as she told Higginson, it embarrassed her and her dog. It was not that she spurned the "Hallowed things" she read about or heard people talk about; she simply withdrew in order to give these things a life that so many of the writers and the talkers failed to give them. This took time, concentration, and solitude.

By a good chance, we can occasionally catch a glimpse of another phase of her reading. In a poem of about 1862 she wrote:

A Book I have—a friend gave—
Whose Pencil—here and there—
Had notched the place that pleased Him— . . .
                                        (#360)

Apparently, the habit of notching passages was hers, too. A good number of the books that have come down to us from the library in the Homestead and a few from the Evergreens that she almost certainly shared with Austin and Sue have markings that seem to be hers: thin pencil lines in the margin, parallel to the column of print, and sometimes barely discernible. Sometimes a passage is marked with a tiny "x." The trouble is, other people in the Dickinson circle had pencils too, and followed the same practice. Sue's copy of *Aurora Leigh*, for instance, is marked, but with heavier lines than Emily's. *Of the Imitation of Christ*, given her for Christmas by Sue in 1876, is marked with much heavier lines than the marks, presumably hers, in two books of her youth, *Kavanagh* (1849) and Ik Marvel's *Reveries* (1850). Copies of both of these, with Austin's signature on the flyleaves, have come down to us from him by way of Mabel Todd. One can only guess that both the fine, thin lines and the later bold ones are Emily's.[3]

Assuming they are (and at least we can be fairly sure that they were done by one or another of the *young* Dickinsons), what kind of passage is marked? Not, usually (to take the *Reveries* first), the glowing word or ringing phrase so much as meditative passages on subjects mighty and minuscule: life and death, time and eternity, love frustrated or fulfilled; marriage versus the solitary life; silence; hiding one's

---

[3]There are some thirty marked books in the Dickinson Collection in the Houghton Library, Harvard. In the library's short-title registry of the books, the markings are described as "probably" or "perhaps" by Emily Dickinson. Though the markings must be approached cautiously, the general scholarly agreement on their authenticity is impressive. The markings in a few of the volumes consist simply of several pages turned down at the corner. The marked volumes (dates indicate editions) are: Matthew Arnold, *Essays in Criticism* (1866 ed.); Elizabeth Barrett Browning, *Aurora Leigh* (1857), *Poems* (1852), *Prometheus Bound*, tr. (1851); Robert Browning, *Dramatis Personae* (1864), *The Ring and the Book* (1869), *Selections* (1884), *Sordello*, (1864); William Cullen Bryant, *Poems* (1849); Thomas Carlyle, *Heroes and Hero Worship* (1853); Arthur Hugh Clough, *Poems* (1869), *Confessions of an English Opium-Eater* (1855), *Literary Reminiscences* (1854); George Eliot, *The Mill on the Floss* (1860), *Romola* (1863), *Scenes from Clerical Life* (1859); Ralph Waldo Emerson, *The Conduct of Life* (1861, 1879), *Society and Solitude* (1879), *May-Day* (1867), *Essays* (1861); Theodore Parker, *Prayers* (1862); Coventry Patmore, *The Angel in the House* (1856, 1857, 1877); Adelaide Ann Procter, *Legends and Lyrics* (1860); Jean-Paul Richter, *Titan* (1862); Shakespeare, *Comedies, Histories, Tragedies, and Poems* (1853); Alexander Smith, *Poems* (1853); Alfred Tennyson, *Poems* (1853), *The Princess* (1848); Thomas à Kempis, *Of the Imitation of Christ* (1857); James Thomson, *The Seasons* (1817); Henry David Thoreau, *Walden* (1863); John Wilson, *Noctes Ambrosianae* (1855). . . .

feelings; home; Past and Present; dreams; letter writing; or the plight of a woman without Religion (much worse, says Ik Marvel, than that of a man!). Sentimentalities perhaps, but matters that the young people had to deal with on their own, with little help from father, mother, or the Sunday sermon. Apparently, Ik Marvel played the role (among others) of today's psychological counselors. Here he is, for instance, on marriage:

> Shall this brain of mine, careless-working, never tired with idleness, feeding on long vagaries, and high, gigantic castles, dreaming out beatitudes hour by hour—turn itself at length to such dull task-work, as thinking out a livelihood for wife and children?
>
> Where thenceforward will be those sunny dreams, in which I have warmed my fancies, and my heart, and lighted my eye with crystal? This very marriage, which a brilliant working imagination has invested time and again with brightness, and delight, can serve no longer as a mine for teeming fancy: all, alas, will be gone—reduced to the dull standard of the actual! No more room for intrepid forays of imagination—no more gorgeous realm-making—all will be over!
>
> Why not, I thought, go on dreaming?[4]

Some such misgivings as these may have been behind Emily's anxieties about marriage in her letter to Sue in 1852, when (only a few months after reading the *Reveries,* and obviously engaged in something of a reverie herself) she confessed that "I tremble lest at sometime I, too, am yielded up." Time after time Marvel's dreamer broaches thoughts similar to her own. She boasted to Joseph Lyman that "space and time are things of the body. . . . My Country is Truth." The Dreamer says of his imaginings,

> Are not these fancies thronging on my brain, bringing tears to my eyes, bringing joy to my soul, as living, as anything human can be living? What if they have no material type—no objective form? All that is crude,—a mere reduction of ideality to sense,—a transformation of the spiritual to the earthy,—a levelling of soul to matter.

Reading, says the Dreamer, is "a great, and happy disentangler of all those knotted snarls—those extravagant vagaries, which belong to a heart sparkling with sensibility," and he recommends, for solace, or sympathy, or "soul-culture" (his phrase), many of those "strongest friends of the soul" to whom Emily turned.

One can imagine the following (marked) passage disentangling a knotty snarl in Emily's consciousness at this crucial time in her development. For all that can be said about her Puritan heritage of Duty and Work, about Mary Lyon's exhilarating example, or even Emerson's insistence, of which she surely was aware, upon the Now, "the almost unbelievable miracle"[5] of the moment, the likelihood is that at a time when she was dreaming of fame Ik Marvel spoke most directly to her:

---

[4]This passage is not "notched," but it is close to a cluster of those that are.

[5]Cf. Francis Otto Matthiessen, *American Renaissance* (1941), p. 12, where he describes Emerson's discovery (after he had turned his back on the "pale negations" of Unitarianism) of "what, after long and quiet listening to himself, he knew that he really believed. The first and recurrent upsurge of his conviction was that 'life is an ecstasy,' that the moment was an almost unbelievable miracle, which he wanted, more than anything else, to catch and to record."

Stop not, loiter not, look not backward, if you would be among the foremost! The great Now, so quick, so broad, so fleeting, is yours;—in an hour it will belong to the Eternity of the Past. The temper of Life is to be made good by big honest blows; stop striking, and you will do nothing: strike feebly, and you will do almost as little. Success rides on every hour: grapple it, and you may win: but without a grapple it will never go with you. Work is the weapon of honor, and who lacks the weapon, will never triumph.

These stirring words come toward the end of the section in *Reveries* called "Noon"—preceded, of course, by "Morning" and followed by "Evening," each with its appropriate thoughts. It may well be that Emily Dickinson's long-time fascination with the phenomenon of noon had its start here. (The section is marked in several places.) Marvel begins,

> The Noon is short; the sun never loiters on the meridian, nor does the shadow on the old dial by the garden, stay long at XII. The Present, like the noon, is only a point; and a point so fine, that it is not measurable by grossness of action. Thought alone is delicate enough to tell the breadth of the Present.

Or, as he puts it a few paragraphs later, "Thought ranges over the world, and brings up hopes, and fears, and resolves, to measure the burning NOW."

Such "measuring" was to become Emily Dickinson's life work, but she carried Marvel's notion of the "breadth of the Present" much further. Noon became a token of the instantaneous, arrested present which is timelessness, or eternity, or heaven, when all accident, or "grossness," is discarded and there is nothing but essence. In the poem "A Clock stopped," "Degreeless Noon" is the timelessness of death. Another poem equates noon with perfection, the ideal world of pure essence, or Heaven:

> There is a Zone whose even Years
> No Solstice interrupt—
> Whose Sun constructs perpetual Noon
> Whose perfect Seasons wait—
>
> Whose Summer set in Summer, till
> The Centuries of June
> And Centuries of August cease
> And Consciousness—is Noon.
>   (#1056, about 1865)

"When Water ceases to rise—[she once wrote] it has commenced falling. That is the law of Flood"—another statement of the idea of "Degreeless Noon." Much of what is often called the breathlessness of Emily Dickinsons's poems comes from the urgency of her attempts to arrest the moment, to catch and preserve its essence. The exercise kept her nimble. "Forever—," she began a poem that further dignifies Ik Marvel's exhortations, "is composed of Nows."[6] . . .

---

[6]Roland Hagenbüchle, "Precision and Indeterminacy in the Poetry of Emily Dickinson" (*Emerson Society Quarterly* xx [1974], pp. 10–11), elevates this idea into a major component of her poetics:

> The . . . concentration on the "critical" moment [the "Now"] is a crucial element in Emily Dickinson's poetry. . . . It finds expression, first iconically, in the epigrammatic shortness of her

Kavanagh was the book, according to Higginson's report of his conversation with Emily in 1870, that Austin smuggled into the house for one of those feasts of reading when they were all young together. The time must have been about 1849, the year the book appeared and the date of Austin's copy. We have already noted the passage in *Kavanagh* describing a friendship between two girls—Alice Archer and Cecilia Vaughan—so close to what Emily felt for Sue as, it would seem, to have been unmistakable, at least to Emily: "They sat together in school; they walked together after school; they told each other their manifold secrets; they wrote long and impassioned letters to each other in the evening; in a word, they were in love with each other." The passage is marked, apparently by two hands—first, by two faint, parallel, but slightly wavy lines next to the column of print and following the length of the paragraph; and then by one very short, straight line, also fine, outside the parallel ones. The book went the rounds: no less than four kinds of markings are discernible—short, heavy, firm; long, light, wavy; long, straight, intermittent light and heavy; and the wavy parallels, which give the impression of being the most emphatic of all.

At the very least the markings show how carefully these young people pored over the book and for much the same kind of sustenance they found in *Reveries*. Longfellow's romance strings together in its loose narrative the same kind of animadversions on life, love, and literature—often little sententious bits that have only slight relevance to the story, like these (marked with the parallel lines):

> The same object, seen from the three different points of view,—the Past, the Present, and the Future,—often exhibits three different faces to us; like those sign-boards over shop doors, which represent the face of a lion as we approach, of a man when we are in front, and of an ass when we have passed. . . .
> The rays of happiness, like those of light, are colorless when unbroken.

These are the thoughts of Mr. Churchill, the village schoolmaster, a would-be poet and novelist, whose projected romance never gets beyond the Casaubon stage and thus provides the theme of the story, summed up in Longfellow's epigraph on the title page,

---

poems, second thematically, in the numerous descriptions of unstable phenomena in nature such as the rising and setting of the sun or its precarious poise at the meridian hour of noon, the changing of the seasons at the solstices and certain fleeting effects of light in general. It can further be observed in the elliptical and often ambiguous syntax (including the hyphen), and finally in the use of polysemantic and often precariously unstable words and expressions. The world's drama is enacted before her eyes as a process or, to use her own words, as "God's Experiment" [*P* #300, about 1862]. The reversal from being into nothingness (and vice-versa) takes place anew at every moment, as "a gun . . . that touched 'goes off' " [*L* III, 670, to Louise Norcross, early September 1880]. This eminently *dialectic* principle foredooms every attempt to pursue the romantic quest by means of analogy or metaphor. The poet experiences each instant of life and, even more so, that of death as a "critical" turning point or crisis:

> Crisis is a Hair
> Toward which forces creep
> Past which forces retrograde
> [#889, about 1864]

The flighty purpose never is o'ertook,
Unless the deed go with it.
                        Shakespeare.

Kavanagh, by contrast, the brilliant young preacher whose marriage to Cecilia
Vaughan (the Sue figure in the story) leads to Alice Archer's brokenhearted death,
represents achievement, the man who follows purpose with deed. On the outside
of his study door is the "vigorous line of Dante, 'Think that To-day shall never
dawn again!' " and on the inside some lines by "a more modern bard," including
the following (marked by parallel lines):

And days are lost, lamenting o'er lost days.
Are you in earnest? Seize this very minute!
What you can do or think you can, begin it!
Boldness has genius, power, and magic in it!

Kavanagh lingered long in Emily's imagination. "Adolphus Hawkins, Esq.," the
simpering village poet in love with Cecilia Vaughan, became the type of the senti-
mentalist. In the fall of 1853 she showed signs of consciously discarding the mode.
She wrote the Hollands: "I wrote to you last week, but thought you would laugh at
me, and call me sentimental, so I kept my lofty-letter for 'Adolphus Hawkins,
Esq.' " Earlier that year (February 24, 1853), a letter to Susan Gilbert, still thoroughly à la Hawkins, quotes the device Mr. Churchill once used for reckoning on
what day of the week the first of December would fall: " 'At Dover dwells George
Brown, Esquire, / Good Christopher Finch and Daniel Friar!' " (As Emily has it,
however, Christopher becomes Carlos, Daniel becomes David, and Friar becomes
Fryer; her memory was burrlike but not photographic.) The experience of reading
the book was still alive enough in her mind to come up in her conversation with
Higginson in 1870; and in 1879 she compared Austin and Sue's driving off to the
Belchertown Cattle Show to "Mr and Mrs 'Pendexter,' turning their backs upon
Longfellow's Parish." . . .

To Emily Dickinson in her mid-twenties, already feeling estranged from certain aspects of things spiritual and temporal in her small, self-conscious community, *Of the Imitation of Christ* must have come with a jolt. Yet there is no word
about the book in her surviving letters, early or late. The clue to the time of her
first experience of it is a copy of an edition of 1857, though it is not certain that the
book was acquired that year. It bore her name but was owned by Sue and apparently shared with her. Although it has markings similar to those in the 1876 copy
that Sue gave Emily for Christmas that year, whether they are Sue's or Emily's or
both, it is impossible to tell. It may have been that Sue, hearing of the new edition
in 1876, presented Emily with a book that had long interested them both.[7]

---

[7]The copy of the 1857 edition is in the Dickinson Collection, Houghton Library, Harvard. The title
page is inscribed "Emily Dickinson," in Sue's handwriting. The copy of the 1876 edition is in the
Beinecke Library, Yale. It is inscribed, in Sue's hand, "Emily with love / Dec 26th 76." The translations
differ slightly. I have followed the 1857 edition except for a few marked passages in the 1876 edition.

Reveries and *Kavanagh* touched on many of Emily's problems and may have helped her to some resolutions, but the *Imitation* presented her with an all-or-nothing choice far more radical in its demands than the mild inspirations of Marvel's Dreamer or Kavanagh's literary advice to Mr. Churchill. The issue of choice was sharpening for her, as she saw her friends taking paths very different from anything she was inclined to follow—matrimony, or careers, or the kind of piety she saw in Abiah Root. She could explain her refusal to become "a christian" (in Abiah's sense) by saying that the world held her affections, but it was not the world of the Amherst sewing society or august assemblies or Boston and Bostonians. For whatever reasons, normal or neurotic, she was withdrawing more and more from the community. The *Imitation* was the sternest kind of challenge to certain tendencies she felt in herself. Her remark to Higginson in 1869 that her life "has been too simple and stern to embarrass any," suggests the degree to which she had answered it. "By two wings," says the *Imitation*, "a man is lifted up from things earthly, namely, by Simplicity and Purity." The passage is marked in the 1876 copy.

"Despise the world." "Fly the tumultuousness of the world as much as thou canst." "Take refuge within the closet of thine heart." These and similar exhortations echo and reecho throughout the *Imitation*. For a girl with religious and social problems, with a burgeoning talent still unfocused, this manual for the dedicated life must have had an attraction quite apart from its doctrinal basis. Its insistence on innate depravity (the doctrine of "corruption" that the minister preached to Father and Vinnie), on the purging away of the sins of the flesh, on the dangers of succumbing to the wiles of the devil—all this she could deal with as she dealt with similar doctrines in the Amherst sermons. But its pattern of life was adaptable to purposes other than monastic. She had not yet, it seems, found a discipline, a way of implementing the "work of a life" she read about in *Reveries*. Here in the *Imitation* was the same urgency: "Why wilt thou defer thy good purpose from day to day? Arise and begin in this very instant, and say, Now is the time to be doing"—and here was a touch of Mary Lyon's teaching: "Do what lieth in thy power and God will assist thy good affection"; and here, even, was something of her own scorn of people (as Higginson recorded her conversation in 1870) who were only half alive ("How do most people live without any thoughts"). The *Imitation*, lamenting "lukewarmness of spirit," slothfulness and apathy, had an answer: "For that is the reason why there are few contemplative men to be found, because few have the knowledge to withdraw themselves fully from perishing creatures."

The *Imitation* prescribed a daily regimen and a locale. "Things private are practised more safely at home." "The more thou visitest thy chamber, the more thou wilt like it; the less thou comest thereunto, the more thou wilt loathe it." In "daily exercises" the cloistered one penetrates those "things internal"—Emily

---

A few pages in the 1857 edition are uncut (Bk. II, ch. eleven; Bk. III, ch. 3; pp. 147–48). Bk. III, ch. 5, and Bk. IV, ch. 7 and 12, are the most heavily marked, often in the same wavy parallel lines noted in *Kavanagh*. The passages marked in the 1876 edition are indicated later in my discussion.

Dickinson's phrase was "the Being's Centre"—and (according to another passage in the *Imitation*) he "must diligently search into, and set in order both the outward and the inward man, because both of them are of importance to our progress in godliness." Then comes a verse, especially marked in the 1876 copy, much to her purpose: "Never be entirely idle; but either be reading, or writing, or praying, or meditating, or endeavouring something for the public good."

She never learned to pray, she said, and she persisted in calling herself a pagan. She interpreted the common good differently from the organized charity or sewing circles of her day and perhaps from what the *Imitation* here implied. Something closer to her notion of the common good came in another passage, where the *Imitation* urges that "we may learn to bear one another's burdens . . . to bear with one another, comfort one another, help, instruct, and admonish one another." This she did with the balsam word, the healing word, the wise word, but, above all, with the living word in hundreds of letters and poems. "Let Emily sing for you because she cannot pray," she wrote the Norcrosses in their bereavement. The *Imitation,* expanding on the Gospels, states her "business" and suggests her method:

> Love feels no burden, thinks nothing of trouble, attempts what is above its strength, pleads no excuse of impossibility; for it thinks all things lawful for itself and all things possible. . . . Love is watchful, and sleeping slumbereth not. . . . Let me sing the song of love. . . .

With one exception, the two chapters on love in the *Imitation* are the most heavily marked in the 1876 copy.

"Sumptuous Destitution"

Richard Wilbur

At some point Emily Dickinson sent her whole Calvinist vocabulary into exile, telling it not to come back until it would subserve her own sense of things.

Of course, that is not a true story, but it is a way of saying what I find most remarkable in Emily Dickinson. She inherited a great and overbearing vocabulary which, had she used it submissively, would have forced her to express an established theology and psychology. But she would not let that vocabulary write her poems for her. There lies the real difference between a poet like Emily Dickinson and a fine versifier like Isaac Watts. To be sure, Emily Dickinson also wrote in the metres of hymnody, and paraphrased the Bible, and made her poems turn on great words like Immortality and Salvation and Election. But in her poems those great words are not merely being themselves; they have been adopted, for expressive purposes; they have been taken personally, and therefore redefined.

The poems of Emily Dickinson are a continual appeal to experience, motivated by an arrogant passion for the truth. "Truth is so rare a thing," she once said, "it is delightful to tell it." And, sending some poems to Colonel Higginson, she wrote, "Excuse them, if they are untrue." And again, to the same correspondent, she observed, "Candor is the only wile"—meaning that the writer's bag of tricks need contain one trick only, the trick of being honest. That her taste for truth involved a regard for objective fact need not be argued: we have her poem on the snake, and that on the hummingbird, and they are small masterpieces of exact description. She liked accuracy; she liked solid and homely detail; and even in her most exalted poems we are surprised and reassured by buckets, shawls, or buzzing flies.

But her chief truthfulness lay in her insistence on discovering the facts of her inner experience. She was a Linnaeus to the phenomena of her own consciousness, describing and distinguishing the states and motions of her soul. The results of this "psychic reconnaissance," as Professor Whicher[1] called it, were several. For one thing, it made her articulate about inward matters which poetry had never so sharply defined; specifically, it made her capable of writing two such lines as these:

"Sumptuous Destitution" by Richard Wilbur. From *Emily Dickinson: Three Views* (Amherst: Amherst College Press, 1960) by Richard Wilbur, Louise Bogan, and Archibald MacLeish. Copyright © 1960 by the Amherst College Press. Reprinted by permission of the author and Amherst College Press.

[1]George Frisbie Whicher, *This Was a Poet* (New York: Charles Scribner, 1938). Reprint ed. Hamden, Conn.: The Shoe String Press, 1980.—Ed.

A perfect, paralyzing bliss
Contented as despair.

We often assent to the shock of a paradox before we understand it, but those lines are so just and so concentrated as to explode their meaning instantly in the mind. They did not come so easily, I think, to Emily Dickinson. Unless I guess wrongly as to chronology, such lines were the fruit of long poetic research; the poet had worked toward them through much study of the way certain emotions can usurp consciousness entirely, annulling our sense of past and future, cancelling near and far, converting all time and space to a joyous or grievous here and now. It is in their ways of annihilating time and space that bliss and despair are comparable.

Which leads me to a second consequence of Emily Dickinson's self-analysis. It is one thing to assert as pious doctrine that the soul has power, with God's grace, to master circumstance. It is another thing to find out personally, as Emily Dickinson did in writing her psychological poems, that the aspect of the world is in no way constant, that the power of external things depends on our state of mind, that the soul selects its own society and may, if granted strength to do so, select a superior order and scope of consciousness which will render it finally invulnerable. She learned these things by witnessing her own courageous spirit.

Another result of Emily Dickinson's introspection was that she discovered some grounds, in the nature of her soul and its affections, for a personal conception of such ideas as Heaven and Immortality, and so managed a precarious convergence between her inner experience and her religious inheritance. What I want to attempt now is a rough sketch of the imaginative logic by which she did this. I had better say before I start that I shall often seem demonstrably wrong, because Emily Dickinson, like many poets, was consistent in her concerns but inconsistent in her attitudes. The following, therefore, is merely an opinion as to her main drift.

Emily Dickinson never lets us forget for very long that in some respects life gave her short measure; and indeed it is possible to see the greater part of her poetry as an effort to cope with her sense of privation. I think that for her there were three major privations: she was deprived of an orthodox and steady religious faith; she was deprived of love; she was deprived of literary recognition.

At the age of 17, after a series of revival meetings at Mount Holyoke Seminary, Emily Dickinson found that she must refuse to become a professing Christian. To some modern minds this may seem to have been a sensible and necessary step; and surely it was a step toward becoming such a poet as she became. But for her, no pleasure in her own integrity could then eradicate the feeling that she had betrayed a deficiency, a want of grace. In her letters to Abiah Root she tells of the enhancing effect of conversion on her fellow-students, and says of herself in a famous passage:

> *I* am one of the lingering bad ones, and so do I slink away, and pause and ponder, and ponder and pause, and do work without knowing why, not surely, for this brief world,

and more sure it is not for heaven, and I ask what this message *means* that they ask for so very eagerly: *you* know of this depth and fulness, will you try to tell me about it?

There is humor in that, and stubbornness, and a bit of characteristic lurking pride: but there is also an anguished sense of having separated herself, through some dry incapacity, from spiritual community, from purpose, and from magnitude of life. As a child of evangelical Amherst, she inevitably thought of purposive, heroic life as requiring a vigorous faith. Out of such a thought she later wrote:

The abdication of Belief
Makes the Behavior small—
Better an ignis fatuus
Than no illume at all—
(1551)

That hers *was* a species of religious personality goes without saying; but by her refusal of such ideas as original sin, redemption, hell, and election, she made it impossible for herself—as Professor Whicher observed—"to share the religious life of her generation." She became an unsteady congregation of one.

Her second privation, the privation of love, is one with which her poems and her biographies have made us exceedingly familiar, though some biographical facts remain conjectural. She had the good fortune, at least once, to bestow her heart on another; but she seems to have found her life, in great part, a history of loneliness, separation, and bereavement.

As for literary fame, some will deny that Emily Dickinson ever greatly desired it, and certainly there is evidence, mostly from her latter years, to support such a view. She *did* write that "Publication is the auction/Of the mind of man." And she *did* say to Helen Hunt Jackson, "How can you print a piece of your soul?" But earlier, in 1861, she had frankly expressed to Sue Dickinson the hope that "sometime" she might make her kinfolk proud of her. The truth is, I think, that Emily Dickinson knew she was good, and began her career with a normal appetite for recognition. I think that she later came, with some reason, to despair of being understood or properly valued, and so directed against her hopes of fame what was by then a well-developed disposition to renounce. That she wrote a good number of poems about fame supports my view: the subjects to which a poet returns are those which vex him.

What did Emily Dickinson do, as a poet, with her sense of privation? One thing she quite often did was to pose as the laureate and attorney of the empty-handed, and question God about the economy of His creation. Why, she asked, is a fatherly God so sparing of His presence? Why is there never a sign that prayers are heard? Why does Nature tell us no comforting news of its Maker? Why do some receive a whole loaf, while others must starve on a crumb? Where is the benevolence in shipwreck and earthquake? By asking such questions as these, she turned complaint into critique, and used her own sufferings as experiential evidence about the nature of the deity. The God who emerges from these poems is a God who does not answer, an unrevealed God whom one cannot confidently approach through Nature or through doctrine.

But there was another way in which Emily Dickinson dealt with her sentiment of lack—another emotional strategy which was both more frequent and more fruitful. I refer to her repeated assertion of the paradox that privation is more plentiful than plenty; that to renounce is to possess the more; that "The Banquet of abstemiousness/Defaces that of wine." We all know how the poet illustrated this ascetic paradox in her behavior—how in her latter years she chose to live in relative retirement, keeping the world, even in its dearest aspects, at a physical remove. She would write her friends, telling them how she missed them, then flee upstairs when they came to see her; afterward, she might send a note of apology, offering the odd explanation that "We shun because we prize." Any reader of Dickinson biographies can furnish other examples, dramatic or homely, of this prizing and shunning, this yearning and renouncing: in my own mind's eye is a picture of Emily Dickinson watching a gay circus caravan from the distance of her chamber window.

In her inner life, as well, she came to keep the world's images, even the images of things passionately desired, at the remove which renunciation makes; and her poetry at its most mature continually proclaims that to lose or forego what we desire is somehow to gain. We may say, if we like, with some of the poet's commentators, that this central paradox of her thought is a rationalization of her neurotic plight; but we had better add that it is also a discovery of something about the soul. Let me read you a little poem of psychological observation which, whatever its date of composition, may logically be considered as an approach to that discovery.

> Undue Significance a starving man attaches
> To Food—
> Far off—He sighs—and therefore—Hopeless—
> And therefore—Good—
>
> Partaken—it relieves—indeed—
> But proves us
> That Spices fly
> In the Receipt—It was the Distance—
> Was Savory—
>
> (439)

This poem describes an educational experience, in which a starving man is brought to distinguish between appetite and desire. So long as he despairs of sustenance, the man conceives it with the eye of desire as infinitely delicious. But when, after all, he secures it and appeases his hunger, he finds that its imagined spices have flown. The moral is plain: once an object has been magnified by desire, it cannot be wholly possessed by appetite.

The poet is not concerned, in this poem, with passing any judgment. She is simply describing the way things go in the human soul, telling us that the frustration of appetite awakens or abets desire, and that the effect of intense desiring is to render any finite satisfaction disappointing. Now I want to read you another well-known poem, in which Emily Dickinson was again considering privation and possession, and the modes of enjoyment possible to each. In this case, I think, a judgment is strongly implied.

> Success is counted sweetest
> By those who ne'er succeed.
> To comprehend a nectar
> Requires sorest need.
>
> Not one of all the purple Host
> Who took the Flag today
> Can tell the definition
> So clear of Victory
>
> As he defeated—dying—
> On whose forbidden ear
> The distant strains of triumph
> Burst agonized and clear!
>
> (67)

Certainly Emily Dickinson's critics are right in calling this poem an expression of the idea of compensation—of the idea that every evil confers some balancing good, that through bitterness we learn to appreciate the sweet, that "Water is taught by thirst." The defeated and dying soldier of this poem is compensated by a greater awareness of the meaning of victory than the victors themselves can have: he can comprehend the joy of success through its polar contrast to his own despair.

The poem surely does say that; yet it seems to me that there is something further implied. On a first reading, we are much impressed with the wretchedness of the dying soldier's lot, and an improved understanding of the nature of victory may seem small compensation for defeat and death; but the more one ponders this poem the likelier it grows that Emily Dickinson is arguing the *superiority* of defeat to victory, of frustration to satisfaction, and of anguished comprehension to mere possession. What do the victors have but victory, a victory which they cannot fully savor or clearly define? They have paid for their triumph by a sacrifice of awareness; a material gain has cost them a spiritual loss. For the dying soldier, the case is reversed: defeat and death are attended by an increase of awareness, and material loss has led to spiritual gain. Emily Dickinson would think that the better bargain.

In the first of these two poems I have read, it was possible to imagine the poet as saying that a starving man's visions of food are but wish fulfillments, and hence illusory; but the second poem assures us of the contrary—assures us that food, or victory, or any other good thing is best comprehended by the eye of desire from vantage of privation. We must now ask in what way desire can define things, what comprehension of nectars it can have beyond a sense of inaccessible sweetness.

Since Emily Dickinson was not a philosopher, and never set forth her thought in any orderly way, I shall answer that question by a quotation from the seventeenth-century divine Thomas Traherne. Conveniently for us, Traherne is thinking, in this brief meditation, about food—specifically, about acorns—as perceived by appetite and by desire.

> The services of things and their excellencies are spiritual: being objects not of the eye, but of the mind: and you more spiritual by how much more you esteem them. Pigs eat acorns, but neither consider the sun that gave them life, nor the influences of the heavens by which they were nourished, nor the very root of the tree from whence they came. This being the work of Angels, who in a wide and clear light see even the sea that gave them moisture: And feed upon that acorn spiritually while they know the ends for which it was created, and feast upon all these as upon a World of Joys within it: while to ignorant swine that eat the shell, it is an empty husk of no taste nor delightful savor.

Emily Dickinson could not have written that, for various reasons, a major reason being that she could not see in Nature any revelations of divine purpose. But like Traherne she discovered that the soul has an infinite hunger, a hunger to possess all things. (That discovery, I suspect, was the major fruit of her introspection.) And like Traherne she distinguished two ways of possessing things, the way of appetite and the way of desire. What Traherne said of the pig she said of her favorite insect:

> Auto da Fe and Judgment—
> Are nothing to the Bee—
> His separation from His Rose—
> To Him—sums Misery—
>   (620)

The creature of appetite (whether insect or human) pursues satisfaction, and strives to possess the object in itself; it cannot imagine the vaster economy of desire, in which the pain of abstinence is justified by moments of infinite joy, and the object is spiritually possessed, not merely for itself, but more truly as an index of the All. That is how one comprehends a nectar. Miss Dickinson's bee does not comprehend the rose which it plunders, because the truer sweetness of the rose lies beyond the rose, in its relationship to the whole of being; but she would say that Gerard Manley Hopkins comprehends a bluebell when, having noticed its intrinsic beauties, he adds, "I know the beauty of Our Lord by it." And here is an eight-line poem of her own, in which she comprehends the full sweetness of water.

> We thirst at first—'tis Nature's Act—
> And later—when we die—
> A little Water supplicate—
> Of fingers going by—
>
> It intimates the finer want—
> Whose adequate supply

Is that Great Water in the West—
Termed Immortality—

(726)

Emily Dickinson elected the economy of desire, and called her privation good, rendering it positive by renunciation. And so she came to live in a huge world of delectable distances. Far-off words like "Brazil" or "Circassian" appear continually in her poems as symbols of things distanced by loss or renunciation, yet infinitely prized and yearned-for. So identified in her mind are distance and delight that, when ravished by the sight of a hummingbird in her garden, she calls it "the mail from Tunis." And not only are the objects of her desire distant; they are also very often moving away, their sweetness increasing in proportion to their remoteness. "To disappear enhances," one of the poems begins, and another closes with these lines:

The Mountain—at a given distance—
In Amber—lies—
Approached—the Amber flits—a little—
And That's—the Skies—

(572)

To the eye of desire, all things are seen in a profound perspective, either moving or gesturing toward the vanishing point. Or to use a figure which may be closer to Miss Dickinson's thought, to the eye of desire the world is a centrifuge, in which all things are straining or flying toward the occult circumference. In some such way, Emily Dickinson conceived her world, and it was in a spatial metaphor that she gave her personal definition of Heaven. "Heaven," she said, "is what I cannot reach."

At times it seems that there is nothing in her world but her own soul, with its attendant abstractions, and, at a vast remove, the inscrutable Heaven. On most of what might intervene she has closed the valves of her attention, and what mortal objects she does acknowledge are riddled by desire to the point of transparency. Here is a sentence from her correspondence: "Enough is of so vast a sweetness, I suppose it never occurs, only pathetic counterfeits." The writer of that sentence could not invest her longings in any finite object. Again she wrote, "Emblem is immeasurable—that is why it is better than fulfilment, which can be drained." For such a sensibility, it was natural and necessary that things be touched with infinity. Therefore her nature poetry, when most serious, does not play descriptively with birds or flowers but presents us repeatedly with dawn, noon, and sunset, those grand ceremonial moments of the day which argue the splendor of Paradise. Or it shows us the ordinary landscape transformed by the electric brilliance of a storm; or it shows us the fields succumbing to the annual mystery of death. In her love-poems, Emily Dickinson was at first covetous of the beloved himself; indeed, she could be idolatrous, going so far as to say that his face, should she see it again in Heaven, would eclipse the face of Jesus. But in what I take to be her later work the beloved's lineaments, which were never very distinct, vanish entirely; he becomes pure emblem, a symbol of remote spiritual joy, and so is all but absorbed into the idea of Heaven. The lost beloved is, as one poem declares, "infinite when gone," and in such lines as the following we are aware of him mainly as an instrument in the poet's commerce with the beyond.

> Of all the Souls that stand create—
> I have elected—One—
> When Sense from Spirit—files away—
> And Subterfuge—is done—
> When that which is—and that which was—
> Apart—intrinsic—stand—
> And this brief Tragedy of Flesh—
> Is shifted—like a Sand—
> When Figures show their royal Front—
> And Mists—are carved away,
> Behold the Atom—I preferred—
> To all the lists of Clay!
>
> (664)

In this extraordinary poem, the corporeal beloved is seen as if from another and immaterial existence, and in such perspective his earthly person is but an atom of clay. His risen spirit, we presume, is more imposing, but it is certainly not in focus. What the rapt and thudding lines of this poem portray is the poet's own magnificence of soul—her fidelity to desire, her confidence of Heaven, her contempt of the world. Like Cleopatra's final speeches, this poem is an irresistible demonstration of spiritual status, in which the supernatural is so royally demanded that skepticism is disarmed. A part of its effect derives, by the way, from the fact that the life to come is described in an ambiguous present tense, so that we half-suppose the speaker to be already in Heaven.

There were times when Emily Dickinson supposed this of herself, and I want to close by making a partial guess at the logic of her claims to beatitude. It seems to me that she generally saw Heaven as a kind of infinitely remote bank, in which, she hoped, her untouched felicities were drawing interest. Parting, she said, was all she knew of it. Hence it is surprising to find her saying, in some poems, that Heaven has drawn near to her, and that in her soul's "superior instants" Eternity has disclosed to her "the colossal substance/Of immortality." Yet the contradiction can be understood, if we recall what sort of evidence was persuasive to Emily Dickinson.

"Too much of proof," she wrote, "affronts belief"; and she was little convinced either by doctrine or by theological reasoning. Her residual Calvinism was criticized and fortified by her study of her own soul in action, and from the phenomena of her soul she was capable of making the boldest inferences. That the sense of time is subject to the moods of the soul seemed to her a proof of the soul's eternity. Her intensity of grief for the dead, and her feeling of their continued presence, seemed to her arguments for the reunion of souls in Heaven. And when she found in herself infinite desires, "immortal longings," it seemed to her possible that such desires might somewhere be infinitely answered.

One psychic experience which she interpreted as beatitude was "glee," or as some would call it, euphoria. Now, a notable thing about glee or euphoria is its gratuitousness. It seems to come from nowhere, and it was this apparent source-lessness of the emotion from which Emily Dickinson made her inference. "The 'happiness' without a cause," she said, "is the best happiness, for glee intuitive and lasting is the gift of God." Having foregone all earthly causes of happiness, she could only explain her glee, when it came, as a divine gift—a compensation in joy for what she had renounced in satisfaction, and a foretaste of the mood of Heaven. The experience of glee, as she records it, is boundless: all distances collapse, and the soul expands to the very circumference of things. Here is how she put it in one of her letters: "Abroad is close tonight and I have but to lift my hands to touch the 'Hights of Abraham.' " And one of her gleeful poems begins,

'Tis little—I could care for Pearls—
Who own the ample sea—

How often she felt that way we cannot know, and it hardly matters. As Robert Frost has pointed out, happiness can make up in height for what it lacks in length; and the important thing for us, as for her, is that she construed the experience as a divine gift. So also she thought of the power to write poetry, a power which, as we know, came to her often; and poetry must have been the chief source of her sense of blessedness. The poetic impulses which visited her seemed "bulletins from Immortality," and by their means she converted all her losses into gains, and all the pains of her life to that clarity and repose which were to her the qualities of Heaven. So superior did she feel, as a poet, to earthly circumstance, and so strong was her faith in words, that she more than once presumed to view this life from the vantage of the grave.

In a manner of speaking, she *was* dead. And yet her poetry, with its articulate faithfulness to inner and outer truth, its insistence on maximum consciousness, is not an avoidance of life but an eccentric mastery of it. Let me close [with] a last poem, in which she conveys both the extent of her repudiation and the extent of her happiness.

The Missing All, prevented Me
From missing minor Things.
If nothing larger than a World's
Departure from a Hinge
Or Sun's extinction, be observed
'Twas not so large that I
Could lift my Forehead from my work
For Curiosity.

(985)

Thirst and Starvation
in Emily Dickinson's Poetry

Vivian R. Pollak

"Emily Dickinson I did like very much and do still," wrote her friend Joseph Lyman to his fiancée in 1858. "But she is rather morbid and unnatural."[1] Lyman, who lived with the Dickinsons during the winter of 1846, had formed a close platonic attachment with Emily at that time and continued to use her as his touchstone of a superior woman throughout his life. In singling out unnatural morbidity as the single defect in an otherwise flawless character, he was referring, I think, not merely to Dickinson's early and lifelong fascination with illness, with death, and with dying. He was suggesting also the absence of inner vitality, the emotional numbness which was the subject of many of her greatest poems and the enabling wound to her artistic bow. Her poetry was an attempt to keep herself alive by memorializing a range of feeling and experience threatened with extinction from without and within. The relationship between the "Death blow" aimed by God, nature, and human beings, and the "funeral" in the brain was one to which Dickinson addressed her sharpest creative intuitions. She explored this relationship with particular subtlety and sophistication through images of thirst and starvation.

Dickinson uses thirst and starvation metaphorically to represent a broad spectrum of needs: spiritual, emotional, and intellectual. The characteristic response of her deprived persona is to strive for self-sufficiency, for intellectual mastery, and for esthetic sublimation of the debilitating emotions occasioned by neglect or persecution. To this end, her starving-thirsting "I" cultivates a strategy of renunciation, a "Banquet of Abstemiousness," which is an attempt to deny the needs of the social self. However, the Dickinsonian persona cannot depend on the religious, social, and moral context which made the economy of compensation work for such Puritan poets as Anne Bradstreet and such transcendental philosophers as Emerson and Thoreau. Thus her persona also responds to deprivation imposed by God, by nature, and by humans, involuntarily. The strategy of shrinking vital needs to the point where crumbs and drops suffice, if pushed to the limit, results

Reprinted from *On Dickinson* (1990) by permission of the author and Duke University Press.
[1]*The Lyman Letters*, ed. Richard B. Sewall (Amherst, Mass., 1965), p. 65.

in the extinction of appetite. What Dickinson portrays, in her most psychologically complex poems, is that loss of life-hunger causes the death of the self.

The "Death blow" in Dickinson's poetry is typically inflicted on a powerless, guiltless self. Her poetry incorporates a wide range of references to such deaths as crucifixion, drowning, hanging, suffocation, freezing, premature burial, shooting, stabbing, and guillotinage. Perhaps because of her deep religiosity, she excludes images of sudden, overt self-destruction from her poetic universe. She does not eliminate images of lingering, covert self-destruction, "Murder by degrees." The most thoroughly worked out of these images is the "I" whose response to privation imposed from without is abstinence to the very point of death, if not beyond. Starving and thirsting occur because of the parsimony of a stingy god; the inaccessibility of nature; and the failure of human love. Or starving and thirsting occur without identifiable cause. Starving and thirsting can also be the unconscious response of a self conditioned by deprivation. Striving desperately for self-reliance, the Dickinsonian persona finds itself unable to respond when

> Victory comes late—
> And is held low to freezing lips—
> Too rapt with frost
> To take it—
> How sweet it would have tasted—
> Just a Drop—
> Was God so economical?
> His Table's spread too high for Us—
> Unless We dine on tiptoe—
> Crumbs—fit such little mouths—
> Cherries—suit Robins—
> The Eagle's Golden Breakfast strangles—Them—
> God keep His Oath to Sparrows—
> Who of little Love—know how to starve—
>
> (690)[2]

Thus death from thirst or starvation can represent extinction from without and from within, as in the poem just cited. It is the interface of murder and suicide.

While the backgrounds of Puritanism and transcendentalism have been fully explored in discussions of Dickinsonian renunciation, the importance of gender has not been sufficiently recognized. Throughout the nineteenth century, the compensatory ethic of "woman's sphere" incorporated the tensions of self-sacrifice and self-affirmation which Dickinson characterized as "The Battle fought between

---

[2]All references to Dickinson's poems are taken from *The Poems of Emily Dickinson*, ed. Thomas H. Johnson, 3 vols. (Cambridge, Mass., 1955). The parenthetical numbers refer to the chronological numbering in this work. Citations from Dickinson's letters are taken from *The Letters of Emily Dickinson*, ed. Thomas H. Johnson, 3 vols. (Cambridge, Mass., 1958). The letter "L" precedes such citations to differentiate letters from poems.

the Soul / And No Man."[3] The imagery of eating and drinking is especially appropriate to this theme, drawn as it is from woman's sphere. If the persona of her food and drink poems appears devoid of gender and history, her letters make it clear that the strategy of shrinking vital needs to the point where crumbs and drops must suffice developed as a defense against the sexual politics of Victorian America, especially as represented by the Dickinson family. Like her poems, her letters show that this defense was not fully adequate to the monumental task of negating the cultural and psychological tensions it was designed to contain. In 1859, writing to her friend Elizabeth Holland, whose husband was about to return from a lecture tour promoting his best-selling books, she commented, "Am told that fasting gives to food marvellous Aroma, but by birth a Bachelor, disavow Cuisine" (L204). Emily Dickinson was not by birth a bachelor, as even the most superficial reading of her poems and letters indicates.

As John Cody has remarked in a psychoanalytic discussion of oral imagery in *After Great Pain*, Dickinson's letters reveal her preoccupation with oral nourishment.[4] She refers to food and drink in approximately three hundred letters, a ratio of almost one in three. Humans, animals, literary, historical and Biblical figures hunger, feed, drink, thirst, starve. Uninterested in housework, she took to cooking easily and naturally. In 1845, at the age of fourteen, she explained to her friend Abiah Root, "You asked me if I was attending school now. I am not. Mother thinks me not able to confine myself to school this term. She had rather I would exercise, and I can assure you I get plenty of that article by staying at home. I am going to learn to make bread to-morrow. So you may imagine me with my sleeves rolled up, mixing flour, milk, salaratus, etc., with a deal of grace" (L8). Fine cooking became her forte. Her father, so she told T. W. Higginson "*very* dreamily" in 1870, would have no bread but hers, "& people must have puddings" (L342a).

Emily Dickinson's letters tell another story as well. Her descriptions of herself stress her smallness, her frailty, her thinness. Especially during her teens and early twenties, the figure of the starved, stunted child, unable or unwilling to take on the plumpness of true womanhood, is essential to her self-characterization. She uses smallness to disguise and to suppress appetites Victorian America was attempting to refine out of "Woman's Sphere": especially anger and aggressive sexuality. In

---

[3]Three recent works defining nineteenth-century American attitudes toward women are Nancy R. Cott, *The Bonds of Womanhood: "Woman's Sphere" in New England, 1789–1835* (New Haven, Conn., 1977); Ann Douglas, *The Feminization of American Culture* (New York, 1977); and Barbara Welter, *Dimity Convictions: The American Woman in the Nineteenth Century* (Athens, Ohio, 1976).

[4](Cambridge, Mass., 1971). Cody believes that Dickinson suffered a total mental collapse just before the onset of her great creative period 1858–1862, and that this breakdown was due, in no small measure, to the inadequacies of Emily Norcross Dickinson as a mother during the poet's childhood. Cody sees in Dickinson the characteristics of the emotionally starved child, and has found her oral imagery especially compelling. He writes, "Her insatiable love needs and their frustration saturate the poetry and the letters, and one finds her forever deriving new images of emotional want and fulfillment from the basic metaphor of food and drink," p. 39. Unlike Cody, I believe that Dickinson's gradual withdrawal from the social world was primarily a political response to the extreme sex segregation of mid-century Victorian America, and that the psychodynamics of the Dickinson household represented cultural, rather than personal, disease.

"The 'Scribbling Women' and Fanny Fern: Why Women Wrote," Ann Douglas describes the ruses resorted to by popular women writers during the 1840's and fifties, to obscure their effective competition with men.[5] Fearful of rendering themselves unfeminine in their own eyes and in the eyes of society, they insisted on their own passivity, helplessness, and weakness, while functioning effectively and aggressively in the literary market place. Hawthorne, writing to his publisher in 1855, protested, "America is now given over to a d—d mob of scribbling women, and I should have no chance of success while the public taste is occupied with their trash." Grace Greenwood, a member of the flowery sisterhood enraging Hawthorne, defined "true feminine genius" as "ever timid, doubtful, and clingingly dependent; a perpetual childhood." She concluded, "A true woman shrinks instinctively from greatness."[6]

The ethic of abstinence Dickinson came to employ grew out of cultural tensions she shared with the women of her generation. A paradigmatic letter of the early 1850's shows her withdrawing from confrontation with her father and brother by invoking the protection of smallness. Letter 45, to Austin, begins with an excited observation on the female usurpation of male prerogatives. At a time when Edward Dickinson was comparing Austin's letters home from Harvard Law School to Shakespeare's, and threatening to publish his correspondence because of its literary merit, his sister was replying,

> I have just finished reading your letter which was brought in since church. *Mr.* Pierce [the postmaster] was not out today, the wife of this same man took upon her *his* duties, and brought the letter *herself* since we came in from church. I like it grandly—very— because it is so long, and also it's *so* funny—we have all been laughing till the old house rung again at your delineations of men, women, and things. I feel quite like retiring, in presence of one so grand, and casting my small lot among small birds, and fishes—you say you dont comprehend me you want a simpler style. *Gratitude* indeed for all my fine philosophy! I strove to be exalted thinking I might reach *you* and while I pant and struggle and climb the nearest cloud, you walk out very leisurely in your slippers from Empyrean, and without the *slightest* notice request me to get down! As *simple* as you please, the *simplest* sort of simple—I'll be a little ninny—a little pussy catty, a little Red Riding Hood, I'll wear a Bee in my Bonnet, and Rose bud in my hair, and what remains to do you shall be told hereafter.

Two years later, when Austin's letters are still the focus of family praise (there isn't a single description of family approval of *her* writing), she asks him, "Are you getting on well with 'the work,' and have you engaged the Harpers? Shall bring in a bill for my Lead Pencils, 17, in number, disbursed at times to you, as soon as the

[5]*American Quarterly*, XXIII (Spring, 1971), 3–24. Elaine Showalter's analysis of "feminine" literature in England, represented by such writers as the Brontë sisters, Elizabeth Barrett Browning, and George Eliot, whom Dickinson especially admired, advances the same sort of argument for the conflict between the vocation of the artist and the vocation of the true woman. See *A Literature of Their Own* (Princeton, N.J., 1977).

[6]The citations are from "The 'Scribbling Women' and Fanny Fern: Why Women Wrote."

publishment" (L110). No Freudian eye is necessary to see that the humor, like her insistence on her smallness, disguises jealousy.

The autobiographical sources of Dickinson's starving-thirsting persona, and the culturally sanctioned, defensive denial of appetite, are evident by the time she had begun organizing her poetry into packets in 1858. The following cycle of deprivation, self-deprivation, and attempted self-sustenance emerges from her poems. The chronology is psychological and internal, and bears no significant relation to the probable order of composition. It does, however, bear a strong relationship to Dickinson's life experience, as my discussion of her letters has suggested.[7]

The Dickinsonian speaker, contrary to all expectations, has been deprived of ordinary "food." Her hunger absorbs all of her attention, and the value of food is inordinately inflated. When she finally approaches a full table, she finds it strongly distasteful. She watches others eat, unable to understand their savage appetites, while she makes do with her "crumbs." She is surprised and awed to discover that she has lost her appetite when invited to partake of the "feast," and concludes that while there may be something profoundly distasteful about the feast, there may also be something wrong with her. She expends a good deal of psychic energy insisting that anyone in her situation would make the same observations, but one of the satisfactions denied her is a steady sense that others are really responding as she does. Appetite which she identifies with both the desire to live and the imagination, always dies as soon as it is gratified, and satiation, even disgust, then sets in. The sensuous apprehension of reality depends, in her view, on distance and denial. Prudence and happiness consist in knowing that the feast is available but untouched. The highest gratification is the ecstasy of the realization that, at last, the feast is available, but wisdom consists in not eating, since eating will destroy the self. This, then, is the "Banquet of Abstemiousness."

In all, slightly more than 10 percent of Dickinson's poems employ images of food and drink, but because these poems are among her best, incorporating as they do the basic tensions of her experience, the qualitative impression exceeds numerical weight.[8] The chief interest of these poems is the way in which they document the changes in the self wrought by deprivation; that is, the internalization of

---

[7]For an intelligent justification of the virtues of viewing Dickinson's lyrics as "one long poem," see Robert Weisbuch, *Emily Dickinson's Poetry* (Chicago, 1975), pp. xi–xxv. He writes, "I choose to view Dickinson's lyrics as one long poem, to the same extent that Whitman's lyrics constitute a *Leaves of Grass*. It is a key tenet of romanticism, put forth by Emerson in the past century and by Yeats in ours, that a writer's work, in its totality, should constitute a biography of his consciousness. To treat such a 'life' critically, categories and subcategories may be necessary, but they had best be willing to destroy themselves by merging finally into a totality."

[8]David Luisi came to similar conclusions in "Some Aspects of Emily Dickinson's Food and Liquor Poems," *English Studies*, LI (Feb., 1971), 32–40. He established that "Among the poems of Emily Dickinson are an impressive number which deal directly or indirectly with food and liquor. Of the more than two hundred poems which employ this kind of imagery, approximately three quarters of them do so in a subordinate fashion. The remaining fifty or more poems, however, provide a sufficient number in which this imagery supplies the basic metaphors for her thoughts." Luisi concentrates primarily on the "spare richness" of this imagery, seeing in it the conjunction of both the Puritan and Epicurean strains of Dickinson's sensibility.

deprivation by the poetic persona. Thus the term "compensation," which critics such as Whicher, Gelpi, Sherwood, and Wilbur have employed, while of historical value, is misleading as a characterization of Dickinson's meaning, since it fails to take account of the vulnerability and threatened deterioration of the self.[9] "Compensation" implies, at least by omission, that the suffering soul remains constant while waiting for its ultimate reward. The Dickinsonian persona concentrates its energies on redefining the normal meaning of starvation and repletion, and in the process attempts to redefine and recreate the self.

Excluded from the feast, excluded from raw experience and especially from human love, the loss of appetite and the romantic aggrandizement of appetite confront her. Obsessively, she watches bees drink from flowers, cattle being led to pasture by boys, apples being harvested, birds dining off worms, dogs sucking the marrow out of bones, while she is starving silently and helplessly. Why is she starving? Why did God give a loaf to every bird, while she has only a crumb, why do gnats get more to "eat" than she does? These are the fixed parameters of her world, and she doesn't always question their genesis. She clings to the vestiges of hunger, to the gnawing pain within, as a vital sign. Hunger seems, *in extremis*, her only link with the living.

It becomes clear that, whatever interest Dickinson had in daily life in baking for her father and in winning prizes for her rye and Indian bread, in her poetry eating and drinking are symbolic, highly stylized acts. Solitary rituals concern her, not the actual or immediate sensuous properties of any particular kind of food or drink. The specific foods her poems record, cocoa, berries, dates, bread, are few. On the other hand, she describes "feeding" off of improbable substances such as her lexicon, hermetically sealed minds, and logarithms, observing wryly, " 'Twas a dry Wine" (728). She capitalizes on the capacity of liquors to alter consciousness and to arouse sacramental associations. Spices, stimulating and insubstantial, have a special fascination for her.

Dickinson's food and drink images are not closely observed, detailed representations of actual sense properties. Food has no taste, no texture, no color, no shape. What it has is size, which she manipulates to great effect to symbolize status; and odor, which can be perceived from afar. The perception of these qualities does not depend on ingestion. The poet is concerned with the acquiring of food and the retention of it, and with its psychosocial effects on the communicant, but implicitly her poems announce that she never gets close enough to it to describe

---

[9]George Frisbie Whicher, *This Was a Poet* (Ann Arbor, Mich., 1960); Albert Gelpi, *Emily Dickinson* (Cambridge, Mass., 1965); William R. Sherwood, *Circumference and Circumstance* (New York, 1968). The most extended study of Dickinsonian compensation is Richard Wilbur's essay, " 'Sumptuous Destitution' " in *Emily Dickinson: Three Views* (Amherst, Mass., 1960). Wilbur discusses the poet's "repeated assertion of the paradox that privation is more plentiful than plenty; that to renounce is to possess the more; that 'the Banquet of abstemiousness/Defaces that of wine.' " When he goes on to observe, "The frustration of appetite awakens or abets desire, and that the effect of intense desiring is to render any finite satisfaction disappointing," he anticipates some of my concerns. [See Wilbur's essay, pp. 53–61 in this text.—Ed.]

its immediate sensuous properties. The very lack of elaboration of her imagery illustrates one form of abstemiousness, of the poet's distancing of the world.[10]

Let us examine more closely the concept of the Banquet of Abstemiousness, as set forth in a poem written about 1877, in the highly compressed, antinarrative manner of Dickinson's late style:

> Who never wanted—maddest Joy
> Remains to him unknown—
> The Banquet of Abstemiousness
> Defaces that of Wine—
>
> Within it's reach, though yet ungrasped
> Desire's perfect Goal—
> No nearer—lest the Actual—
> Should disenthrall thy soul—
>
> (1430)

The setting is formal: a banquet for one. "Abstemiousness" serves as food and drink, and is superior, in its ability to confer pleasure, to wine. "Wine" represents anything rare and fine, implying the esthetic connoisseurship the poem endorses. The shocking negative abstraction, "Abstemiousness," coming after a sequence which prepares for the introduction of some actual food or drink, startles the reader into attending closely to what follows. The image itself brings the banquet tantalizingly near, then whisks it away. The images in the second stanza, where Desire, another abstraction, grasps like a hand, again brings the material world up close, yet distances it. The second stanza indicates that the banquet of life is to remain untouched, except by the imagination. This notion that anticipation is always superior to fulfillment, that fantasy is the only fulfillment, is the most limited aspect of Dickinson's ethic and one which her poetry as a whole, in its concern for preserving and gratifying the urgent thirsts and hungers of the instinctual self, refuses to accept.[11]

Having established a psychlogical law in this representative poem, which in effect posits an absolute cleavage between reality and imagination, Dickinson predictably violates the tenets of this rigid dualism in much of her poetry. The need for closure which her philosophy of renunciation attempts to satisfy is but one

---

[10]This perspective enables her to describe any abstraction as food or drink. Success is a nectar, best understood by dying soldiers who will never actually taste it (67). "Fame is a fickle food," scorned by crows, coveted by men (1659). "The Consciousness of Thee" is a "single Crumb" (815). "Impossibility" is like wine, "Possibility/Is flavorless," "Enchantment" is an "ingredient" (838). "Victory comes late—/ And is held low to freezing lips—" (690). "Surprise is like a thrilling—pungent—/Upon a tasteless meat" (1306). Thoughts are "signal esoteric sips/Of the communion Wine" (1452). "Grief is a Gourmand" (793). "Hope is a subtle Glutton" (1547): "His is the Halcyon Table—/That never seats but One—/And whatsoever is consumed/The same amount remain."

[11]Other food and drink poems which affirm the central Dickinsonian paradox of possession through renunciation are "Who never lost, are unprepared" (73); "Water, is taught by thirst" (135); "To learn the Transport by the Pain" (167); "I taste a liquor never brewed" (214); "Exhiliration—is within" (383); "A Prison gets to be a friend" (652); "Deprived of other Banquet" (773); "God gave a Loaf to every Bird" (791); "The Luxury to apprehend" (815); "To disappear enhances" (1209); "Art thou the thing I wanted" (1282); "I took one Draught of Life" (1725).

aspect of the unstable flow of experience. If one compares this paradigmatic poem to earlier formulations of the theme of renunciation, it is evident that this is a weak poetic statement. In the famous "Success," for example, written in 1859, and subsequently extorted from the poet for publication by Helen Hunt Jackson, Dickinson poises perfectly between the extremes of morbid cynicism and naive idealization. In that poem, published anonymously and attributed by reviewers to Emerson, intellectual clarity is balanced against agonized defeat. The poet does not assert the superiority of defeat to victory, as is sometimes supposed.[12] Rather, she juxtaposes the perception of victory to the experience of defeat, making perception and experience interdependent antagonists. And while Dickinson writes a good many poems asserting the inviolability of the soul and the educative value of suffering, she also recognizes that clarity of vision is not a necessary or even a probable consequence of exclusion:

> Undue Significance a starving man attaches
> To Food—
> Far off—He sighs—and therefore—Hopeless—
> And therefore—good—
>
> Partaken—it relieves—indeed—
> But proves us
> That Spices fly
> In the Receipt—It was the Distance—
> Was Savory—
>
> (439)

Both "Who never wanted—maddest Joy" and "Undue Significance" do, in fact, reflect some loss of the life-hunger which is the inevitable consequence of the atrophy of the social self. Despite Dickinson's intermittent adherence to a religion of art, this religion must feed on the vitality of ordinary human appetitiveness. Thus her philosophy of renunciation receives its strongest poetic embodiment when the starving-thirsting "I" is still capable of imagining what freedom and amplitude might mean. Such a poem as the following, for example, invokes self-restraint only in response to an inflexible economics of scarcity:

> God gave a Loaf to every Bird—
> But just a crumb—to Me—
> I dare not eat it—tho' I starve—
> My poignant luxury—
>
> To own it—touch it—
> Prove the feat—that made the Pellet mine—
> Too happy—for my Sparrow's chance—
> For Ampler Coveting—

---

[12]Wilbur asserts that "the more one ponders this poem the likelier it grows that Emily Dickinson is arguing the superiority of defeat to victory, of frustration to satisfaction, and of anguished comprehension to mere possession."

It might be Famine—all around—
I could not miss an Ear—
Such Plenty smiles upon my Board—
My Garner shows so fair—

I wonder how the Rich—may feel—
An Indiaman—An Earl—
I deem that I—with but a Crumb—
Am Sovreign of them all—

                              (791)

Dickinson's fullest poetic statement of the relationship between external deprivation and internal inhibition is poem 579, "I had been hungry, all the Years." It
was written in 1862, before her own seclusion had hardened into an unalterable
mannerism, at a time when her hopes for love and literary recognition were still
very much alive. The narrative structure provided by the journey allows her to
incorporate the entire cycle of deprivation, self-deprivation, and self-sustenance.
The poem records the death of the social self. After years of unsatisfied hunger,
the speaker's "Noon" has come "to dine." The wonderful ambiguity of the phrase
perfectly identifies her own effort with the cooperation of external circumstance.
The moment she has been enlarging through anticipation, her moment of fulfillment, is before her. She had imagined this chance often enough, as she stared
through windows into opulent houses where people were "eating" as a matter of
course, knowing that she could not even hope for such abundant happiness.
Trembling with eagerness, she draws the table close to her and merely touches the
strange wine. Having anticipated some ultimate communion, her reaction startles
her:

I did not know the ample Bread—
'Twas so unlike the Crumb
The Birds and I, had often shared
In Nature's—Dining Room—

The Plenty hurt me—'Twas so new—
Myself felt ill—and odd—
As Berry—of a Mountain Bush—
Transplanted—to the Road—

Nor was I hungry—so I found
That Hunger—was a way
Of Persons outside Windows—
The Entering—takes away—

In the past she has successfully shared "crumbs" with birds, and it is possible to
read the poem as contrasting this overwhelming "ample Bread" with her accustomed spare, yet life-sustaining ration. But the poem goes further. Since the
crumbs always left her hungry and frustrated, exiled from human society and
reduced to the company of birds, the really significant event is the loss of appetite
she experiences when the opportunity to merge intellectual anticipation and sen-

suous realization occurs. The self has been so completely defined by its starvation that food threatens to destroy it. The speaker cannot, in the end, conceive of the relaxation of restrictions as enabling growth and change. Thus she resists food in order to survive. A berry transplanted from a mountain bush to the public highway dies. Eating crumbs in nature's dining room is better than not eating at all. But the loss in human relatedness is awesome.

The paralyzing consequences of prolonged emotional starvation are subjected to further scrutiny in poem 612, where the low comedy analogy with the gnat controls the poet's despair. Here, the attempt to renounce natural hunger is thwarted, as is the ability to gratify instinctual urges.

> It would have starved a Gnat—
> To live so small as I—
> And yet I was a living Child—
> With Food's necessity
>
> Upon me—like a Claw—
> I could no more remove
> Than I could coax a Leech away—
> Or make a Dragon—move—

This hunger surprises her, as the single unavoidable confirmation that she is alive. Her hunger symbolizes her vitality, but it also serves to emphasize her powerlessness. The gnat has "The privilege to fly / And seek a Dinner" for himself: "How mightier He—than I—". She is totally dependent on mysterious forces beyond her control to supply her wants and enlarge her existence. The gnat can be forthrightly aggressive and acquisitive: she can only wait. Furthermore, the gnat can kill himself on the imprisoning window pane, ensuring the cessation of all consciousness. As a human being, she recognizes that, even after contriving her own death, she might have to "begin—again." In context, this suggestion of life after death is not comforting. The life that would begin again, she implies, would be a life so small, so constricted by want, that she would continue to envy gnats.

In her poetry as in her life, Emily Dickinson pursued a strategy of containing hungers, in response to externally imposed deprivation, beneath which the pressures of a volcanic self continually threatened to erupt. This strategy, as she recognized when her poetic vision was most comprehensive, became an active agent in the death of the psychosocial self. Like the paralyzed speaker in "It would have starved a Gnat," she was unable either to extinguish such inevitable hungers as the desire for literary recognition and for sexual gratification, or to renounce them. As late as 1881, she jotted down the poignant lines, "Let me not thirst with this Hock at my Lip / nor beg, with Domains in my Pocket—" (1772). Thomas Johnson describes them as "the rough draft of lines on a scrap of paper in an envelope containing messages which in their final draft presumably were sent to Judge Lord." Striving to accept celibate obscurity, she wrote each of nearly eighteen hundred poems as though it were her last, and as though she were encapsulating a final vision. However, just as she could not accept the death of love and fame for herself, or the postponement of such rewards until eternity, neither could she wish such a fate on others. The desire to nurse the dying back to life with "food and drink" is everywhere recorded in her poems and letters.

What is not recorded is a single instance where this effort is unquestionably rewarded. Ranging from occasional verse to Samuel Bowles ("Would you like summer? Taste of ours. / Spices? Buy here! / Ill? We have berries, for the parching!") to private, confessional threnodies ("I am ashamed—I hide— / What right have I—to be a Bride— / So late a Dowerless Girl—"), these efforts are at best inconclusive.[13] Poem 773, "Deprived of other Banquet, / I entertained Myself—", is representative of these unconsummated transactions, with its "Berry" reserved for charity. The offering is made to an unrepresented other whose response is unknown. Even the manic exuberance of "Doubt Me! My Dim Companion!" results in a conditional phrasing when Dickinson attempts to describe herself as food offered to her lover (275).

None of these efforts yields a single poem in which the poet's summer is unmistakably tasted. Despite the fact that, from 1875–1882 Emily Dickinson was nursing her stroke-ridden mother with obvious fidelity; despite her Indian summer romance with the widowed Judge Lord; despite the lowering of gingerbread for children; despite the incessant exchanges of food and wine with the women of Amherst; none of these efforts yields a single poem where the offering of self as woman or as poet is accepted.

Inevitably, the starved self does not have the emotional or the practical resources to function effectively as a nurturer. The following poems, "A Dying Tiger—moaned for Drink—," and "I bring an unaccustomed wine," will serve as examples. The first is a brilliant vision of the frustration of generous nurturing impulses in a dreamlike setting charged with anxious sexuality. The second attempts to revivify moribund humanity, and fails. Verbal echoes of a distant religious tradition of charity cannot be reattached to present human sympathy. In both poems, the imaginative distance between Emily Dickinson and her persona has collapsed. The hardiness of response she describes, the legacy of conflict, is unquestionably hers.

> A Dying Tiger—moaned for Drink—
> I hunted all the Sand—
> I caught the Dripping of a Rock
> And bore it in my Hand—
>
> His Mighty Balls—in death were thick—
> But searching—I could see
> A Vision on the Retina
> Of Water—and of me—
>
> 'Twas not my blame—who sped too slow—
> 'Twas not his blame—who died

[13]Poems 691 and 473.

While I was reaching him—
But 'twas—the fact that He was dead—
                    (566)

The tiger, a potent threatening masculine symbol, has been rendered harmless because he is dying. The speaker carries the life-giving water in her bare hands, and the very sparseness of the wasteland makes this an elemental meeting. There are no cups or glasses. She has to offer herself, her hand, in offering the "dripping" of the rock. She arrives too late, the tiger is dead by the time she has returned to him, yet he arouses vague feelings of guilt in her. His last sight was "Of Water—and of me—" and she is haunted by his unfulfilled longing. Tiger and speaker are leagues away from parlor niceties. The last stanza attempts, somewhat lamely, to shift the blame away from the tiger and the tardy nurse "who sped too slow" onto a impersonal universe: "the fact that He was dead." The hardness of response, here, is a denial of feeling, a this-has-nothing-to-do with me statement. Yet the guilt is there, despite the denial. If there were no guilt, there would be no poem.

Wine functions as a potential medicine in "I bring an unaccustomed wine," just as water was a medicine in the preceding poem, but again, the speaker is neither Jane Eyre ministering to a blinded Rochester, nor Florence Nightingale:

I bring an unaccustomed wine
To lips long parching
Next to mine,
And summon them to drink;

Crackling with fever, they Essay,
I turn my brimming eyes away,
And come next hour to look.

The hands still hug the tardy glass—
The lips I w'd have cooled, alas—
Are so superfluous Cold—

I w'd as soon attempt to warm
The bosoms where the frost has lain
Ages beneath the mould—

Some other thirsty there may be
To whom this w'd have pointed me
Had it remained to speak—

And so I always bear the cup
If, haply, mine may be the drop
Some pilgrim thirst to slake—

If, haply, any say to me
"Unto the little, unto me,"
When I at last awake.
                    (132)

At the beginning of the poem two figures, nurse and patient, are dying of thirst. This thirst is a compound of physical need and lovelessness. Both people are unused to "wine," let alone an ample supply of water. The patient is feverish and physically ill, the nurse is nominally healthy. Each has been, in some measure, dehumanized by thirst. Devoid of "Circumstances— / And a name" (382), they are both merely "lips." As the poem progresses, the speaker loses the ability to sympathize. At first her eyes are brimming with tears, but she turns them away, and when she takes another look at the striving lips an hour later, the patient is dead. Her tears were futile water. By stanza four she is describing the dead patient as "this" and "it." Cloaked with cheerfulness, hers is the frozen bosom of the automaton do-gooder. She dies emotionally, while the patient dies physically. Ironically, "its" spirit may have survived, while hers has been denied the sense of useful relatedness.

What kind of regrets does this situation engender? The speaker is eager once again to absolve herself of all responsibility for the death. She does this by the comparison between the just dead corpse and "The bosoms where the frost has lain / Ages beneath the mould." In addition, she emphasizes her willingness to help by asserting that, if only the just dead corpse had remained to speak, it could have directed her to someone else in need of her ministering. This attempt to profit from misfortune, to bring good out of evil, becomes morally obnoxious when she goes on to explain that she intends to use a whole series of patients to ensure the welfare of her soul. She always tries to help dying people because, perhaps, her good deeds will be rewarded after her own death. Notice, however, that all she is able to describe is bearing the cup, and that the image of the cup of sympathy refused is the one the poem leaves us with, along with the eyes and lips and hands that never connect.

Dickinson's food and drink imagery, then, describes a cycle of deprivation, self-deprivation, and attempted self-sustenance. Typically, her persona is starving, unaccountably and unjustly, in a world of plenty. This prolonged exclusion causes her appetite to shrivel so that when the external restriction is removed, she no longer desires "food." She discovers that the only way she can sustain her desire to live and the vitality of her imagination is to welcome the absence of food and drink, symbolic of the desires of the social self. Inverting the normal meaning of starvation and repletion, she insists that the ideal constructs of her imagination are more vitalizing than any outer wine. However, although both her ability to be nourished and to nourish others has been impaired, she never fully renounces the thirsts and hungers of the social self.

While it is perhaps unnecessary to explain why the near contemporary of Emerson, Thoreau, Hawthorne, and Poe should have attempted to create an invulnerable artistic persona out of the ashes of a vulnerable human identity, Emily Dickinson's strategy of self-deprivation is best understood as a specifically female response, conditioned by American Victorian definitions of true womanhood. More isolated during her years of creativity than any of her literary contemporaries, "Homeless at home," she nevertheless emerges as the spokeswoman for a whole generation of nineteenth-century women. Her recoil from the world, her attempt to live in a separate sphere, and her obsessive fascination with the sexual and social power she could never attain was theirs. In *Literary Women*, Ellen Moers identifies "that vexed question of access to experience, the worst limitation, it is always assumed, that society has imposed upon the woman writer." She hastens to add that "It was by reading, of course, that women writers acquired the remarkable quantity and quality of information about workaday realities that they brought to literature."[14] Dickinson was alert to the compensatory function of art, to satisfy the thirsts and hungers of a deprived persona; but she was ever more insightful into the changes in the self wrought by exclusion. Struggling against the extremes of naive idealization and deadening cynicism, she would have understood the point of Joseph Lyman's comment, "Emily Dickinson I did like very much and do still. But she is rather morbid and unnatural." Virtually all of her critics have disagreed with this assessment, preferring instead to cast her in the role of a detached clinician of death. The starving-thirsting "I" of Emily Dickinson's poetry expresses its bitterness toward God, toward nature, and toward human society through the language of withdrawal. This language controls the impulses to murder and to create. "Renunciation," she tells us, "is a piercing Virtue" (745).

[14](Garden City, N.Y., 1976).

Emily Dickinson and the
Economics of Desire

Joan Burbick

The writings of Emily Dickinson are often interpreted as a pristine expression of individual consciousness or a narrative of the autonomous self bent on an ever-deepening quest for power and freedom. As such, her voice stands beyond culture in the lyric landscape of mythic yearning. Instead, this study presumes to read Dickinson's words as a cultural text that attempts to explore and resolve on an aesthetic level pressing ideological conflicts of her social class.[1] Dickinson's Amherst, no matter how disembodied we would like to perceive her participation, was marked by the fervor of evangelical Christianity, the ethos of the Christian Gentleman and Lady, and the determined desire for social order and class stability, emerging from the Protestant vision of industrial capitalism.[2]

At the heart of the developing managerial and professional class was a strongly articulated need for the rational control of human actions and emotions whose language was frequently encased in an economic metaphor of use.[3] As Henry May has reminded us, the language of rational control is not unique to nineteenth-century America, having a long history in enlightenment thought.[4] What is distinctive,

Reprinted from *On Dickinson* (1990) by permission of the author and Duke University Press.

[1]As Fredric Jameson, *The Political Unconscious: Narrative as a Socially Symbolic Act* (Ithaca: Cornell Univ. Press, 1981), writes, the literary act is "a way of doing something to the world, to that degree what we are calling 'world' must inhere within it, as the content it has to take up into itself in order to submit it to the transformation of form," p. 81.

[2]Besides the biography of Richard B. Sewall, *The Life of Emily Dickinson*, 2 vols. (New York: Farrar, Straus and Giroux, 1974), of relevance to an understanding of Dickinson's social context is Polly Longsworth's book, *Austin and Mabel: The Amherst Affair and Love Letters of Austin Dickinson and Mabel Loomis Todd* (New York: Farrar, Straus, and Giroux, 1984) in which the language of desire is justified in a highly antinomian manner by means of the rhetoric of evangelical Christianity.

[3]Of general interest see in particular, Gilles Deleuze and Felix Guattari, *Anti-Oedipus: Capitalism and Schizophrenia* (New York: Viking, 1972); Albert O. Hirschman, *The Passions and the Interests: Political Arguments for Capitalism before Its Triumph* (Princeton: Princeton Univ. Press, 1977), and Max Weber, *The Protestant Ethic and the Spirit of Capitalism* (New York: Scribner's, 1958). More specifically, Dickinson's father, Edward Dickinson, is fairly representative when he writes to Emily Norcross two months before their marriage: "Let us prepare for a life of rational happiness. I do not expect, neither do I desire a life of *pleasure*, as some call it—I anticipate pleasure from engaging with my whole soul in business," Sewall, *The Life of Emily Dickinson*, I, p. 47.

[4]*The Enlightenment in America* (New York: Oxford Univ. Press, 1976).

however, is its increasing emphasis on cultural prescriptions concerning sexual behavior. Charles Rosenberg points out that during the years between 1830 and 1870, after the Second Great Awakening, a new interest was placed upon the social need to manage sexuality, both within and without marriage. He identifies the medical and biological literature of this period as at first expressing a "tone of repressiveness" which by the 1870s has "moved from the level of individual exhortation to that of organized efforts to enforce chastity upon the unwilling."[5] By analyzing the mode of authority used by these social commentators, Rosenberg notes how "apparent is the emotional centrality of a fundamental expository metaphor, one which might best be called 'mercantilist.' " This economic language led to, what Rosenberg calls, a "logic of sexual frugality."[6]

In the economic language of sexual frugality, the unmarried woman represented a puzzling, if not disturbing, cultural fact. As a woman, she was equated with sexuality, having access to its use, but as a single woman without the sanction of marriage, she had no proper guidelines for how to "manage" its use.[7] As a result, the unmarried woman was in need of severe regulation: all sexual feelings, thoughts, and actions had to be contained. In particular, desire, if it existed for the unmarried woman, was "dangerous" and, as Dickinson would write, needed to be "handled with a Chain." Without the legitimation of marriage, the single woman was forced into a controlled abstinence of both her emotional and social self. Desire must not be felt or thought, let alone acted upon.

---

[5]*No Other Gods: On Science and American Social Thought* (Baltimore: Johns Hopkins Univ. Press, 1976), p. 73.

[6]*No Other Gods*, p. 87. In addition, John S. Haller and Robin M. Haller, *The Physician and Sexuality in Victorian America* (Urbana: Univ. of Illinois Press, 1974), pp. 91–137, claim that seventeenth- and eighteenth-century manuals of love and marriage stress "pleasure" as a legitimate need and emotion between marriage partners, but that mid-nineteenth century manuals stress the utilitarian aspects of sex. Women are accordingly seen as "indifferent" to both desire and sexual activity. Carl N. Degler, *At Odds: Women and the Family in America from the Revolution to the Present* (New York: Oxford Univ. Press, 1980), however, considers the portraits in health manuals as idealized renderings of how woman should behave. Instead, Degler claims that women increasingly controlled the means of reproduction through policies of sexual purity and male self-restraint. Gerda Lerner, ed. *The Female Experience: An American Documentary* (Indianapolis: Bobbs-Merrill, 1977), also points out that nineteenth-century feminists often attacked sexuality because "for most women, the perils, travails, and hardships of frequent pregnancies far outweighed the benefits and pleasures of sexual intercourse," p. 47. Sexual abstinence was turned to as the most reliable form of birth control. But Lerner does not see the drop in birth rate at the end of the nineteenth century as a signal of woman's power in domestic matters. Rather, she cites economic reasons for restricting the size of families. Desire in this historical debate, however, quickly becomes subservient to the issues of birth control and the functions of adult marital sexuality. See also Nancy Cott, "Passionlessness: An Interpretation of Victorian Sexual Ideology, 1790–1850," *Signs: Journal of Women in Culture and Society*, 4 (1978), 223; and Anita Clair Fellman and Michael Fellman, *Making Sense of Self: Medical Advice Literature in Late Nineteenth-Century America* (Philadelphia: Univ. of Pennsylvania Press, 1981), p. 105.

[7]A revealing set of letters between Lucy Stone, the nineteenth-century women's rights leader who early in her life embraced spinsterhood, and her family shows how strongly women were considered "unnatural" if they did not marry. Luther Stone wrote to Lucy these words of wisdom, telling her that it was "As Great A Sin To Not Suffer These Organs To Be Used At All As To Use Them Too Much." Gerda Lerner, ed., *The Female Experience: An American Documentary* (Indianapolis: Bobbs-Merrill, 1977), p. 85.

Recent critics have shown how Dickinson transforms religion, art and death into Eros and how she rivals Walt Whitman's litanies to the senses.[8] Yet few have bothered to examine how Dickinson often analyzes desire through economic tropes that ultimately determine the "cost" of longing.[9] Through what might be called her "economics of desire," Dickinson describes longing in terms of poverty and wealth, loss and gain, producing poems that both mimic and deprecate the mercantilist vision of her social class.[10]

In general, Dickinson's writings can be seen as expressing four logical, not chronological, visions of desire that imply a specific theory of use or economy. The first dreams about an extravagant wealth and joyful consumption of pleasure without regulation: delight becomes an end in itself, producing nothing other than its own "greedy" enjoyment. The second ponders the tension of not-having: loss and restraint promise greater "gain" by deferring possession and, at times, by embracing asceticism. The third analyzes and renders ironic patterns of not-having until they assume nightmare proportions of need: the "true cost" of restraint is revealed to be the mutilation of the body. The fourth pushes even further into irony: desire is denied until only the "dead" body remains as the "price" of wanting.

As presented in this study, each successive voice widens further the gap between desire and delight until the power to have is eliminated. At its worst, delight rests finally within death. Nonetheless, what is remarkable about her poetry is the extent to which Dickinson depicts the bliss of consummatory pleasure and constructs an economy that equates it with absolute "riches." As "Debauchees of Dew," her speakers exist in a state of animated sensuality. She

---

[8]Rebecca Patterson, *Emily Dickinson's Imagery* (Amherst: Univ. of Massachusetts Press, 1979), claims that there is "no more erotic poetry in the English language" than Dickinson's, p. 30. While Karl Keller, *The Only Kangaroo Among the Beauty: Emily Dickinson and America* (Baltimore: Johns Hopkins Univ. Press, 1979), compares Dickinson directly to Whitman and finds her vision of sex "as many things: overwhelming monster, plaything, object of perplexity, escapist high, symbol of disillusionment, spiritual tease, productive pain—any and all of these," p. 267.

[9]Some critics have written on Dickinson's economic language as it pertained to family, friends, and New England society. Robert Meredith, "Emily Dickinson and the Acquisitive Society," *New England Quarterly*, 37 (1964), 436, suggests that her language attacks "the counterfeit values of her time." Vivian R. Pollak, " 'That Fine Prosperity': Economic Metaphors in Emily Dickinson's Poetry," *Modern Language Quarterly*, 34 (1973), 171, also finds that Dickinson's economic language functions as "oblique social criticism." It establishes "the resistance of the private self to public values, the resistance of the self to any form of authority, human or divine." But Cynthia Chaliff, "The Psychology of Economics in Emily Dickinson," *Literature and Psychology*, 18 (1968), 93, finds instead that the "capitalistic system" became a part of Dickinson's "psychological dynamics." Though these studies connect Dickinson's language with the terms of mercantile New England culture, they overlook the specific tension between economic language and expressions of desire.

[10]As an unmarried woman, Dickinson was in a particularly acute social role. Degler, *At Odds*, points out that the "highest proportion of women who never married for any period between 1835 and the present were those born between 1860 and 1880," p. 152. There was a rising incidence of single women during the second half of the nineteenth century, but despite this increase, these women were still generally characterized as living in an "unnatural" state, conducive to "unpleasant eccentricities" and "queer fancies." In this regard, Thomas Wentworth Higginson is famous but hardly unique for his "dread" of printing "Wild Nights." His inability to reconcile the psyche of an unmarried woman with expressions of desire is merely symptomatic of the times. See Millicent Todd Bingham, *Ancestor's Brocades: The Literary Debut of Emily Dickinson* (New York: Harper, 1945), p. 127.

knew that the "Heart" asks "Pleasure" first but also described how afterward comes the menacing "will of its Inquisitor." Her work is never far from describing the tension of delayed desire as well as the horror of deprivation. In her quest for adequate expressions of delight, spectres of regulation stalk the poetry. They can appear at any moment as the frowning mask of the "Keeper" or the "Sexton" who guards the keys to life. But most provokingly, they figure as economic metaphors that imply a system of controlled "values." Desire is often encased in a "costly" standard of measure that robs the body of delight.

I

Hardly a strategy of restraint, this lyric voice, tinged with "greed," unabashedly proclaims the desire to "hoard" the love of family and friends. This opulent language that describes those desired as gold and priceless jewels, challenges the world of carefully measured mercantilist wealth. Not uncommonly, women writers at mid-nineteenth century often described their domestic spheres as the locus of value in the culture, equating wealth with home and friends bound together by love. The wealth of men in the marketplace was, hence, inferior to the wealth of women in extended households.[11] Dickinson too, from an early age, links her family and friends with gold, the ultimate social sign of value, and declares the domestic sphere the citadel of wealth. She writes to Jane Humphrey in 1842: "I miss my beloved Jane—I wish you would write to me—I should think more of it than of a mine of gold—."[12] Elsewhere her friends, as part of a domestic circle of love, are jewels and precious gems often bound together with golden chains which she covets as avidly as the greediest miser.[13]

These letters to her family and friends during the 1840s and 50s also express an economic language particularly imbued with biblical imagery. Equating extreme wealth with her friends, Dickinson frequently envisions them as precious treasures, echoing the language of Matthew: "For where your treasure is, there will your heart be also."[14] Dickinson, in turn, describes the heart as "such hard little creditors—such real little misers," without equal in the "whole, wide world" (L 85). In its greed, the heart yearns to possess its earthly treasure, and in this way, actually inverts the biblical language it echoes. In Matthew, the dictum is clear: "Lay not up

---

[11]Nancy Cott, *The Bonds of Womanhood: Women's Sphere in New England, 1780–1835* (New Haven: Yale Univ. Press, 1977), p. 69, describes how women praised the value of the home, but she sees in their praise no direct challenge to "the modern organization of work and pursuit of wealth." Nina Baym, *Woman's Fiction: A Guide to Novels by and about Women in America, 1820–1870* (Ithaca: Cornell Univ. Press, 1978), pp. 48–49, however, assigns women a slightly more activist role. Their "special concept of home" with its perception of wealth as human bonds of affection attempts to reform the mercenary principles of larger American society.

[12]*The Letters of Emily Dickinson*, ed. Thomas H. Johnson and Theodora Ward, (Cambridge: Harvard Univ. Press, 1958) I, 7. Hereafter cited in the text with corresponding letter number.

[13]L 26; L 39; L 74; L 77; L 193.

[14]King James Version, Matthew 6:21.

for yourselves treasures upon earth, where moth and rust doth corrupt, and where thieves break through and steal: But lay up for yourselves treasures in heaven, where neither moth and rust doth corrupt, and where thieves do not break in and steal."[15] Equating friends with gold is idolatrous, yet Dickinson continues to evoke her desire for friendship and love with an earthly economy of extravagant wealth. Writing to Samuel Bowles, she boldly asserts: "My friends are my 'estate.' Forgive me then the avarice to hoard them!" (L 193). This economy knows no restraint; friends are "mints" and "precious stones" meant to be possessed entirely.

Dickinson clearly understands how she is inverting this biblical language, and in a letter to Abiah Root, her conflict over where to place "value" is apparent: "perhaps the treasure *here* would be *too dear* a treasure—couldn't 'the moth corrupt, and the thief break thro' and steal'—" (L 50). The "*subtle* moth" that has invaded her "treasurehouse" performs an "errand," fulfilling its "mission"; "it taught me dear Abiah to have no treasure here, or rather it tried to tell me in it's little mothy way of another *enduring* treasure, the robber cannot steal which, nor time waste away" (L 50). Ending on a note that embraces the evangelical enthusiasm of her Abiah, Dickinson nonetheless hints at another reason why the moth exists. A fatal reminder of mortality, corruption warns against the placing of value on earthly delights since, after all is experienced, they may indeed be the most valuable treasure. Attempting to restrain herself from desiring too strongly this earthly treasure, Dickinson nonetheless cannot let go of its magical hold.

The earthly treasure is indeed so priceless, the theme of its robbery and loss preoccupies Dickinson's poetic imagination. In "I never lost as much but twice," the accused is the "Burglar! Banker!—Father!" (P 49), who like other poetic marauders or thieves continually pillages human life.[16] Friends are such precious jewels that their loss leaves at best "an Amethyst remembrance" (P 245), at worst a searing emptiness: "Without this—there is nought— / All other Riches be / As is the Twitter of a Bird— / Heard opposite the Sea—" (P 655). Those desired are "Gigantic Sums" whose value brings distress: "Heaven is so presuming that we must hide our Gems" (L 535). In the economic and biblical language of robbery, Dickinson seems particularly anxious: "No Verse in the Bible has frightened me so much from a Child as 'from him that hath not, shall be taken even that he hath.' Was it because it's dark menace deepened our own Door?" (L, 788).

Dickinson also carries economic metaphors of golden domestic treasure into the terrain of explicit sexual experience. Writing a "saucy page" to her future sister-in-law, Susan Gilbert, she dares to bring up the taboo topic: "How dull our lives must seem to the bride, and the plighted maiden, whose days are fed with gold, and who gathers pearls every evening. . ." (L 93).[17] This metaphor of extreme

---

[15]King James Version, Matthew 6:19–21.

[16]All quotes from the poetry are from *The Poems of Emily Dickinson*, ed. Thomas H. Johnson (Cambridge: Harvard Univ. Press, 1955), cited in the text by the appropriate poem number.

[17]Rebecca Patterson, *Emily Dickinson's Imagery*, p. 86, thinks that "the most sexually charged of Emily Dickinson's jewels is the pearl—and from at least as early as the girlhood days when she first began to think of writing poetry."

wealth as sexual knowledge informs her classic poem about desire: "Wild Nights— Wild Nights! / Were I with thee / Wild Nights should be / Our luxury!" (P 249).

Dickinson's speakers also supplicate and entreat the lover to experience a consummatory sexuality that implies total depletion. In P 211, the speaker entreats: "Come slowly—Eden!" and is eventually lost in the experience of sexual pleasure. Indeed, her speakers often dwell on the act of consummatory joy: "Oh Sumptuous moment / Slower go / That I may gloat on thee—" (P 1125). Some of her poetic voices eat and drink with abandon: they ask to be brought the "sunset in a cup" (P 128); their hands ache to practice "*Gem*-Tactics" in order to learn to possess jewels of love (P 320); they declare themselves "wives," claimants of sexual knowledge (P 461). And desire can ultimately become part of "nature," an aspect of being that like beauty "is." "Longing is like the Seed / That wrestles in the Ground" (P 1255); unavoidable, inexplicable, desire is one with life.

II

The language of hoarding, greed, and consumption stands in stark contrast to a strictly mercantilist language that "measures" desire in terms of "loss" and "gain," a closed system of monetary value in which gain is increased through not-consuming.[18] In an economic language of asceticism, Dickinson's speakers often embrace a posture of self-denial for which they are rewarded. Only by not-having does that which is desired "gain" in value. A rationale for the management of wealth structures and regulates the emotions. The consumption of what is desired is continually deferred, and the activity of striving acquires value over the satisfaction of obtaining the goal. The second voice, unlike the first that consumes in excess, glorifies the language of economic restraint necessary for the accumulation of wealth.

These strategies of restraint, depicting "consummation" as the "hurry of fools,"[19] instead exalt the state of not-having. Writing to Susan Gilbert in 1871, Dickinson asserts: "To miss you, Sue, is power. The stimulus of Loss makes most Possession mean" (L 364). In "Go not too near a House of Rose—" (P 1434), the speaker concludes that "In insecurity to lie / Is Joy's insuring quality." On one level, such statements about desire fit into the larger schemas of opposition throughout her poetry. Critics have long analyzed the poems that base their tension on the enticement of polarities in which "Opposites—entice."[20] Her speakers

---

[18]I am using Max Weber's concept of asceticism as a metaphor for consumption in the post-Reformation world, but it is a metaphor in the process of dissolving by Dickinson's time. As America is thrust into a world of necessary consumption, where consumer palaces dot the landscape of the late nineteenth century, great contradictions pervade the Victorian milieu. Rational restraint on sexuality stands in great contrast to the burgeoning affluence of the post-1870s.

[19]Prose fragment noted in *The Letters of Emily Dickinson*, ed. Johnson, III, 922.

[20]See in particular the discussion of "compound vision" by Robert Weisbuch, *Emily Dickinson's Poetry* (Chicago: Univ. of Chicago Press, 1975), who writes that Dickinson's poetry "contrasts and sometimes, remarkably, combines a self which is powerful, autonomous, and godlike with a self which is all-vulnerable, limited, and victimized," p. xi.

thirst, hunger and fail and only through their state of deprivation truly value what they desire: "Water, is taught by thirst" (P 135) and "To comprehend a nectar / Requires sorest need" (P 67).

But what is of interest in this language of opposites is the way in which the desired goal "gains" through destitution. This economics of asceticism is often a way of allowing loss, danger, and uncertainty to increase both the cost and the value of what is desired. Dickinson's speakers can define desire as the mere realization of absence. Simply put, " 'Heaven'—is what I cannot reach!" (P 239). Striving for the unobtainable forms the very basis of incredible worth. Delight becomes "More fair—because impossible / That any gain—" (P 572). Elsewhere, Dickinson writes: "Danger—deepens Sum—" (P 807) and "That Possession fairest lies that is least possest" (L 359).

This "spirit" of not-having that enhances the desired is also expressed as a series of obstacles, each provoking greater worth. In "I cross till I am weary," the speaker depicts the weariness of the mind confronted with "Mountains," "Seas," and a "Desert" while continuing to search and scan the horizon for the desired. Midway through the poem the following rationale is given for the deferment of satisfaction: "What merit had the Goal— / Except there intervene / Faint Doubt—and far Competitor— / To jeopardize the Gain?" (P 550). The logic of a carefully planned asceticism not only validates the struggle but claims that the goal will increase in "merit." Value increases in direct ratio to the threat of competition. Intervention, the necessary obstruction to the movement of desire, is found in "Faint Doubt" and "far Competitor." Whose doubt it is, however, is left in abeyance; Dickinson does not make clear whether it belongs to the desirer or the desired or if it is a shadow across the very act of the search. Hardly a conventional "rival," doubt nonetheless adds "value" to the goal.

The activity of not-having can, however, gain such importance that it begins to rival consumption. Each denial builds the prize to such proportions that actual possession pales in relation to the struggle to acquire. Consummation is denied, and instead asceticism emerges as a means to defer and increase the value of what becomes an impossible goal. In P 1430, the "Banquet of Abstemiousness" becomes so precious that it paradoxically "Defaces" the value of the inebriating wine. The "perfect Goal" is made transcendent and hence is never consumed; it exists in a perpetual state of denial. The speaker is finally left without the ability to have; only a fantasy about the ideal is possible.

III

Though it animates the search and adds value to the ideal, continually deferred goal, the economic language of restraint easily transforms into a third, deeply ironic vision in which self-denial becomes simply the expression of dire need. Temporary deferment, leading to a more valued or idealized gratification, becomes instead a permanent impoverishment, if not a psychic or physical wounding. The rationales for not-having become insidious and are exposed for their "true costs." In this economic description of desire, the system of deferred possession nullifies the purpose of the search and confines the pursuer within a maze of deprivation:

From Blank to Blank—
A Threadless Way
I pushed Mechanic feet—
To stop—or perish—or advance—
Alike indifferent—

If end I gained
It ends beyond
Indefinite disclosed
I shut my eyes—and groped as well
'Twas lighter—to be Blind—
(P 761)

By having the goal permanently out of reach, always one step beyond the speaker, the state of desiring and the object of desire create a terrifying impoverishment.

Restraint, a form of self-control or self-robbery, that regulates the desire to consume can as easily become a form of deprivation. In Dickinson's famous definition poem, "Renunciation—is a piercing Virtue—," the speaker who desires to drink and to see is required to thirst and blind herself for the sake of a goal beyond the reach of human hands. "Renunciation" becomes a "Not now— / The putting out of Eyes— / Just Sunrise—," a landscape of mutilation and envy. This form of renunciation is further expressed as necessary because "Sunrise" might have more value than "Day's Great Progenitor—." As a result, the activity of renunciation is presented less as a glorious triumph over earthly consumption than as a tormented process of self-denial: "Renunciation—is the Choosing / Against itself— / Itself to justify / Unto itself—" (P 745).

Vivian Pollak points out in her discussion on images of thirst and starvation in Dickinson's poetry that such moments of renunciation have too easily been labeled as "compensation." Renunciation implies for many critics the image of a suffering soul "who remains constant while waiting its ultimate reward." But Pollak finds that such labeling misses the "vulnerability and threatened deterioration of the self" that accompanies renunciation.[21] Such deterioration is not

[21]"Thirst and Starvation in Emily Dickinson's Poetry," *American Literature*, 51 (1979), 48, finds that Dickinson's "starving self" wants the absence of food and drink but never "fully renounces the thirst and hungers of the social self." In general, she challenges the critical viewpoint of George Whicher, Albert Gelpi, William R. Sherwood and Richard Wilbur. Although I agree with much that Pollak writes, I believe that to free the social self from a system of restraint is to interiorize unnecessarily the problems of deprivation that Dickinson's speakers articulate. See also chap. 4 of Pollak's . . . *Dickinson: The Anxiety of Gender* (Ithaca: Cornell Univ. Press, 1984). In addition, Robert Weisbuch has commented on how Dickinson's poetry bravely emphasizes "the hero's act of questing over against his successful completion of the quest." In his final interpretation, "Success is irrelevant." Poems that deprecate the quest are seen as "momentary" failures, laments of the "low comforts of the 'Daily mind,'" p. 166. Not only does this interpretation quickly overlook the pain and disillusionment of the failure while retaining an ideal of "heroism," but it also disregards the function of memory within quest activity. . . . [See Pollak's essay, pp. 77–90—Ed.]

explained by labeling Dickinson's biographical sexuality "pathological"; rather she accurately describes the *effects* of a system of restraint endemic to female sexuality in the nineteenth century.[22] Dickinson sees clearly that the social demand of "renunciation," especially as it is interiorized by women, actually requires physical and mental wounding.

IV

Dickinson's most insidious voice involves the cost of desire as nothing less than death. Instead of displaying the scars of renunciation or remorse, Dickinson's speakers require death as the response to the mere thought of desire. Enthralling fantasies instantly kill (P 1291) and thrust the speaker into a deadly landscape of economic measure: "Utmost is relative— / Have not or Have / Adjacent Sums / Enough—the first Abode / On the familiar Road / Galloped in Dreams—." Desire for Dickinson's speakers, as for the heroines of Kate Chopin and Edith Wharton, ruins life and destroys the female body through suicide or fantasies of extinction.[23]

Dickinson also writes poems, however, in which the death of the desiring self becomes the necessary prerequisite to prove love. "The Test of Love—is Death—" (P 573) refers not only to the religious paradigm of Jesus's willingness to sacrifice

[22]It is difficult today to look into the Victorian household without the eyeglasses of pathology, which we inherited from the medical sociology of the nineteenth century. In *The History of Sexuality* (New York: Random House, 1978), Michel Foucault notes that the nineteenth century found "sexuality" everywhere and produced a medical pathology to classify and hence regulate the "secret" of sex. He discusses this process as the "hysterization of women's bodies" where the feminine body was "analyzed—qualified and disqualified—as being thoroughly saturated with sexuality," p. 104. Not merely a repressive society, the nineteenth century was obsessed with the knowledge of sexual emotions and behavior and produced a *scientia sexualis* bent on differentiating and regulating all aspects of sexual experience. For the woman, and even the man, pathology and sexuality were wedded. Accordingly, many of Dickinson's critics and biographers find her living within a nexus of "pathological" female types: her mother, the "hysterical" married woman; her sister and herself, perverse "old maids"; her sister-in-law, the "frigid" wife; and her brother's mistress, the "libidinous" female. But as we have seen, these images of women reflect an economy of use, implying either the extremes of excess or inappropriate reserve. It is through her writings on desire that Dickinson explores the economic language underlying the tensions among desire, restraint, and use.

[23]Writing a number of years after Dickinson, Kate Chopin in *The Awakening* and Edith Wharton in "The Bunner Sisters" and *Ethan Frome* were also fascinated by the ruin of contentment. Their heroines are reasonably, though superficially, happy until the realization of desire sets off an inevitable wanting that leads to self-destruction. The fact alone of "more," the process of desiring, is in itself fatal. Desire destroys not only the basis of the heroines' social status and their expectations of duty, but also their desiring selves. A tremendous fear of desire is interiorized in these stories; threats of punishment and agonizing guilt create situations in which desire sets off an inevitable process of destruction. In sharp contrast, according to Nina Baym, pp. 22–50, the women writers of the mid-century in America practically eliminated desire from their stories. The sexual purity of women in the home was assumed. Heroines were often portrayed as intelligent and moral, capable of surviving financial and personal hardship and of acquiring rational mates. Dickinson's poetry in this way prefigures Wharton's and Chopin's work. Dickinson was, of course, familiar with British and French women novelists whose works did not assume sexual purity. Ellen Moers, *Literary Women: The Great Writers* (Garden City, N. Y.: Anchor Books, 1977), pp. 84–95, stresses Dickinson's reading of Browning, Eliot and Sand as well as her preoccupation with the theme of love.

his life for love, but also to the reality of "death" as the event which verifies desire. In another strangely tormented poem, the speaker urgently insists that her love can be proved in the face of impending doom. While the speaker watches the waters rise, threatening her extinction, the negation of her life is proof of love: "Oh Lover—Life could not convince— / Might Death—enable Thee—" (P 537).

Again, the cost of realizing desire is precisely self-annihilation. Desire is a fatal emotion for many Dickinson speakers; in a sense, it is much more dangerous than the Oedipal struggle. Whereas the son is threatened with castration, the daughter is threatened with the destruction of the entire body. The woman, of course, cannot be restrained through the cutting of a part. Her body in its entirety must be suppressed if she is to be made sexually ineffective. In working through the maze of wanting and the obstacles to desire, the woman must chart a system of punishment that does not seek to diminish power but to annihilate the body. The wounds on the body that "commemorate" its death are indeed the greatest threat to the attainment of desire. To want is to face intimately the "subtle suitor," Death. Put another way, what Dickinson seems to describe with unhalting repetition is the fact that restraint in its logical extreme demands as its price the total cancellation of the body.

Another variant to this economy that demands death for desire is the expression of desire in relation to the dead body. In some poems, the speaker imagines a space and time in which restraint from desire evaporates and the articulation of desire is allowed, if what one wants is dead. In a relatively early poem, Dickinson establishes how to "value" the lover without the presence of inhibiting restraint:

> As by the dead we love to sit,
> Become so wondrous dear—
> As for the lost we grapple
> Tho' all the rest are here—
>
> In broken mathematics
> We estimate our prize
> Vast—in it's fading ratio
> To our penurious eyes!
> 　　　　　(P 88)

In the language of exchange and measure, the other increases in price as it recedes into death. In a simple economy of desire, death ironically enhances the value of the desired; the corpse is most precious. In death all desire can be thought and spoken, freeing the speaker's voice to "value" the lover; but, of course, once spoken it cannot be acted upon in any other way than the drama of necrophilia. Basically, it frees only the voice: speakers are allowed to speak the words of desire to the dead precisely because they are dead and outside human action. In this way Dickinson describes how death ironically sanctions desire but forbids its consummation.

Some of Dickinson's speakers, however, often seek to outwit the threat of death. They envision a union of loved ones in the grave. Possession of the dead by

the dead is a grim solution to an overwhelming social demand for the denial of
pleasure:

> If I may have it, when it's dead,
> I'll be contented—so—
> If just as soon as Breath is out
> It shall belong to me—
>
> Until they lock it in the Grave,
> 'Tis Bliss I cannot weigh—
> For 'tho they lock Thee in the Grave,
> Myself—can own the key—
>   (P 577)

In the first two stanzas, the death scene not only lifts the sanctions against articulating desire but insures possession of it. Death frequently is seen as an interdic-
tion to action, but here it becomes the place where desire is enacted. The dead
body is capable of possession. "Back from the cordial Grave I drag thee / He shall
not take thy Hand" (P 1625). Such aggressiveness is necessary because "Never the
treasures in her nest / The cautious grave exposes" (P 141). If the speaker in the
poem is also dead, her bliss is ensured by the death of the loved one. Conversing
in their graves, these phantom lovers communicate by "signs" and freely admit
their desire. The poem ends: "Forgive me, if the Grave come slow— / For
Coveting to look at Thee— / Forgive me, if to stroke thy frost / Outvisions paradise!" (P 577). For the fulfillment of desire, death is required. A middle space
between earth and Paradise, the grave becomes a sanctioned meeting place for
love. Celestial love in this bizarre poem is undone by the materiality of the body.

But necrophilism is not the only response to an internalized system of restraint.
Death is also presented as a figure of intense power which stops desire, not merely
robbing it of anticipated pleasure but transforming desire into dread. Like the
"Sexton" or the "Keeper," death holds in check the experience of desire. In this
way, horror can become the most menacing form of restraint. In P 512, desire is
indeed haunted; it must "Sip, Goblin, from the very lips / The Lover—hovered—
o'er— / Unworthy, that a thought so mean / Accost a Theme—so—fair." This
frightening substitution, goblin for lover, immobilizes the speaker as she watches
helplessly the advances of Death. The "Goblin" invades the intimate space shared
by the lovers and accosts the lips, formerly warmed by love. The ability of the
speaker's "Soul" to flip between images of lover and goblin is unnerving. To depict
desire as always vulnerable to control by death equates desire with threat.

These elaborate, internalized systems of restraint, constraining desire and pre-
venting its full enjoyment, are often reduced to a simple warning against consumption and joy: "For each extatic instant / We must an anguish pay / In keen and
quivering ratio / To the extasy" (P 125). Desire is restrained merely through an
inflated assignment of cost. The reason the cost of joy is so high is not disclosed;
only the harsh ratio that rigidly extracts "years" of payment for "hours" of bliss is
articulated. The punishment of joy by pain is measured in time and emotional
strain. Ecstasy like life is fatal: " *'Tis* Costly—so are *purples*! / 'Tis just the price of

Breath— / With but the 'Discount' of the *Grave* / Termed by the *Brokers*— 'Death' " (P 234).

This reasoning, not dialectical but coldly mercantile, assigning clear-cut relationships of measure to human emotions, recurs throughout Dickinson's poems on immortality. Like joy, the cost of immortality is immense. Dickinson's speakers remind us of cultural heroes such as Christ who "thought no / Extravagance / To pay—a Cross—" (P 571). For the chance of immortality "All—is the price of All—" (P 772). Dickinson could parody the religio-business language of immortality (P 234) as well as take it with complete seriousness (P 522). She could also present a speaker aloof from the responsibility of the payment system of death: "Is Heaven an Exchequer? / They speak of what we owe— / But that negotiation / I'm not a Party to—" (P 1270). Someone outside the self has computed this economics of desire and life. In a number of the immortality poems, then, the original force behind restraint is not interiorized but belongs to a cosmic economy, planned by a "transcendent" actor. Although the speaker claims no responsibility for assigning prices, she nonetheless must fall victim to the fatal demand that such eternal gains as immortality or ecstasy be paid in full.

The economics of immortality is, however, interwoven with that of desire, for implicit in the wish for life-after-death is the desire for reunion with earthly lovers. Immortality, then, is repayment not only for the loss of life, but for the loss of human bonds. Although Dickinson sometimes resents and stands indifferent to the "new Equation" found in Heaven, she also presents speakers who demand specific repayments from the celestial Exchequer. Precisely, he must "refund us finally / Our confiscated Gods—" (P 1260). The God that extracts enormous sums for human joy and robs earth in jealous glee must at last return the stolen treasures.

Immortality becomes then, in one sense, deferred desire. The responsibility of union is placed on the will of the celestial banker who pillages life and is then appealed to for amends. Restoration of the desired is out of the hands of the poetic speakers. Possession of the desired is projected into a cosmic drama beyond life, and restraints against consumption are blamed on a competitor who makes human desire futile.

The origin of the ascetic economics of desire and its punishing system of restraint is identified in some of the poetry with the figure of a death-God—a "blond Assassin," a "Burglar," a "Thief"—who has set up a dictatorship of rules that produces an internal system of bondage. Obliquely pointing to the religious dictums of her class, Dickinson presents speakers of individual poems as victims within a value system that teaches the virtue of renunciation. As a result, this value system requires self-mutilation and finally death as payment for life.

Dickinson often leaves unnamed in the poems the power that defines these economic rules. Sometimes the controllers have social masks, like the "Keeper" and the "Sexton," at other times they appear as forces "within" the self that hold desire in check. At best, they attain focus as figures in a celestial economy. In one sense theology, society, and the personal psyche are indistinguishable players in the game of regulation. In this way, Dickinson's writings expose how mutilation and death stand as insidious checks within an economy of desire and are potent precisely because they cannot be projected easily beyond the self.

Late in her life, Dickinson writes to Judge Otis P. Lord: "I feel like wasting my Cheek on your Hand tonight—Will you accept (approve) the squander—Lay up Treasures immediately—that's the best Anodyne for moth and Rust and the thief whom the Bible knew enough of Banking to suspect would break in and steal" (L 843). To the end suspicious of celestial "gains," Dickinson parodies the religio-economic language of her social class. The dictum to "Lay up Treasures immediately" undoes both the evangelical fervor of heavenly reward and the mercantilist need for ascetism. Daring to dream a new economics of desire in which the cup is drunk and the joy consumed, Dickinson boldly asserts the right of the female body to speak and to have.

This economic system in which all life is finally reduced to a mortal payment is, at times, only redeemed by the voice of the poet. Through the magic of her art, Dickinson expresses "having" without the fear of deprivation or the necessity of restraint:

> Take all away from me, but leave me Ecstasy,
> And I am richer then than all my Fellow Men—
> Ill it becometh me to dwell so wealthily
> When at my very Door are those possessing more,
> In abject poverty—
>
> (P 1640)

Through the affirmation of "Ecstasy," often implying poetic reverie, the speaker poet stands beyond vulnerability, where even robbery cannot harm: "Himself—to Him—a Fortune— / Exterior—to Time—" (P 488).

We cannot, however, merely assume that Dickinson rests for long in this poetic triumph, compensating for life through a quest for aesthetic pleasure. More frequently, her poems and letters describe and expose an economic idiom of regulation that prevents "Ecstasy." Ever attentive to the language of her social milieu, Dickinson probes the nineteenth century's effort to "manage" sexuality and the emotional experience of desire. As an unmarried woman in Victorian America, refused any sanctioned "use" of sexuality, Dickinson records the internalized system of regulation, controlling desire. Her speakers are often psychological accountants, checking the ledger of human emotions, attempting to fix the "price" of desire. Checking their "busy pencil," they face bafflement and perplexity (P 69). The costs are, as we have seen, often morbidly high. When used to regulate the emotions, economic language often goes beyond producing an ethos of sexual frugality, creating instead sexual impoverishment. In this way, Dickinson's writings delineate the cultural language of desire for the Victorian woman in an age that attempted to "rob" the female body of delight.[24]

---

[24]It is no wonder that Mabel Loomis Todd, Dickinson's editor and the mistress of her married brother, a woman who had broken the social mores of her times, eventually found relief in Dickinson's words and a map for her worst fears. In her diary, Mabel Loomis Todd wrote: "The poems were having a wonderful effect on me, mentally and spiritually. They seemed to open the door into a wider universe than the little sphere surrounding me which so often hurt and compressed me—and they helped me nobly through a very trying time," quoted in Bingham, *Ancestor's Brocades*, p. 31.

Emily Dickinson and the Calvinist Sacramental Tradition

Jane Donahue Eberwein

One of the characteristic features of Emily Dickinson's poetry is its idiosyncratic employment of religious vocabulary—including diction associated with Christian sacraments. Although she used sacramental terminology in relatively few poems, it dominates some of her most interesting ones, "These are the days when Birds come back—," "There came a Day at Summer's full," "I'm ceded—I've stopped being Their's—," and "Further in Summer than the Birds" among them.[1] Such poems have been subjected to numerous readings that attend thoughtfully to the religious language resonating within them but have never been systematically examined within the specific context of Calvinist sacramental theology as understood by the nineteenth-century Congregational community within which Dickinson received her Christian formation. Examining the poems in that context, attempting to read the words as she would have recognized them and to exclude meanings appropriate only to related Christian traditions with which she was barely acquainted, casts useful light on the poet's religious thinking.[2]

Overall, when one considers Emily Dickinson's use of sacramental language within the context of her antebellum Congregationalist religious formation, the most remarkable fact is that she used such language at all. Hers was not a sacramentally-centered church, and she held aloof from most of the limited sacramental experience it offered her. Yet, in making her poems, she called frequently, imaginatively, and memorably upon the idea of sacrament. There were religious concepts emphasized within her culture that she virtually disregarded—foremost

Reprinted from *ESQ: A Journal of the American Renaissance*, Vol. 33, 2nd Quarter, 1987. By permission of the author and the editors.

[1] Dickinson's poems are identified according to the numbering in *The Poems of Emily Dickinson*, ed. Thomas B. Johnson, 3 vols. (Cambridge and London: Belknap of Harvard Univ. Press, 1955), here Poems 130, 322, 508, and 1068; her letters are cited according to the numbering in *The Letters of Emily Dickinson*, ed. Thomas B. Johnson and Theodora Ward, 3 vols. (Cambridge: Belknap of Harvard Univ. Press, 1958).

[2] I am grateful to Harold F. Worthley and the staff of the Congregational Library in Boston and to Daniel Lombardo of the Jones Library, Amherst, for access to materials related to Dickinson's religious heritage. In general, materials cited here with reference to Calvinist doctrine and to Dickinson's college readings derive from the Congregational Library, while those related to Amherst town and church history and involving devotional readings available within Dickinson's community are to be found in the Jones Library.

among them the idea of total human depravity. Softening that preeminent Calvinist doctrine into her characteristically penetrating awareness of personal limitation, she dispensed with the concern for sin and fear of damnation that were emphasized within her church and that especially dominated its appeals to the young. But while neglecting much of her Calvinistic legacy, she proceeded to rediscover other aspects of it, including the sacramental tradition. She invoked that tradition in her poems, amplifying it in the process, and used it for assistance in her quest for assurance of immortality.

Misconceptions of Dickinson's sacramental experience abound. Some scholars tell us that Dickinson was never baptized—an assumption presumably based on her failure to seek admission to any church.[3] Others, thinking in terms of Catholic sacramental practice, both Roman and Anglo-Catholic, read Dickinson's marriage poems in sacramental terms without regard for Calvin's limitation of sacraments to baptism and the Lord's Supper.[4] Richard Chase gets the number right but its constituents wrong in identifying "only two important sacraments" in Dickinson's writing—"the ceremony of 'marriage' and the ceremony of death." Charles R. Anderson and Sharon Cameron interpret the liturgical references in "Further in Summer than the Birds" as though Dickinson were well acquainted with the mass and sympathetic to its rituals.[5] Yet Calvin's *Institutes* assailed the mass as "a Sacrilege" (II, 1429), and the New England poet lived in an atmosphere that, if no longer so violently hostile to Catholic ritual, still had no place for it. It is instructive to remember the limitations of her environment when reading Emily Dickinson. The only religious tradition she knew well enough to speak its language was that of Connecticut Valley Congregationalism. And that language employed a more theologically precise vocabulary than E. Miller Budick utilizes in her extensive study of Dickinson's reaction to the "sacramental symbolism" linking New England's Puritan and Transcendentalist traditions.[6]

---

[3]Those who assume the poet was never baptized include Richard Chase, *Emily Dickinson*, American Men of Letters Series (New York: William Sloane Associates, 1951), p. 156; Albert Gelpi, "Emily Dickinson and the Deerslayer: The Dilemma of the Woman Poet in America," *Shakespeare's Sisters: Feminist Essays on Women Poets*, ed. Sandra Gilbert and Susan Gubar (Bloomington and London: Indiana Univ. Press, 1979), p. 132; and John Emerson Todd, *Emily Dickinson's Use of the Persona* (The Hague, Paris: Mouton Press, 1973), p. 44.

[4]Chase handles the marriage poems this way (pp. 150–151), as does Charles R. Anderson in *Emily Dickinson's Poetry: Stairway of Surprise* (New York: Holt, Rinehart & Winston, Anchor Books, 1966), p. 200. Their readings conflict with John Calvin's position: "Marriage is a good and holy ordinance of God; and farming, building, cobbling, and barbering are lawful ordinances of God, and yet are not sacraments. For it is required that a sacrament be not only a work of God but an outward ceremony appointed by God to confirm a promise. Even children can discern that there is no such thing in matrimony"; *Calvin: Institutes of the Christian Religion*, 2 vols., ed. John T. McNeill, Library of Christian Classics (Philadelphia: Westminster Press, 1960), II, 1481. The *Institutes* is hereafter cited parenthetically within the text.

[5]Anderson, pp. 170–171; Cameron, *Lyric Time: Dickinson and the Limits of Genre* (Baltimore and London: Johns Hopkins Univ. Press, 1979), p. 182.

[6]*Emily Dickinson and the Life of Language: A Study in Symbolic Poetics* (Baton Rouge and London: Louisiana State Univ. Press, 1985).

In Calvinist theology, a sacrament is a seal of the covenant by which God affirms his promise of salvation to the elect. From the time of the 1648 Cambridge Synod, the Westminster Assembly's Catechism, by which generations of New England Puritan children learned the rudiments of their faith, provided this definition: "A sacrament is a holy ordinance instituted by Christ, wherein by sensible signs Christ and the benefits of the new covenant are represented, sealed, and applied to believers." In the Reforming Synod of 1679–80, the Congregational churches in America adopted the Savoy Declaration of 1658, which defined sacraments as "holy Signs and Seals of the Covenant of Grace, immediately instituted by *Christ* to represent *him* and his benefits and to confirm our interest in him, and solemnly to engage *us* to the service of God in Christ, according to his Word."[7]

At the time Dickinson was growing up in Amherst, nothing significant had changed in Calvinist theology or diction with regard to sacramental understanding. A *Young Communicant's Catechism* of 1830 reminded those young converts who would be preparing themselves for their first reception of the Lord's Supper that the sacraments were "seals of the covenant of grace" appointed by God "to be sacred signs, memorials, and pledges of his mercy to us through a crucified Jesus, he being the great surety and sacrifice, to which we are directed constantly to look for pardon, grace, and glory."[8] If Dickinson associated any specific vocabulary with her idea of sacrament, then, it would have emphasized the words "seal," "covenant," "ordinance," and "promise." A few phrases demonstrate both her access to this vocabulary and her ingenuity in deploying it: "a Holiday— / Crowded—as Sacrament—," "the Seal Despair—," the sailor's "Covenant Needle," "Humming—for promise—when alone—," and "No Ordinance be seen" (Poems 495, 258, 851, 503, and 1068 respectively). The concluding lines of "It will be Summer—eventually" (Poem 342), with their reference to the way "Priests— adjust the Symbols— / When Sacrament—is done—," redirect attention to an earlier pattern of diction introduced in the third stanza by which Dickinson grounds her hopefulness about nature's renewal in the concept of divine promise that is central to Calvin's definition of sacrament:

> The Lilacs—bending many a year—
> Will sway with purple load—
> The Bees—will not despise the tune—
> Their Forefathers—have hummed—
>
> The Wild Rose—redden in the Bog—
> The Aster—on the Hill

[7]This definition comes from a book available in Amherst during Dickinson's childhood, Joseph Emerson's *The Evangelical Primer, Containing a Minor Doctrinal Catechism: and a Minor Historical Catechism, to which is added the Westminster Assembly's Shorter Catechism* (Boston, 1825), p. 63. The Savoy Declaration, along with other major statements of Congregational doctrine and practice, may be found in Williston Walker, *The Creeds and Platforms of Congregationalism*, originally published in 1893 (Boston: Pilgrim Press, 1960), p. 397.

[8]John Willison, *The Young Communicant's Catechism; with Questions and Counsel for Young Converts* (New York, 1830), pp. 6–7.

Her everlasting fashion—set—
And Covenant Gentians—frill—

Till Summer folds her miracle—
As Women—do—their Gown—
Or Priests—adjust the Symbols—
When Sacrament—is done—

(ll. 9–20)

Those "Covenant Gentians" of the fourth stanza represent a pledge of new birth following the apparent death of the botanical year, just as the bees humming the traditional hymns of their "Forefathers" demonstrate continuity. Even though the promise it seals will continue, however, an actual sacrament concludes—just as the year does. Priests "adjust the Symbols" after communion to signify the end of one incident of interchange between the material and spiritual worlds and to leave all in readiness for the next.

The words "seal" or "sealed" did not always express sacramental ideas for this poet. Sometimes "sealed" simply meant closed tightly. Even when a religious resonance attends this word, readers should be aware of the Lamb's sealed book in Revelation—the poet's favorite source of biblical allusions. That, for instance, seems to be the origin of the lines "Some pale Reporter, from the awful doors / Before the Seal" (Poem 160) and perhaps also "Divinity dwells under seal" (Poem 662). There is a distinction, however, between two kinds of seals: the kind that the Lamb breaks open to reveal the future (presumably tight metal clasps) or the other kind, the official implements used to certify the authenticity of royal documents. Calvin referred to the latter in his explanation of sacraments (II, 1280). Earthly princes' edicts, he remarked, "are concerned with frail and fleeting things"—unlike God's promises, "which are spiritual and eternal."

It is the first of these meanings—that from Revelation—that Brita Lindberg-Seyersted applies to the passage of "There came a Day at Summer's full," (Poem 322) in which the speaker reports that, during her interview with her lover, "Each was to each The Sealed Church, / Permitted to commune this—time— / Lest we too awkward show / At Supper of the Lamb."[9] By speaking in terms of the Lamb's book (and perhaps his marriage also), the poet would be projecting her thoughts forward to the final judgment and the fulfillment of this love in heaven. The final reference to "that new Marriage, / Justified—through Calvaries of Love—" substantiates this reading (especially through its allusion to the "justification" of the elect through the imputation of Christ's righteousness). But what if Dickinson were using the idea of "The Sealed Church" in a sacramental way as well as by reference to scripture? The phrase was familiar to her as representing all the elect included within the Covenant of Grace as sealed by the two sacraments. In this case, however, the elect are limited to two: the speaker and her lover, and they have ordained a new sacrament to consecrate their private promise of fidelity. As

---

[9]*The Voice of the Poet: Aspects of Style in the Poetry of Emily Dickinson* (Cambridge: Harvard Univ. Press, 1968), p. 86.

members of this unique church, they have become eligible for their own Lord's Supper, "Permitted to commune this—time—." Biographically minded critics tend to raise questions about the identity of the lover here, with some identifying one or another man as the beloved and others thinking the poet refers to Jesus. Analysis of the poem's sacramental language supports the latter possibility. If there is anything orthodox about the sacrament presented here, we must assume that the lover is Christ, since sacraments involve the sealing of a bond between God and man. On the basis of this diction, I tend to agree with Ruth Miller, whose analysis of syntax convinced her that such is the case, that "it is the Lord and the Poet that combine to make the sealed Church."[10] His "Calvaries of Love" justify the speaker, even though her sanctification remains invisible on earth.

Calvin's discussion of the prince's seal does even more to help us unriddle one of Dickinson's most powerful but perplexing poems:

Mine—by the Right of the White Election!
Mine—by the Royal Seal!
Mine—by the Sign in the Scarlet prison—
Bars—cannot conceal!
Mine—here—in Vision—and in Veto!
Mine—by the Grave's Repeal—
Titled—Confirmed—
Delirious Charter!
Mine—long as Ages steal!

(Poem 528)

The "Royal Seal" validates Christ's promise in the way Calvin explained: "a sacrament is never without a preceding promise but is joined to it as a sort of appendix, with the purpose of confirming and sealing the promise itself, and of making it more evident to us and in a sense ratifying it" (II, 1278). What would that promise be? Surely nothing trifling. The speaker's ecstatic claims to something wonderful as "Mine—" resound throughout the poem to proclaim her sense of herself as supremely gifted. She is elect, like one of the saints privileged in Revelation to wear white garments. And she is titled or named—with her name presumably inscribed on the white stone. In addition, she holds a legal title to eternal life. The seal is that of the covenant, thereby explaining the legal language that also suffuses the poem by linking it with the traditional Puritan metaphors of covenant theology. A bargain has been struck for the speaker with God. The contract committing her soul to him and granting assurance to her of immortality has been sealed by Christ through his atonement. The "Scarlet prison— / Bars—cannot conceal!" is his empty tomb, proof to the elect of "the Grave's Repeal" for them as well as for the saints he liberated in the harrowing of hell while supposedly entombed beneath a different sort of seal. Read in the light of Calvinistic sacramental theology, the poem can be identified as a proclamation of grace achieved and immortality promised. Whether it celebrates an actual experience of

---

[10]*The Poetry of Emily Dickinson* (Middletown, Conn.: Wesleyan Univ. Press, 1968), p. 80.

assurance or is simply an imaginative rendering of what conversion would feel like to the saved, it shows the poet working brilliantly within an enduring Puritan system of language.

Calvinist theologians understood both sacraments in terms of Christ's sealing of his promise, but they tended to place special stress on the word "seal" in their discussions of baptism. This was the seal of the Covenant of Grace by which Christ extended his promises to the children of saints, just as God had included Abraham's seed in his covenant with that patriarch and had encompassed all the people of Israel in his covenant with Moses. Despite the cleansing ritual of sprinkling the child with water, Calvin and his successors recognized no efficacy in baptism for removing the pollution of man's depraved nature. Only converting grace could accomplish that—usually two decades or so afterward. What baptism did was to extend a symbolic promise to children of church members who were "baptized into future repentance and faith"—the seeds of both lying "hidden within them by the secret working of the Spirit" (Calvin, II, 1343). None of the theological statements I have found in materials available to the poet makes any reference to naming—an action that Noah Webster associated only with the related word "christen" that Dickinson never used in her poems.[11]

Of the two sacraments recognized within her religious culture, Dickinson received only the first. She was baptized as an infant in accordance with her parents' sense of duty and their hope, along with the church's, that she would eventually prove a member of the Covenant of Grace.[12] Her poetry gives little evidence that the sacrament was important to her, although she demonstrated awareness of the church's triumph in gathering its ranks of saints: "Snatches, from Baptized Generations— / Cadences too grand / But for the Justified Processions / At the Lord's Right hand" (Poem 367; see also 503).

One poem holds special interest for its apparently autobiographical reference back to Dickinson's own initiation into the church and for its renunciation of that parentally and societally imposed identity:

> I'm ceded—I've stopped being Their's—
> The name They dropped upon my face
> With water, in the country church
> Is finished using, now,
> And They can put it with my Dolls,
> My childhood, and the string of spools,
> I've finished threading—too—
>
> Baptized, before, without the choice,
> But this time, consciously, of Grace—
> Unto supremest name—

---

[11]*An American Dictionary of the English Language* (Springfield, Mass., 1849).

[12]Sister Regina Siegfried, "Conspicuous by Her Absence: Amherst's Religious Tradition and Emily Dickinson's Own Growth in Faith," unpublished dissertation, St. Louis Univ., 1982 (Ann Arbor: UMI, 1982), 8223729, p. 93.

Called to my Full—The Crescent dropped—
Existence's whole Arc, filled up,
With one small Diadem.

By second Rank—too small the first—
Crowned—Crowing—on my Father's breast—
A half unconscious Queen—
But this time—Adequate—Erect,
With Will to choose, or to reject,
And I choose, just a Crown—

(Poem 508)

Ever since its initial publication in the 1890 *Poems* as "Love's Baptism" (a title presumably reflecting the interpretations of Mabel Loomis Todd and Thomas Wentworth Higginson), this poem has commonly been read in terms of marriage.[13] Some readers, however, find it a more general proclamation of mature status—as independent woman, as poet, or as saint.[14] The assumption of a marital context depends upon a presumed sacramental parallel best articulated by Anderson, who reasons that "two sacraments, baptism and marriage, are set against one another and out of the comparison two kinds of status emerge. Both are name-giving ceremonies and the names are the signs by which she is identified, first in life then in love." His argument would be more persuasive if we had any reason to think that Dickinson regarded marriage as a sacrament—aside from the startling phrase she once used, "Baptized—this Day—A Bride—" (Poem 473), with its implication that marriage ought to be sacramental and must, therefore, be associated somehow with one of the existing ordinances. When considering the continuities in life and its gradual progressions, it is appealing to imagine the baby girl in her christening robe and then to project her as reentering the church a few years later in the white dress and veil of First Communion and eventually pacing down the same aisle in the white gown and train of the bride. Only the first of these visions, however, would conform to the Amherst poet's experience. Marriage was no sacrament among the Calvinists, and the weddings Dickinson seems to have known the most about (Susan Gilbert's, Emily Fowler's, and Eliza Coleman's, anyway) took place in private homes. Nor would the new name given by a husband replace that conferred at baptism (Emily), even though it would set aside that transmitted by

[13]Anderson, pp. 200–201; Chase, pp. 156–157; Clark Griffith, *The Long Shadow: Emily Dickinson's Tragic Poetry* (Princeton: Princeton Univ. Press, 1964), pp. 174–175; William H. Shurr, *The Marriage of Emily Dickinson* (Lexington: Univ. Press of Kentucky, 1983), pp. 23–24.

[14]Karl Keller, *The Only Kangaroo among the Beauty: Emily Dickinson and America* (Baltimore and London: Johns Hopkins Univ. Press, 1979), pp. 36, 244–245; Barbara Antonina Clark Mossberg, *Emily Dickinson: When a Writer is a Daughter* (Bloomington: Indiana Univ. Press, 1982), pp. 158–160; Jean McClure Mudge, *Emily Dickinson and the Image of Home* (Amherst: Univ. of Massachusetts Press, 1975), pp. 155–156; Richard B. Sewall, *The Life of Emily Dickinson,* 2 vols. (New York: Farrar, Straus and Giroux, 1974), II, 504–505; William R. Sherwood, *Circumference and Circumstance: Stages in the Mind and Art of Emily Dickinson* (New York and London: Columbia Univ. Press, 1968), pp. 146–148; and Robert Weisbuch, *Emily Dickinson's Poetry* (Chicago and London: Univ. of Chicago Press, 1972), pp. 82–83.

her father; in fact, a marriage name seems more to erase a woman's existing identity than to award a grander one.

What we have here is a willed, adult sealing of a covenant that supersedes the ritual Dickinson associates with infancy and parental choice. Whereas before she participated as a passive—if actually wailing—beneficiary of other persons' good will ("Crowned—Crowing—on my Father's breast—") and was enrolled as a putative member of the covenant, she now proclaims that she has experienced its fulfillment in "Grace." If we are to look for a sacramental parallel to this second baptism she claims here, it would be confirmation rather than marriage; but confirmation is also a Catholic ritual and probably not in her consciousness despite its name-giving aspect and its enrollment of the newly adult Christian as a soldier of Christ ("Adequate—Erect, / With Will to choose, or to reject"). Hers is, instead, a private baptism by which the speaker seals her own covenant and triumphantly assumes a new identity and elevated status: the "supremest name" that may be written on the white stone of Revelation.

When discussing the other sacrament, communion or the Lord's Supper, Calvin rejected both the Catholic doctrine of transubstantiation and the Lutheran alternative of consubstantiation, emphasizing instead the spiritual nourishment drawn by the faithful from eating and drinking the food of the soul under physical symbols of bread and wine. He stressed the obligation of mutual caring associated with communion, echoing Augustine in calling this sacrament "the bond of love" (II, 1403–1404, 1414–1415). The American Congregational churches accepted this theology—like that of baptism—essentially unchanged. The Lord's Supper, according to a catechism that circulated in Amherst during Dickinson's youth, should be recognized as "a great privilege and precious legacy to his [Christ's] church, seeing it as a bright memorial of his dying love, a sure pledge of his second coming, and a quickener of all the graces"; it conferred "a remission of sin, freedom from wrath, peace with God, peace of conscience, adoption into God's family, increase of grace, perseverance therein, sanctified mercies and crosses, and a title to eternal life."[15] The power of the sacrament would act far less favorably on those who approached it unworthily, however. Questions of eligibility for the Lord's Supper arose urgently and frequently from the time of Jonathan Edwards, and much of the advice available in Dickinson's formative years—from devotional manuals as well as pastoral counsel—probably did more to foster insecurity and scrupulosity than confidence in the promises of the covenant and the loving community of Christians.[16]

---

[15]Willison, pp. 10–11.

[16]Edwards' 1749 "Inquiry Concerning Qualifications for Communion," reprinted in *The Works of President Edwards*, 8 vols., Research and Source Work Series no. 271 (New York: Burt Franklin, 1968), VII, 3–171, touched off extensive controversy. Solomon Williams argued with Edwards' attempted limitation of the Lord's Supper to the most assuredly converted church members in *The True State of the Question . . .* (Boston, 1751). In doing so, he was upholding the innovations of Solomon Stoddard, Edwards' grandfather and ministerial predecessor in the Northampton church. Other voices prominently heard in this enduring debate were those of Moses Mather, Moses Hemmenway, and Nathanael Emmons.

Between the Savoy Declaration of 1658, adopted by the 1680 synod as the official doctrinal statement of the New England churches, and the Burial Hill Declaration of 1865, which represented the next attempt by American Congregationalists to formulate their shared understanding, no official statement of belief was established for American Congregational churches as a whole; thus, local churches were left with responsibility for determining their own qualifications for membership and stipulating the conditions under which both sacraments would be celebrated within each congregation. Nor did the Burial Hill Declaration attempt to define such qualifications for Congregationalists in general.[17]

The practices of the First Congregational Church in Amherst, therefore, become central to our understanding of Dickinson's religious formation.[18] Like other congregations in the theologically conservative Connecticut Valley, this one adhered to the Edwardsean tradition as it had gradually evolved. During the poet's youth in the midst of the Second Great Awakening, the Amherst church experienced wave after wave of revivals (1831, 1834, 1841, 1845, 1850)—all of them encouraging insistence on experiential religion, as convincing experience came to seem so commonplace, so much to be expected in the children of church members like the young Dickinsons.[19] The successive church manuals published during the poet's lifetime record a very gradual liberalization of membership standards, although these remained quite rigid for the period before she ceased attending services in the late 1850's or early 1860's. The 1834 "Articles of Faith" admitted to communion "none but those who furnish satisfactory evidence of their faith in Christ." In 1859, the "Creed, Covenant, and Rules" spoke a bit more gently of qualifications for full church membership and communion—these privileges now being reserved simply for those who "in the judgment of Christian charity, shall appear to be the subject of divine grace, and to live according to the requirements of the gospel." By the terms of the 1869 "Manual," however, almost anyone might

---

[17] This statement, aimed at reinforcing church unity after the Civil War, expressed basic agreement of the nineteenth-century Congregational churches with the historic synods of 1648 and 1680. Its formulation of sacramental theology, however, gave little guidance to particular churches, saying only that "We believe . . . in the sacraments of Baptism and the Lord's Supper" (Walker, p. 564).

[18] Dickinson's college reading would have done little to expand her awareness of alternative sacramental traditions beyond what her local church provided. Of the books on religious topics assigned for the Mount Holyoke curriculum, only John Marsh's *An Epitome of General Ecclesiastical History from the Earliest Period of Antiquity to the Present Time,* 7th ed. (New York, 1843) gave even the slightest attention to sacraments, and it did so simply to point out Old Testament types of baptism and to discuss some of the sacramental disputes in the colonial New England churches. The religious argumentation to which Dickinson was exposed attacked tendencies toward deism and Unitarianism rather than responding to any perceived threats from sacramentally oriented churches. In their determination to prove the existence and nature of God through discovery of the order in his creation, Archibald Alexander, Joseph Butler, and William Paley (like Amherst's Edward Hitchcock) could have taught Dickinson much about analogical reasoning and even about science but nothing about sacramental theology or practice. A listing of textbooks used during the poet's year at Mount Holyoke appears in Jack L. Capps, *Emily Dickinson's Reading, 1836–1886* (Cambridge: Harvard Univ. Press, 1966).

[19] *An Historical Review: One Hundred and Fiftieth Anniversary of the First Church of Christ in Amherst, Massachusetts, November 7, 1889* (Amherst, 1890), p. 32.

qualify.[20] No wonder the Reverend Jonathan Jenkins, who ministered to the parish from 1866 to 1877, found Dickinson spiritually "sound" when he examined her; she easily could have qualified for church membership by that time, had she chosen to apply.[21]

Dickinson family members entered the church gradually during the poet's lifetime, so that she surely never grew up with the assumption that every respectable and God-fearing person must necessarily belong. Her mother joined in 1830 while pregnant with Emily; she was one of forty-five new members who were received into communion in July 1830.[22] Edward Dickinson, by contrast,—although active on parish committees and a stalwart worker for the church's interests—waited to join officially until the revival of 1850. Lavinia followed him a few months later, Austin during his engagement to Susan Gilbert. From 1856 until her death thirty years later, Emily Dickinson remained the only noncommunicant adult in her family.

She had spent her youth in an intensely religious atmosphere, with Sundays reserved for churchgoing. Although nonmembers were dismissed after the sermon and barred from the communion service, she occasionally witnessed such sacramental ritual as the First Church offered (letters 46 and 80, note to letter 926). Within this environment, however, she would have heard many more sermons on depravity and the need for conversion than about sacramental theology. Unconverted and thus ineligible for church membership, Dickinson experienced the communion ritual only from the vantage point of the excluded.[23]

Yet the poet's abstention from the Lord's Supper may not demonstrate indifference to sacramental nurture. It is instructive to notice how often Dickinson's poems dealing with hunger use the eucharistic foods as their symbols of nutrition. In "I had been hungry, all the Years—" (Poem 579), the speaker "trembling drew the Table near— / And touched the Curious Wine—" before approaching "the ample Bread," only to find these goods less appetizing in experience than in expectation. Other poems (159, 1077, 1240, 1314) repeat the theme. It is not cake that Dickinson's beggars and starving children lack—or even meat and vegetables—but the nutriments associated with communion. Were bread her only example, it could be explained on the basis of its being the most basic and universal food.

[20]The First Parish of Amherst (Congregational), *The Articles of Faith and Government of the First Church in Amherst, Mass.* (Amherst, 1834), pp. 4–5; *The Creed, Covenant and Rules and List of Members of the First Congregational Church* . . . (Amherst, 1859), p. 8; *Manual of the First Congregational Church, Amherst* (Amherst, 1869), pp. 3–4.

[21]MacGregor Jenkins gives no date for the interview between his father and the poet but sets it late in Edward Dickinson's life. It was for her parents' peace of mind rather than Emily Dickinson's own that the spiritual interview took place; *Emily Dickinson: Friend and Neighbor* (Boston: Little Brown, 1930), pp. 80–82. Jay Leyda locates the event around 1873; *The Years and Hours of Emily Dickinson,* 2 vols. (New Haven; Yale Univ. Press, 1960).

[22]*Catalogue of the Pastors and Deacons and Members of the First Church of Christ in Amherst, Mass.,* manuscript copy from the original compiled by Rev. G. S. Dickerman, April 23, 1891, p. 68.

[23]I have discussed her situation in more detail in *Dickinson: Strategies of Limitation* (Amherst: Univ. of Massachusetts Press, 1985), pp. 185–188.

Wine, however, would have seemed a different matter for a poet raised in a temperance-minded household. It obviously symbolized something needed to appease a more-than-physical thirst: " 'Tis Beggars—Banquets best define— / 'Tis Thirsting—vitalizes Wine— / Faith bleats to understand—" (Poem 313). She concluded, characteristically, that the parched and starving outsider was the one who most appreciated the feast—presumably the communion feast as well as other blessings that are normally shared among those who love one another. She concluded, also, that it was possible to make do with far less nourishment than others thought essential. One who recognized that "A little Bread—a crust—a crumb— / A little trust—a demijohn— / Can keep the soul alive—" (Poem 159) might find austere satisfaction even in "signal esoteric sips / Of the communion Wine" (Poem 1452). Finding, in church circles anyway, that "Bread is that Diviner thing / Disclosed to be denied" (Poem 1240) and that "Bread of Heaven resents bestowal / Like an obloquy—" (Poem 1314), she sought alternative sources of succor and exhilaration—both in nature with "Her invitation broad / To Whosoever famishing / To taste her mystic Bread—" (Poem 1077) and within her own consciousness: "There can no Outer Wine / So royally intoxicate / As that diviner Brand / The Soul achieves—Herself— / To drink—or set away / For Visiter—Or Sacrament—" (Poem 383).

One of Dickinson's most famous poems applies eucharistic language to the natural world as though attempting to find compensation there for her alienation from the church. The situation presented tends to deepen that sense of exclusion, however, rather than relieve it. Here the speaker responds to the blaze of autumnal glory that only intensifies her Indian Summer forebodings of loss:

These are the days when Birds come back—
A very few—a Bird or two—
To take a backward look.

These are the days when skies resume
The old—old sophistries of June—
A blue and gold mistake.

Oh fraud that cannot cheat the Bee—
Almost thy plausibility
Induces my belief.

Till ranks of seeds their witness bear—
And softly thro' the altered air
Hurries a timid leaf.

Oh Sacrament of summer days,
Oh Last Communion in the Haze—
Permit a child to join.

Thy sacred emblems to partake—
Thy consecrated bread to take
And thine immortal wine!

(Poem 130)

There is a major division in this poem, best described by Anderson, between exposition of natural changes—with the speaker's recognition of the fraudulence of the hope that summer's slide into death can be halted or reversed—and the speaker's prayerful response to her troubling perceptions. Dissatisfied with the reality of biological decline that she, as a knowledgeable adult, understands as evidence of encroaching winter, she reverts to a childlike religious faith and implores inclusion in a naturalistic sacrament.[24]

Within the context of Dickinson's sacramental experience, however, the hopefulness of the concluding stanzas turns out to be strangely muted. What sort of communion service is taking place in the speaker's garden? What authority has sealed the apparent promise of exemption from death? Perhaps nature has its own covenant with God. Or perhaps, in its dying, the summer pledges itself to come again, reassures its anxious friends of its everlasting love, and somehow releases its own variety of transformative grace—thereby achieving a natural parallel with Christ's gift at the Last Supper. The speaker seems to be making just such assumptions without specifying the basis for her hope. Sensing that some natural ritual is taking place, she begs inclusion as a child. A child, presumably, would be closer to nature than an adult—less invasive, less threatening. A child would also feel greater need for inclusion, having less experience of seasonal renewal to rely on and therefore suffering greater dread at the loss of birds, bees, and leaves. She would not as yet fully understand that seeds bear witness to rebirth even more than to death. One critic observes that "this season of the year evokes in the speaker the same awe and reverence experienced by a child at the sacrament of communion," evoking images of tiny, white-clad first communicants.[25] But children in Dickinson's day did not receive communion—not even in the Catholic church until Pope Pius X (reigning 1903–14) lowered the age of eligibility for the sacrament. They were especially ineligible in a Congregational church like the one in Amherst that required conversion as a condition of membership. The poet's personal experience of exclusion—her memory of herself "fleeing from Sacrament" (letter 412)—makes this childlike petition especially ironic and unpromising. And the speaker requests admission to this "Last Communion in the Haze" rather than the first of her new spiritual life. This phrase may refer to "the last rites," as Anderson speculates, or to Christ's Last Supper that was also a sacramental beginning, as Sandeen argues, or it may simply recognize that the first Sunday of November annually marked the final celebration of communion in the First

[24]Anderson, pp. 164–167; also Budick, pp. 54–60; Paul Ferlazzo, *Emily Dickinson*, Twayne's United States Authors Series no. 280 (Indianapolis: Bobbs-Merrill, 1976), p. 115; David T. Porter, *The Art of Emily Dickinson's Early Poetry* (Cambridge: Harvard Univ. Press, 1966), p. 13; Ernest Sandeen, "Delight Deferred by Retrospect: Emily Dickinson's Late-Summer Poems," *New England Quarterly*, 40 (1967), 489.

[25]James E. Mulqueen, "Is Emerson's Work Central to the Poetry of Emily Dickinson?" *Emily Dickinson Bulletin*, 24 (1973), 215.

Church, Amherst.[26] Nothing in the poem, however, suggests that this prayer will be answered favorably or that the sacrament will prove a seal to any promise.

The liturgical contexts of this poem and its frequent companion piece, "Further in Summer than the Birds" (Poem 1068), raise interesting questions. Might Dickinson have come under some non-Calvinistic Christian influence, some Protestants of the Oxford stamp or even Roman Catholics? Her references to the mass liturgy have encouraged readers to suppose so. Yet it is hard to discern high-church influences in her environment.[27] One might be Bishop Frederick Dan Huntington of Boston, an Amherst College alumnus and Austin Dickinson's friend. In 1860, Edward Dickinson presented his daughter with a gift of Huntington's sermons, *Christian Believing and Living* (Boston, 1860), in which she might have read welcome reflections on the vocation to "the true inward life" (p. 261) rather than the more active callings approved by Mary Lyon, and in which she would also have found an 1858 sermon on the dedication of Harvard's Appleton Chapel that made a cautious plea for reinstitution of religious ritual into post-Puritan New England.

Although Bishop Huntington helped to found Grace Episcopal Church in Amherst, Dickinson would have been unlikely to attend its services. The church opened its doors in 1864, after she had already closed those to the Homestead. St. Bridget's Church, the Roman Catholic house of worship, was built in 1871.[28] Servants in the Dickinson home belonged to that parish, once it was organized. Could Dickinson have had access to a missal, then? Records exist of her own family's books but not those belonging to lesser members of the household—that "minor Nation" of Irish workers like Maggie Maher and Thomas Kelley. We do not know how many of them were literate—aside from Maggie Maher, who joined the household too late to have influenced "Further in Summer than the Birds" (Poem 1068), written in 1866. In any event, the movement to put a missal in every Catholic home was an early twentieth-century one, making it improbable that Dickinson would ever have encountered this guide to the mass.

Such questions gain interest when one considers "Further in Summer" and the criticism it has elicited. Despite the assumptions many have made about Dickinson's familiarity with the Anglican or Roman liturgy, however, in interpret

---

[26]Anderson, p. 166; Sandeen, p. 489; *The Articles of Faith and Government of the First Church in Amherst, Mass.,* p. 11.

[27]Conceivably, Dickinson's familiarity with British literature, the metaphysical poets in particular, might have extended her liturgical outlook. Dorothy Huff Oberhaus makes a persuasive case for Dickinson's kinship with George Herbert in " 'Engine against th' Almightie': Emily Dickinson and Prayer," *ESQ,* 32 (1986), 152–172.

[28]*The History of the Town of Amherst, Massachusetts, Published in Two Parts* (Amherst, 1896), pp. 246, 249–250.

ing, for example, the phrase "So gradual the Grace,"[29] it seems sound to forgo the search for hidden references to liturgical and sacramental traditions different from Dickinson's own, and to recognize instead that, when she referred to the mass in this poem, she did so forthrightly for its shock value.

"Further in Summer than the Birds" focuses on an earlier stage of summer's departure than "These are the days when Birds come back—" (Poem 130). Here it is crickets who are said to conduct a liturgy, and the speaker makes no attempt to join them. The "unobtrusive Mass" she intuits seems to be a requiem that confers peace on its participants by affirming a cosmic order that both accepts and transcends death:

Further in Summer than the Birds
Pathetic from the Grass
A minor Nation celebrates
It's unobtrusive Mass.

No Ordinance be seen
So gradual the Grace
A pensive Custom it becomes
Enlarging Loneliness.

Antiquest felt at Noon
When August burning low
Arise this spectral Canticle
Repose to typify

Remit as yet no Grace
No Furrow on the Glow
Yet a Druidic Difference
Enhances Nature now

[29]Could Dickinson have known the meaning of "gradual" as noun? Charles Anderson and Sharon Cameron both suggest that she did, although he carefully points out that the word occurs adjectivally in her poem and may have no direct liturgical reference. If it does point to a liturgical source, it would be a rich one in the Anglican tradition. Anderson identifies the Gradual as "the oldest and most important chant by the choir during the Proper of the Mass" (p. 170); Cameron observes that it "dominates" the Proper (p. 182). Yet an 1850 American edition of *The Book of Common Prayer*, belonging to an Amherst citizen and now in the collection of the Jones Library, contains no reference anywhere to that chant, raising questions about whether the poet's few Episcopalian contacts would have opened much insight to her about high-church rituals. The Gradual occurs less prominently in the Roman Catholic mass as a brief scriptural response to the Epistle. It would, of course, have been proclaimed in Latin and would be an improbable topic of pantry conversation from an Irish cook or laundress returning from church. Nor was it one of those liturgical rituals to which American travelers in France and Italy responded with mixed curiosity and reproach. Although taking the word "gradual" as another reference to the mass deepens our sense of unity in the poem by connecting the sixth line with the eleventh, the poem loses no essential merit without this connective, and it seems more honest to forgo it. Not even Noah Webster comes to our aid here. Even though our contemporary unabridged dictionary features the liturgical meaning of gradual as a noun, an edition from the poet's day defines it simply as "an order of steps" or, secondarily, "a grail; an ancient book of hymns and prayers, so called because some of the anthems were chanted on the steps (*gradus*) of the pulpit." There is no explicit reference to the mass. Perhaps some of Dickinson's reading in English novels could have filled the gap in her vocabulary, but this seems doubtful.

Although no specific sacramental actions are recorded here, any mass is a communion service that celebrates the closeness of the community while symbolically
reenacting sacrificial death. The poet, however, stands outside, listening: the ritual
intensifies her "Loneliness" rather than assuaging it.

As readers have long recognized, this poem acknowledges Dickinson's sense of
the cleavage between man and nature.[30] She is an outsider, unable to draw spiritual nourishment from the natural sacrament she senses taking place just outside
her doors. There seems to be a contradiction here between the liturgy's purpose of
"Repose" and the speaker's experience of conflict; yet that contradiction dissolves
when we find Dickinson deliberately invoking a foreign ritual as a symbol for her
alienation. Nothing in her background prepared her to expect consolation from
Catholic liturgy or to attribute to it any salvific power. Rather than thinking of such
a service as sublime and uplifting, she had been taught to regard it as evidence of
superstition, the quasi-magical expedient of "minor" nations like Irish servants or
inhabitants of backward European countries.[31] The masses said in Amherst during
the mid-1866's, when this poem was written, were themselves "unobtrusive,"
being celebrated on an irregular basis in private homes.[32]

The Calvinist language with which Dickinson herself would have felt comfort-
able appears only three times in this poem. It lends an ironic twist to the line "No
Ordinance be seen," implying that it refers not only to the invisibility of the crickets' sacramental action but also to its heretical quality. Nothing that happens here
was ordained by Christ. The purpose of the activity is also called into question by
her juxtaposition of Calvinistic and Catholic concepts in the line "Repose to typify." Christ is the antetype to whom all typological emblems should point in
Puritan thinking, and Christ's presence should itself be the reality of the sacrament for Catholics. Yet this ritual typifies nothing but the emotion of finite creatures, thereby draining communion of its spiritual power. The result of sacramental action ought to be grace; but, at best, this liturgy avoids diminishing its existing
sum. No grace has been remitted or lost. If we take "remit" in its alternative sense,
as verb rather than adjective, the speaker tells us that this liturgy gives back no
grace either. In Calvinist terms, the sacramental activity recorded here accom-
plishes nothing of value and should never have been expected to do any good.

Recognizing how foreign and strange Catholic liturgy would have seemed to
Dickinson refreshes our perspective on her concluding reference to "Druidic

---

[30]Yvor Winters, "Emily Dickinson and the Limits of Judgment," *In Defense of Reason* (Denver:
Alan Swallow, 1943), p. 292; Anderson, pp. 169–171; Sandeen, pp. 489–490.

[31]"Pathetic" would be a kind word for it, to judge from her spiteful if comically hyperbolic remarks
to Austin about the disciplinary practices he adopted while teaching in Boston: "Vinnie and I say
masses for poor Irish boys souls. So far as *I* am concerned I should like to have you kill some—there
are so many now, there is no room for the Americans, and I cant think of a death that would be more
after my mind than *scientific destruction, scholastic dissolution,* there's something lofty in it, it smacks
of *going up!*" (letter 43).

[32]The origins of the Amherst Catholic church are detailed in an unpublished student paper by
Patricia Leal, "The History of St. Brigid's Church" (Univ. of Massachusetts, 1974) in the Jones Library
collection of Amherst historical materials. Records of early masses appear on pp. 249–250.

Difference." Druid rituals, poorly understood by historians of her time and still mysterious even to modern anthropologists, probably summoned ideas of primitive magic. Dickinson might have made grim associations with the Druids, thinking in terms of human sacrifice that would connect with Christ's sacrifice on Calvary (reenacted in the Catholic mass but not in Calvinist services) and also with the crickets' apparent acceptance of the necessity for autumnal dying.[33] She could also have known that the Druids worshiped the sun, celebrating solstices as they marked the transitions of the solar calendar with ritual observances. In its own way, Catholic liturgy is seasonal and cyclic as well—with its year beginning with Advent in early winter and thereby (for the northern hemisphere, anyway) affirming renewal in the midst of natural death. The Congregational church of Dickinson's experience disregarded even Christmas and Easter. Its calendar made no attempt either to mirror or to counteract the cycles of the natural year. The Roman and Anglo-Catholic churches, by contrast, acknowledged seasonal progressions with their succession of feast days and their alternating seasons of penitence and jubilation. Although Dickinson probably chose the liturgical imagery of this poem to intensify the sense of her alienation from nature, she employed the language in a nonjudgmental way and obviously recognized the profound appeal of a worship pattern different from her own. The crickets draw upon long-buried impulses. They elicit "Antiquest" feelings, sentiments like those the Druids embodied in their rituals and that monks in the Dark Ages expressed through the mass. Cut off from such possibilities of worship, the speaker expresses a wistfulness here—not only, as has long been recognized, for union with nature, but also for reunion with ancient religious traditions from which she feels isolated.

The driving question of Emily Dickinson's life was the one she apparently directed to the Reverend Washington Gladden: "Is immortality true?" (letter 752a). Everlasting life was the one great promise of Christianity that she kept testing in her poems, letters, and conversations. The sacraments were known to her as seals of Christ's promise. As I have reasoned elsewhere, the cooperation between God and man entailed in sacramental action and the concept of divine penetration into the material forms of natural substances (baptismal water), and the products of human making (communion bread and wine) challenged her imagination.[34] She began with the symbols provided within her religious culture but refused to be limited by Congregational church practices or by Calvin's insistence on following Christ's few specific ordinances. Instead, Dickinson revitalized the concept of sacrament to include those imaginative processes by which the poet—recognizing occasions of grace in the natural world, within her own consciousness, and in her relationships with other people—demonstrated the multifarious ways in which spirit surcharges matter, thereby giving symbolic expression to her hope for immortality. By "adjusting the symbols" of her Calvinist heritage in this imaginative way (Poem 342), Emily Dickinson converted doctrine into her own distinctively religious art.

---

[33]Cynthia Griffin Wolff, *Emily Dickinson* (New York: Knopf, 1986), pp. 310–311. See also Frank D. Rashid, "Emily Dickinson's Voice of Endings," *ESQ*, 31 (1985), 32.
    [34]Eberwein, p. 187.

"Tender Pioneer": Emily Dickinson's Poems on The Life of Christ

Dorothy Huff Oberhaus

Emily Dickinson's poems on the life of Jesus Christ, written from early to late in her canon, reflect a poetic concern spanning her entire creative life. When read together as a group allowing each to illuminate the others, these meditations on Jesus' birth, life, Crucifixion, and Resurrection form something like a nineteenth-century American Gospel.[1] By recreating the Gospels, often with wit and American colloquial language, Dickinson assumes the role of that "warbling, typic Teller" her "supposed person" observes the Bible needs to "captivate" readers.[2] As "little 'John,' " her persona in one of many poems addressed to Jesus, she stresses the Gospels' contemporary relevance and makes them freshly available to her "Sweet countrymen" (497, 441). But while spoken "New Englandly" (285) and in her unique voice, the deep structure of her Gospel poems places them in the poetic tradition of Christian devotion, a tradition extending from the "Dream of the Rood" and *Pearl* poets, through the medieval lyricists, Herbert, Vaughan, Crashaw, and Hopkins, to Eliot and Auden in our own day. The salient feature uniting Christian poets in a single identifiable poetic mode is their reverential attention to the life of Jesus Christ and their acceptance of such données as the Trinity, the Incarnation, and the Redemption. They regard the life of Christ as not merely a picturesque fable providing vivid metaphors but rather as their model. In the language of Christian typology, they see both a fulfillment of Old Testament figures and a prefiguration or foreshadowing of the lives of His followers.[3] Dickinson's Christology in her poems on the life of Christ is that of the devo-

Reprinted from *On Dickinson* (1990) by permission of the author and Duke University Press.

[1]Charles R. Anderson, *Emily Dickinson's Poetry: Stairway of Surprise* (New York: Holt, Rinehart & Winston, 1960), p. xiii, first posited that Dickinson's poems are best read in thematic groups to allow each to illuminate the others.

[2]"Typic" is a variant word for "warbling" in Poem 1545, *The Poems of Emily Dickinson*, ed. Thomas H. Johnson, 3 vols. (Cambridge: Harvard Univ. Press, 1955). Hereafter poems are cited in parentheses in the text according to Johnson's numbering. Letter 268, *The Letters of Emily Dickinson*, ed. Thomas H. Johnson and Theodora Ward, 3 vols. (Cambridge: Harvard Univ. Press, 1958). Hereafter letters preceded by "L" are cited in parentheses in the text according to Johnson's numbering.

[3]I am indebted here and throughout for my definition of the poetic tradition of devotion to Miriam K. Starkman, director of my 1980 doctoral dissertation. See her "Noble Numbers and the Poetry of Devotion" in *Reason and the Imagination: Studies in the History of Ideas 1600–1800*, ed. J. A. Mazzeo

tional tradition and so are many of her most arresting tropes in portraying Him, her own versions of recurring Christian figures.

Paradigmatic of her way of imaginatively recreating while maintaining the essence of traditional material is the following meditation's epithet for Jesus, "Tender Pioneer," summing up her loving portrait of Him in this poem and throughout the canon. According to the "Lexicon," whose importance to her poetic thought she herself acknowledged (L-261), "tender" means loving, compassionate, kind, and "anxious for another's good"; a "pioneer" is "one that goes before another to remove obstruction or to prepare the way for another."[4] Dickinson thus describes Jesus in her own words, but her underlying meaning is that of the New Testament and of other devotional poets: Jesus Christ is the loving and courageous Redeemer.

Life—is what we make it—
Death—We do not know—
Christ's acquaintance with Him
Justify Him—though—

He—would trust no stranger—
Other—could betray—
Just His own endorsement—
That—sufficeth Me—

All the other Distance
He hath traversed first—
No New Mile remaineth—
Far as Paradise—

His sure foot preceding—
Tender Pioneer—
Base must be the Coward
Dare not venture—now

(698)

This meditation's meaning centers on its astonishingly varied verb forms. The first two sentences, in the general present, introduce the themes of life, created by our own choices, and death, as yet unknown. But "Christ's acquaintance" with death "Justify Him." "Him" punningly refers not only to death, personified as "Him" in line 3, but to Christ, "He" in line 5. Christ's Atonement both vindicated God by proving His love and vindicated death by transforming its meaning, a recurring

---

(New York: Columbia Univ. Press, 1962), pp. 1–27, and "The 'Grace of the Absurd': Form and Concept in W. H. Auden's *For the Time Being,*" *Harvard Theological Review,* 67 (1974), 275–88. Donald Davie, ed. *The New Oxford Book of Christian Verse* (New York: Oxford Univ. Press, 1981), p. xxi, stresses the centrality of attention to the life of Christ and acceptance of Christian doctrines to a definition of Christian poetry. For a discussion of Christian typology, see A. C. Charity, *Events and Their After-life: The Dialectics of Christian Typology in the Bible and Dante* (Cambridge: Cambridge Univ. Press, 1966).

[4]Noah Webster, *An American Dictionary of the English Language* (1848 ed.; rpt. Ann Arbor: University Microfilms International, 1979). Hereafter, definitions are Webster's.

Christian donnée expressed less succinctly and more prosaically in the title of Isaac Watts's hymn, "A Prospect of Heaven makes Death easy."[5] Dickinson's uninflected verb, "Justify," expresses grammatically the eternal meaning of Christ's redemptive death: it did, does, and always will prove His love and transform the meaning of death.

Returning to the theme of choice in the first two lines of the second stanza, the single sentence's verbs are conditional: Christ "would" trust no other because another "could" betray. Though He "could" have done otherwise, He willingly chose human life and death, another donnée of the poetic tradition of devotion. As George Herbert's Jesus "sweetly took / Our flesh" and the "Dream of the Rood" poet's Jesus was "eager to mount the gallows,"[6] Dickinson's "Savior" voluntarily chose to come to earth for the sake of His "little Fellowmen" and even "coveted" the Crown of Thorns (1487, 1735, to be discussed later). The third and fourth lines of stanza 2 return from the conditional to the present tense but in the specific rather than general sense: Christ's endorsement "sufficeth" for the speaker who here therefore accepts death.

Beginning with the third stanza, Jesus is conqueror of life as well as death. When the reader regularizes its syntax and supplies its elliptical words, stanza 3 reads, "[Because] He hath traversed first / All the other Distance [of human life,] / No New Mile remaineth [from birth, through life and death, and ultimately as] Far as Paradise." The initial spondee, "No New Mile" underscores the importance of Christ's having "traversed first": by typologically foreshadowing His followers' pilgrimage, He has provided a model for their imitation and extended the way as far as Paradise. The meaning of the Incarnation is restated but intensified in stanza 4: "[Because] His sure foot is preceding [,] / Tender pioneer [,] / Base must be the Coward [who does not] / Dare [to] venture—now—." "His sure foot," another spondee, is one of many Dickinson synecdoches drawing attention to the actual physical body of Christ and His real humanity; in other poems, He has a "second [human] face" (225), the "highest head" (1735), and even stands on "divinest tiptoe" (317). The past biblical form "hath traversed" becomes in stanza 4 "[is] preceding," placing Christ's life in the ongoing present. Here Dickinson adapts the recurring devotional figure of anachronism to stress the ever-present significance of Christ's life; as Herbert's speaker is present at both the Nativity and the Crucifixion and Auden's Nativity takes place in twentieth-century New York City, Dickinson's Christ is preceding now and as "Pioneer," with its connotations of the American frontier, on this very continent.[7]

"Tender Pioneer," foregrounded as a single line, is one of Dickinson's many original, often witty kennings for Christ. As Robert Alter points out, the kenning, a recurring biblical figure, is in reality a riddle that has been transformed from the

---

[5] In Davie, *Oxford Book of Christian Verse*, p. 149.

[6] "Faith," *The Works of George Herbert*, ed. F. E. Hutchinson (Oxford: Clarendon Press, 1941), p. 49. "The Dream of the Rood" in Davie, *Oxford Book of Christian Verse*, p. 1.

[7] Herbert, "Christmas" and "Redemption," *Works*, pp. 80, 40. Auden, "For the Time Being," *Collected Poetry* (New York: Random House, 1945), pp. 407–66.

interrogative into the declarative. This is obvious, as Alter explains, when one turns the declarative back into the interrogative: "What is a whale-road? The sea. What is fruit of the loins? A child."[8] Dickinson's kennings for Jesus are similarly illuminated when returned to the interrogative: Who is the "Tender Pioneer," the "docile Gentleman," the "Largest Lover"? The reader must then in the context of the poem answer, Jesus Christ, of course (1487, 573, to be discussed later).

Concluding as it began with the theme of choice and in the general present, the meditation's final two lines retrospectively draw together the poem's widely disparate verb forms: because Christ did, does, and will "Justify" death as well as His love; because He who could have done otherwise willingly chose human life and death; because He "hath traversed" first, defeating both life and death; because "His sure foot [is] preceding"; in short, because He is the "Tender Pioneer," "Base must be the Coward" who does not choose to imitate Jesus' courage and "dare venture" both life and death—"now."

As "Tender Pioneer," Jesus thus tested the "Bridge" of faith for the sake of the "Crowd" who follow:

How brittle are the Piers
On which our Faith doth tread—
No Bridge below doth totter so—
Yet none hath such a Crowd.

It is as old as God—
Indeed—'twas built by him—
He sent his Son to test the Plank,
And he pronounced it firm.
                    (1433)

An emblem poem, a form favored by the religious poets of the seventeenth century as well as by Dickinson, its visual image for meditation is the bridge of faith. One of her many inner dialogues, its two quatrains are united by this visual image, by their identical metrical and rhyme patterns, and by the regularity of the poem's iambic trimeters and tetrameters expressing the steady, ongoing "tread" of the faithful. Yet each stanza concludes with a period, and the two voices assume opposing attitudes toward the bridge. The bridge is "brittle," vacillating, and crowded, reflects the first voice; the second responds, reminding the first voice (as well as the reader), the bridge was built by God and tested and endorsed by Jesus. That God the Father is the craftsman who built the bridge and Jesus the "Son" sent to test it manifests Dickinson's acceptance of the Christian Trinity, implicit in all her Christocentric poems but more specifically stated here and elsewhere. In a seldom-considered meditation on prayer, Deity is both the singular "God" and the plural "Jehovahs," including Father, "Son," and "Spirit" (626); in another, the speaker declares herself "Bride" of the Trinity, naming in turn "Father," "Son," and "Holy Ghost" (817).

---

[8]*The Art of Biblical Poetry* (New York: Basic Books, 1985), pp. 15–16.

In a Nativity poem, Dickinson's kenning for the "Son" is "docile Gentleman." Far less solemn than the "Tender Pioneer" and bridge of faith meditations, its reverential-playful tone brings to mind the "saintly impertinence" often attributed to George Herbert.[9] After wittily titling the meditation "Christ's Birthday," she is believed to have sent it next door to her best friend and sister-in-law, Susan Dickinson, at Christmas 1876 with an iced cake, presumably intended as the Savior's birthday cake:[10]

> The Savior must have been
> A docile Gentleman—
> To come so far so cold a Day
> For little Fellowmen—
>
> The Road to Bethlehem
> Since He and I were Boys
> Was leveled, but for that twould be
> A rugged billion Miles—
>
> (1487)

The first stanza focuses on the Nativity, the second more generally on the meaning of the Incarnation. The witty near-rhyme, "docile Gentleman" / "little Fellowmen" stresses that Jesus' pilgrimage was human but precedes those of His followers in importance as well as in time. In other poems, she similarly contrasts Him with His followers in terms of size: our crucifixions are "smaller" versions of His (225); His is the "highest head" (1735); the speaker's attempts to imitate Him are of necessity "smaller" because she has "less Infinity" (573). Here Dickinson's "Savior" willingly came to earth for the sake of His "little Fellowmen" on a cold New England day, another instance of her use of anachronism, a figure further developed in the second stanza where the speaker and the "Savior" were "Boys" together.

The second stanza's "Bethlehem," puzzling at first because it seems to refer to the scene of Jesus' birth, is a metonymy for the entire human life and death of Christ and typologically for those of his followers. By conflating Jesus' birth, life, and Crucifixion, Dickinson stresses that in choosing birth He chose human life, suffering, and death, another recurring devotional theme, as in Eliot's "Journey of the Magi" where the kings journey to Bethlehem to find upon their arrival a foreshadowing of the Crucifixion, "three trees on the low sky" and men "dicing for pieces of silver."[11] Dickinson similarly conflates Christ's entire life in a dialogue between Jesus and Daisy, often the speaker of her Christocentric poems. The poem begins with Jesus' saying, " 'They have not chosen me . . . But I have chosen

---

[9]William Empson, *Seven Types of Ambiguity*, 3rd ed. (New York: New Directions, 1955), p. 238.

[10]See my "In Defense of Sue," *Dickinson Studies*, No. 48 (Bonus 1983), pp. 1–25, for a refutation of the widely held belief that Emily and Susan Dickinson's girlhood friendship ended in indifference or even hostility.

[11]T. S. Eliot, *The Complete Poems and Plays, 1909–1950* (New York: Harcourt, Brace, and World, 1952), p. 68.

them!' ", according to Daisy, the "Broken hearted statement [He] Uttered in Bethleem!" (*sic*, 85). Jesus spoke these words, of course, not as an infant, but in Jerusalem shortly before His Crucifixion.[12] Elsewhere, "Bethlehem" refers typologically to the lives of Christ's followers whose birth, like His, necessitates suffering and death. In a meditation on I Corinthians 15.35, "Paul knew the Man that knew the News," another kenning for Jesus, because "He passed through Bethlehem," not meaning that he was present at Jesus' birth but that he followed the way of the Cross (1492). "The Road to Bethlehem," then, refers both to Jesus' human life and death and to those of every human pilgrim whose "Road" would be a "rugged billion Miles" had Jesus not "leveled" the way.

The speaker of the following meditation reflects upon the Cross that proved God's love, asserts that she attempts to imitate His love, confesses her imitation is imperfect, and finally asks for salvation not because she has earned it but because Christ promised and won it:

> The Test of Love—is Death—
> Our Lord—"so loved"—it saith—
> What Largest Lover—hath—
> Another—doth—
>
> If smaller Patience—be—
> Through less Infinity—
> If Bravo, sometimes swerve—
> Through fainter Nerve—
>
> Accept it's Most—
> And overlook—the Dust—
> Last—Least—
> The Cross'—Request—
>
> (573)

The first stanza is meditatively spoken by the speaker to herself, the second and third are prayerfully addressed to the "Largest Lover." The first line echoes Jesus' words, "Greater love hath no man than this, that a man lay down his life for his friends" (John 15.13). The second blurs the distinction Dickinson usually makes between Father and Son. By "Lord," she almost always means Jesus, as in number 538 where "Christ" is the variant word for "Lord" and 571 where "Our lord— thought no / Extravagance / To pay—a Cross—"; yet the apparent biblical analogue for "so loved" is John 3.16, "For God so loved the world, that he gave his only begotten Son." The "Largest Lover" whom the speaker subsequently addresses is thus the Son, but it also alludes to that New Dispensation's loving Father described by Jesus. She "doth" / He "hath" is a near-rhyme drawing attention to her imperfect imitation. In turn, "doth" / "hath" nearly rhyme with the first

---

[12]John 15.16, King James version. Hereafter biblical references are noted in parentheses in the text.

two lines' "Death" and "saith," drawing attention to what it is she attempts to imitate, the love Christ proved by His death and attributes to God the Father.

She then apologizes to the "Largest Lover" for her imperfect imitation and asks His forebearance: "If smaller Patience—be— / Through [my having] less Infinity [than you, and] / If Bravo, sometimes swerve— / Through [my having] fainter Nerve— / [Please] Accept it's Most [my imperfect attempt] / And overlook—the Dust." The uninflected "be" and "swerve" express the ongoing nature of the human condition. As representative of humanity, the speaker was, is, and always will be imperfect because she is after all only "Dust," a recurring trope for imperfect mortality in Dickinson, the Bible, and the poetic tradition of devotion.

In the poem's penultimate line, like the first a highly condensed biblical allusion, the speaker boldly quotes Scripture to the "Largest Lover" to support her plea, reminding Him that He Himself promised "the last shall be first" and the "least among you . . . great" (Matthew 19.30, Luke 9.48). Foregrounded as a spondee and the poem's only monometer, "Last—Least" alliteratively recalls "Largest Lover," contrasting her "Dust" with His "Infinity," a juxtaposition underscored by the poem's intricate rhyme pattern. "Last—Least," an internal near-rhyme, nearly rhymes with "Most" and "Dust," referring to human imperfection. All are near-rhymes with the poem's first accented word, "Test," and its final word, "Request," true rhymes referring to Christ's redemptive Crucifixion. Though the speaker attempts to imitate the "Largest Lover," she does not rely upon her own merit for salvation but rather upon the "Cross' Request," the unexplainable but all-consuming love for His creatures Jesus proved by His Atonement.[13]

As in the "Tender Pioneer" meditation, Christ's Atonement proves His love and promises redemption, but His Passion is also for Dickinson as for other devotional poets an awesome event of unparalleled significance to be contemplated sorrowfully. The hieroglyph and meditational focus of the following emblem poem is the Crown of Thorns Jesus wore when presented to Pontius Pilate, who then turned Him over to the mob to be crucified (John 19.2):

> One crown that no one seeks
> And yet the highest head
> Its isolation coveted
> Its stigma deified
>
> While Pontius Pilate lives
> In whatsoever hell
> That coronation pierces him
> He recollects it well.
>   (1735)

As the initial spondee, "One crown," juxtaposed alliteratively with the spondee, "no one," contrasts human reluctance to suffer with Christ's uniquely coveting its

---

[13]Compare Richard Strier's discussion of Herbert's "Artillerie," *Love Known: Theology and Experience in George Herbert's Poetry* (Chicago: Univ. of Chicago Press, 1983), pp. 97–104.

"isolation," so "coveted" and "stigma deified" contrast Old Testament with New Testament connotations. According to Christian typology, Old Testament figures foreshadow those of the New, but often there is considerable tension between old and new meanings. In the Tenth Commandment, "covet" means "to desire inordinately" in a negative sense, but in the New Testament the word is used in a positive sense, as in I Corinthians 12.31 where Paul advises, "covet earnestly the best gifts." Similarly, the oxymoron "stigma deified" contrasts the usual negative biblical connotation of "thorns" with their meaning when worn by Christ. "Thorns" in the Old Testament signify God's anger; after the Fall, He tells Adam, "Cursed is the ground for thy sake. . . . Thorns also and thistles shall it bring forth to thee" (Genesis 3.17–18). The word retains some of its negative meaning in the New Testament; even Jesus asks, "Do men gather grapes of thorns?" (Matthew 7.16). But by wearing the Crown, Christ transformed "thorns" into a symbol of His glory—though they retain their old meaning for Pontius Pilate who in hell is still "pierced" by them.[14]

Neither the meditation on the Crown of Thorns, the "Tender Pioneer," the bridge of faith, the "docile Gentleman," nor the "Largest Lover" has received more than passing critical attention, yet these poems where Dickinson's discourse is most clearly that of Christian devotion are crucial to understanding her other poems on the life of Christ. One better known poem whose secular interpretations are called into question when read in light of these five includes a dramatization of Peter's denial of Christ:

> He forgot—and I—remembered—
> 'Twas an everyday affair—
> Long ago as Christ and Peter—
> "Warmed them" at the "Temple fire".
>
> "Thou wert with him"—quoth "the Damsel"?
> "*No*"—said Peter, 'twas'nt me—
> Jesus merely "looked" at Peter—
> Could I do aught else—to Thee?

(203)

This poem has elicited much speculation as to who it was that forgot Dickinson, John Cody supposing it a lover and Rebecca Patterson a woman friend.[15] But Dickinson does not disclose what if any personal event inspired the poem; nor does it concern the speaker's experience, mentioned only in the first and final lines, but rather her mental process in a disappointing situation.

She begins, "He forgot," reflects such experiences are common, then in line 3 turns to the typic denial of Peter. Again, "No New Mile remaineth" because Jesus

---

[14]See Chana Block, *Spelling the Word: George Herbert and the Bible* (Berkeley: Univ. of California Press, 1985), pp. 50–51, for a discussion of Old and New Testament meaning for "thorn."

[15]John Cody, *After Great Pain: The Inner Life of Emily Dickinson* (Cambridge: Harvard Univ. Press, 1971), p. 374; Rebecca Patterson, *The Riddle of Emily Dickinson* (Boston: Houghton Mifflin, 1951), p. 203.

has experienced denial first. Vividly recreating Peter's denial in lines 3 through 7, she draws attention to its contemporary relevance by fusing American colloquial language with the biblical language of all four Evangelists: The "damsel" appears in Matthew and John, Peter "warmed himself" in Mark and John, "the Lord . . . looked upon Peter" in Luke (Matthew 26.69–75, Mark 14.66–72, Luke 22.55–62, and John 18.16–27), yet Peter responds to the damsel's charge in unmistakably nineteenth-century American colloquial terms: " 'No'—said Peter, ' 'twas'nt me.' " Remembering Jesus' response to Peter solves the problem of how to respond to her delinquent friend whom she directly addresses in the final line: she will imitate Jesus and "merely" look at him.

Secular interpretations of another better known poem, a meditation on the Crucifixion, are similarly called into question when read in light of the Bible, the poetic tradition of devotion, and the five clearly devotional meditations:

> One Crucifixion is recorded—only—
> How many be
> Is not affirmed of Mathematics—
> Or History—
>
> One Calvary—exhibited to Stranger—
> As many be
> As Persons—or Peninsulas—
> Gethsemane—
>
> Is but a Province—in the Being's Centre—
> Judea—
> For Journey—or Crusade's Achieving—
> Too near—
>
> Our Lord—indeed—made Compound Witness—
> And yet—
> There's newer—nearer Crucifixion
> Than That—
>
> (553)

Brooks, Lewis, and Warren see this meditation biographically as "a fine instance of Emily Dickinson's capacity to bend the Biblical vocabulary to an account of her own psychic condition." Robert Weisbuch, too, diminishes Christ's importance to the poem, arguing that Dickinson finds His Crucifixion "unique only in that it was made historically public" and " 'newer-nearer Crucifixion'. . . most worthy of attention."[16] But, though crucifixion is here the common lot for all humanity as well as for the human-divine Jesus and though in the final stanza the speaker alludes obliquely to her own, Dickinson keeps the Crucifixion of Christ before the reader's attention throughout the poem.

---

[16]Cleanth Brooks, R. W. B. Lewis, and Robert Penn Warren, eds. *American Literature: The Makers and the Making* (New York: St. Martin's, 1973), pp. 1245–46. Weisbuch, *Emily Dickinson's Poetry* (Chicago: Univ. of Chicago, 1975), pp. 80–81.

As number 1735 begins "One crown," this meditation begins "One Crucifixion." "One Calvary" and "Our Lord" are similarly stressed as initial spondees. "Calvary," "Gethsemane," "Province," and "Judea" metonymically allude to the geographical place where Christ's life and death took place. Even the poem's shape is that of the typic Cross, its long pentameters and tetrameters the upright post, its short alternating dimeters and monometers the transverse piece. The uniqueness of Christ's sacrifice is expressed by the uniqueness of the ringing first line of the last stanza, "Our Lord—indeed—made Compound Witness." The other stanzas begin with a pentameter, but this is a tetrameter; the other verbs are either in the passive voice or forms of "to be," but this line is in the active voice and contains the poem's only strong verb, "made," accented by "indeed." The line's apparent biblical analogues are I John 5.6–9 where Christ is He that "beareth witness" (Dickinson's variant for "made" is "bore") and Revelation 1.5 where He is the "faithful witness and the first begotten of the dead." To the biblical "Witness," Dickinson adds "Compound," creating another kenning. Christ's "Witness" is "Compound" because, as in the "Tender Pioneer" and "Largest Lover" meditations, He gave His life both as evidence of God's love and of His transformation of death.

Stanza 1, the first three lines of stanza 2, and stanza 4 are parallel, each beginning with a clause concerning Christ's Crucifixion, then the adversative "And yet" (specifically stated in stanza 4 and understood in 1 and 2), and finally a clause concerning those unrecorded. The uninflected "be" of stanzas 1 and 2 and "is" of stanza 3 assert the universal nature of personal suffering both before and after Christ, typologically placing His at the center of time.[17] Thus, "One Crucifixion is recorded," and yet how many there have been, are, and will be remains unknown; "One Calvary" is exhibited, and yet there are as many as have been, are, and will be persons. "Our Lord—indeed—made Compound Witness," and yet there is antitypical crucifixion taking place right now, presumably including that of the speaker.[18]

These parallel stanzas provide an envelope structure for the poem's central insight: "Gethsemane— / Is but a Province—in the Being's Centre." As Christ in "One crown" suffered in "isolation," so all human suffering takes place alone and within. Seven lines precede and seven follow this sentence, Dickinson's pun, "Centre," drawing attention to its centrality in form as well as meaning. "Province," another pun, uniting all crucifixion with that of the human-divine Jesus, is a verbal play she explains in the following lines: one does not have to journey to the province of Judea because the province of suffering is within. The poem's metrical pattern underscores this epiphany: up to and including "Gethsemane," the short alternating lines are dimeters, but thereafter monometers, expressing union with Christ, a union all humanity attains through the sameness of their crucifixions.

---

[17]Weisbuch, pp. 80–81, argues that for Dickinson, Christ is no longer the center of time.
[18]Note that "antitype" does not mean opposite type, but fulfilled type.

Dickinson thus internalizes the meaning of the Crucifixion, but not in the sense of "bend[ing] the Biblical vocabulary to an account of her own psychic condition." Nor, as Weisbuch argues, does her "internalization" of biblical texts and Christian typology distinguish her from other religious poets.[19] Robert Alter cites George Herbert, "arguably the greatest Protestant poet in English," as adapting not only biblical ideas and phrases but the "dynamics of biblical poetry and its relation to the life of the spirit." Noting that even the Psalms include many poignantly personal allusions, Alter explains that there is a tendency in biblical poetry to move "from outer to inner," "from heaven to earth . . . to [the human] heart" standing at the "center of the great picture" recorded in biblical poetry.[20] Dickinson's internalization of biblical texts is thus not that of an eccentric nineteenth-century American spinster searching for metaphors to express her personal angst but that of the great poets of the Bible and that of the epitome of Christian poets, George Herbert.

As type, awesome event demanding sorrowful contemplation, and "Compound Witness" to Christ's love and transformation of death, the Crucifixion is Dickinson's most frequent subject and allusion in her poems on the life of Christ. His Resurrection, understood in the preceding poems by His transformation of death, is the subject of the previously undiscussed retrospective narrative concluding this study. Drawing on all four Evangelists' accounts, Dickinson recreates the first Easter. After announcing the enormous import for all time of Christ's gift of Himself, the narrator recounts the aftermath of the Crucifixion, the disciples' discovery of the empty tomb, their despair when believing their Master dead, and their ultimate joy when He suddenly appears among them:

He gave away his Life—
To Us—Gigantic Sum—
A trifle—in his own esteem—
But magnified—by Fame—

Until it burst the Hearts
That fancied they could hold—
When swift it slipped it's limit—
And on the Heavens—unrolled—

'Tis Ours—to wince—and weep—
And wonder—and decay
By Blossoms gradual process—
He chose—Maturity—

And quickening—as we sowed—
Just obviated Bud—
And when We turned to note the Growth—
Broke—perfect—from the Pod—

(567)

[19]Weisbuch, pp. 80–81.
[20]*Art of Biblical Poetry*, pp. 209–11.

Though not named, Christ is obviously He who "gave away his Life" and "Broke—perfect—from the Pod," but the identity of the similarly unnamed narrator, a far more fully drawn dramatic figure than the preceding poems' speakers, is less clear. As her first person plural pronoun indicates, she participated in the events she describes. Though Dickinson may have had in mind Mary Magdalene, a favorite protagonist of Christian poets in poems about the Resurrection, more likely, as line nine's colloquial " 'Tis" suggests, she anachronistically painted into the biblical scene a nineteenth-century American disciple, perhaps "little 'John' " or Daisy (497, 85).[21] Whether a nineteenth-century disciple, Mary Magdalene, or a fusion of both, the narrator has a complex point of view. From the beginning, she knows the narrative's happy outcome, but she shifts between this omniscient perspective and the first person view of a participant. This double perspective heightens the ironic disparity between what the disciples perceive and what in reality is taking place.

From a universal viewpoint, she begins with the "Gigantic Sum" or summary of the meaning of Christ's Atonement, "He gave away his Life— / To Us," a variation of Jesus' saying He "came . . . to give his life a ransom for many" (Matthew 20.28, Mark 10.45). But He spoke these words as a prediction of His approaching death and Resurrection, and the narrator speaks after His prediction has been fulfilled. As the poem later makes clear, however, she no more than the others remembered while the events were taking place that He not only predicted His death but that on the third day He would rise again (Matthew 20.19, Mark 10.34). "Gigantic Sum," foregrounded as a kenning, is a pun meaning both summary and the enormous price or value of Christ's life given as ransom, its second meaning the subject of the following sentence and the referent of its three third-person-singular pronouns.

This sentence works as a kind of zoom lens, quickly relating what happened after the Crucifixion until the disciples found the empty sepulchre. Decompressed, it reads, "[The 'Gigantic Sum' of Christ's life given as ransom was] A trifle—in his own esteem—But [it was] magnified—by Fame— / Until it burst the Hearts / That fancied they could hold— / When swift it slipped it's limit— / And on the Heavens—unrolled." The first line counters the narrator's estimate of the enormous value of Christ's gift of Himself with His own: He "thought [it] no / Extravagance / To pay—a Cross" (571). "But," she continues, His death on the Cross was "magnified—by Fame," a dark fame so great that when Christ appeared unrecognized and asked the disciples why they were sad, ironically pretending not to know what had taken place, Cleopas replied He must be a stranger in Jerusalem not to have heard of the Crucifixion (Luke 24.17–18). The disciples were overwhelmed with grief at Christ's awful death, their courage further eroded by its notoriety "Until" their hearts finally "burst" "When" they discovered the empty sepulchre, though as Dickinson interjects they had incorrectly believed they could "hold" the faith in face of any adversity. From the enlightened viewpoint of one

---

[21]Bloch, *Spelling the Word*, p. 30, describes Herbert as "painting himself into the biblical scene."

who knows why the tomb is empty, the narrator explains its meaning: Christ "slipped it's limit." Though the disciples saw the stone "unrolled" ("rolled away" in Matthew 28.2, Mark 16.4, Luke 24.2) and assumed His body stolen, in reality Christ "unrolled," on the heavens as the bird of another Dickinson poem "unrolled" his feathers in flight (328).

The first three lines of stanza 3, the poem's only lines in the present tense, are spoken in both the immediate and general present. On one level, the narrator intensifies her story, reliving it in the telling; on another, she succinctly and powerfully describes the despair of all who live without the hope of salvation. Dickinson accentuates the lines' dual biblical-contemporary significance by interweaving Gospel words with her own. The colloquial " 'Tis" sounds more contemporary than biblical, and two of the sentence's four verbs are Dickinson's. By alliterating biblical words with her own, she further fuses the lines' biblical and contemporary meanings: "weep" echoes Mary Magdalene's "weeping" outside the sepulchre (John 20.11) and "wonder" Peter's "wondering in himself" after discovering the empty tomb (Luke 24.12). However, "wince" is Dickinson's, though as a tactile verb it recalls how the women "trembled" when they fled from the sepulchre (Mark 16.8). Her own verb "decay" introduces the poem's concluding botanical imagery. The disciples (including the narrator) expect their bodies to decay with their hopes, like "Blossoms." But in the stanza's final line, the narrator, resuming the omniscient perspective, tells how Christ countered this expectation: "He chose Maturity," a pun drawing together the poem's initial commercial language inspired by Christ's "ransom" and its concluding botanical language. By choosing "Maturity," defined both as "the time when [a note or bill of exchange] becomes due" and as a state of "ripeness . . . as of corn or grass," Christ fulfilled His promise alluded to in lines 1 and 2 of rising on the third day and assured His disciples—then and now—they would not die like "Blossoms."

The final stanza contrasts the disciples' perceptions with what, unknown to them, was taking place: even "As [we buried Christ] we sowed [because He was even then] quickening." "Sow" and "quicken" are not words used in the Evangelists' accounts, but they are biblical words. Celebrating the Israelites' release from captivity, the Psalmist exults, "They that sow in tears shall reap in joy" (126), a line summing up the meaning of Easter: the disciples sowed tearfully and reaped joyfully when Christ "slipped" the "limit" of the grave. Paul, too, uses "sow" as well as "quicken" in a sermon on Christ's resurrection as testimony to the resurrection of all: beginning with Christ who "was made a quickening spirit," the dead are "sown in dishonour [but] raised in glory" (I Corinthians 15.42-45). By introducing references to the Psalms and to Paul's sermon on Christ's defeat of death, Dickinson once more places Christ at the center of time as fulfillment of Old Testament figures and prefiguration of the lives of His followers.

Her concluding lines echo three of the Evangelists' sentences describing Christ's sudden appearance among the dejected disciples. According to Matthew, "And as [the women] went to tell his disciples, behold, Jesus met them" (28.9). According to Luke, "And as [the disciples] spake, Jesus himself stood in the midst of them" (24.36). According to John, "And when [Mary Magdalene] had thus said, she turned herself back and saw Jesus standing" (20.14). According to Dickinson, "And when We turned to note the Growth [,] [Jesus] Broke—perfect—from the Pod."

Dickinson's agon in her poems on the life of Christ is with the Bible and the poetic tradition of Christian devotion. Her kennings for Jesus illustrate most dramatically her way of waging this agon, of considering biblical and devotional texts, then responding with her own condensed, original versions. Christian tradition portrays Jesus Christ as the loving courageous Savior, typological prefiguration of the lives of His followers, perfect model for imitation, and herald of the New Dispensation. Dickinson responds that Jesus Christ is the "Tender Pioneer," the "docile Gentleman," the "Largest Lover," and the "Man that knew the News" who gave the "Gigantic Sum" of His life as "Compound Witness" to God's love for His creatures and to the good news that the grave is now only a seed "Pod." By recreating the Gospels, Dickinson makes them freshly available to modern readers and forcefully affirms their ongoing relevance.

[Im]pertinent Constructions of Body and Self: Dickinson's Use of the Romantic Grotesque

Cynthia Griffin Wolff

Once upon a time, most Dickinson scholars took it for granted that the poetry was a direct, unmediated reflection of "Emily Dickinson's state of mind" (whatever they thought it to be) and made no distinction between the speaking "I" of the verse and the woman herself. Today, we are more sophisticated and can reject such modes of misreading: "For all its value in the teacher's preparation," a modern scholar has recently written, "the historical, biographical, and ideological setting of Dickinson's work is something for our student to work toward, not work from."[1]

One must applaud this advance; nonetheless, I wonder whether we have not gone too far in the opposite direction—whether in our sophistication we are missing something when we do not respond to the *apparently* "biographical" element in the poetry. Many naive admirers of Dickinson's work still have a curious preoccupation with her personal effects and her corporeal remains (the one white dress that is believed to have been hers, even the one lock of her dark red hair that is lodged in the archives at Amherst College and sometimes reverentially displayed during her birthday week in December); and the proprietors of Emily Dickinson's material estate preserve and display intimate, personal items with the same attention that they give to manuscripts, almost as if there were some obscure, but intrinsic connection. This attitude is different from the response evoked by other major authors, and if Dickinson's *scholars* generally distinguish between the speaker in a given poem and "Emily Dickinson, herself," the ordinary citizens who still flood into the Dickinson home continue to think they have heard the woman in the work. Perhaps they are in touch with something "real," a unique, "Dickinsonian" tonality.

Reprinted from *The Emily Dickinson Journal*, Vol. II, No. 2, 1993 by permission of the editors.

[1]William Shullenberger, "My Class Had Stood—A Loaded Gun" in *Approaches to Teaching Dickinson's Poetry*, p. 96. Although I use Shullenberger's work as a point of departure, in general I admire not only his essay, but all of the essays in the collection. They represent a splendid collective response to the earlier habit of seeing "Emily Dickinson the person" in each of Dickinson's poems.

More than thirty years ago, Archibald MacLeish commented upon this illusion:

> No one can read these poems . . . without perceiving that he is not so much reading as
> being spoken to. There is a curious energy in the words and a tone like no other most of
> us have ever heard. Indeed, it is the tone rather than the words that one remembers
> afterwards. Which is why one comes to a poem of Emily's one has never read before as
> to an old friend.[2]

MacLeish has conflated a series of separate *constructs* (the poem, the "speaker" of
the poem, and the "author") with the flesh-and-blood *person* who wrote the verse.
And while this is undoubtedly a mistake in poetic analysis, it *does* respond to the
vividness—the perhaps unmatched intensity of Dickinson's work.

Dickinson had a lean, mean imagination, and her irreverent humor slips like a
whippet throughout the work: she loved riddles and jokes, and seems to have
enjoyed making the speaking "self" (and its illusion of corporeal reality) the most
profound riddle (or joke) of all. Thus her verse is saturated with the first person
singular: "Poem after poem—more than a hundred and fifty of them—begins with
the word 'I,' the talker's word."[3] Moreover, there are body parts scattered throughout: one need only consult the *Concordance* entries for "hand," "hair," "foot,"
"brain," and the like to document this phenomenon. (The most extravagant prolif-
eration can be found with "eye" and "eyes"—those playful puns for self; there are
almost two hundred entries for them, one of the longest lists in the book!)
Dickinson assaults us with "identity" at the same time that she deliberately baffles
us with it; and if we entirely ignore issues of "author," "speaker," and their relationship to the "person, Emily Dickinson" ("self" and all of the [im]pertinent constructions of self), we may be missing something important.

Fundamentally, the big question can be construed as an issue of grammar: what
is the referent for "I"? Readers who have responded intuitively, to "the author" or
"Emily Dickinson"—and who have presumed that these entities are the same—
feel that they have "heard" the "author" by virtue of having read the work; moreover, even when this "I" has an extravagant, carnivalesque component, it still tugs
at many sleeves and seems to demand human recognition (this is one of her tricks).
The compelling illusion of intimacy (along with the singular appearance of the
verse upon the page—the unique *"skeleton"* of the poems) may be the most
"Dickinsonian" element of the work.[4] How, then, can we understand the force and
intimacy of "I" in Dickinson's work without falling into simplistic confusions?
More baffling, perhaps, how can we construe the existential nature of "I" in those
most extreme cases when a flesh and blood speaker would be impossible (already
dead, for instance)?

---

[2]MacLeish, 307.
[3]Ibid., 307.
[4]One clue comes from parody, for caricaturists always cut to the quick of the subject in constructing their mockery of it. And two things that all parodies of Dickinson have is this air of breathless fervor and the jagged, unpunctuated lineaments of her "unruly" lines, replete with dashes.

Consider simply the notion of "Emily Dickinson, the author." Unlike an ordinary given name, which links a group of words with the real person who spoke or wrote them (as in the signature of a letter), the name of an "author" identifies both a certain kind of discourse and the public status of that discourse within a given culture; moreover, when the writer's name is used in this way, as in the locution, "a Dickinson poem," it attaches primarily to the works themselves, and only indirectly to the actual person who once created the text in question. We develop notions of what to expect from a "Dickinson poem"—a "Frost poem," a "Shakespeare poem"—and then the work with these expectations in mind. Thus, as Michel Foucault has insisted, the principal importance of this "author-function" is for readers, who use it to anticipate and organize their reading experience.[5]

Although each reader formulates his or her own notion of any given "author," writers generally attempt to influence these readerly constructions. For example, in his preface to the first edition of *Leaves of Grass*, Dickinson's contemporary, Walt Whitman, elaborated a notion of the "poet" as an essentially common man; he even imprinted an image of himself as "author" on the frontispiece—hand on hip, dressed in the clothes of a day-laborer. The photograph is arresting; it appears to be informative. Yet without Whitman's expansive preface to elaborate his definition of both "poetry" and the nature of the "poet/author," this image alone would have told us very little—might even have lured us into pointless speculations about "Walt Whitman the man."

Nor is Whitman unusual. In the case of poets, some kind of poetic has become the conventional index to this author-function, providing readers with an explicit guide to the poetry itself. Thus even those poets who have not written a *Defense of Poetry* or an informative preface have generally found one or another ingenious way to project a construction of themselves as the "author" and to convey this construction to their readers. The Dickinson difference is not merely that she wrote no poetic to construct the "author" and define the mission of her poetry (thus entirely consigning this task to her readers), but that she sometimes deliberately blurred the issue. Her statements about her verse are scarce, scattered, and usually gnomic; almost a form of *camouflage*, they function to obscure both the artist and her work.[6]

Now let us return to the problem of that vexing personal pronoun, "I." In ordinary discourse and in non-literary texts, like a personal letter, that do not have a formal "author," this "shifter" refers to a flesh-and-blood individual and to an actual deictic situation. By contrast, in a piece of "authored literature" (like a novel or a serious poem), the function of "shifters" is more variable: first person pro-

---

[5]Foucault talks about them as "projections . . . of our way of handling texts"; p. 143.

[6]There are undoubtedly many *reasons* for Dickinson's reticence. She was, by her own admission, very shy. More important, however, the culture in which she lived actively *discouraged* any woman from the attempt to become a serious artist; and even in this day of sophisticated understanding, some readers and critics forget the fact that *when a language is explicitly prohibited from a class of individuals*, an artist from that class cannot avail herself of it. Dobson's discussion of Dickinson's plight in a society where the "invisible lady" (bereft of brain and tongue) seemed the ideal is an excellent commentary on Dickinson's plight. See Dobson, esp. Chap. III. Also, see Wolff, pp. 163–179.

nouns ("I/me") do not refer directly or simply to the particular person who has written the text; "they stand for a 'second self' whose similarity to 'the Author' is never fixed and undergoes considerable alteration within the course of a single [work]."[7] In one of the few straightforward statements she ever made about her poetry, Dickinson herself insisted upon precisely this subtle grammatical distinction: "When I state myself, as the Representative of the Verse," she told Higginson, "—it does not mean—me—but a supposed person"—that is, a constructed "second self."[8] Yet Higginson ignored her admonition, assumed that he was dealing with an hysterical amateur (not a serious "author"), read the poems as spontaneous effusions of "Emily Dickinson, individual woman," and failed to understand either her ambition or her subtle genius.[9]

To some extent, Higginson's problem defines the dilemma confronted by all of Dickinson's readers. In the absence of a poetic, how can we identify the boundary conditions within which to concoct an appropriate and useful construct of the "author"?

Let us suppose that the "author" always emerges from an interconnected set of "fields"—almost like force fields—which delimit the circumstances within which the writer works. The first would be individual: the writer's gender, family situation, range of personal concerns, and so forth. A second might be situational: the kinds of problems that typically preoccupied the society in which the writer worked. A third might be narrowly linguistic: the rules of discourse that pertained during the writer's productive life. A fourth might be broadly aesthetic and moral: the totality of forms available to the writer (and their significance within the culture), and the kinds of moral issues with which the culture was concerned. A fifth might be political: the totality of power structures that governed the writer's world and the possibilities for art's intervention into workings of these power structures.

This rather cumbersome procedure has two clear advantages: it moves us radically away from the narrowly personal and encourages us to focus on "work" and "author"; at the same time, it retains a signifying element of biographical—links "I," however indirectly, with the woman herself.

In the case of Dickinson: (1) she was a woman who grew up in a close-knit family of publically empowered men [personal]; (2) she was constrained to consider unexpected death as a condition of everyday life [situational]; (3) she worked with the American language as it had been defined by Noah Webster and the Bible [linguistic]; (4) although she lived in a community that was preoccupied with the aesthetic/moral dilemmas of latter-day Puritanism, she was influenced by a wide

---

[7]Foucault, p. 144. Miller's book on Dickinson's "poetic grammar" is remarkable for the absence of any discussion of shifters.

[8]*Letters*, II., p. 412.

[9]Almost certainly, one of the things that led Dickinson to become so evasive when discussing her poetry and her role as a serious poet was the accumulation of many such mistakes—her experience with the many readers among her family and friends who could not or would not credit her genius (Sam Bowles is notorious).

One cannot resist wondering how work that is similar to this would have been received if it has been "*authored*" by a male!

variety of poetic possibilities—from the Bible, Milton and Shakespeare to Emerson and Poe [aesthetic/moral]; (5) her world was governed by male hierarchies that began with the intimacy of family-life and extended through the church, the township, and the country at large toward that ultimate embodiment of male authority, God the Father [political]. The Dickinsonian "author-function" reflects the convergence of all these forces and reveals a sophisticated, purposive method at work. Thus we can appreciate her most impertinent constructions of "self" only if we take this combination of factors into account.

Consider, for example, a series of lines that have that distinctively "Dickinsonian" air of obscurity—shifters that cry out for recognition, that assail us with (apparently) personal intensity and defy us with a carnivalesque set of impossibilities: "I am alive—I guess—" (470); or "I felt my life with both my hands" (351); or "I heard a Fly buzz—when I died" (465); or " 'Twas just this time, last year, I died" (445); or "As if my life were shaven, / And fitted to a frame" (510). Such poetry exceeds the merely melancholy, eludes our usual categories by virtue of its immense (but immensely effective) exaggeration, and presents a series of experiences so outlandish that they seem to dance along the boundaries of comedy. Of course, this is precisely the kind of poetry that has evoked those caricatures of Emily Dickinson as suicidal or mad at worst, and babbling at best.

Yet if we define "Dickinson" not as "woman" speaking at the height of emotional crisis, but as a meticulous wordsmith plying her trade, we can investigate the various options open to an *"author"* of her time and place. One result is to introduce the possibility that she was working within a popular mid-nineteenth-century mode, the "Romantic grotesque."

> [The Romantic grotesque was] a reaction against . . . official, formalistic . . . authoritarianism. . . . Unlike the medieval and Renaissance grotesque, which was directly related to folk culture and thus belonged to all the people, the Romantic genre acquired a private "chamber" character. It became, as it were, an individual carnival, marked by a vivid sense of isolation.[10]

Why would Dickinson elect to experiment with this modality? Our field survey provides a set of tentative explanations:

1. Unexpected death was both the principal fear of her culture and the most frequent subject of its poetry.
2. Conventional religion provided only the consolation of faith in a life to come [a notion that Dickinson rejected both as a person and as "an Author"—a notion that she found offensive to human dignity].
3. The "poetic" that most clearly expressed this culture's treatment of death, that is the pronouncements of Edgar Allan Poe, took an attitude toward women (and their bodies) that could only be termed bizarre and demeaning.

---

[10]Mikhail Bakhtin, *Rabelais and His World*, trans. Helene Iswolsky (Indiana University Press: Bloomington, Indiana, 1984), p. 37.

4. This combination of factors emphasized several forms of disempowerment: the general disempowerment of the human condition (always under sentence of death) and the highly particular ways in which women were disempowered by the culture of mid-nineteenth century America.

In 1846, Poe's essay, "The Philosophy of Composition," had proclaimed that "The death of a beautiful woman is, unquestionably, the most poetical topic in the world—and equally is it beyond doubt that the lips best suited for such a topic are those of a bereaved lover." Not only did this poetic radically disempower women (by rendering them lifeless); it also betrayed a morbid preoccupation with their *bodies* to the exclusion of any moral or intellectual attributes. They retained importance only insofar as they could become aesthetic objects.

Such a dictum was so dismissive of all actual women (insofar as it was not simply silly) that one might conclude it offered nothing of value to them. Yet in the hands of a woman *"author,"* its very deficiencies might become the occasion for a bold assertion of power (especially, of course, when the woman was a genius). An "author" can do what the "person" cannot: an "author" can dazzle her readers with irresistible inventions of grotesquery as they apply to some *fabricated* "self"— forms of satire that take us always by surprise because they do not betray their aim by lapses into the didactic. The grotesque mode can

> consecrate inventive freedom to permit the combination of a variety of different elements and their rapprochement . . .; [it can] liberate [an artist] from the prevailing point of view of the world, from conventions and established truths, from clichés from all that is humdrum and universally accepted.[11]

In short, it can do a great deal more than criticize the status quo: it can demolish it! All right, Dickinson might have said: I'll play your foolish game; I'll create the aesthetic situation that you seem to need (the death of a beautiful woman)—and then, like the good fairy in the story of Sleeping Beauty, I'll give one extra gift. The dead women of *my* creation will retain the ability to talk!

This much is bravura, defiance, even hilarity. However, Dickinson's elaboration of the grotesque has at least one additional possibility: an exploration of what Bakhtin has termed the "interior infinite" with its "depth, complexity, and inexhaustible resources"—not merely the rational self in pursuit of knowledge, but the untamed, uncivilized, affective self confronting an existential horror of insatiable death:

> "The *interior infinite* could not have been found in the closed and finished world, with its distinct fixed boundaries dividing all phenomena and values."[12]

In this respect, Dickinson could transform Poe's notion from an extremity of female passivity to a form of supreme feminine heroism in which the speaker explores the experiential "reality" of extinction itself. Here defiance takes the form of courage, a clear-headed willingness to probe behind the sentimental pieties with which convention had veiled life's final, terrifying mysteries—precisely those

---

[11]Bakhtin, p. 34.
[12]Ibid., p. 44.

pieties that characterized the sentimental poetry that was considered appropriately "feminine" in mid-nineteenth century America.

Bakhtin has observed that the grotesque is essentially and literally degrading. During earlier periods, this degradation was vigorous and life-giving, preoccupied with strong (and strongly forbidden) language and with the most elementary processes of the body; thus if it acknowledged that mankind exists only in process (always under sentence of death), its very crudeness and lustful vitality affirmed the continuing emergence of life with equal force. By the early nineteenth century, however, this image of life as perpetually poised between creation and destruction had taken on a deeper and more pessimistic tone. The "degradation" of the grotesque pointed only toward dissolution—humanity teetering at grave's edge. In many ways, it was precisely suited for many of Dickinson's purposes.

Her use of the Romantic grotesque is carefully modulated. In poems like "I died for Beauty—" (449) or " 'Twas just this time, last year, I died" (445), the speaker seems to retain the body intact, having embarked upon a sacrilegious course to chart the forbidden territory just beyond the grave's edge. In such work, the voice is methodical and matter-of-fact—apparently rational and proceeding with an almost scientific precision. Such poetic postures capture principally the odd configuration of each individual's mortal state: fear tinged with fascination, life italicized by the ever-constant threat of that ultimate plummet into the unknown realms of death.

At other times, Dickinson *exploits* the body with tantalizing, perverse sexual elegance ("The Soul has Bandaged moments—" [512] or "Because I could not stop for Death—" [712]). Here her intention is bitterly satirical. Such poems mock Poe's vicious aesthetic assumption that any woman's death could be essentially poetical—sentimentalized into an occasion for her still-living lover's expressions of self-pity. They also mock the Christian tradition that promises an ecstatic reunion of Christ and His "bride." Finally, in contrast with those poems that celebrate the unique capacity of [the] feminine body to breed new life ("I tend my flowers for thee—" [339], for example), they denounce the monstrous notion of a sexual encounter that will lead the feminine body to nothing but annihilation.

In its most extreme form "I heard a Fly buzz—when I died" [465] or "I felt a Funeral, in my Brain" [280]), this voice of the talking dead literally *explodes* the body by tracking the process of its dissolution and decay through careful modulations of the verse. In such poems, the gradual loss of corporeal unity and coherent perception creates a form of singular anxiety for the reader—perhaps not the anxiety of death itself (for who can both know that event and tell us of it?), but surely an anxiety that mimics mortal terror. The speaker's fleshly self is subjected to mutilating distortion; consciousness struggles to retain its integrity; and in the end, nightmarish isolation is the only alternative to nothingness.[13]

[13]Not every poem that treats death or the loss of coherence can be termed a use of the "Romantic grotesque." For example, the poem that begins "I felt a Cleaving in my Mind—" (937) has an altogether different timbre; it is noteworthy that *this* poem does not assault us with an awareness of the body or its parts, but rather presents a consciousness that is attempting to make coherent, sequential sense out of the events in its life—trying (to employ the metaphor with which the poem concludes) to spin a yarn.

None of these poems are funny; and although they display immense intelligence and talent, few readers would term them witty. Poems like these, one might say, have given Emily Dickinson her kinky reputation. To some extent, such a reaction "goes with the territory": the Romantic grotesque is often singularly lacking in humor (as Poe's work demonstrates). However, Dickinson's use of the grotesque in constructing the "second-self" of her poetry is not always so somber.

Consider, for example, the cartoon-like quality of the well-known poem about "author" and "reader" that begins: "I would not paint—a picture—" (505). More reminiscent of the Renaissance grotesque than of the Romantic form, the verse presents a speaking self that almost immediately begins to assume gigantically distended proportions. Sexual stimulation and the act of artistic creation are commingled ("And wonder how the fingers feel / Whose rare—celestial—stir— / Evokes so sweet a Torment—"). The combination of artistic work and the delight of aesthetic response are mysteriously combined, and in their juncture recall the distended belly of pregnancy—mother and child still miraculously/monstrously joined ("Myself endued Balloon / By but a lip of Metal— / The pier to my Pontoon—"). And the "climax" (masturbation? hermaphroditic self-stimulation?) devolves into the hilarity of an impossible aesthetic desire: "Had I the Art to stun myself / With Bolts of Melody!"[14]

In this poem a celebration of life, sexuality, parturition, and art are joyously jumbled together; here, the irreverence is less a protest than a jubilant echo of creativity's intrinsic unruliness—an affirmation of the fact that artistic genius never did and never will submit meekly to the strictures of social propriety. Since art may be the only force that can counter the force of death, Dickinson's use of the grotesque in this poem about a *woman* artist seems an appropriate foil for the Romantic grotesquery of so many of the poems about death. Nonetheless, they share this essential similarity: both forms of the grotesque in Dickinson's poetry employ the subversive strategy of using the first-person shifters in ways that will baffle any reader who is inclined to equate this "second self" of the "author" with the actual woman, Emily Dickinson; and nowhere is this bafflement more profound than in Dickinson's riddle poems.[15]

---

[14]See Bakhtin's chapter on "The Grotesque Image of the Body," esp. pp. 343–347. Probably Dickinson would have had access to few (if any) of the specific sources Bakhtin cites. However, New England Puritanism had its own contingent of grotesque religious images—not in *churches*, where graven imagery was prohibited, but in *graveyards*, where grotesquery was abundant.

There were, of course, other sources in the culture for grotesque images of human form. Children's publications like *Peter Parley* often had grotesque, cartoon-like drawings that were meant to convey a moral message. Christian emblem books had pictures of the dismembered body (heart and eyes most often). And American folk art and folk tales were filled with fanciful figures (Paul Bunyan, for example).

[15]Bryant's extended discussion of riddles in his preface gives us many hints that can help us to formulate reasons Dickinson might have found this form attractive. In addition, his book provides an invaluable guide to different *forms* of the riddle—many of which find their way into Dickinson poems.

Traditionally, of course, the riddle is the principal way a "little guy" (some disempowered person) can win against a "bigger guy" (the empowered establishment). In extreme cases, as Bryant points out, *even death* may weigh in the balance:

Scholars have long noted Dickinson's fondness for riddles and her habit of transferring certain "riddling" forms into her poetry; however, none has remarked one singular fact. The grammatical ambiguity of a riddle pivots upon its iconoclastic use of "shifters": the talking "I" in a riddle never refers to some human speaker; "I" is the "thing" that must be guessed—the riddle's *solution*. Consider these examples, taken from game books that Dickinson probably used:

(1) In every hedge my *second* is,
As well as every tree;
And when poor school-boys act amiss,
It often is their fee.

My *first*, likewise, is always wicked,
Yet ne'er committed a sin;
My *total* for my *first* is fitted,
Composed of brass or tin
[Speaker/answer: Candlestick]

(2) Ever eating, never cloying,
All devouring, all destroying,
Never finding full repast,
'Till I eat the world at last.
[Speaker/answer: Fire][16]

In some parts of the world it was once traditionally the custom to grant a condemned man the opportunity of putting a "neck" riddle to his captors which, if they failed to solve it, would literally save his neck. Naturally the riddles tended to be as esoteric as possible, involving enough specialist and personal knowledge to make them virtually insoluable to any but the propounder. (p. 9)

Bryant's discussion of the Judaeo-Christian tradition (pp. 17–20) is especially relevant to Dickinson's work.

[16]These two riddles are drawn from *The Boy's Treasury of Sports, Pastimes, and Recreations*, n.a. (Philadelphia: Lea and Blanchard, 1847). I chose them because they are simple, representative, and short. However, they represent a very large *class* of reading.

The Boltwood Collection at the Jones Library in Amherst has many books and mid-nineteenth century periodicals that contain similar riddles, "charades," and other word games. See, for other examples, *Merry's Gems of Prose and Poetry, Youth's Galaxy*, and *Our Young Folks, An Illustrated Magazine for Boys and Girls*. Although there is no record of these in the Dickinson family library (such books were often "read to death"—like paperbacks or comic books—and an absence tells us very little about the family's reading habits), both the Hitchcocks and the Stearns possessed *Our Young Folks;* and Dickinson was a regular guest of the younger generation in both homes.

Exploration of these riddles is a rich and largely untapped source for many of the poet's linguistic strategies—for example, her habit of focusing upon the possibility of a *single letter's* functioning as a semiotic symbol. Consider the following riddle.

Why is the following puzzle too ridiculously simple to be asked?

guEssEd

ANSWER: because it is guessed
with too [two] great ease [E's]!

This *fluidity* of semiotic manipulation can be found nowhere in Dickinson's culture in such rich and suggestive ways as in Amherst's riddle books.

Similarly, in Dickinson's most extravagant "riddle" poems, the first person singular refers not (of course) to "the person, Emily Dickinson" and not even to some constructed "second self," but to a personification of the *"thing" to be guessed.*[17]

Nowhere is this poetic maneuver more powerfully employed than in that poem which has been Dickinson's most mystifying riddle of all—a poem with Death as its speaker/answer: "My Life had stood—a Loaded Gun—" (754).[18] Here, the grotesque element is principally a habit of mind that is gradually revealed to be dispassionate, lethal, and jubilantly pleased with its cold-blooded work. The puzzle or game-like properties of the verse do not dominate at the outset; however, its conclusion presents the reader with the unmistakable postulation of a puzzle or riddle:

> Though I than He—may longer live
> He longer must—than I—
> For I have the power to kill,
> Without—the power to die—

The clear (if unstated) query is: who am "I" and who is "He"? If we compare this stanza with #2 (above), the signature of a riddle form is difficult to mistake.

What makes *this* riddle-poem so difficult—so almost impossible to comprehend, then? Why has Dickinson preceded this closing riddle-signature with a lengthy (and misleading) introduction? Because *death* is God's most outrageously incomprehensible riddle and/or joke; because human existence begins to seem grotesque principally when we recognize that life teeters always at grave's edge; because the human body, so glorious in its capacity to bring pleasure and to breed life, can nonetheless not be exempted from deterioration and decay.[19]

It is, then, a final jest, a super-added irony, both that every member of Dickinson's community could easily envision Death's "body" and that Death's "body" was grotesque indeed! It had been engraved on countless gravestones: always skeletal, often grinning and generally brandishing its weapons (a scythe and an hourglass) in gloating triumph. No one doubted that Death was life's opponent, the enemy of all fleshy joy; and no one doubted that Death would always conquer the flesh in the end.

---

[17]I find it surprising that although Dolores Dyer Lucas is well aware of the fact that Emily Dickinson often chose to personify Death (see Lucas, p. 69), she fails to make the next logical move—namely, to comprehend that Death (personified) might actually be the speaker in one of Dickinson's poems.

[18]For a complete analysis of this poem—along with an explanation of the "solution" see Wolff, pp. 442–446.

[19]Although not every poem that uses shifters in this way is grotesque, many hint at catastrophe. Thus a poem that presents Nature speaking with the voice of a harried housewife ("The Winters are so short—" [403]) cannot contemplate a summer's conclusion without a glissando into devastation: "Because there was a Winter—once— / And all the Cattle—starved— / And so there was a Deluge— / And swept the World away—."

Mid-nineteenth century Amherst did postulate one form of "exemption" from deterioration and decay: the absolute relinquishment of reason for faith—in Dickinson's view, an intolerable affront to human dignity (grotesque in and of itself!).

For more than a century, readers have been mystified by the boldness with which Dickinson employed this mode of the Romantic grotesque; typically, they have sought to mitigate its message by transforming its import. It is Dickinson who was melancholy (they have sometimes thought), Dickinson who was incomprehensible—perhaps a bit unhinged. Such a response is not surprising; for insofar as we fully understand the grim lesson of these [im]pertinent constructions of self, to that extent we must also acknowledge the frailty of all human life and confront the inevitable mysteries of our shared mortality. Perhaps, then, readers are seeking to displace the pain of insight; for if we can suppose that "Emily Dickinson the woman" was mildly mad or marginally hysterical, we need never acknowledge our own deep fears about the issues that her poetry explores. Perhaps it was even part of her genius that "Emily Dickinson the author" understood her readers' anguished needs. And perhaps that was her deepest reason for suffusing the poetry with such powerful, seductive, and playful illusions for her "self."

Works Cited

Bakhtin, Mikhail. *Rabelais and His World*. Trans. Helene Iswolsky. Bloomington: Indiana University Press, 1984.

Bryant, Mark. *Dictionary of Riddles*. London and New York: Routledge, 1990.

Dickinson, Emily. *The Letters of Emily Dickinson*. Ed. Thomas H. Johnson and Theodora Ward. 3 Vols. Cambridge, Mass.: Harvard University Press, 1958.

———. *The Poems of Emily Dickinson*. Ed. Thomas Johnson. 3 Vols. Cambridge, Mass.: Harvard University Press, 19951, 1955.

Dobson, Joanne. *Dickinson and the Strategies of Reticence*. Bloomington and Indianapolis: Indiana University Press, 1989.

Fast, Robin Riley and Christine Mack Gordon. *Approaches to Teaching Dickinson's Poetry*. New York: The Modern Language Association of America, 1989.

Foucault, Michel, "What Is An Author?" in *Critical Theory Since 1965*. Ed. Hazard Adams and Leroy Searle. Tallahassee: Florida State University Press, 1989.

Lucas, Dolores Dyer. *Emily Dickinson and Riddle*. DeKalb, Illinois: Northern Illinois University Press, 1969.

MacLeish, Archibald, "The Private World," in *The Recognition of Emily Dickinson*. Ed. Caesar R. Blake and Carlton F. Wells. Ann Arbor: The University of Michigan Press, 1968.

Miller, Cristanne. *Emily Dickinson: A Poet's Grammar*. Cambridge, Mass., and London, England, 1987.

The Boy's Treasury of Sports, Pastimes, and Recreations, n.a. Philadelphia: Lea and Blanchard, 1847.

Wolff, Cynthia Griffin. *Emily Dickinson*. New York: Alfred A. Knopf, 1986.

"The Landscape of the Spirit"

Suzanne Juhasz

> Soto! Explore thyself!
> Therein thyself shalt find
> The "Undiscovered Continent"—
> No Settler had the Mind.
>
> [832]°

The "Undiscovered Continent" is one of Emily Dickinson's descriptions of the mind. Another, from a letter to her friend Mrs. Holland, is "the Landscape of the Spirit."¹ Poem and prose statement indicate both the centrality of her exploration of self and also how the place where it occurred, the mind, is conceived of as actual, substantial, there. "Continent," "Landscape"—these words grant spatial dimension to the mind, the setting for Dickinson's most significant experience.

In this [essay] I take literally Dickinson's assessment of the mind as tangible space. I am concerned with how she defines the mind as a place in which to live and with what happens to her, living there. . . .

The fact that Dickinson lived primarily in the mind is not a new observation. It has long been acknowledged as a factor central to her biography and to her art. Yet critics of Dickinson have interpreted the situation variously. In particular, there is a radical difference of perspective, and opinion, on this subject between feminist critics and traditional critics that is based in their understanding of gender.

Traditional criticism frequently begins with the assumption that Dickinson's move into the mind was a retreat. For example, George Whicher, in his "classic" biography, *This Was a Poet*, sees her reclusiveness as a self-imprisonment occasioned by a failed love affair (his vote goes to Charles Wadsworth, among the several candidates proposed over the years). "Only a Robert Browning could have released the Lady of Shalott, and no Robert Browning came her way." Her unhappiness in love, which he labels "a death blow to her heart," turns into "a life blow to her mind," so that her poetry, the result of living in that mind, is seen as

Reprinted from *The Undiscovered Continent: Emily Dickinson and the Space of the Mind* by permission of the author and Indiana University Press.

¹*The Letters of Emily Dickinson*, 3 vols., ed. Thomas H. Johnson and Theodora Ward (Cambridge: The Belknap Press of Harvard University Press, 1958), II, #315, p. 450.

compensatory activity: "Perhaps as a poet she could find the fulfillment she had missed as a woman."[2]

John Cody, whose *After Great Pain: The Inner Life of Emily Dickinson* is psychoanalytic in orientation, takes Whicher's position even further. He labels Dickinson's retreat into the mind madness, a "psychotic breakdown" occasioned by her "sexual bewilderment, anxiety and frustration," which in turn was caused by her mother's "failure as a sufficiently loving and admirable developmental model." Because Dickinson could not emulate her mother, she experienced, says Cody, strong identification with her father and later, her brother. It was this abnormal masculine identification that "although blocking her completion as a woman, stimulated her to use her mind." This ongoing abnormality—she never settled into either a "thoroughgoing and 'mature' masculine identification" or a female one— gave rise to, in his opinion, her latent homosexuality, sexual terror, and general craziness; *but*, he announced, "The point, important for American literature, is that threatening personality disintegration compelled a frantic Emily Dickinson to create poetry—for her a psychosis-deflecting activity."[3]

A study [such as] David Porter's . . . *Dickinson: The Modern Idiom* also considers the famous "withdrawal" to be responsible for a major difficulty with her poetry, the separation it effects between language and reality.

> The autogenerative concentration on language both reflects and was caused by Emily Dickinson's withdrawal from the world. She withdrew in all the physical ways with which we are familiar, and we must at long last consider what the effect was on her poems. Most crucially, her language became idiosyncratic, disengaged from outside authority, and thus in its own way inimitably disordered. The lack of architecture is a consequence of the linguistic reflexiveness, and both are part of the harsh artistic freedom that opens up when reality and language undergo a separation. . . . When she disengaged her idiom from the complicated texture of social existence, she made it self-conscious, private, and momentary in its grasp.

Ultimately, Porter claims, "when language breeds, removed from exterior referents, it becomes almost pure locution, and meaning cannot be established."[4]

It is clear that behind the various "assessments" of Dickinson in these books are operating some very powerful assumptions about gender and art. If to be a fulfilled woman is to follow the model of Mrs. Dickinson, wife, mother (and invalid), to marry some Robert Browning, or at least somebody, then Dickinson's refusal to leave her father's house, her own bedroom, and her own mind is decidedly "unfeminine." At the very least, according to these writers, it leads to frustration and unhappiness. It may also lead to madness and to a severed connection with

---

[2]George Whicher, *This Was a Poet* (Ann Arbor: University of Michigan Press, 1938), pp. 139, 272, 113.

[3]John Cody, *After Great Pain* (Cambridge: The Belknap Press of Harvard University Press, 1971), pp. 484, 103, 171, 391.

[4]David Porter, *Dickinson: The Modern Idiom* (Cambridge, Mass., and London: Harvard University Press, 1981), pp. 114, 121.

reality (probably these are the same). The mind, on the other hand, is masculine (according to Cody), and, according to both Whicher[5] and Cody, so is poetry. Porter, on the other hand, makes a point of applauding Dickinson for being a woman poet, for understanding and writing about a woman's life, but he never looks to see any connections between the acts of her life, like the famous withdrawal, the acts of her poetry, such as its concern with mental experience, and her womanhood.

The mind may be thought of by some as "masculine," but men, even male poets, rarely *live* in the mind, as if it were, let us say, a house and they the householders there, the house*wives*. Although Dickinson's move into her mind is usually classified as "unfeminine," the way in which she made use of her mind is suspiciously "feminine." It's confusing, and worrisome, even when the poetry that was produced by all of this isn't. Because Dickinson is not a man, and is not a "real" woman, either, the complications that her situation creates for many critics results in either a radical schism in their thinking between "Dickinson the woman" and "Dickinson the poet" or in a total concentration on what resulted from all of this, her poems, with little or no acknowledgment that anybody at all wrote them.[6]

Of course, not all writing on Dickinson is so judgmental. Richard Sewall's eminently intelligent biography, *The Life of Emily Dickinson*, for example, begins by emphasizing "the degree to which her way of life represented a conscious choice. . . . More than is true of almost any other poet in the tradition, her life, like the major vehicle of her poetry, was metaphoric; and as she grew older, it became more and more deliberately so."[7] Sewall's portrait of Dickinson is sensitive to her traits and her techniques; it persists as an invaluable source of information about her. What it does not do is analyze the poetry, and it does not raise the question of gender—that is, look at how Dickinson's womanhood affects either her life choices, for example, the suggestive fact that her life was "metaphoric," or her poetry.

A concern with gender is central to feminist criticism, which characterizes Dickinson's move into the mind as strategy rather than retreat. Feminist criticism begins with the assumption that gender informs the nature of art, the nature of biography, and the relation between them. Dickinson is a woman poet, and this fact is seen as integral to her identity. . . .

"Strategy" means that Dickinson chose to keep to her house, to her room, to live in her mind rather than in the external world, in order to achieve certain goals and to circumvent or overcome certain forces in her environment and experience

---

[5]George F. Whicher, *This Was a Poet* (New York: Charles Scribner, 1938)—Ed.

[6]I have analyzed more copiously the styles of sexism in traditional Dickinson criticism in " 'A Privilege So Awful': The Poetry of Emily Dickinson," *Naked and Fiery Forms: Modern American Poetry by Women, A New Tradition* (New York: Harper and Row, 1976), pp. 7–32. I have treated the same subject more recently in my introduction to *Feminist Critics Read Emily Dickinson*, ed. Suzanne Juhasz (Bloomington: Indiana University Press, 1983).

[7]Richard Sewall, *The Life of Emily Dickinson*, 2 vols. (New York: Farrar, Straus and Giroux, 1974), p. 4.

that were in opposition to those goals—particularly, the expectations and norms that a patriarchal society creates for women, especially problematic when a woman wants to be a poet.

In my first study of women poets, *Naked and Fiery Forms: Modern American Poetry by Women, A New Tradition*, I use the phrase, "the double bind of the woman poet," to talk about the conflict and strain experienced by women poets in our society, because "woman" and "poet," as much traditional literary criticism indicates, denote opposite and contradictory qualities and roles.[8]

Dickinson's way of declaring her vocation, from her early letters to friends and to her brother to her famous dialogue with the editor, Thomas Wentworth Higginson, is a good example of the effects of the double bind. Dickinson cloaks her avowals in various metaphors; she attests at once to her bravery and her wickedness; she apologizes for herself; but through it all she keeps declaring herself to be a writer.

In 1850, when she is twenty, she characterizes her friend Abiah Root as a good, proper, "real" girl, making Abiah a foil for her own self-portrait as deviant.

> Now my dear friend, let me tell you that these last thoughts are fictions—vain imaginations to lead astray foolish young women. They are flowers of speech, they both *make*, and *tell* deliberate falsehoods, avoid them as the snake, and turn aside from the *Bottle* snake, and I don't *think* you will be harmed. Honestly tho', a snake bite is a serious matter, and there cant be too much said, or done about it. The big serpent bites the deepest, and we get so accustomed to its bites that we dont mind about them. "Verily I say unto you fear *him*." Wont you read some work upon snakes—I have a real anxiety for you! I love those little green ones that slide around by your shoes in the grass—and make it rustle with their elbows—they are rather my favorites on the whole, but I would'nt influence *you* for the world![9]

Margaret Homans has shown in convincing detail how Dickinson associates language, lies, sin—and portrays herself as Eve, sinner and poet—in this passage.[10] She is bad to Abiah's good, in every way; but how proudly she declares it: "I love those little green ones . . ."!

A similar irony and tension are manifest in another letter to Abiah from the same year.

> . . . You are growing wiser than I am, and nipping in the bud fancies which I let blossom—perchance to bear no fruit, or if plucked, I may find it bitter. The shore is safer, Abiah, but I love to buffet the sea—I can count the bitter wrecks here in these pleasant waters, and hear the murmuring winds, but oh, I love the danger! You are learning control and firmness. Christ Jesus will love you more. I'm afraid he don't love me *any*! . . .[11]

---

[8]Juhasz, *Naked and Fiery Forms*, pp. 1–6.
[9]*Letters*, I, #31, p. 88.
[10]Homans, pp. 166–71.
[11]*Letters*, I, #39, p. 104.

Most critics assume these "fancies" to be her plans to become a poet. I agree, yet find it equally significant that she needs the veil of allegory to say so, while at the very same time announcing her daring, her sinfulness.

A letter to her brother Austin in 1853 shows her very much aware of the male's prerogatives in the world of poetry yet also asserting her own claims, which turn out to be prior, and superior, to his.

> And Austin is a Poet, Austin writes a psalm. Out of the way, Pegasus, Olympus enough "to him," and just say to those "nine muses" that we have done with them!
>
> Raised a living muse ourselves, worth the whole nine of them. Up, off, tramp!
>
> Now Brother Pegasus, I'll tell you what it is—I've been in the habit *myself* of writing some few things, and it rather appears to me that you're getting away my patent, so you'd better be somewhat careful, or I'll call the police![12]

Ten years later, in her correspondence with Higginson, the constant humility that she adopts ("My size felt small—to me—I read your Chapters in the Atlantic—and experienced honor for you—") is accompanied by statements that yet reveal her stubborn pride in herself and sense of self-worth, although, as always, these unladylike assertions are masked: "If fame belonged to me, I could not escape her"; "I do not let it go, [a line of poetry] because it is mine."[13]

From all of these examples it is clear that Dickinson knows full well what a proper girl is and how one should behave; knows equally well that her sense of her own self is profoundly deviant. Yet still she persists in becoming herself, adopting strategies of language (her truth told slant) that reveal the double bind she experiences as much as they deal with it.

Language, of course, turns out to be Dickinson's greatest power and best weapon. But in order to use it properly and most effectively as a means of control and of creation, Dickinson needs to develop strategies of living as well as writing.

John Cody is probably correct in observing that Dickinson found little in her mother to emulate, and that she did indeed identify in rather powerful ways with her father and, especially, her brother. What is misleading is his evaluation of the situation as "abnormal." As a Freudian, Cody insists that a woman acquires female identity through positive identification with her mother. If this does not happen, he maintains, if she has suspicions "that to be a female is to be secondrate," if she cannot find another woman to act as a role model (though what is her fascination with the great English women writers—George Eliot, the Brontës, Elizabeth Barrett Browning—but that?), "she may at last be driven to pattern herself on a masculine model," which will lead to "an almost insurmountable crisis in sexual identity."[14]

But for Dickinson to feel that "to be a female is secondrate" was surely accurate, even as it was probably more "normal" than otherwise for her not to want to be like her mother, to see in her male relatives important qualities that she possessed as well, to seek to be like those few other women who did not tend to marry

---

[12]*Letters*, I, #110, p. 235.
[13]*Letters*, II, #261, p. 405; #265, p. 408; #271, p. 415.
[14]Cody, p. 55.

and to bear children and who were writers. Cody's gender definitions do, however, reflect those of Dickinson's society as well as his own, so that her so-called "crisis in sexual identity" would indicate, not her craziness, but the predictable result of her own personality coming into conflict with society's norms.

One way in which Dickinson attempted to deal with this situation was to try *not* to grow into a "woman." In their chapter on Dickinson, Sandra Gilbert and Susan Gubar have observed: "She must have decided that to begin with she could try to solve the problem of being a woman by refusing to admit that she was a woman."[15] The child persona who so persists in her poetry, her sometimes identification of herself with a boy, her refusal, after a certain time, to enter seriously into the courtship games of her social set—and then, of course, the notorious although, it must be emphasized, *gradual* withdrawal—all exemplify how she kept herself, on both psychic and social grounds, from ever having to enter into the arena of adult womanhood as her society decreed it to be.

In the same letter to Abiah Root from which I have quoted Dickinson's announcement of the fancies she is letting blossom and of how she loves to buffet the sea, she speaks as well of another friend, remarking: "She is more of a woman than I am, for I so love to be a child—Abby is holier than me—she does more good in her lifetime than I shall ever do in mine—she goes among the poor, she shuts the eye of the dying—she will be had in memorial when I am gone and forgotten."[16] Her identification with the child (she is twenty), because it is contrasted to what a "woman" does—good works, once again underlines her sense of herself as deviant, not young. The woman who goes among the poor would not be out buffeting the sea. . . .

Barbara Mossberg, in "Metaphysics of a Yankee Mother Goose: Emily Dickinson's 'Nursery Rhymes,' " points to Dickinson's persistent "saying 'no.' "

> If Dickinson does not feel she has much authority or power in her culture, she can at least say "no" to the demands her culture makes upon her and women in general. Thus we see Dickinson winning a freedom of sorts for herself by *not* joining sewing societies, music groups, or church groups, by *not* becoming "born again," by *not* getting married, by *not* leaving home. Saying "no" to a conventional life as a woman necessarily keeps Dickinson in a kind of childhood; childhood in this sense is not only a metaphor for confinement and repression, but also a retreat from the world's limiting expectations for women. "No" is for Dickinson "the wildest word we consign to Language" because it makes for possibility. Dickinson's child persona is in large measure a crucial aspect of her systematic refusal to become bound in a conventional woman's life.[17]

Nevertheless, Dickinson was attracted to people, men and women. Her friendships were never casual. Her letters as well as her poems, written to the friends of her girlhood, to male friends both identified and unidentified, to older women and younger nieces, all show how overwhelmingly significant those she loved were to

---

[15]Gilbert and Gubar, p. 590.
[16]*Letters*, I, #39, pp. 104–5.
[17][Clark] Mossberg, in [Barbara Antonina,] *Feminist Critics Read Emily Dickinson*, p. 60.

her. Love itself was for her an essential, and consuming, emotion. She did not choose not to marry and bear children because she could not, or would not, love. Her choice seems to have had more to do with her greater need to maintain her self and also with the way in which she did experience love. Sewall comments on her friendships as follows: "All her life she demanded too much of people. Her early girlfriends could hardly keep up with her tumultuous letters or, like Sue, could not or would not take her into their lives as she wanted to be taken. They had other concerns. The young men, save for a few who had amusing or edifying intellectual exchanges with her, apparently shied away. Eliza Coleman's fear that her friends in Amherst 'wholly misinterpret' her, was a polite way of saying, perhaps, that they would not respond with the intensity she apparently demanded of everyone." Sewall continues: "meetings themselves became ordeals . . . in her own economy, she found that she had to ration them very carefully."[18]

Given her propensity for passions more intense than their recipients could return, Dickinson used physical distance, and language, to deal with love. "After you went," she wrote to her friend Mrs. Holland, "a low wind warbled through the house like a spacious bird, making it high but lonely. When you had gone the love came. I supposed it would. The supper of the heart is when the guest has gone."[19]

Thus, because of her own temperament, her intensity and sensitivity; because of her ambitions for herself, her stubborn dedication to her sense of vocation; because of her situation as a woman in middle-class Amherst society in nineteenth-century America with its expectations for normal womanhood; Emily Dickinson, a woman who wanted to be a poet, chose to withdraw from the external world and to live her most significant life in the world of her mind. This decision was surely what enabled her to be the poet that she became. It gave her control over her own experience: she could select, apportion, focus, examine, explore, satiate herself exactly as she wished and needed to do, such that poetry could result. In the outer world, this manner of control would have been impossible. It gave her, as well, the possibility for complete and thorough experience, for risk, intensity, range, and depth, that as a woman she could never have achieved in the world at large. She could not wander across the continent, like Walt Whitman; but she could move freely in the "undiscovered continent," the mind.

Such a description of mental experience assumes, categorically, that these events are real. Even as Dickinson wishes to think of the mind itself as actual space, so she is insistent throughout her poetry that mental experience is in no way less real than what happens in the world outside. When David Porter writes of Dickinson's poems, "There is no final reality, and the loss of that reality is a function of a language intent on saying itself and not on signifying a specific world," or, "Dickinson had no subject, least of all reality," he is using a definition of reality that is based upon what he calls "the things outside her window,"[20] one which does

---

[18]Sewall, pp. 517–18.
[19]*Letters*, II, #318, p. 452.
[20]Porter, pp. 55, 129, 245.

not include in its domain mental experience. This approach does a profound disservice to the poetry Dickinson did write, because its subject is so often exactly that: what happens in the mind.

What happens in the mind is also the subject of this book. It is common enough to hear, of Emily Dickinson's life, that "nothing happened to her." "Nothing," in fact, tends to happen to most women, because, as we know, patriarchal history has a propensity for cataloguing battles and not dinner parties. Feminist history has begun to write the events of women's lives and call them real—not only their battle to get the vote but their daily domestic occurrences. Yet Dickinson's most important life took place not when she was baking the family's bread, but when she was adventuring, dangerously and alone, in the very deep and very wide terrain of her mind: having experiences so profound and powerful that they could be the subject of great poetry. For Dickinson did not choose to be a "normal" woman, even as she did not try to pretend that she was a man. She did not choose to live where men live, in the public world, or where women live, in the domestic world. She found another place, at once more private and expansive than either of those others: the mind.

And yet I do not think that Dickinson was the first woman to discover the mind's potential as a place particularly suited for significant experience. As Patricia Meyer Spacks writes in her study of the female imagination, "The cliché that women, more consistently than men, turn inward for sustenance seems to mean, in practice, that women have richly defined the ways in which imagination creates possibility: possibility that society denies . . . women dominate their own experience by imagining it, giving it form, writing about it."[21]

To live in the mind, an actual and occupied place, was for Dickinson the key to solving the problem of how to be a poet, of how to achieve the self-knowledge, the self-awareness, the self-fulfillment that her vocation demanded. Certainly Dickinson's tactics were extreme; but then, they were more successful than moderation might have brought. She became an extraordinary poet, as few women before or since have done. Nevertheless, I think that Dickinson was capitalizing upon a technique that women have always known and used, for survival, using the imagination as a space in which to create some life other than their external situation. What Dickinson did was to make art from it. . . .

Dickinson's poems frequently assert her sense of the mind's actuality with images of caverns and corridors (777, 670), windows and doors (303, 657), even cellars (1182). Because she took the mind to be her dwelling place, it is appropriate that she use these domestic figurative correspondences to describe it. Yet her poems using such architectural analogues go beyond pointing out how a mind might be like a house. They set out to show, as well, what happens in a mind that is as a house, so that the solidity which door and window frame provide grants substance both to the setting and to the events occurring within. The architectural

[21]Patricia Meyer Spacks, *The Female Imagination* (New York: Alfred Knopf, 1975), pp. 315, 322.

vocabulary usually portrays the mind as an enclosed space, its confinement responsible for power, safety, yet fearful confrontation.

Poem 303 is a strong statement about the power of the self alone. The soul is shown living within a space defined by door, gate, and mat. The external world, with its nations and their rulers, is kept outside.

> The Soul selects her own Society—
> Then—shuts the Door—
> To her divine Majority—
> Present no more—
>
> Unmoved—she notes the Chariots—pausing—
> At her low Gate—
> Unmoved—an Emperor be kneeling
> Upon her Mat—
>
> I've known her—from an ample nation—
> Choose One—
> Then—close the Valves of her attention—
> Like Stone—

Traditional ideas about power are reversed here. Not control over vast populations but the ability to construct a world for oneself comprises the greatest power, a god-like achievement, announces the opening stanza. Not only is the soul alone "divine," but it is also identified as "Society" and "Majority": the poem also challenges our ideas about what constitutes a social group. Consequently, the enclosed space of the soul's house is more than adequate for a queenly life, and ambassadors of the external world's glories, even emperors, can easily be scorned. Yet while the speaker claims her equality with those most powerful in the outer world—they may be emperors, but she is "divine Majority," at the same time she asserts her difference from them; for her domestic vocabulary of door, low gate, and mat establishes her dwelling as not a grand palace but rather a simple house.

While associating power with the enclosed space of the mind, the poem also implies how isolation is confinement, too. When the soul turns in upon her own concerns, she closes "the Valves of her attention— /Like Stone—."

Valves permit the flow of whatever they regulate in one direction only: here, from outside to inside. Either of the halves of a double door or any of the leaves of a folding door are valves. Valves seen as doors reinforce the poem's house imagery, while their association with stone makes the walls separating soul from world so solid as to be, perhaps, prison-like.

Prison-like because they allow no escape from the kinds of conflict, the kinds of terror, even, that must occur within. Poem 670, exaggerating the architectural vocabulary, compares the chambers of the mind to the haunted castle of gothic fiction, a stereotypical setting for horror.

> One need not be a Chamber—to be Haunted—
> One need not be a House—
> The Brain has Corridors—surpassing
> Material Place—

Far safer, of a Midnight Meeting
External Ghost
Than its interior Confronting—
That Cooler Host.

Far safer, through an Abbey gallop,
The Stones a'chase—
Than Unarmed, one's a'self encounter—
In lonesome Place—

Ourself behind ourself, concealed—
Should startle most—
Assassin hid in our Apartment
Be Horror's least.

The Body—borrows a Revolver—
He bolts the Door—
O'erlooking a superior spectre—
Or More—

The poem assumes that the mind is substantial, possessing corridors and chambers, because it is the dwelling place of "oneself." The extended comparison that is developed, between two kinds of dwellings, two kinds of hauntings, is for the purpose of dramatizing how there can be something more frightening than the most frightening situation usually imaginable.

Both the second and third stanzas begin with the same phrase: "Far safer." Safer are the supernatural events of gothic castles, meeting ghosts at midnight; we are warned about "interior confronting," the everyday moments of the mind, another lonesome place, when "one's a'self encounter." One clue to the degree of difference in horror is the word, "Unarmed." We come prepared to find ghosts in spooky old castles, but not in what Dickinson calls in another poem "That polar privacy/A soul admitted to itself" (1695).

There is, in fact, no way one can be armed against this particular kind of ghost. The murderer seeking to kill the body can be vanquished—one can borrow a revolver, bolt the door. But this assassin is hidden within oneself—is oneself. There is no escape. As Dickinson comments in poem 894, "Of Consciousness, her awful Mate / The Soul cannot be rid."

In the final stanza, the quintessence of this horror is revealed. The rhetoric of the poem has been dramatic as well as concrete. Two dramas, in fact, have been enacted and contrasted. The external self has been venturing into lonesome abbeys, discovering hidden assassins in her chamber, even as the internal self has become aware of the existence of the "Cooler Host." Now the two plots turn into one. The self, who is, after all, body and mind at once, bolts the door, only to discover that she has locked herself in with herself. Adventuring in the external world, one need not confront one's own consciousness. But when one turns from "Horror's least" to live in the mind, that "superior spectre" can never be avoided again.

Because consciousness is self-confrontation, it establishes a "society" within, of "ourself" with "ourself." To represent the conflict and struggle engendered here, poem 642 uses an architectural vocabulary that provides a setting, fortress, for a drama of siege and defense. Yet even as "One need not be a Chamber—to be Haunted—" constructs a comparison between external and internal ghost stories only to conflate them, so the following poem's distinctions between inner and outer, protagonist and antagonist, turn out to be fictions.

Me from Myself—to banish—
Had I Art—
Impregnable my Fortress
Unto All Heart—

But since Myself—assault Me—
How have I peace
Except by subjugating
Consciousness?

And since We're mutual Monarch
How this be
Except by Abdication—
Me—of Me?

[642]

The speaker of the poem "Myself" wishes for the ability to banish from her castle an enemy, called "Me." In the second stanza she admits to the complexity of the problem; more than skill is required to maintain the defense, because there is a profound connection between the combatants. Reversing their titles—"Me" is now the speaker, "Myself" the opponent—the poem acknowledges their interchangeability while at the same time continuing to deal with them as separate entities. The enemy is also identified as "Heart" in the first stanza, "Consciousness" in the second. That these are as much aspects of "Me" as they are of "Myself" the poem will not yet admit.

Although we know that the poem is discussing one person and not two, its dramatic fiction of attacker and attacked creates a situation that is surely war, albeit civil. When the dichotomy itself is collapsed in the final stanza, the effect is to intensify the situation, the pain, the impossibility of victory. "Mutual Monarch," the antagonists are revealed to be in actuality both within. There is nobody without. Without doesn't matter. Victory is impossible, is not a mere matter of "art," because enemy and friend are one. "Consciousness" is the self's awareness of itself and could be vanquished only through the annihilation of self, which would leave no victor, since no self is left. The very naming of the characters in this drama articulates and also anticipates this conclusion. If in stanza one the defender was Myself, the attacker, Me; and in stanza two the attacker was Myself, the defender, Me; in the final stanza they, as mutual Monarch, are "Me" and "Me."

The poem's structure dramatizes an experienced conflict. If the fictional dichotomy of within and without is necessary so that we might understand the problem, so is the final denial of the fiction, that we might better understand the conclusion: that self-consciousness means precisely the encounter of the self with itself, and that this is a perpetual struggle.

Strangely Abstracted Images

David Porter

Abstraction, we are told repeatedly, is inimical to poetry. Yet in images that are so abstract they have given up their sensuous immediacy to pure meaning, Dickinson asserted her poetic individuality. Featureless, inconsistently successful, these peculiar figures with no light-catching body perform in her poems on occasion so audaciously as to reveal the interior moment when for her events became apprehended by language.

The paradigmatic image of this abstract sort is also one of Dickinson's most familiar. It appears in a simile at the end of "Safe in their Alabaster Chambers" and signifies in that terminal position the unarguable proposition that mighty Doges, even as the meek of the earth, shall fall to death in cold silence.

> Diadems—drop—and Doges—surrender—
> Soundless as dots—on a Disc of Snow—

The problem with the image "dots—on a Disc of Snow" takes the form of a paradox: while no exact image will form in the mind's eye (what sort of dots? what sort of disc?), the figure works superbly as poetry. The poem as a whole is an elegy for the senses that death extinguishes, but the poem does not console. The assured doctrinal belief posited by the opening word "Safe" is stealthily dislodged by negatives as the lines proceed one by one and is resolutely nullified by the contrived inanimation of the final image. It is a marvelous endgame.

> Safe in their Alabaster Chambers—
> Untouched by Morning—
> And untouched by Noon—
> Lie the meek members of the Resurrection—
> Rafter of Satin—and Roof of Stone!
>
> Grand go the Years—in the Crescent—above them—
> Worlds scoop their Arcs—
> And Firmaments—row—
> Diadems—drop—and Doges—surrender—
> Soundless as dots—on a Disc of Snow—
>
> (P-216)

Reprinted from *Dickinson: The Modern Idiom* (1981) by permission of Harvard University Press.

Dickinson tried out a large assortment of variant images of deadness for the second stanza: silence, echoes, frost, a "numb" door, eclipse, marble, icicles, and polar caverns, but she settled for "dots—on a Disc of Snow." It is difficult to imagine another figure that does so much so well as this bleak endscape. The sweep and grandeur of the cosmic visions of Crescent, Worlds, Arcs, and Firmaments which begin the second stanza are shrunk and contained by the small geometry of the dots and disc and then quietly obliterated by the snow. In addition, the falling motion of the dots (they trail the verbs "drop" and "surrender") reverses the lofty connotations and pomposities of Resurrection and Firmaments. The six single syllables of the dots-and-disc image neutralize the splendid polysyllables Alabaster and Diadems. Snow inexorably deprives "Safe" of its coziness, and "Soundless," the lefthand term of the final simile, rests appropriately opposite and linked to the substanceless image. Not identifiably visual, but rigorously composed of clipped consonants and repealed sibilants, the image "dots on a Disc of Snow" expresses in phonetic preciseness and geometric abstraction the qualities of slight matter, minuscule size, and the feel of cold inert insignificance. It is a dead image that constitutes a ghostly knowledge.

Archibald MacLeish has attended to Dickinson's drained images most ably of all her readers. Some of the images, he writes, are "so strangely abstracted as to be almost transparent." Of the illogical coupling of her images "either in metaphor or out of it," he says, "it takes more than a second reading or even a third to demonstrate that there are images at work at all." He gives examples:

> "Amethyst remembrance," "Polar expiation," Neither of these exists upon the retina. Neither can be brought into focus by the muscles of the eye. The "blue and gold mistake" of Indian summer seems to exist somewhere in the visible—or would if one could only get rid of that "mistake." And so too does "The Distance / On the look of Death" and "Dying—is a different way— / A Kind behind the door." But who can describe the graphic shape of "that white sustenance / Despair"? And yet all of these present themselves as images, do they not?—*act* as images? Where can remembrance be amethyst? Where but in the eye?[1]

Of Dickinson's customary use of abstractions like Grace and Bliss and Balm and Circumference, MacLeish says with delightful conviction: "The poems of almost any other poet would go down, founder, if they put to sea in generalizations as leaky as these." He inspects as an example Dickinson's poem about the early morning songbird's disappearance, which ends with these lines:

> At Half past Seven, Element
> Nor Implement, be seen—
> And Place was where the Presence was
> Circumference between.

>   (P-1084)

---

[1]This passage and those that follow are from the chapter entitled "Private World: Poems of Emily Dickinson" in *Poetry and Experience* (Boston: Houghton Mifflin, 1961).

What saves Emily Dickinson's abstractions from shipping water? MacLeish says it is the Dickinson's *voice* in the poems, its "extraordinary mastery of tone," the "laconic restraint" appropriate to New England, the "wholly spontaneous tone," the "liveness in the voice." Universal words, he writes, "generalizations, abstractions, made particular in a particular voice, can be poetry. As Emily Dickinson proved once for all."

But when she fails in the launching of her abstractions, they sink lifeless and undecipherable. Or, as in her slogan "My business is Circumference," they drift, inaccessibly subjective, cryptic, and opaque. A model of these faceless blocks to understanding is the subject phrase "Contemplation for / Cotemporaneous Nought" in poem 982.

> No Other can reduce
> Our mortal Consequence
> Like the remembering it be nought
> A Period from hence
> But Contemplation for
> Contemporaneous Nought
> Our Single Competition
> Jehovah's Estimate.

Extant versions indicate that Emily Dickinson struggled for as long as three years in the mid-1860s with this curiously impacted poem. It is an impossible object, transfixing readers with a sphinx's stony gaze. . . .

Dickinson achieved varying degrees of success with figures made of abstractions: "Brooks of Plush—in Banks of Satin," for example, to suggest the sound of the satisfied laughter of the happy dead in their coffins (P-457); "Great Streets of silence" and "Neighborhoods of Pause" for the expanse of timelessness (P-1159); "a maritime conviction" for the feel of the sea in the air (P-1302); "the obligation / To Electricity" for the debt owed revelation (P-1581). For the most part, they *mean* but do not *be*. Such resort to disembodied conceptual figures presents itself whenever we look for it in Dickinson. Two further examples, small successes of a comparable sort, though derived from different grammatical structures: "No Goblin—on tbe Bloom" from poem 646 and "no film on noon" from letter 235. Only by great transfusions of implication from their contexts does it become clear that each means there is no diminution of beauty, no apprehension, no alteration of the perfect.

The exemplar of this particular form of abstraction, now doubly deobjectified by its negative, is the image "No Furrow on the Glow" in the spendid poem of the cicada's hum . . . "Further in Summer than the Birds" (P-1068). The last eight lines seek the instinctual sensation of seasonal change.

> Antiquest felt at Noon
> When August burning low
> Arise this spectral Canticle
> Repose to typify

Remit as yet no Grace
No Furrow on the Glow
Yet a Druidic Difference
Enhances Nature now

The image "No Furrow on the Glow" succeeds for a reader after he has known this poem a long time. Like the examples cited just previously, it similarly means there is no decline from the ideal. Specifically in this poem of high summer it means there is no evident break in summer's full brilliance (though there is simultaneously the felt turn of the season toward fall, winter, and death—-which is what the poem is *about*). It is an idea image (what sort of furrow? what sort of glow?), Dickinson having floated out this figure as an unattached trope in free linguistic orbit.

Ezra Pound, in an essay on Cavalcanti, described a realm beyond the plastic where the poet's aesthetic requires something more than simple visual mass, not limiting itself to "the impact of light on the eye." He characterized this lost domain of Cavalcanti's as a "radiant world where one thought cuts through another with clean edge, a world of moving energies '*mezzo oscuro rade,*' '*risplende in se perpetuale effecto,*' magnetisms that take form, that are seen, or that border the visible, the matter of Dante's *paradiso*, the glass under water, the form that seems a form seen in a mirror, these realities perceptible to the sense, interacting."[2]

Dickinson's plunge into such obscurity, which Yvor Winters cited as the source of her "nonsense," produced her drained images. To the extent they were habitual, they are radical signs of her peculiar stance before reality. A reader thus would gain valuable insight by perceiving the motion of her mind in that crucial engagement. Is it possible to be present at the making of one of those impalpable images, to locate ourselves, as Roland Barthes says, "at that very fragile and rather obscure moment when the relation of a real event is about to be apprehended by literary meaning"?[3] There perhaps, the hidden coupling of sensation and language would be revealed. It would take us closer to the elemental act of bonding language to discrete experiences that are both inescapable and unlitterable.

Dickinson's worksheet trials for a poem dated about 1861 enable us to go behind one of her opaque figures, to pierce the text to the situation that is the image's raw material. Poem 291, beginning "How the old Mountains drip with Sunset," is copied on two sides of a single sheet that the poet threaded into one of her dresser-drawer packets when she was about thirty-one. It is a popular anthology piece because the imagery of sunset and night coming on is exquisitely various and evocative ("Mountains drip with Sunset / . . . the Hemlocks burn"), the metaphors are fresh and offbeat ("the Houses blot"), and the sounds exotic and syncopated ("How the Dun Brake is draped in Cinder"). But at its core, the poem is the old artful dodge, the speaker protesting she can never do

[2]*Literary Essays of Ezra Pound* (London: Faber and Faber, 1954), pp. 151, 154.
[3]*Critical Essays* (Evanston: Northwestern University Press, 1972), p. 157.

justice in words to the scene facing her ("Have I the lip of the Flamingo / That I dare to tell?") even as she proceeds to do just that. Virtuoso performance is the poem's reason for being. In this respect, of course, it is an honorable descendant in a line that includes *The Divine Comedy* ("my vision was greater than our speech, which fails at such a sight"—*il mio veder fu maggio / che 'l parlar nostro ch'a tal vista cede*)[4] and a fit sibling to "When Lilacs Last in the Dooryard Bloom'd" ("How shall I deck my song for the large sweet soul that has gone?")

Dickinson's language in the poem explores with sensuous abundance the sunset and the coming of night (her constant analogue of death), "visions" that the voice says "paralyzed" the great painters.

> How the old Mountains drip with Sunset
> How the Hemlocks burn—
> How the Dun Brake is draped in Cinder
> By the Wizard Sun—
>
> How the old Steeples hand the Scarlet
> Till the Ball is full—
> Have I the lip of the Flamingo
> That I dare to tell?
>
> Then, how the Fire ebbs like Billows—
> Touching all the Grass
> With a departing—Sapphire—feature—
> As a Duchess passed—
>
> How a small Dusk crawls on the Village
> Till the Houses blot
> And the odd Flambeau, no men carry
> Glimmer on the Street—
>
> How it is Night—in Nest and Kennel—
> And where was the Wood—
> Just a Dome of Abyss is Bowing
> Into Solitude—
>
> These are the Visions flitted Guido—
> Titian—never told—
> Domenichino dropped his pencil—
> Paralyzed, with Gold—

The image that occupies the crucial last position—after the mountains, the hemlocks, the village, and the yard—represents the severest test of the artist's skills. Just at this point, in this preferred position, we encounter the image that stops us cold.

---

[4]*Le Point de départ* (Paris: Plon, 1964), p. 40, translation from Sarah N. Lawall, *Critics of Consciousness* (Cambridge, Mass.: Harvard University Press, 1968), p. 83.

And where was the Wood—
Just a Dome of Abyss is Bowing
Into Solitude—

Eye muscles will not bring into focus a "Dome of Abyss," much less its "Bowing into Solitude." Such apparent humbug sends a diligent reader to the worksheets in search of an editor's transcription error or signs of some acute word block in the face of which the poet let the effort collapse. The search yields the poet's variants, and they in turn lead through the "Dome of Abyss" to the literal occasion behind the image. A more recognizable landscape begins to emerge from the fairly pedestrian metaphor she rejected: "Acres of Masts are standing / back of Solitude." By rectifying the inverted syntax in line 18 we see that the complete variant sentence visualizes, in fact, woods being swallowed up in night.

where the Wood was[,]
Acres of Masts are standing
back of Solitude

Her use of "Masts" in place of "trees" begins the habitual motion of abstracting away from perceived reality that culminated in the impossibly abstract "Dome of Abyss" image. "Dome," we discover from a poem that she attached to a cocoon and sent to her nephew Ned about 1864 (P-893), holds an extraordinary cluster of associations for the poet. Not only is it intended to suggest the otherness of natural creation—she called the cocoon "Dome of Worm"—but the figure also stands in apposition to "Drab Habitation," "Tabernacle," "Tomb," "Porch of Gnome," and "Elf's catacomb," thus for her combining with alienness (were there domes in Amherst?) qualities of miracle, mystery, and death. "Abyss," we know from other Dickinson poems, signifies a feeling.

There is a pain—so utter—
It swallows substance up—
Then covers the Abyss with Trance—
So Memory can step
Around—across—upon it—

(P-599)

Bonded together then in the new anatomy of "Dome of Abyss" is Dickinson's *feeling* of deep darkness within an enclosure that itself is wrapped in obscurity. "It is Night—in Nest and Kennel." It is darkness folded within night. We are near the realm of Milton's famous *palpable obscure* or what our contemporary Ted Hughes in his poem "Pike" calls the *darkness beneath night's darkness*. Emily Dickinson, moreover, attempted to perceive the very process that produces the complicated experience of a felt world beyond the visible world just disengaging itself from our sensory receptors.

The raw material, then, of the "Dome of Abyss" image is not only a preverbal but a preconscious sensation: the feel of woods unseen that one yet knows are there. What shall we compare to this habitual Dickinson moment of a presence conceived as an absence? An impalpable thickness? Perfume, fog, a window pane?

It is the felt presence of the invisible, a sensuous absence, or, indeed, as in the "Dome of Abyss" poem, *an absence felt as a presence*. What linguistic shell games one must engage in to suggest what Dickinson, in her art of saying where a thing had been, distilled in such phrases as "Miles of Stare"! The death of the gods is an inflated but comparable thing. Place was where the Presence was.

Abstract expressionist artists since Kandinsky have sought representations of this sort of experience that unknowably *is*. Materialization of incipient abstract forms occurs in Jackson Pollock's poured paintings, where he abandoned the brush (especially in *Blue Poles*, 1952), and in the motifless shapes of Robert Motherwell, Franz Kline, and Mark Rothko. The closest parallel in recent sculptural art to Dickinson's abstractions is the glass and steel construction of Christopher Wilmarth called "Nine Clearings for a Standing Man." It is abstraction made strikingly expressive without a trace of figurative quality. With Dickinson's "Dome of Abyss" we stand at a comparable threshold of both verbal and figurative consciousness. The variant readings show us the poet attempting to haul instinctual feelings into language and thus into consciousness. In those trial words of hers for poem 291 we witness the stages by which she labored to grasp a sense of her own existence.

Dickinson's conceptual attempt at this threshold moment is discernible in variant expressions on a worksheet from about 1870. In this least finished draft of poem 1165, written perhaps as long as nine years after "Dome of Abyss," Dickinson labored to speak the idea of apogean experiences the senses are unequipped to handle. The completed version of the poem has eight lines.

> Contained in this short Life
> Are magical extents
> The soul returning soft at night
> To steal securer thence
> As Children strictest kept
> Turn soonest to the sea
> Whose nameless Fathoms slink away
> Beside infinity

In the least finished worksheet, the poet applied herself to defining that stunning moment referred to in line two. She tried terms of invisibility, power, and vast distance. The trip metaphor had already lodged in the ninth line of the worksheet version.

> Contained in this short Life
> Were wonderful extents
> Discernible to not a friend
> Except Omnipotence
> A friend too straight to stoop
> Too distant to be seen
> Come unto me enacted how
> With Firmaments between
> The soul came home from trips
> That would to sense have dazzled

Variants for "wonderful extents" in line two of this worksheet indicate how she sought repeatedly to name the moment's full and contradictory impact. Besides "wonderful" and "magical," she sorted through "terrible," "miraculous," "tenderest," and "exquisite." In the final line of the worksheet, however, she is reduced to making a literal statement of the problem we as readers have wrestled with: experience that will not link up with language or sense. Those "wonderful extents" are "trips that would have dazzled sense" (*to* is an awkwardness left over from the syntax of variant experiments). The variants for the lines explicitly define for us as they did for the poet the limits of sense-linked images. The revelations not only fatigue response (producing "the tired sense," another variant), but they are trips "Unmanifest to sense" and "Unwitnessed of the sense."

In these literal assertions and amid all the trials and rejections is the chronicle of Dickinson's attempts, as in "Dome of Abyss," to ambush experience outside cognitive capacities and beyond linguistic grasp. Those terribly abstract images that puzzle us, to her mind possessed these experiences. . . .

The Riddles of Emily Dickinson

Anthony Hecht

Emily Dickinson's metrics and prosody . . . are considerably more various and interesting than has been commonly allowed. Anyone who has read through the entire body of her work can testify that she by no means confined herself to the tetrameter quatrains of the standard anthology pieces. And I am convinced that one of the commonplaces that is due for serious revision is her supposedly narrow indebtedness to the hymnals, and to Dr. Watts in particular. Dr. Watts, at one of his pinnacles of eloquence wrote,

> Hark! She bids all her friends adieu;
> Some angel calls her to the spheres;
> Our eyes the radiant saint pursue
> Through liquid telescopes of tears.

To be sure, Watts was not always up to that level, as his parodists have suggested; but I delight to think how well and comfortably that stanza of his might have appeared among Samuel Johnson's anthology of the blemishes of metaphysical poetry. Watts, as I say, was not always so inspired and adventurous. Like most of the hymnodists his stanzas were mostly short, singable quatrains, with a syntax that perfectly conformed to the simplicity of the verse: the full stops always at the end of the stanza, and often of the individual line—a simple necessity for the untrained voices of a congregation. But Emily Dickinson did not work under those particular compulsions, and she did some violence to them. Here, for example, is a poem about a butterfly, composed to be sure, in quatrains, but with some telling surprises for all that.

> He parts himself like leaves,
> And then he closes up,
> Then stands upon the bonnet
> Of any buttercup,
> And then he runs against
> And oversets a Rose,
> And then does nothing.
>   Then away

From *Obbligati* (New York: Atheneum, 1986). Reprinted by permission of the author.

Upon a jib he goes,
And dangles like a mote
Suspended in the noon,
Uncertain to return below
Or settle in the moon.
What come of him at night
The privilege to say
Be limited by ignorance.

What come of him that day
The frost possess the world,
In cabinets be shown:
A sepulchre of quaintest floss—
An abbey—a cocoon.
                                    517

    The first full stop here comes in what is metrically (for this is poulter's measure) the midst of the seventh line with "And then does nothing." Or another way to describe the effect is to say that the first sentence runs to six and one-half lines, the next five and one-half, the next three, and the last five; so that nowhere in the poem does the syntax conform to the quatrain. I have not found a comparable freedom among the hymns. In addition to poulter's measure, the measure of

I lothe that I did love,
In youth that I thought swete:
As time requires for my behove
Me thinkes they are not mete,

and the familiar tetrameter quatrains, Emily Dickinson employed various other stanza forms and line lengths. There is one stanzaic pattern she uses a number of times that interests me especially.

Bring me the sunset in a cup,
Reckon the morning's flagons up
And say how many Dew,
Tell me how far the morning leaps—
Tell me what time the weaver sleeps
Who spun the breadths of blue!
                                    128

Into this Port, if I might come,
Rebecca, to Jerusalem,
Would not so ravished turn—
Nor Persian, baffled at her shrine
Lift such a Crucifixial sign
To her imperial Sun.
                                    506

    I am obliged to admit that the hymnals, and Dr. Watts himself, exhibit this form; but I prefer to think that Emily Dickinson might have come upon it in an anthology of religious poetry, and in the incarnation of a poem of which these are two stanzas.

> Rich almonds colour to the prime
> For adoration; tendrils climb,
> And fruit trees pledge their gems:
> And Ivis with her gorgeous vest
> Builds for her eggs a cunning nest
> And bell-flowers bow their stems.
> . . . .
>
> But stronger still, in earth and air,
> And in the sea, the man of prayer;
> And far beneath the tide;
> And in the seat to faith assigned
> Where ask is have, where seek is find,
> Where knock is open wide.
>   (Christopher Smart, "A Song to David")

There has, of course, been a good deal of investigation into, and speculation upon, her reading; and a number of influences upon her work now seem almost inarguable. Of these, one of the strongest and most recognizable is George Herbert.

> Where Thou art—that—is Home—
> Cashmere—or Calvary—the same—
> Degree—or Shame—
> I scarce esteem Location's Name—
> So I may Come—
>
> What Thou dost—is Delight—
> Bondage as Play—be sweet—
> Imprisonment—Content—
> And Sentence—Sacrament—
> Just We Two—meet—
>
> Where Thou art not—is Wo—
> Thou' Bands of Spices—row—
> What Thou dost not—Despair—
> Tho' Gabriel—praise me—Sir—
>   725

The carefully balanced rhetorical and syntactical structure of this poem is far nearer Herbert's practice than Emily Dickinson's. The two initial five-line stanzas, each beginning with its topic phrase—"Where Thou art"; "What Thou dost"—followed in each case by a series of paradoxes; the inverted or negative versions of the topic phrases—"Where Thou art not"; "What Thou dost not"—each followed by a noun that represents the opposite of the corresponding noun in the positive version—for Home, Wo; for Delight, Despair—compressed into a quatrain, this neatness and intricacy of form, together with the intimacy of address, strongly suggests the Herbert influence. And her poem "'Unto Me?' I do not know you—" (968) seems to me directly indebted to Herbert's "Love."

From her antecedents let me turn to her descendants, who are more numerous and various than you might at first think. Richard Wilbur has honorably confessed to burglaries from her work. And it is hard for me to believe that the following, by Theodore Roethke, would have been written without her practice to emulate.

Thought does not crush to stone.
The great sledge drops in vain.
Truth never is undone;
Its shafts remain.

The teeth of knitted gears
Turn slowly through the night,
But the true substance bears
The hammer's weight.

Compression cannot break
A center so congealed;
The tool can chip no flake;
The core lies sealed.

I think I detect in some of her comic and ironic poetry (in 1461 and 1207) notes of impertinence and attitudes that I encounter also in the work of Robert Frost. But I should like to make the claim for a couple of even unlikelier candidates: W. H. Auden and e. e. cummings. We have the testimony of Christopher Isherwood that some of Auden's early poetry was influenced by hers, and I find these lines of hers strikingly like some of Auden's early work. This is about a child.

Credits the world—
Deems His Dominions
Broadest of Sovereignties—
And Caesar—mean—
In the Comparison—
.   .   .   .
Grown bye and bye
To hold mistaken
His pretty estimates
Of Prickly Things
He gains the skill
Sorrowful—as certain—
Men to anticipate
Instead of Kings—

637

The dimeter line, the widely spaced rhymes, elision of articles, inversions, these were all early Auden trademarks. And as for cummings, hear this:

Love—is that later Thing than Death—
More previous than life
Confirms it at it's entrance—And
Usurps it—of itself

924

Surely there is an intimate connection between these lines of Emily
Dickinson's and the following by cummings.

love is more thicker than forget
more thinner than recall
more seldom than a wave is wet
more frequent than to fail

I adduce these foster children with no litigious motives, but merely to
demonstrate that her own work was far more various in its styles and forms than
is commonly supposed. And even with regard to her regular tetrameter quatrains, I would claim, with Robert Frost, that "The possibilities for tune from
the dramatic tones of meaning struck across the rigidity of a limited meter are
endless." . . .

In preparation for this paper I have devoted my attention almost entirely to
Emily Dickinson's poems. I made a personal selection of those I liked best, as
well as those that might best serve the topic's purposes, and the two groups coin-
cided in a sufficiently reassuring way. For it became increasingly my conviction
the more I read that "riddles" of identity, of voice, of definition, abounded in her
work as almost a technique. And whatever psychological gratifications they may
have had for her, they had the sanction not only of her dictionary but of her
Bible.

The grand one is, of course, the Bible, not only for many an ultimate riddle, but
containing many diverse riddles, themselves richly compounded by controversies
of doctrine and commentary, of which Emily Dickinson seems to have been sufficiently aware. A second and humbler one is that body of children's fairy tales and
verse which we also know her to have had some acquaintance with, for she refers
to some of it in her letters. And I should like to deal with the humbler one first.

The best known verses of "Mother Goose" date from the eighteenth century
and before. It is a literature that abounds in riddles, and for my present purposes I
wish to do no more than recall some characteristic examples. There are explicit
riddles, formulated as questions to which answers are expected.

As I was going to St. Ives
I met a man with seven wives,
Each wife had seven sacks,
Each sack had seven cats,
Each cat had seven kits;
Kits, cats, sacks, and wives,
How many were going to St. Ives?

To which, of course, the answer is, "one," the speaker. But not all such riddles take the shape of questions; they are preponderantly enigmatic statements, requiring interpretation. Were Tenniel's drawings not so familiar to all of us, it might not be so utterly transparent that Humpty Dumpty, whom all the king's horses and all the king's men could not reassemble, was a broken egg.

> How many miles to Babylon?
> Three score miles and ten.
> Can I get there by candle-light?
> Yes, and back again.

As soon as we recognize that Babylon is "baby-land," and that the three score and ten miles are the three score and ten years biblically allotted to the lifespan of man, the enigma disappears, and we have a little runic statement about the pilgrimage of life from the first childhood to the second, with a strong memento mori flavor of life's brevity. And here is another which might, superficially, appear to be about the same topic.

> Solomon Grundy,
> Born on Monday,
> Christened on Tuesday,
> Married on Wednesday,
> Took ill on Thursday,
> Worse on Friday,
> Died on Saturday,
> Buried on Sunday,
> And that was the end of
> Solomon Grundy.

Commentators have remarked that this verse is no more than a mnemonic device to teach small children the names of the days of the week. But I am inclined to suspect that it is something more; that it is in fact an account of the diet of a poor family, obliged to budget out carefully over the space of a whole week a single salmagundi stew.

Let me turn now to the Scriptures; specifically to the fourteenth chapter of the book of Judges.

> And Samson said unto them, I will now put forth a riddle unto you. . . . And he said unto them, Out of the eater came forth meat, and out of the strong came forth sweetness. And they could not in three days expound the riddle.

That riddle of the lion and the honeycomb was more subtle and complicated than even Samson knew at the time he asked it. It was a riddle he was to solve for good and all only at the end of his life, through pain, humiliation and self-sacrifice. It may be the most famous of biblical riddles, yet it is only one of many, and of many biblical references to riddles.

> Son of man, put forth a riddle, and speak a parable unto the house of Israel; . . .
> (Ezekiel 17:2)

I will open my mouth in a parable: I will utter dark sayings of old:
Which we have heard and known, and our fathers have told us.

                                                        (Psalms 78:2–3)

The locusts have no king,
yet they go forth all of them by bands;
The spider taketh hold with her hands,
and is in kings' palaces.

                                    (Proverbs 30:24–28)

I close this brief list with a paradox.

Answer not a fool according to his folly,
lest thou also be like unto him.
Answer a fool according to his folly,
lest he be wise in his own conceit.

                                    (Proverbs 26:4–5)

Let me point directly at two poems of Emily Dickinson's that seem, at least to
me, to bear intimate family resemblances to the two models I have posited.

Who is the East?
The Yellow Man
Who may be Purple if He can
That carries in the Sun.
Who is the West?
The Purple Man
Who may be Yellow if He can
That lets Him out again.

                                    1032

This is neither a compelling poem nor a very complex riddle, but I submit that in
its formal and personified presentation of sunrise and sunset it might be easily be mistaken for a "Mother Goose" rhyme. And here is a poem which imitates, as I think,
some of the formal principles of the riddles in the Book of Proverbs that I just cited.

Some things that fly there be—
Birds—Hours—the Bumblebee—
Of these no Elegy.

Some things that stay there be—
Grief—Hills—Eternity—
Nor this behooveth me.

There are that resting, rise.
Can I expound the skies?
How still the Riddle lies!

                                    89

Let me labor, for a moment, the parallels to the Proverbs: the general statement that there are certain unnamed "things" that share a common characteristic,

that are never satisfied or that fly; that statement stands for the "question" which will be answered by the list, the discontinuous series, which will not only satisfy the conditions of the so-called question, or initial statement, but redefine it— sometimes through puns or double meanings. So "fly" in the first line means both "perish" and "take wing." But the first two tercets about things impermanent and permanent, riddling and surprising as they are, are merely preliminary riddles to contrast with the insoluble paradox of the last stanza, which I presume refers to the souls who have seen "salvation." The last line is a riddle all by itself, and may refer either to the soul or to God. In either case, it seems to insist that the living are denied any sure sign of their own salvation.

The word "Riddle" itself appears in some four or five of her poems, but rather than discuss those, let me turn instead to her more familiar riddling practice. These are poems which either provide their own surprising answers, or in which we are challenged to identify a thing metaphorically described.

Most commonly the "answer" was omitted altogether, though sometimes the poems accompanied gifts (a cocoon, a pine needle, some apples) which were themselves the subject of the poem and the answer to its riddle. So abundant are examples of this kind of poem in her work that I shall do no more than list a few representative ones and their answers.

> It sounded as if the Streets were running (1397)—a gale
> She slept beneath a tree (25)—a flower
> It sifts from Leaden Sieves (311)—snow
> The Guest is gold and crimson (15)—sunset
> A route of Evanescence (1463)—a hummingbird
> A Narrow Fellow in the Grass (986)—a snake
> A Visitor in Marl (391)—frost
> He fumbles at your Soul (315)—the wind

Lovely as some of these poems are, ingenious or powerful in their descriptive or imaginative language as they may be, I wish instead to examine a few others that seem to me both more puzzling and more interesting.

> The Soul selects her own Society—
> Then—shuts the Door—
> To her divine Majority—
> Present no more—
>
> Unmoved—she notes the Chariots—pausing—
> At her low Gate—
> Unmoved—an Emperor be kneeling
> Upon her Mat—
>
> I've known her—from an ample nation—
> Choose one—
> Then—close the Valves of her attention—
> Like Stone—

This poem is not usually conceived of as a riddle, but rather as a description of those instinctive preferences and choices, those defiantly nonrational elections and allegiances, like love, that we all make, without regard to personal advantage, to rank or to estate. To the degree that the poem has been construed as a private and guarded revelation of the poet's emotional life, and to some circumstantial events in it, there is a dispute about whether the choice of "one" means someone else or the poet herself; whether she is electing the solitude of a society of one, or committing herself to another. And it is not out of place, I think, to construe the poem as being about love. The mixed metaphor of the last two lines ("Then close the valves of her attention/Like stone") could be rather comfortably resolved if we substituted "heart" for "soul," since hearts can be "stony" and they have valves.

But I suggest that the power of this poem derives from a suppressed riddle, an unstated but implied parallel. As the soul is to its society (absolute, arbitrary, ruthless) so is God in His election and salvation of souls. Moreover, it seems to me that the second stanza not improbably suggests the adoration of the Magi, though I have no care to press that point. Still, the ominous quality of the final words is considerably amplified when the ultimate mystery of election is taken into account. We play at being God; it is characteristically human of us to do so.

Tell all the Truth but tell it slant—
Success in Circuit lies
Too bright for our infirm Delight
The Truth's superb surprise
As Lightning to the Children eased
With explanation kind
The Truth must dazzle gradually
Or every man be blind—

1129

Again, this poem has been read as an instance of Emily Dickinson's deliberate tact and poetic strategy "in a generation which did not permit her, without the ambiguity of the riddle, to 'tell the truth' . . . she early learned that 'success in circuit lies.' " I cannot disprove that notion, nor do I feel obliged to; but the poem seems to me to have a good deal of religious significance that such a statement inclines altogether to flout.

And it came to pass on the third day in the morning, that there were thunders and lightning and thick clouds upon the mount. . . . And the Lord said unto Moses, Go down, charge the people, lest they break through unto the Lord to gaze, and many of them perish.

(Exodus 19:16–21)

The blinding effect of direct access to the Godhead, which is to say the Truth (except in the case of selected few, and Moses one of them), has been a commonplace of religious poetry from long before Emily Dickinson to our own century. And there is what might be called a New Testament version of the same idea. Jesus has just told his followers the parable of the sower and the seed:

And he said unto them, He that hath ears to hear, let him hear. And when he was alone,
they that were about him with the twelve asked of him the parable.
And he said unto them, Unto you is given to know the mystery of the kingdom of God:
but unto them that are without, all these things are done in parables.

(Mark 4:9–11)

Christ himself has been seen as that human manifestation of the Godhead
which allows all men to look upon that Truth which would otherwise be blinding.
Milton clearly has such a meditating notion in mind in the "Nativity Ode."

> That glorious form, that light unsufferable,
> And that far-beaming blaze of majesty,
> Wherewith he wont at Heaven's high council-table
> To sit the midst of Trinal Unity,
> He laid aside; and here with us to be,
> Forsook the courts of everlasting day,
> And chose with us a darksome house of mortal clay.

The same idea is, as I understand it, somewhat blasphemously paralleled by
John Donne in "The Extasie," in which, like Christ undergoing human incarnation, the Truth and the Word becoming flesh, so must the pure lovers' "souls
descend/T'affections and to faculties," and he continues, "To our bodies turne we
then, that so/Weak men on love revealed may look."

I am not asserting an influence of either Milton or Donne on Emily Dickinson.
I am, however, convinced that the success that lies in circuit, that dictates that all
the truth must be told, but told slant, has behind it the authority of both the Old
and New Testament: that parables, riddles, the Incarnation itself are but aspects of
a Truth we could not comprehend without their mediation.

> As if some little Arctic flower
> Upon the polar hem—
> Went wandering down the Latitudes
> Until it puzzled came
> To continents of summer—
> To firmaments of sun—
> To strange, bright crowds of flowers—
> And birds, of foreign tongue!
> I say, As if this little flower
> To Eden, wandered in—
> What then? Why nothing,
> Only, your inference therefrom!

180

"All virtue in 'as if,'" wrote Robert Frost, in parody of Falstaff, and about some lines
by Edwin Arlington Robinson. And here the same words shyly amplify, or multiply,
the inferences that might be drawn from this curious, cryptic little poem. Half of a
comparison has been omitted, and we are invited to supply the missing part by careful
attention to what is given. Yet we are on very uncertain ground: the poem is conversationally casual, reticent, and daring in the double sense of boldness and challenge.

I find at least two ways to read the poem, which are not mutually exclusive, and which may neither of them be right. One may suppose, to begin with, that "Arctic flower" is itself a metaphoric description for something like an Indian Pipe, one of those curious white plants or flowers that have no chlorophyl or pigmentation, that are identifiable interlopers among the more familiar plants of summer, and that are, as it happens, rather rare. One may further surmise that Emily Dickinson, who had adopted a white habit, who had written of her "white election," who was "different" from virtually everyone she knew, could, without great strain, have identified with such a flower. In which case, the poem appears to be about a state of beatitude on the part of one who might have thought herself exempt from it, given the outward signs. And the daring consists in the almost explicit claim to having found salvation. So daring a boast would that be that it would have to be said circumspectly. And the poem is all innuendo. All virtue in "as if."

Let me now propose a radically different reading. Thomas Johnson dates the poem "about 1860." This is only a year after the publication of *The Origin of Species*, and I have no safe grounds to suppose that Emily Dickinson entertained any notions whatever about theories of evolution at this stage of her life, though she clearly knew of Darwin and his work at some point. But let us suppose that the poem is in fact about the evolutionary process of survival with regard to the flower. How but by chance, patience, strength and mystery has it persisted to arrive at last in an alien, Edenic climate? And if a single human soul were like that flower, how uncertain its election to God's grace, how mysterious and chancy its survival, how very long and ruthless is the process by which many might be called but few are chosen. This second reading is far less complacent than the first. But Emily Dickinson was capable of adopting so many attitudes and tones toward her immortal longing that we cannot confirm or deny anything by appealing to other poems of hers.

> I read my sentence—steadily—
> Reviewed it with my eyes,
> To see that I made no mistake
> In its extremest clause—
> The Date, and manner, of the shame—
> And then the Pious Form
> That "God have mercy" on the Soul
> The jury voted Him—
> I made my soul familiar—with her extremity—
> That at the last, it should not be a novel Agony—
> But she, and Death, acquainted—
> Meet tranquilly, as friends—
> Salute, and pass, without a Hint
> And there, the Matter ends.

> 412

We have here a small drama, with its peripeteia, and with a surprisingly large cast, all of whom but one are versions or facets or personae of the poet. There is a judge, an Accused, a clergyman, the soul of the Accused, and Death. And all of them but the soul are male. Moreover, it is the soul and Death who, in the course of the drama, overturn the entire "official" proceedings, and turn out to be cooperative friends, when the mortal and judicial world had counted upon them to be enemies. I take the first eight lines to be spoken by the persona as judge pronouncing sentence on the Accused (who is, of course, part of the same person) and pronouncing that sentence with a chilling jest which seems to doubt that the malefactor could possess such a thing as a soul, though one must ceremoniously take account of the jury's expression of compassion ("and may God have mercy on his soul")—much as officers in the United States Army are made "gentlemen" by an act of Congress. The tone is lofty, inflexibly cool, and slightly jesting. I take the next lines to be no more unbending but clearly more compassionate.

> I made my soul familiar—with her extremity—
> That at the last, it should not be a novel Agony—

This is the office of the clergyman, to prepare the Accused to face the inevitable, and at least to spare him the additional terror of uncertainty or the unexpected. It is a more charitable tone than the judge's, and altogether lacking in his judicial contempt. But these two, the judge and the clergyman, are mere mortals. The immortals have an understanding which makes a mockery of the trial. As such, it is a little allegorical pageant, but it also clearly speaks of a mind frighteningly divided, without an external orthodoxy to appeal to or to judge by, the nightmarish solipsism of the lonely who must work out their salvation without help or tradition. And the light-hearted comradeship of the soul and Death at the end may not be so light-hearted after all.

I want to deal with one more poem (568) and I beg leave to approach it slowly, stanza by stanza. Here is the first of the three stanzas.

> We learned the Whole of Love—
> The Alphabet—the Words—
> A Chapter—then the mighty Book—
> Then—Revelation closed—

There will be nothing to come in the poem that will firmly determine for us whether the first word here, "We," refers to two people or to a larger group, a community, a congregation. And I want to suggest that part of the excitement of the poem resides precisely in this uncertainty. In any case, it appears that in this first stanza, "the Whole of Love" may be read as either sexual or spiritual, and that the stanza presents us with an experience of education, of maturation and of growing up, beginning with the most elementary units and graduating from alphabet to words to chapter to book. The last line "Then—Revelation closed," is ambiguous, depending on whether we suppose the poet to have used an inversion or not—and inversions are common enough in her practice. The difference, though slight, seems important. If the word order is inverted, then the subject of the verb, "closed," is the "We" of the first line; and the sense is that "We" have completed a sort of education from beginning to end. But if the word order is "normal," there is a far more moot and edgy sense to the stanza: we read through the great book, or we grew up, or we made discovery upon discovery, and then revelation ceased. These two alternatives, which, in a rough way, incline to exclude each other, are maintained in the second stanza.

> But in Each Other's eyes
> An Ignorance beheld—
> Diviner than the Childhood's—
> And each to each, a Child—

If we conceive the first stanza to be about a species of education, the second stanza seems to suggest that the "We" who were educated either learned and understood or did not learn and understand. It seems to me very probable that a reference is intended here to a familiar passage in the Gospels.

> Suffer the little children to come unto me, and forbid them not: for of such is the kingdom of God.
> Verily I say unto you, Whosoever shall not receive the kingdom of God as a little child, he shall not enter therein.
>
> (Mark 10:14–15)

The Christian and pastoral paradox is well known: children, in their sublime innocence and ignorance, are "wiser" than the rest of us, who have been corrupted by worldly wisdom. In order to attain to that original purity, which would allow us to enter into the kingdom of God, or to experience true love, we would have to go through a process of education which would uneducate us, and return us to a perfect state of ignorance. This state is "Diviner than the Childhood's" because consciously and deliberately sought for and attained with the careful patience that begins with the alphabet, instead of being the natural condition of infancy. Still, the poem is playing powerfully with the paradox that the infinitely painstaking efforts of education serve to uneducate. The last stanza:

> Attempted to expound
> What Neither—understood—
> Alas, that Wisdom is so large—
> And Truth—so manifold!

I should guess that a good deal of the tension and success of the poem derives from the double sense of the word "love" in the first line as both eros and agape. And the further paradoxical feeling that the growth or maturation of one of these senses is the necessary annihilation of the other. It is not only that, in the terms of this poem, divine love unfits us for worldly love; it is the further paradox that a perfect understanding of love (which is ignorance) makes love inexpressible, an ineffable mystery, a riddle. In this sense, such "ignorant knowledge" is not unlike, perhaps, the Book of Revelations, which, despite its name, is revelation in the ambiguous sense that what was revealed to Saint John is not absolutely intelligible to us; it is a complicated revealing with its mystery somehow intact. And coming, as it does, at the end of the Bible, as the last chapter of the Book of Love, it both reveals and conceals at once, educates us to ignorance, and leaves us incapable of articulating the ambiguous love we have striven toward from childhood. The poem seems to me full of awe; and full of frustration.

The scope of these remarks may seem modest or narrow, given the enormous volume and range of Emily Dickinson's work, and might suggest that any grandiose conclusions on my part would be ludicrously out of place. And no doubt the reader will be grateful, in these painful days, to someone who will go out of his way to avoid inflation. But I would want, even minimally, to urge the idea that it was not nineteenth-century debased puritan gentility, nor "tact" as the word is commonly employed, nor lonely eccentricity that accounts for Emily Dickinson's use of riddles. Not ladylike reticence, but rather a religious seriousness, however unorthodox, and a profound sense that neither life itself nor the holy text by which we interpret it is altogether intelligible, and both require a riddling mind or inter-pretative skill. And that "identity" has something to do with "certainty," in a world where certainties are hard to come by.

The Art of Peace

Barton Levi St. Armand

Dickinson's unique "black light" stood for the dark night of the soul that followed the detonation of sunset or preceded the rosy flush of dawn. Night was necessarily black, yet because it could harbor hope and faith as well as doubt and despair, it became either the sum of all colors or the complete negation of them:

> The Red—Blaze—is the Morning—
> The Violet—is Noon—
> The Yellow—Day—is falling—
> And after that—is none—
>
> But Miles of Sparks—at Evening—
> Reveal the Width that burned—
> The Territory Argent—that
> Never yet—consumed—
>
> [J 469]

The "color" of night—of imprisonment, of New England, of Winter—was the heraldic hue of "Argent," a silver or snow-white field upon which any meaningful figure could be emblazoned by whatever recording angels still existed in this dour realm. Yet Dickinson sought most in her sunset poetry to express not the polarities of her mythology but rather their compromise, the mystery of their organicism. The sunset was ultimately not to be analyzed, only "arrested" or apprehended, and then presented in the veiled medium of words or paint. In perhaps the most inclusive of her sunset poems, Emily Dickinson expressed her conviction that the ghost or spirit that presided over the death of the day demanded the exercise of the imagination as well as the fancy. In this case the color of reverie or recollection in tranquillity became an equally inseparable mixture of blue tinged with red and silver, a "firmamental" lilac or crowning "royal purple":

> The Lilac is an ancient shrub
> But ancienter than that
> The Firmamental Lilac
> Upon the Hill tonight—

Reprinted from Barton Levi St. Armand, *Emily Dickinson and Her Culture, The Soul's Society* (1983) by permission of the author and Cambridge University Press.

The Sun subsiding on his Course
Bequeaths this final Plant
To Contemplation—not to Touch—
The Flower of Occident.
Of one Corolla is the West—
The Calyx is the Earth—
The Capsules burnished Seeds the Stars
The Scientist of Faith
His research has but just begun—
Above his synthesis
The Flora unimpeachable
To Time's Analysis—
"Eye hath not seen" may possibly
Be current with the Blind
But let not Revelation
By theses be detained—

[J 1241]

This poem is a remarkable example of that close botanical, meteorological, or geological attention to detail linking together . . . three related nineteenth-century modes of thought: . . . the writings of the American poet-naturalists, the paintings of the Hudson River school, and the aesthetics of John Ruskin. To Dickinson, the great amateur of sunsets, what is seen hovering upon the western hills is imaged (and preserved) as an immense floral specimen, a blossom related to that most persistent and characteristic of New England exotics, the lilac. The crucifixion that is implicit in the romantic typology of sunset is here subsumed by Dickinson's study of the overwhelming, passional color of the scene. To analyze this phenomenon, in fact, would itself be a kind of crucifixion of her subject by the devoted artist, who can only admire and try her skill in her chosen medium of poetic reproduction. As Emerson wrote in "Nature" of a similar visionary moment, "The beauty that shimmers in the yellow afternoons of October, who ever could clutch it? Go forth to find it and it is gone; 't is only a mirage as you look from the windows of diligence" (*Works of R. W. Emerson*, ed. Edward Waldo Emerson [Boston: Houghton Mifflin, 1904], 1:19). Dickinson's "windows of diligence," like those of Durand, Thoreau, Turner, and Ruskin, are the materials of her art, mastered by a long training and intimacy with nature. She uses the highly technical botanical terms of "Corolla" and "Calyx" in order to express as precisely as possible the fanciful image that first presents itself to her. In painting with words the bursting bloom of the sunset, she may capture as well its presiding "ghost," and some of the meaning of its hidden secret or prophecy. Where in his description of the January sunset in "Nature" Emerson had noted with Pre-Raphaelite accuracy the "stars of the dead calices of flowers" around him, touched by flame and frost (*Works* 1:18), Dickinson transfers this image to the firmament itself, elaborating, multiplying, and cosmicizing it.

The danger once again is so concentrated an intellectual approach that the butterfly may be crushed in the hands of the student, or the flower crumbled when it is plucked for the collecting box. Here the discipline that Ruskin speaks of in his

Preface to the second edition of *Modern Painters*, volume one, comes into play: the difference between the botanist's knowledge of plant life and that of the great poet or painter is that

> the one counts the stamens, and affixes a name, and is content; the other observes every character of the plant's color and form; considering each of its attributes as an element of expression, he seizes on its lines of grace or energy, rigidity or repose; notes the feebleness or the vigor, the serenity or tremulousness of its hues; observes its local habits, its love or fear of peculiar places, its nourishment or destruction by particular influences; he associates it in his mind with all the features of the situations it inhabits, and the ministering agencies necessary to its support. Thenceforward the flower is to him a living creature, with histories written on its leaves, and passions breathing in its motion (*MP* 1:xxxv–xxxvi).

Even the conservative Charles Wadsworth, in his sermon entitled "Songs in the Night," thundered that the age was "an era of cold, material, skeptical philosophy. We have quenched the fire in the bush, that we may achieve its botany; and we have classified the star of Bethlehem with the meteors, because of our astronomy; and would walk Zionward rather lighted by Gideon's lamps of conflict than cheered by David's harp of victory" (*Sermons* [Philadelphia: Presbyterian Publishing Co., 1882], 45). Emerson also condemned this skeptical approach to pure natural history when he wrote in his essay "Beauty" in *The Conduct of Life* that

> the bird is not in its ounces and inches, but in its relations to nature; and the skin and skeleton you show men is not more a heron than a heap of ashes or a bottle of gases into which his body has been reduced, is Dante or Washington. The naturalist is led *from* the road by the whole distance of his fancied advance. The boy had juster views when he gazed at the shells on the beach or the flowers in the meadow, unable to call them by their names, than the man in the pride of his nomenclature . . . Chemistry takes to pieces, but it does not construct. Alchemy, which sought to transmute one element into another, to prolong life, to arm with power,—that was in the right direction. [*Works* 6:281–2]

Echoing both Ruskin and Wadsworth in " 'Arcturus' in his other name—" (J 70), Dickinson also encapsulated Emerson's sentiment in appropriately chemical or alchemical terms when she wrote:

Banish Air from Air—
Divide Light if you dare—
They'll meet
Whiles Cubes in a Drop
Or Pellets of Shape
Fit.
Films cannot annul
Odors return whole
Force Flame
And with a Blonde push
Over your impotence
Flits Steam.
[J 854]

The profane scientist who cast nature into a crucible and attempted to force its secrets by the fire of intellect alone would soon find that he was impotent to capture the elusive ghost, spirit, essence, or "steam" that flitted into new forms above his dead and blackened residues. It was this same spirit that inhabited and animated the landscape, a spirit whose own method was one of synthesis, of spheres and cubes that melted into whole and inseparably transmuted entities. If the artist was to practice the method of nature as part of her strategy of physiognomy (another one of those supposedly outmoded sciences that actually was in "the right direction" for both Emerson and Dickinson), then her study must be a living anatomy rather than a deadly dissection:

A science—so the Savans say,
"Comparative Anatomy"—
By which a single bone—
Is made a secret to unfold
Of some rare tenant of the mold,
Else perished in the stone—

So to the eye prospective led,
This meekest flower of the mead
Upon a winter's day,
Stands representative in gold
Of Rose and Lily, manifold,
And countless Butterfly!
                    [J 100]

The wisdom that applied to the "meekest flower of the mead" also held for the gigantic lilac-blossom of the sunset. Dickinson's botanical terms were a means only of placing or fixing the specimen, not of destroying it. Rising above analysis, the artist had to be a "Scientist of Faith" whose science was the living anatomy of the sunset and whose faith was that the sunset was "prospective," that it stood for more than itself. Just as the lilac hue of this transcendent sunset was an indecipherable synthesis or blend of other colors, so was the artist's approach one of balance and fusion. For a state in which the cloudy mysteries must prevail, the revelation of this scene was enough for Dickinson. In this world, at least, the sunset was the closest that the human could come unto the divine. A kingly purple proved to be the most fitting trophy in Dickinson's royal hunt of the sun.

In Dickinson's private mythology of the mystic day, there was only one other state or condition that matched the time of sunset in its aura of mystery and veiled revelation. This was the occurrence of the northern lights, a brilliant but constantly changing veil of color that overspread the void of the night as the stain of the dying sun did that of day's end.[1] The sun in all its variety of atmospheric veils—

mist, haze, fog, and cloud—was replaced at nighttime by a host of walpurgisnacht entities, among which were the moon, the stars, meteors, and the aurora borealis. Of these "lamps" the northern lights were the most hopeful ministers, for they shone forth in the iridescence of a magical fire, a consuming Wagnerian love-death. Like the great curtains of color in Frederic Church's *Aurora Borealis* of 1865, they were a sign that, even in the midst of potential darkness and engulf-ment, a cold, pure, elusive hope stood burning, a vestal flame of the almost forgot-ten faith in dawn and resurrection. The northern lights revealed a spirit or a ghost

---

leaves," she also reports: "There was quite an excitement in the village Monday evening. We were all startled by a violent church bell ringing, and thinking of nothing but fire, rushed out in the street to see. The sky was a beautiful red, bordering on a crimson, and rays of a gold pink color were constantly shooting off from a kind of sun in the centre. People were alarmed at this beautiful Phenomenon, sup-posing that fires somewhere were *coloring* the sky. The exhibition lasted for nearly 15 minutes, and the streets were full of people wondering and admiring. Father happened to see it among the very first and rang the bell *himself* to call attention to it. You will have a full account from the pen of Mr Trumbell, whom I have not a doubt, was seen with a large lead pencil, noting down the sky at the time of it's highest glory" (*L* 1:139). Leyda excerpts part of J. R. Trumbell's account of this "beautiful Phenomenon" published in the *Hampshire and Franklin Express* on October 3: "AURORA BORE-ALIS.—One of the most splendid displays of this kind we remember ever to have witnessed, was visi-ble on Monday night . . . The rays converged at the zenith and extended over the concave above like folds of crimson attached to the center by a ring" (*YH* 1:214).

It is interesting to observe that while Dickinson was more attuned to the remarkable colorism of this event, Trumbell was more concerned with fixing a fanciful image in his reader's mind. Later Dickinson would learn to combine both techniques in her own meteorological shorthand, but she was conditioned to study such events not only by her father's Puritan attention to signs and wonders (matched by the fervent natural theology of Edward Hitchcock) but by such lyrics as the following, which appeared in *Parley's Magazine* 8 (1840):136. This song, "Aurora Borealis," originally published with music, was furnished by Lowell Mason, "Professor in the Boston Academy of Music":

See the Northern light! the Northern light!
To the zenith of the skies,
How the glowing columns rise!
Brightly gleaming, Brightly gleaming, Brightly gleaming,
Through the veil of the night.

See the Northern light! the Northern light!
See the dark clouds round the base,
Brilliant streaks from place to place,
Ever changing, Ever changing, Ever changing,
Now 'tis dim, now bright.

See the Northern light! the Northern light!
Like the dawning day it shines,
Shooting stream from stream combines,
Brightly gleaming, Brightly gleaming, Brightly gleaming
Through the veil of the night.

See the Northern light! the Northern light!
Plainly telling He is great
Who did all its beams create
Never changing, Never changing, Never changing
Source of life and light.

Mason was coeditor, with Austin Phelps and Edward Park, of *The Sabbath Hymn Book* (1858), Edward Dickinson's favorite hymnal. He was also the composer of the music for the famous "Missionary Hymn" beginning "From Greenland's icy mountains," whose lyrics were written in 1819 by the English bishop of Calcutta, Reginald Heber.

that was entirely unique, a deity who inspired paradoxically fervent yet coldly crystalline dreams of fulfillment:

> The Sunrise runs for Both—
> The East—Her Purple Troth
> Keeps with the Hill—
> The Noon unwinds Her Blue
> Till One Breadth cover Two—
> Remotest—still—
>
> Nor does the Night forget
> A Lamp for Each—to set—
> Wicks wide away—
> The North—Her blazing Sign
> Erects in Iodine—
> Till Both—can see—
>
> The Midnight's Dusky Arms
> Clasp Hemispheres, and Homes
> And so
> Upon her Bosom—One—
> And One upon her Hem—
> Both lie—
>
>   [J 710]

The northern lights too provided a synthesis, but it was a dark communion of souls involved in death or dream. Night was the climax of the cloudy mysteries of doubt—the entombment of Phoebus—as dawn was the fulfillment of the cloudless mysteries of redemption—his resurrection. The frigid blaze of the northern lights was the only consolation for those too terrified to keep the faith. Like the sunset, the aurora borealis could confirm the prophecy of heavenly reunion that was engendered at summer's full, the high solstice of the season of love. It became not a false dawn but a kindly light that led to the triumph of belief, strengthening the resolve of the poor in spirit:

> Of Bronze—and Blaze—
> The North—Tonight—
> So adequate—it forms—
> So preconcerted with itself
> So distant—to alarms—
> An Unconcern so sovereign
> To Universe, or me—
> Infects my simple spirit
> With Taints of Majesty—
> Till I take vaster attitudes—
> And strut upon my stem—
> Disdaining Men, and Oxygen,
> For Arrogance of them—

My Splendors, are Menagerie—
But their Completeless Show
Will entertain the Centuries
When I, am long ago,
An Island in dishonored Grass—
Whom none but Beetles—know.

[J 290]

The sunset, with the northern lights, was only one of the splendors of the mystic day, but Dickinson took some pride in realizing that if she could but once capture the true "effect" of this phenomena, her art would be as permanent and "firmamental" as the incredibly difficult and elusive subjects that she chose to depict. Sunrise, noon, and midnight were all important stations on the *via crucis* that she traveled every day, but sunset was the most important, because most prophetic, of her private appassionata. One might even compare the depth of her attachment and her truly consanguineous relation to the mystery of the dying, bleeding sun to what was said of the death of George Inness, that great Hudson River artist equally attracted to sunset scenes. Inness was a Swedenborgian, a mystic who believed in a theory of correspondence among the look of a landscape, the mind of God, and the soul of man. He was another romantic artist who placed the capturing of effect above all, and whose pictures, as his son, George Inness, Jr., noted in his biography, "breathed forth the poetic side of all he saw, but his special interest was for the elusive beauties of lights and shades, of atmospheric conditions, and for the rich, full, throbbing life of earth and sky." It was equally prophetic and appropriate that he should have died with the sun itself as his companion. As George Inness, Jr., wrote of his father's passing:

> Late on the afternoon of August 3 [1894] he suggested to my mother that they take a drive, and that while she was dressing he would stroll about and look at the sunset. He went out to a point where he could best see the flaming sky, which was unusually beautiful that evening. A sunset had always moved him to the deepest emotions, and as he gazed he was filled with an ecstacy too profound, a pain too exquisite, for the frail earthly body. Just as the big red ball went down below the horizon he threw his hands into the air and exclaimed, "My God! ah, how beautiful!" and fell stretched on the ground.[2]

As melodramatic as this incident may seem to us today, it is an entirely appropriate analogue to the sensibility of an Emily Dickinson who could write, after a similarly long and intensive study of the evening sky:

The Sun kept setting—setting—still
No Hue of Afternoon—
Upon the Village I perceived—
From House to House 'twas Noon—

---

[2]George Inness, Jr., *Life, Art and Letters of George Inness*, intro. by Elliott Daingerfield (New York: Century, 1917), 209.

The Dusk kept dropping—dropping—still
No Dew upon the Grass—
But only on my Forehead stopped—
And wandered in my Face—

My Feet kept drowsing—drowsing—still
My fingers were awake—
Yet why so little sound—Myself
Unto my Seeming—make?

How well I knew the Light before—
I could not see it now—
'Tis Dying—I am doing—but
I'm not afraid to know—

[J 692]

Sunset was the ultimate dress rehearsal for death, and in focusing on it the fundamental question that Dickinson, Ruskin, and the Hudson River school were asking, in spite of the monumentality of their aesthetics, was not "What is the nature of art" but rather "What shall I do to be saved?" In Ruskin's chapter in *Modern Painters* entitled "The Dark Mirror," where the critic finally abjures art for nature, he does so from an increasing humanist motivation that soon was to lead him into those very paths of reform already trodden by the most active of the New England Transcendentalists. Art alone cannot save, unless it is tied to specifically human concerns: the salvation of the soul through a redemption of the general quality of life. Ruskin at last arrives very nearly at Emerson's position, especially when he admits that "in these books of mine, their distinctive character, as essays on art, is their bringing everything to a root in human passion or human hope" (5:196). "Fragrant tissue of flowers, golden circles of cloud," he writes, "are only fair when they meet the fondness of human thoughts, and glorify human visions of heaven." Moreover, "the essential connection of the power of landscape with human emotion is not less certain, because in many impressive pictures the link is slight or local. That the connection should exist at a single point is all that we need" (197). This connection, as I have before stated, is fundamentally a connection of soul with soul and spirit with spirit. But in "The Dark Mirror," Ruskin also makes an open declaration of the massive change in emphasis that has been occurring throughout the five volumes of *Modern Painters*, the shift of his thought from an interest in theology to an interest in psychology.

In a willful attempt at accommodating himself to the dark glass of self, Ruskin entitles the final chapter of *Modern Painters* "Peace," yet the whole thrust of his last volume is a restlessness, a frustration, and a growing despair at the condition of man in the nineteenth century. The best he can do is to find, through his aesthetics and his steadily enfeebled Christianity, some kind of justification through works, though his confession is eventually to be one of life without hope.[3] The book of nature is superseded by the even more mysterious leaves of the book of self:

[3]See George Landow's chapter "Ruskin's Religious Belief," in *Aesthetic and Critical Theories of John Ruskin* (Princeton, N.J.: Princeton Univ. Press, 1971), 241–317.

"But this poor miserable Me! Is *this*, then, all the book I have got to read about God in?" Yes, truly so. No other book, nor fragment of book, than that, will you ever find;—no velvet-bound missal, nor frankincensed manuscript;—nothing hieroglyphic nor cuneiform, papyrus and pryamid are alike silent on this matter;—nothing in the clouds above, nor in the earth beneath. That flesh-bound volume is the only revelation that is, that was, or that can be. In that is the image of God painted; in that is the law of God written; in that is the promise of God revealed. Know thyself; for through thyself only thou canst know God.

Through the glass, darkly. But except through the glass, in no wise. [5:200]

Since the Puritans, American thinkers and artists had been studying the book of the self as intensively as they looked for images and shadows of divine things in the revelations of landscape. What they had discovered was a truth that Ruskin came to only too late, when the mirror of his individual being had already been fatally clouded by the lengthening shadow of madness. For if as Poe had suggested, the soul too was a veil, then the lifting of this veil had as dire consequences as the rending of the natural mantle of the atmosphere, or the parting of the film of matter that covered the spirit of visible creation. The human soul itself was capable of hauntedness; it had its peculiar genii and local spirits—invisible, intangible, elusive, beneficent, or sinister—as did the closets of the general house of nature. Dickinson surely could join with Ruskin in hoping that the ultimate reward of the anguish of art was, if not faith, a deep abiding peace. "Another kind of peace I look for than this, though I hear it said of me that I am hopeless" (*MP* 5:351), he wrote, and she who had also often been deemed "hopeless" replied:

> The Martyr Poets—did not tell—
> But wrought their Pang in syllable—
> That when their mortal name be numb—
> Their mortal fate—encourage Some—
>
> The Martyr Painters—never spoke—
> Bequeathing—rather—to their Work—
> That when their conscious fingers cease—
> Some seek in Art—the Art of Peace—
> [J 544]

Ruskin announced in "The Dark Mirror" that "all the power of nature depends on subjection to the human soul," that "man is the sun of the world; more than the real sun. The fire of his wonderful heart is the only light and heat worth gauge or measure. Where he is, are the tropics: where he is not, the ice-world" (*MP* 5:200-1). Emily Dickinson, however, had already tested this assertion and rejected it. For she knew from experience that within the soul itself were the possibilities of a tropical paradise or a polar world of despair, with glacial mountain ranges composing infinitely lone landscapes. If in her late poetry Dickinson still sought the light, it was because she had already struggled with the darkness that was soon to overwhelm the unfortunate Ruskin. That light, like that darkness, was internal as well as external, an illumination defined by one of her favorite lines from Wordsworth, his "Elegiac Stanzas, suggested by a Picture of Peele Castle, in a Storm, painted by Sir George Beaumount."[4] Its meaning had been perfectly explicated by none other than Emerson himself, for in his essay "Beauty," Emerson wrote: "Wordsworth rightly speaks of 'a light that never was on sea or land,' meaning that it was supplied by the observer" (*Works* 6:303). It was just such an observer that Emily Dickinson became. For whether she gloried in the Red Deeps of sunset or traversed the wintry wastelands of the self, her inward eye remained steadfastly, obediently open, keeping her soul both alive and awake. This was the final secret of her art, of her peace, and of her greatness.

[4]*Works*, 452–3. . . . There are only three quotations from Wordsworth in Emily Dickinson's surviving letters. One is from "We Are Seven," but the other two fasten on "the light that never was on sea or land" from "Elegiac Stanzas." The first is an altered version of the lines and the second an extract quotation (see *L* 2:449, 510). In an 1872 essay called "French Pictures in Boston," Henry James declared that Wordsworth's mysterious light "is simply the light of the mind" (*The Painter's Eye*, 47).

Dickinson's Experimental Grammar: Nouns and Verbs

Cristanne Miller

Because much of her language sounds extraordinary, Dickinson is assumed to coin a large number of words and to use words from exotic sources. For the most part, however, the unusual sound of her language stems from the transposition of classes of words by simple appropriation (a verb is used as a noun, for example, without a change in its form), from the transformation of words from one class to another by adding or omitting suffixes, and from unusual juxtapositions of words (the violation of selectional restrictions). In his vocabulary study, Howard reports that coined words amount to only slightly more than 2 percent of Dickinson's total vocabulary (a percentage comparable to that in poetry by Keats, Lanier, and Emerson), and that her vocabulary does not contain an uncommon proportion of words from special sources. The poet's vocabulary is uncommon, he finds, because of its small number of "high-frequency" words (words that occur eight times or more per thousand lines of poetry), because of its high ratio of verbs to nouns and adjectives, and because of the poet's "singular" experimentation with the form and class of words.[1]

Most of Dickinson's form/class grammatical experiments involve adjectives and nouns: adjectives, verbs, and adverbs function as nouns, and nouns function, most often, as adjectives. Dickinson will transform anything into a noun or adjective. Action becomes object in "The Daily Own—of Love" (580),[2] "The overtakeless-ness" (1691), or with "Piles of solid Moan—" (639). Adjectives may act as nouns: "Brow to Barefoot!" (275), "I sometimes drop it, for a Quick—" (708) and "The fairer—for the farness— / And for the foreignhood" (719). Adverbs become nouns: "an Until—" (779), "a Sportsman's Peradventure—" (925). Nouns and verbs become adjectives with the addition of the suffix -less: competeless, record-less, postponeless, repealless, stopless, graspless, pauseless, perturbless, report-

Reprinted from *Emily Dickinson, A Poet's Grammar* (1987) by permission of Harvard University Press.

[1]William Howard, "Emily Dickinson's Poetic Vocabulary," *PMLA*, 72 (March 1957), 230, 240–243, 248.

[2]Numbering of poems as in Thomas H. Johnson, ed., *The Poems of Emily Dickinson* (Cambridge, Mass.: Harvard University Press, 1955)—Ed.

less, floorless—to name just a few of Dickinson's uses of this suffix.[3] Noun becomes adjective in the famous snake poem "A narrow Fellow in the Grass" (986): "His notice instant is"; and with "more angel" in "The World—stands—solemner—to me—" (493). An abstract noun becomes capable of action, or quantified, in "The Plenty hurt me—'twas so new" (579); "But Epoch had no basis here / For Period exhaled." (1159); "across the June / A Wind with fingers—goes—" (409); and with "a blame" (299). Transforming an insubstantial property into a noun—as in "The Adequate" of hell (744)—implies that the object, quality, or event in question can only be named indirectly, through a grammatical subversion of the distinction between quality and object.

Using a word of one grammatical class to function as another disguises a complex predication. Juxtaposing words that do not function together in normal usage creates a kind of parataxis, for which the reader must work out the appropriate relationship. To give a simple example: "The Daily Own—of Love" gives distinct body to possessiveness, perhaps in reflection of the physical quality of the feeling, and certainly in analogy with the ownership of more mundane and quantifiable possessions. "The Daily Own—of Love / Depreciate the Vision—" suggests that once love becomes a daily affair (and is in that sense "owned") it decreases in worth. Or the unusual "Own" and uninflected "Depreciate" may imply that allowing love to be possessive, especially in a constant or "Daily" way, decreases one's appreciation of love generally; or more simply that any love gained is less desired than a love that remains unrequited. Making a noun function as an adjective, a verb function as a noun, and so on requires a semantic explanation provided only by lengthy and speculative paraphrase. The discourse of the poem indicates the direction these reconstructions of meaning and syntax should take, but it does not clarify the ambiguity altogether. Form/class experimentation, in other words, is a particularly effective and metaphorical form of compression. Through these unusual combinations, Dickinson may create resonant and complex predications using just a few words.

The "gift of Screws" provides a semantic instance of Dickinson's play with form and meaning. Here each word is used grammatically, but because Dickinson uses the copular (or abbreviated auxiliary) "is" for the previous notional "Be . . . expressed," the action of creating in the line "It is the gift of Screws" is carried implicitly by the noun "Screws." "Screws" is a metonymy for a process that involves screwing; Attar is expressed through, or as a gift of, that process. In the same poem, "Ceaseless Rosemary" gives Rosemary an unexpected temporal and active edge. "Ceaseless" ordinarily describes only activities or time-bound events (as in ceaseless motion). "Ceaseless Rosemary," then, is not just immortal (the logical synonym for "Ceaseless") but ceaselessly active with whatever rosemary may do—produce its own scent? keep the corpse smelling like a living part of the earth? grow in kitchen gardens? represent the common work of a housewife? As a

---

[3]These adjectives occur in poems 290, 298, 390, 409, 510, 627, 721, 724, 1382, and 1400.

combination of adjective and noun, "Ceaseless Rosemary" is entirely grammatical. The combination of these words, however, violates semantic rules of selectional restriction, thereby implicitly predicating qualities of the noun (in this case predicating motion of Rosemary) that are inappropriate to it. The same jar in expectation of how one word will modify or join with another occurs in the phrase "Vesuvian smile" or in the predications "Your Breath has time to straighten— / Your Brain—to bubble Cool"; normally, a smile does not explode destructively, nor does breath have form capable of controlled flexibility nor the brain share properties of motion and temperature with water. Like her grammatical form/class substitution, Dickinson's semantic violation of selectional restrictions increases the complexity and metaphorical density of a poem.

Dickinson's liberties with the standard singular and plural number of nouns, like her form/class experimentation, affect the possibilities for direct unambiguous reference and hence generally move the poem in the direction of the metaphorical. By altering the expected use of number, the poet at times makes her subject more diffuse and at others creates a more particular sense of her subject, giving the illusion of increased referentiality. Both effects alter one's conventional perception of things in the world.

To begin with the greater particularity of the singular number: when a speaker wishes she were "a Hay—" (333), for example, or has the bird on her "Walk" drink "a Dew / From a convenient Grass—" (328), the indefinite article "a" sharpens the image otherwise created by these mass nouns. Making a plural or mass noun singular does not identify any dew or grass, but it suggests that one could. "Hay," for example, does not grammatically distinguish its parts except in the separate categories of "stalks," "bundles," and so on. A *hay* is not possible in English.[4] By making her speaker "a" hay, however, Dickinson implies that she would stand out from the rest of the grasses—even if the point of difference existed only in her own imagined singularity. In "a Glee among the Garret" (934), the singular glee seems specifiable, perhaps traceable to a particular cause, and the plural Garret seems more a repeated event than a place repeatedly returned to. Through her casual use of the singular where one expects a plural number, Dickinson suggests that even under the apparently most anonymous circumstances single reference, and singularity, is possible.

Marking a plural noun as singular or making a singular noun plural (as with "among the Garret" or "thronging Mind—", 751, or "Whole Chaoses," 806) disrupts the possibility of reference. The poet's favorite combination of singular and plural reference occurs in the pronouns "ourself" and "themself." The singular "self" attached to a reflexive plural pronoun seems to undermine individuality by identifying numbers of people in a symbolic one. For example, in a poem later

---

[4]For a description of the apparent irrationality of English determinations that some nouns may be counted (shoes, chairs, coins) and others may not (footwear, furniture, money), see James D. McCawley's "Lexicographer and the Count-Mass Distinction" in *Adverbs, Vowels, and Other Objects of Wonder* (Chicago: University of Chicago Press, 1979), 165–173.

containing the unambiguously singular "And so I bear it big about / My Burial—"
Dickinson writes:

> If we demur, it's gaping sides
> Disclose as 'twere a Tomb
> Ourself am lying straight wherein
> The Favorite of Doom.
> (858)

Here the speaker includes her lover, and perhaps also the reader, in her experience ("Ourself") without departing from the narration of her own singular position
("am lying"). Reversing this multiplication of herself in "Those fair—fictitious
People" (499), Dickinson begins with the plural "we" and "ourselves" and ends
with the stanza:

> Esteeming us—as Exile—
> Themself—admitted Home—
> Through gentle Miracle of Death—
> The Way ourself, must come—

In this poem, "Themself" and "ourself" emphasize that although we all die, each
instance of death involves only one solitary "self." Similarly, we "deem ourself a
fool—" (320) and "We" question, "What, and if, Ourself a Bridegroom—" (312).
The disruption of conventional number (is it I or we who act and speak?) places
these poems in the universal spectrum of common human experience but maintains the particularity of an immediately active and experiencing "I.". . . .

[T]he poet's nouns are on the whole both the most and the least substantial
aspect of her verse. When capitalized, they occur with a deliberate, suggestively
referential presence, but that distinctive prominence gives them a larger than life
or symbolic undertone that detracts from a single referentiality. When mass or
plural nouns are made singular and when adjectives and nouns are transposed,
they lose as much specificity from the impossibility of literal reference as they gain
from the suggestion that some new distinction of singularity or reference is possible. Nouns create the illusion of thingness in Dickinson's poems, but they do not
direct us to particular events or things. They give, instead, the sense that the world
is as mobile and flexible as her perception of it. The events of her brain are as con-
cretely and substantially present as the events in her garden or those of her
friends' lives.

Critics tend to notice Dickinson's foregrounding techniques involving nouns
more readily than they do her less ostentatious experimentation with verbs. It is
true that Dickinson capitalizes primarily nouns; that nouns are the class of major
focus in her contrasts of latinate and native, or polysyllabic and monosyllabic
vocabulary; and that she coins far more nouns than verbs and experiments more
with substitutions and transformations of nouns and adjectives than with verbs.
Nonetheless, the poet does experiment with the forms of verbs in her poems; furthermore, she uses an unusually high proportion of verbs to nouns and adjec-

tives.[5] Unlike her foregrounding of nouns, Dickinson's innovation with verbs sounds more ungrammatical than poetic or semantically significant: for example, she will drop or change a verb's marked features (its inflections of voice, tense, person, and mood) or alter the transitive and intransitive properties of verbs. This difference in her types of experimentation with nouns and verbs has both a semantic and a formal cause.

First, and obviously, Dickinson's interest in action corresponds to those aspects of meaning carried by a verb's inflection. She writes of how action is perceived, what its agent may be, what transformations it effects, and the process of change, or action, itself. Inflections mark the context, and thus generally the direction and boundaries, of a verb's predication. Second, in English verbs as a class tend to be less stable syntactically than nouns, although they are more flexible than nouns in incorporating other meaning. As we know from common usage, verbals operate syntactically as adjectives or nouns; adding the infinitive "to" or a participial or gerundive suffix transforms a verb grammatically into a substantive. Lindberg-Seyersted states that "the noun-class in English is capable of incorporating any part of speech" to explain why the largest number of Dickinson's neologisms belong to the category of the noun.[6] Josephine Miles apparently operates on this theory in her analysis of syntax in English and American poetry; she counts nouns used as adjectives in poetry as nouns, but verbs used as adjectives (that is, participial forms of verbs) as adjectives: the noun is syntactically more stable than the verb. Dickinson could easily have discovered from her own sensitivity to language that nouns lend themselves to greater syntactic play and verbs to greater stability in meaning. The verb provides the basis for most meaning; it lends itself to greater semantic than structural experimentation.

To take a familiar example, in

Essential Oils—are wrung—
The Attar from the Rose
Be not expressed by Suns—alone—

"Be" at the beginning of the third line of this poem provides a sight rhyme with the E of "Essential" that begins the first line. The rhyming echo in this line-initial position calls attention to the unexpected form of the auxiliary "Be." In ordinary prose the sentence would read: Attar *is* not expressed by suns; "Be" is the infinitive or subjunctive or uninflected form of the expected, standard "is." Three other uninflected verbs occur in the poem's remaining five lines: the "Rose *decay*," "This *Make*," and "the Lady *lie*." Leaving these verbs unmarked for person, function, or tense suggests that they represent essential or primary process and activity. Without the restrictions of person and tense, the verb's action is unlimited; its ref-

---

[5]Both Howard and Lindberg-Seyersted comment on this fact as one of the primary characteristics of Dickinson's poetry. Josephine Miles, in *Eras and Modes in English Poetry*, rev. ed. (Berkeley: University of California Press, 1964) provides statistical evidence that the ratio of Dickinson's verbs to her nouns and adjectives is very high in comparison with that of most poets.

[6]Lindberg-Seyersted, *Voice of the Poet*, 116.

erence is essential, not historical. "The General Rose" will always "decay," and both the capital letters of the substantives and the uninflected verb make the proposition more definitive.

Because Dickinson's use of uninflected verbs is among her most unusual language disruptions, critics have singled it out for comment. In early criticism the poet's uninflected verbs were generally assumed to be ungrammatical and therefore regrettable, or else a modified form of the subjunctive voice. Subjunctive verbs, like the ungrammatical verbs above, often take the form of the infinitive without its auxiliary "to." Dickinson frequently creates the subjunctive mood with the conventional change of the verb "to be." A few examples are: "As if my life were shaven" (510); "if there were / A time" (650); "Then 'Great' it be—if that please Thee—" (738); "If we had ventured less / The Gale were not so fine" (1175). The subjunctive mood contributes importantly to the speculative and qualifying tone of her verse. Because the subjunctive does appear often in Dickinson's poems in its standard form, a reader might be inclined to read questionable uses of "be" in particular as subjunctive—an option the poet doubtless intends. For the most part, however, there is a tonal and semantic difference between Dickinson's regular use of the subjunctive mood and her irregular use of uninflected verbs.

Grace Sherrer is the most persuasive proponent of the argument that most of Dickinson's uninflected verbs are grammatically regular, primarily as subjunctive verbs but also as colloquial or archaic forms well known to the poet and her contemporaries.[7] Because critics—informally if not in print—still deplore Dickinson's ungrammaticality or still defend her from claims of irregularity by trying to make her usage conventional, I will linger over Sherrer's argument longer than it alone would warrant. At times Sherrer reveals grammaticality that is helpful in understanding a poem. For example, in the lines ". . . 'Whatsoever Ye shall ask— / Itself be given You'—" (476), the addition of "shall" to the final line accounts for the poet's use of "be." The omitted auxiliary "shall" makes "be" sound ungrammatical, whereas in fact it is not. Generally, however, Sherrer's claim for verbal regularity made more sense in 1935 than it does today. Sherrer was working from an altered edition of Dickinson's poems (the only editions then available) and thus did not see many of Dickinson's irregular verbs.

In the poem "You've seen Balloons set—Hav'nt You?" (700), for example, Sherrer points out that "Crowd" in the line "The Crowd—retire with an Oath—" may take the plural, in accordance with common understanding of the noun as plural and with common usage. In the next line of this poem, however, Dickinson uses an uninflected verb with a noun that is not acceptable as a plural: "The Dust in Streets—go down—". For Sherrer this verb creates no problem because her

---

[7]Grace Sherrer, "A Study of Unusual Verb Construction in the Poems of Emily Dickinson," *American Literature*, 7 (1935), 37–46. Sherrer sees most of Dickinson's uninflected verb constructions as archaic forms of the subjunctive. According to Lindberg-Seyersted, altering a verb to create the subjunctive mood was already out of style in the nineteenth century. There was some inclination to revive that form from 1855 to 1880, but even then the use of any verb but "be" in the subjunctive mood was considered archaic. She takes her information from Thyra Jane Bevier's "American Use of the Subjunctive" in *American Speech*, 6 (February 1931), 211.

text gives "dust . . . goes." The echoing "Crowd—retire" and "Dust . . . go" lead me to see both verbs as unusual. "Crowd" and "Dust" are mass or collective nouns and thus normally take singular verbs. Making both verbs plural in this poem doubly emphasizes the contrast between the tragic but "imperial" singularity of the poet/balloon and the plural anonymity of the members of the crowd. Like particles of dust, they have recognizable shape as an entity, they assume importance, only when they are indistinguishable members of a group. Particularly when repeated, the combination of mass noun and plural or uninflected verb calls attention to a disparity, thereby encouraging the reader to ask why these forms were chosen.

The question of correctness is generally irrelevant as a criterion for judgment in reading Dickinson's work. If one could identify grammaticality with skillful use of language and ungrammaticality with flawed or careless use (as one does in the speech of children), then there would be some point in advocating grammaticality for its own sake. With Dickinson, however, ungrammatical and grammatical uses of language are equally intentional and manipulated with equal precision and skill. Assuming that the poet's unusual sounding constructions are conventional (even if only archaically) and therefore of no special interest in fact hinders the reading of some poems. For example, Sherrer claims that the poet uses "Neighbor" colloquially, as a plural subject, in the first stanza of the following poem:

> The Show is not the Show
> But they that go—
> Menagerie to me
> My Neighbor be—
> (1206)

Sherrer would read the last line: "My Neighbor[s] be." Yet had the poet wanted to use the common plural form, she might have done so without disturbing her meter or any other reference of the poem; she has already used "they that go," and "Menagerie" is a mass noun. More important, seeing the poet's subject as plural detracts from the humor of her metaphor. With the singular subject, the speaker claims to see a collection of exotic animals, another whole circus, in the single person next to her (her neighbor). Identifying "Menagerie" with the entire crowd (all her neighbors) makes them less odd and the speaker correspondingly less amusing, if not less amused.

Unusual uses of language foreground themselves and their effects on the surrounding text. By speculating about these effects, a reader only follows the writer's cue. Consequently, even when a conventional explanation of apparently ungrammatical syntax is convincing, the reader should not be limited by its restrictive view of the poet's intentions from interpreting the construction in other ways, using the context of the poem and the rarity of the construction as guides. In "We will not drop the Dirk— / Because We love the Wound / The Dirk Commemorate—Itself / Remind Us that we died." (379), Sherrer reads "Commemorate" as an adjective participle and would insert "may" before "remind" (the commemorate dirk itself may remind us . . .). But despite its lack of inflection and thus ungrammatical form, "Commemorate" functions equally well as a verb in this sentence (we love

the wound that the dirk commemorates; or we love the wound that commemorates the dirk). Furthermore, the assertive "We will not drop" at the beginning of
the sentence makes it unlikely that the speaker would turn to the subjunctive
mood for this statement at the end. The stark roughness of "Because We love the
Wound / The Dirk Commemorate—Itself / Remind Us . . ." suits the painful
speech of the (apparently) wounded speaker. Combining these readings, we see in
this poem another instance of syntactic doubling—here unusually complex
because "Commemorate" changes grammatical class (from uninflected verb to
adjective) as well as function (from predicate to modifier of subject).

The subjunctive typically functions to connote either conditionality or univer-
sality. Interestingly, Dickinson critics tend instead to see it as connoting uncertainty and therefore read the poet's uninflected verbs as signifying doubt even
when they are not strictly subjunctive. Lindberg-Seyersted, for example, accepts
in modified form George Whicher's argument that uninflected verbs mark the
poet's "chronic trepidation"; "it is unquestionable," she says, "that in some poems
this idiosyncratic 'subjunctive' carries a strong element of uncertainty and doubt."[8]
Other critics, however, are more apt to interpret the poet's use of uninflected
verbs symbolically: it is an attempt to "universalize her thought"; the poet returns
to "the basic stem" of verbs, escapes "from all particularity . . . into the Absolute;
she attempts a verbal, and indeed a visual (for the inflections are visibly pared
away), correlative for the insight into essences at the core of meaning and experience."[9] The suggestion that Dickinson escapes from particularity into the absolute
gives insufficient recognition to her repeated emphasis on the singular and the
(especially domestic) particular. She uses the particular, however, as David Porter
observes, to reach its essence. By using uninflected verbs Dickinson moves both
out, to the actual rose, and in, to essences; she brings the universal and the personal into immediate play. She unhinges words and ideas from conventional syntax
and hence indirectly from a conventional conceptualization of the world, calling all
rules into question.

"Essential Oils" thematically supports this interpretation of its uninflected
verbs. The uninflected *Be, decay, Make,* and *lie* embody the process of transformation from time-bound Rose to essential Attar that is the subject of the poem.
These verbs present their root meaning fully but leave their action universalized,
unfinished, unspecified. "Essential Oil" is continuously "expressed."

Uninflected verbs function similarly in another poem (515). It begins:

No Crowd that has occurred
Exhibit—I suppose

[8]George Whicher, *This Was a Poet: A Critical Biography of Emily Dickinson* (New York:
Scribner's Sons, 1938), 93; Lindberg-Seyersted, *Voice of the Poet*, 248.

[9]Thomas H. Johnson, *Emily Dickinson: An Interpretive Biography* (New York: Atheneum Press,
1967), 93; David Porter, *The Art of Emily Dickinson's Early Poetry* (Cambridge, Mass.: Harvard
University Press, 1966), 139. Charles R. Anderson reads the verb forms of "Essential Oils" as signs of
the permanence of art and the "absolute truth" of her claim in *Emily Dickinson's Poetry: The Stairway
of Surprise* (New York: Holt, Rinehart and Winston, 1960), 67.

There we stop. It should be "No Crowd . . . has exhibited," we think. These past crowds seem still to exist. As befits a meditation on resurrection, this poem repeatedly undercuts any clear sense of time or of number. In twenty lines, Dickinson uses eight uninflected verbs: "No Crowd . . . Exhibit," "Circumference be full," the "Grave / Assert," "The Dust—connect—and live—," "Solemnity—prevail—," its "Doom / Possess," and "Duplicate—exist—". The atemporality of these verbs is magnified by the even more unusual "All Multitudes that were / Efface in the Comparison" (lines 10–11). What should logically be either a reflexive or a passive voice construction (efface themselves or were effaced) is instead intransitive, active, unmarked. Singular "Dust" and plural "Multitudes" describe the same crowd of dead and take the same unrestricted verb form of active, continuing, timeless presence. Those crowds do still exist, and resurrection is not clearly an event of the future or of any other single time. It is ongoing, universal, like the poem's verbs. Authoritative pronouncements about the boundaries of the living and the dead do not hold in this poem.

In "To pile like Thunder," the uninflected form again opens a timeless, nonreferential space around the action. Here Dickinson's uninflected verb is a logically passive verb used intransitively, or transitively without a direct object, and with only an implied subject; "Experience either [Poetry or Love] and consume— / For None see God and live—". "Consume" appears to be command, statement, and prophecy (depending on whether "Experience" is an imperative to the reader or a truncated form of "we experience" or "if you experience"). The logically passive "you will be consumed" appears active, a matter of your volition: [you] consume. There is no simple way to integrate that shifting of responsibility for the action of consuming easily into the rest of the poem. Thus the verb's ambiguous form leaves the effect of poetry (and love) uncertain.

Assuming a subjunctive mood in every truncated verb in Dickinson's poetry leads to a skewed perception of the poet. Dickinson writes several poems of hesitation or doubt and uses explicit and implicit questions as a major semantic and structural device. Her questions, however, are frequently rhetorical, and her speakers' doubts often have more to do with undercutting an established truth than with real doubt on the part of the poet. Regarding Dickinson's unusual verbs as uninflected allows the reader to respond to the unusual sound of the construction; the reader's interpretation may then be directed by its unexpectedness and by the context of the poem. The uninflected form, furthermore, corresponds to the poet's tendency to value process and continuation over specified event. Other language use in Dickinson's poetry makes one more apt to expect multiplicity and surprise from this poet than uncertainty and archaism, so why should expectations differ here? The verbs of "All Multitudes that were / Efface in the Comparison" and "Experience either [Poetry or Love] and consume" carry little hesitation and rich ambiguity, as do the poet's uninflected verbs generally.

The lines from these two poems reveal another of Dickinson's frequent experiments with verbs: the alteration of tense and mood. With "Efface" and "consume" the poet uses verbs that should logically be passive intransitively or as transitive verbs without a direct object. In other poems she moves from present to past tense, or from the indicative to the conditional mood without explanatory conjunctions or prepositions. As with the verbs discussed above, changes in the properties or tense of a verb may have the effect of stripping a verb of its inflections; making "consume" imperative or active and intransitive rids it of the need for marked inflection. Both forms of alteration create semantic ambiguity through a process akin to nonrecoverable deletion. Beyond this, however, the semantic effect differs. Where lack of inflection causes confusion with regard to person or number and tense, the uninflected verb takes on an atemporal, unhinging quality and the subject, by implication, tends to expand. Where lack of inflection makes a verb ambiguously transitive and intransitive or marks a change in tense within the poem, its effect depends more closely upon the context of change.

In the rhythmically experimental "Four Trees—upon a solitary Acre," the nonrecoverable deletion that results from using the transitive verb "Maintain" intransitively or without an obviously apparent direct object takes the form of syntactic doubling. Leaving "Maintain" (line 4) ambiguously transitive, Dickinson causes "The Sun" to serve doubly as the direct object of "Maintain" (four trees maintain the sun) and as subject of "meets" (the sun meets them):

> Four Trees—upon a solitary Acre—
> Without Design
> Or Order, or Apparent Action—
> Maintain—
>
> The Sun—upon a Morning meets them—
> The Wind—
> No nearer Neighbor—have they—
> But God—
>
> The Acre gives them—Place—
> They—Him—Attention of Passer by—
> Of Shadow, or of Squirrel, haply—
> Or Boy—
>
> (742)

To some extent, however, "Maintain" may take not just the sun but the whole world as its object. The last stanza of the poem speculates indirectly along these lines:

> What Deed is Their's unto the General Nature—
> What Plan
> They severally—retard—or further—
> Unknown—

These trees may "Maintain" all Nature, themselves, or only a plan that has been discarded by the rest of the universe. Reading "Maintain" as an abbreviation of the passive voice "are Maintained" increases the possibilities: the trees may continue to live because some person tends them, that is, they may owe their existence to some individual's plan at the same time that they may structure some larger plan of Nature's or their own. Because one cannot know, they figure larger in one's imagination than obviously useful or tended trees would. As the speaker dramatizes by hypothesizing that their nearest "Neighbor" is God, the mystery of the trees' purpose leads as directly to all order and meaning as to nothingness.[10]

Familiarity with the conventions of English syntax makes a reader want to provide direct objects for transitive verbs. Consequently, a logically transitive verb used intransitively will almost always create syntactic and semantic ambiguity; the reader will attempt to find a direct object where there is none. This attempt tends to lead the reader to extreme interpretations: "consume" (1247), "Efface" (515), "Maintain" (742) seem to carry complete destruction or all being in their isolation.

In other poems Dickinson changes her verb tense or mood as shorthand for a point that is not ambiguous. In "My Life had stood," for example, Dickinson twice compares an action in the present tense to one in the past or present perfect:

> And do I smile, such cordial light
> Upon the Valley glow—
> It is as a Vesuvian face
> Had let its pleasure through—

> And when at Night—Our good Day done—
> I guard My Master's Head—
> 'Tis better than the Eider-Duck's
> Deep Pillow—to have shared—

In the first instance, the speaker/Gun compares her smile to the aftermath of a volcanic eruption. Her smile is not like the volcano's fire or threat but like its completed act: when she smiles it is as if a volcano had erupted.[11] The past perfect verb is more chilling than the present tense would be because it signals completion, even in the midst of a speculative ("as if") comparison; her smile has the cordiality of ash, of accomplished violence or death, not just of present fire. In the second instance, the speaker prefers guarding the master to having shared his pillow, that is, to having shared intimacy with him—primarily sexual, one would guess from the general structure of the poem. Again, the comparison contrasts action with effect rather than action with action (and when I guard . . . 'tis better than sharing . . .). As a consequence, the speaker seems ironically and almost condescendingly distant from the world of life (here, of potential life-creation or love). Shared intimacy, in her view, would bring nothing better than aggressive self-reliance does. Both uses of the perfect tense in this poem distance the speaker from humanity, perhaps as any skewed analogy would. Yet by allying herself with catastrophic

---

[10]The variant for "Maintain," "Do reign," supports this argument by making the trees sovereign but over nothing in particular.

[11]Dickinson may be using an archaic form of the subjunctive here: "It is as [if] a Vesuvian face were to let [or were to have let] its pleasure through." The archaism is uncommon, however. Furthermore, even if the poet intended the subjunctive here, it remains unclear whether it is past or present subjunctive, and thus the suggestive contrast of present smile with accomplished explosion holds.

power rather than sexual intimacy, she may also be indicating that the former seems more possible or safer to her; even the power of volcanoes may be known. The change in tense alerts the reader to the peculiarity and the importance of the comparisons.

Like most lyric poetry, Dickinson's poems are primarily in the simple present tense—what George Wright calls the "lyric present."[12] As Wright demonstrates, lyric poets' use of the simple present gives an aura of continuing and yet timeless action to their dramas. Wordsworth gazes at Tintern Abbey forever, and Dickinson's poet/gun continues to live "without the power to die." The use of simple present may create temporal ambiguity, however, when ongoing dramatic action is predicated of the reader ("you") rather than of the speaker. For example, the action of "He fumbles at your Soul" seems colored by both major uses of present tense. Simple present verbs portray habitual or repeated action (Jane takes piano lessons). According to this understanding, "He" would fumble at your soul repeatedly, by some unspecified schedule (every day? whenever some other unspecified event occurs?). Simple present is also used for verbs of sense and cogitation that have no clear beginning or end (Jane feels, sees, thinks, knows). In this sense they express timelessness: "you" are continuously touched in the poem. The moment of fumbling and of being scalped is existential: your condition is to suffer this blow. Or the experience is psychological, hence ongoing in the sense that it is consciously felt in suspended memory. The speaker's role in this reading would be prophetic: she knows that "you" cannot escape the described feeling or knowledge. The use of present tense here combined with the direct address to "you" prevents readers from distancing themselves from the poem. "He fumbles" now, as the poet speaks.

Even Dickinson's poems that begin in the past tense often conclude in the present. "One Blessing had I than the rest" (756), for example, ends with three indirect questions: "Why Bliss so scantily disburse— / Why Paradise defer— / Why Floods be served to Us—in Bowls—" and then "I speculate no more—". The movement to the present tense typically involves a reevaluation of, or an attempt to improve upon, the past—either implicit, through questions as in this poem, or explicit. Examples of the latter occur in "It always *felt* to me—a wrong" (597), which concludes "Old Man on Nebo! Late as this— / My justice *bleeds*—for Thee!"; and in "I *cried* at Pity—not at Pain—" (588), which turns to "I *wish* I knew that Woman's name—" (italics mine). "It ceased to hurt me, though so slow" (584) uses the present tense to create a contrast between previous and present feeling: ". . . whereas 'twas Wilderness— / It's better—almost Peace—" (584). The change from past to present tense occurs only in poems with a first-person speaker. As she changes tense the speaker seems to draw a conclusion that disrupts what before had seemed clear; the change makes the speaker seem to be thinking aloud.

---

[12] George Wright, "The Lyric Present: Simple Present Verbs in English Poems," *PMLA*, 89 (1974), 563–579.

The first line of "This was a Poet—It is That" is confusing in its movement from past to present tense because the changing tenses carry nonspecific pronouns as subject and object. If what "was" a poet still "is" that (let us assume: a poet), then the second verb tense asserts that a poet—or at least this poet—does not die. What was a poet, what did "Entitl[e] Us" and so on, will always be one. Each reinterpretation of the pronouns "it" and "That," however, necessitates a new interpretation of the line's "is."

My favorite among Dickinson's multiple unexpected changes in verb tense occurs in the deceptively innocent "I started Early—Took my Dog— / And visited the Sea—" (520). Here the speaker presents herself as walking quietly by the sea, seeing its landscape in childish metaphors, until stanza 3 (italics mine):

> But no Man moved Me—till the Tide
> Went past my simple Shoe—
> And past my Apron—and my Belt
> And past my Boddice—too—
>
> And made as He would eat me up—
> As wholly as a Dew
> Upon a Dandelion's Sleeve—
> And then—I started—too—
>
> And He—He followed—close behind—
> I felt His Silver Heel
> Upon my Ancle—Then my Shoes
> *Would overflow* with Pearl—
>
> Until We met the Solid Town—
> . . . . .

The sudden introduction of the conditional "Would," however, gives the speaker away. This auxiliary changes the mood of the verb and of the poem: what seemed a single action in the past now seems to be either a hypothetical or a customary, repeated action. The speaker's tale becomes a sexual fantasy—repeated either in her imagining of what it would be like to walk by what she sees as a masculine and therefore dangerous sea, or in her imagination as she in fact walks by the sea, or in her metaphorical representation of real dealings with the world of men. The speaker teases the reader, and perhaps herself, just as much as she does the sea/Man. She pretends to be entirely innocent in her motives for going to the sea (walking the dog) and then repeatedly lets it touch her to the point of mutual arousal before she runs away to the "Solid Town." The last lines of the poem give the sea dignity in his lovely but otherwise undignified chase and underline the sexual content of the poem:

> Until We met the Solid Town—
> No One He seemed to know—
> And bowing—with a Mighty look—
> At me—The Sea withdrew—

As with Dickinson's mixture of past and present tenses in other poems, her combination of differing verb tense and mood in this narrative remove it from any simple, temporal context. The poet does not let us place her speaker easily, and the speaker is allowed her coy retreat to apparent innocence and safety.

Dickinson's gravitation toward the simple (habitual) present and toward the uninflected verb may suggest her overriding concern to escape the historicity of time, to make herself in some way timeless and thus safe from the forces of death and loss she feels . . . strongly. . . . It seems to me, however, that these verb forms (and Dickinson's poems) point more toward a concern with ongoing process, revelation, continuous perception, and change than toward the lyric suspension exemplified by the dancers on Keats's Grecian urn or the predictable return of Wordsworth's "Lines Composed a Few Miles above Tintern Abbey." The teasing disappearance of Dickinson's verbs from any single time or person repeats itself in her experiments with other parts of speech, and in the narratives of her poems generally. . . .

Emily Dickinson's Volcanic Punctuation

Kamilla Denman

What a hazard an Accent is! When I think of the
Hearts it has scuttled or sunk, I almost fear to lift my
Hand to so much as a punctuation.[1]

Emerson, in his famous lecture on "The American Scholar," declared: "The human mind . . . is one central fire, which flaming now out of the lips of Etna, lightens the capes of Sicily; and, now out of the throat of Vesuvius, illuminates the towers and vineyards of Naples. It is one light which beams out of a thousand stars. It is one soul which animates all men."[2] The volcano that animates Dickinson's writing, however, is a far more violent force, an image of devastating linguistic expression erupting out of silence: "Vesuvius dont talk—Etna—dont—one of them—said a syllable—a thousand years ago, and Pompeii heard it, and hid forever—" (L 233). Dickinson's volcano emits not only light but consuming lava:

A still—Volcano—Life—
That flickered in the night—
When it was dark enough to do
Without erasing sight—

A quiet—Earthquake Style—
Too subtle to suspect
By natures this side Naples—
The North cannot detect

Reprinted from *The Emily Dickinson Journal*, Vol. II, No. 1, 1993 by permission of the editors and the author.

[1]Penciled draft found among Dickinson's papers at her death. Cited in Emily Dickinson, *The Letters of Emily Dickinson*, ed. Thomas Johnson and Theodora Ward, 3 vols. (Cambridge: Belknap P of the Harvard UP, 1958) 3: 1011. All further references to this source will be cited parenthetically as L, followed by the number of the letter.

[2]Ralph Waldo Emerson, "The American Scholar," *Selections from Ralph Waldo Emerson: An Organic Anthology*, ed. Stephen E. Whicher (Boston: Houghton Mifflin Co., 1960) 67.

The Solemn—Torrid—Symbol—
The lips that never lie—
Whose hissing Corals part—and shut—
And Cities—ooze away—[3]

In contrast to Emerson's image of benevolent spiritual enlightenment, Dickinson's volcano consumes, burns, and destroys. The volcano is an unpredictable, subversive force, more appalling when it erupts because it has been so long silent. Yet the subtlety of the volcano persists even in the eruption, which is only a hiss, and in the destruction, which is an oozing away. Far from being limited by its constraining rock, the volcano's power of expression is so great that it can swallow up the exterior that seems to confine it. As such, it offers an image of Dickinson writing from within the confines of her society, exploding the language by which her culture seeks to limit and define her. . . . Dickinson's disruption of social structures, like her poetic image of the volcano, is primarily a linguistic one. The volcano destroys cities that are, like conventional language and grammar, constructions of civilization. But just as the fiery lava and ash also resculpt the landscape and enrich the soil, Dickinson's disruption of conventional discourse also reshapes and enriches language.

When Dickinson described the effect of attempting to impose order on her own poetry, she expressed it in volcanic terms: "when I try to organize—my little Force explodes—and leaves me bare and charred—" (L 271). The publication history of Dickinson's poems chronicles many subsequent attempts by others to contain her explosive language, and nowhere is this more marked than in the editing of Dickinson's punctuation. Editors usually turn to her punctuation as an area where they can confidently bring some order to her enigmatic poetry. Their assumption is that all writers ought to subscribe to conventional standards of punctuation, and when authors violate these laws, editors must enforce them.[4]

[3]Emily Dickinson, *The Poems of Emily Dickinson*, ed. Thomas H. Johnson, 3 vols. (Cambridge, MA: Belknap P of the Harvard UP, 1955) 2: 601. Further references to Dickinson's poems from this source are referenced parenthetically as P, followed by the number Johnson assigned to the poem.

[4]In Dickinson's day, the punctuation of poetry was not considered separately from that of prose. Joseph A. Turner, a contemporary of Dickinson, remarks in his *Handbook of Punctuation* that "The laws for the punctuation of poetry are the same as those for the punctuation of prose" (Philadelphia: J. B. Lippincott & Co., 1876, 66). It must be stressed that ideas about punctuation were by no means uniform in Dickinson's time. In the eighteenth and nineteenth centuries, there was a lively debate about pointing theory. The elocutionary school held that punctuation had a primarily rhetorical function: to indicate the length of pauses and rises and falls in the voice when declaiming a written piece. But as the medium of print became more widespread, the syntactic school gained increasing support, claiming that the primary function of punctuation was to reveal the grammatical structure of each sentence. In the absence of a voice to clarify ambiguities about the relations of words to one another, the eye must take the place of the ear in receiving and interpreting meaning. Park Honan tells us that by mid-century, the syntactical view had prevailed over the elocutionary (Park Honan, "Eighteenth and Nineteenth Century English Punctuation Theory," *English Studies* 46.2 (1960): 92–102.)

Consequently Dickinson's punctuation is either obscured in earlier editions and made to conform to conventional rules or displayed as a curiosity in later editions and then condemned for deviance.[5]

These editorial practices have sparked a lively debate among critics, some of whom seek to rescue Dickinson by imaging her as an eccentric transcendentalist in opposition to the grammatical reprobate whose punctuation editors have both displayed and sought to correct. In the more traditional editorial approach, John Crowe Ransom gallantly suggests that the editor of the next edition "will respect [her] capitalizations, I think, even while he is removing them," a statement that (especially in the context of a male critic discussing a female writer) is not too far from the old adage, "I'll still respect you in the morning."[6] On the other side of the debate, in the musical and elocutionary theories propounded by such critics as Thomas H. Johnson, Brita Lindberg-Seyersted, Edith Perry Stamm, and Susan Howe, Dickinson's punctuation is lifted into the lofty realm of para-language and relegated to a function secondary to semantics and social discourse, a realm where conventional meanings are consequently safe from Dickinson's volcanic disruption.

I will argue that Dickinson's punctuation is neither a transcendent, purely extra-semantic effect nor a careless transgression of grammatical rules but an integral part of her exploration of language, used deliberately to disrupt conventional grammatical patterns and create new relationships between words; to resist stasis in linguistic expression (whether in the conventions of printing or in her own evolving writing); to create musical and rhythmical effects; and to affirm the silent and the nonverbal, the spaces between words that lend resonance and emphasis to poetry. In the punctuation of her poetry, Dickinson creates a haunting, subversive, impelling harmony of language, wordless sound (emotional tonality and musical rhythms), and silence. Like songs set to music, Dickinson's poems are accompanied by a punctuation of varying pauses, tones, and rhythms that extend, modify, and emancipate her words, while pointing to the silent places from which language erupts.

---

[5]Mabel Loomis Todd, Dickinson's first editor, remarked: "I am not surprised at the success of the poems, for there is nothing like them in English. Their haunting, compelling effect upon me while I was putting the seven hundred into shape was beyond anything I can express." For Todd, putting these compelling poems "into shape" required smoothing rhymes, adding titles, omitting stanzas, altering words, and regularizing punctuation (Millicent Todd Bingham, *Ancestors' Brocades: The Literary Debut of Emily Dickinson*, New York: Harper, 1945, 83). Thomas H. Johnson, after all his efforts to restore the original punctuation in 1955, wrote in the preface to his edition: "Her use of the dash is especially capricious. . . . Within lines she uses dashes with no grammatical function whatsoever . . . Quite properly such 'punctuation' can be omitted in later editions" (Preface to *The Poems of Emily Dickinson*, 3 vols., Cambridge, MA: Belknap P of Harvard UP, 1955, 1:lxiii). R. W. Franklin, who took great pains to order her packets as they had been at her death and produce a facsimile edition of her poems, argues the need for 'a readers' text whose capitalization and punctuation conform to modern usage,' edited by a god-like "editor, critic, and philosopher in one" who has struggled with "editorial and critical principles even to the limits of onotology and epistemology" (*The Editing of Emily Dickinson: A Reconsideration*, Madison: U Wisconsin P, 1967, 128, 143).

[6]Cited in Charles R. Anderson, *Emily Dickinson's Poetry: Stairway of Surprise* (New York: Holt, Rinehart, and Winston), 344.

Punctuation has evolved as a system of rules and principles to establish the relationship of words to one another in a sentence, otherwise arbitrary, and as a means of bringing tone and emphasis to language. The *OED* defines punctuation as "The practice, art, method, or system of inserting points or 'stops' to aid the sense, in writing or printing; division of written or printed matter into sentences, clauses, etc. by means of points or stops. The ordinary sense."[7] Dickinson's definition of a poet, however, is in direct opposition to the idea of ordinary sense:

> This was a poet—It is That
> Distills amazing sense
> From ordinary Meanings—
> (P 448)

Part of Dickinson's own power to distill amazing sense from ordinary language lies in her innovative use of punctuation.

Editors and critics often lament the posthumous publication of Dickinson's poetry, since it leaves so many unanswered questions, while others have used this fact to create elaborate speculations about Dickinson's intentions. But not all of Dickinson's poems were published posthumously. Dickinson's single comment about punctuation and publication was made following the publication of her poem "The Snake" in the *Springfield Republican* in 1866. She wrote to her editor-mentor, Thomas Wentworth Higginson, to explain that she had not deceived him in declaring her reluctance to publish: "Lest you meet my Snake and suppose I deceive it was robbed of me—defeated too of the third line by the punctuation. The third and fourth were one—I had told you I did not print—" (L 316). Though the reference to the punctuation is almost an aside, the complaint is clear. In the fascicles, the lines Dickinson mentions were written:

> You may have met Him—did you not
> His notice sudden is—[8]

The *Springfield Republican* punctuated them:

> You may have met him—did you not?
> His notice instant is.[9]

Cristanne Miller claims that if Dickinson objected to a single editorial alteration in one poem, then she would certainly have objected to all other punctuation changes in her work.[10] But the *Springfield Republican* made many changes in the punctuation of "The Snake" of which Dickinson did not complain. Capitalization

---

[7] J. A. Simpson, and E.S.C. Weiner, eds., *Oxford English Dictionary*, 2nd ed., 20 vols. (Oxford: Clarendon P, 1989) 10: 841.

[8] P 986; fascicle as it appears in R. W. Franklin, *The Manuscript Books of Emily Dickinson* (Cambridge, MA: Belknap P of Harvard UP, 1981).

[9] As printed in the *Springfield Republican*, February 14, 1866.

[10] Cristanne Miller, *Emily Dickinson: A Poet's Grammar* (Cambridge, MA: Belknap P of Harvard UP, 1987), 50.

was entirely regularized; stanzas were made uniform; dashes were changed to commas, semi-colons, and periods; punctuation was added where Dickinson used none and vice versa; and two words were changed. Traditionally, editors are far more reluctant to change words than to edit punctuation; yet Dickinson let the verbal substitutions pass without comment. Why did she complain only of the one editorial change?

To my knowledge, only one critic has attempted to explain Dickinson's protest. Brita Lindberg-Seyersted suggests that Dickinson's punctuation has a purely rhythmic, rhetorical purpose. Unable to make grammatical sense of the punctuation, she assumes it must have an entirely extra-semantic function.[11] However, the effect here is more a case of counter-semantics than extra-semantics. The *Springfield Republican* editor punctuates the lines logically, conversationally, and safely, keeping the "you" fenced off from the snake by a comma, evoking the tone of a casual aside. The sense here is, "You may have met him, didn't you? He gives instant warning of his presence." The sense as Dickinson intended it is something more like, "You may have met him, and if you didn't glimpse him at first, he quickly gives notice of his presence." Dickinson's punctuation pulls the "you" alliteratively ("not/notice") and hissingly ("His notice sudden is") into the same clause with the snake, leaving no space for breath or distance. This effect is verbally echoed in the closing lines: "tighter Breathing / And Zero at the Bone." Dickinson's punctuation breaks down the conventional, conversational groupings of words as well as the safe distance between speaker and snake.[12] While Dickinson certainly did use punctuation for musical, rhythmic, and emphatic purposes, perhaps more than any other poet, her pointing system also sought to disrupt and reassemble the relationships between words, volcanic fashion.

At the time of her most disruptive use of punctuation in the early 1860s, she wrote in exasperation to Samuel Bowles: "The old words are *numb*—and there *a'nt* any *new* ones" (L 252). In the absence of new diction, Dickinson sought to redefine words through dislocating marks of punctuation. In disrupting punctuation, Dickinson reveals the open nature of language that conventional punctuation

---

[11]Brita Lindberg-Seyersted, *The Voice of the Poet: Aspects of Style in the Poetry of Emily Dickinson*, Acta Universitas Upsaliensis, Studia Anglistica Upsaliensia 6 (Upsala: Almqvist & Wiksells Boktryckeri, 1968), 195–196. [See also the same text, published Cambridge, Mass.: Harvard UP, 1968.—Ed.]

[12]The version Dickinson sent to Susan in 1872 shows that the convention of print had no impact on her choice of punctuation, except to reinforce her original intentions. To avoid the intrusive editorial placement of the question mark, she puts her own at a point which would render it impossible under conventional standards to add the *Republican's* question mark:

You may have met him? Did you not
His notice instance is—

Dickinson's re-writing of this poem after its publication offers crucial evidence that her reluctance to publish was based, at least in part, on an aversion to the conventions of print. When Todd and Higginson (the latter the recipient of the protesting letter) published "The Snake" in 1891, they followed the example of the *Republican*, ignoring Dickinson's defense of her punctuation. Other editors followed suit, favoring grammatical sense and conventional practice over Dickinson's "intention." *Bolts of Melody*, edited by Millicent Todd Bingham in 1945, was a notable exception.

seeks to regulate and obscure and makes new groupings and relationships between words apart from linguistic conventions. Thus her punctuation has a semantic as well as an extra-semantic function.

Charles F. Meyer says that the essential function of punctuation can be summed up under the rubrics of separation and enclosure.[13] Words that belong together are enclosed by punctuation and separated from other words.[14] Without changing or moving a single word in a sentence, William Klein, in *Why We Punctuate* (1916), shows how the insertion of two tiny marks of punctuation can make a sentence mean the opposite of its original sense:

> The prisoner said the witness was a convicted thief.
> The prisoner, said the witness, was a convicted thief.[15]

In the first, the witness is implicated by the prisoner; in the second, the implication is reversed. This is no fine, scholarly distinction.

While Dickinson did not go so far as to make words mean their logical opposite, she did disrupt conventional arrangements to create emotional and psychological effects, as in the lines of "The Snake" above. A more extended example of this process appears in poem 341:

> After great pain, a formal feeling comes—
> The Nerves sit ceremonious, like Tombs—
> The stiff Heart questions was it He, that bore,
> And Yesterday, or Centuries before?
>
> The Feet, mechanical, go round—
> Of Ground, or Air, or Ought—
> A Wooden way
> Regardless grown,
> A Quartz contentment, like a stone—
>
> This is the Hour of Lead—
> Remembered, if outlived,
> As Freezing persons, recollect the Snow—
> First—Chill—then Stupor—then the letting go—

The poem begins with words conventionally grouped (though the punctuation marks Dickinson used were not conventional), but by the third line, the grammar of the poem begins to disintegrate with the introduction of an additional comma, leaving only the iambic pentameter as a stabilizing of relentless rhythmic force throughout the first stanza.[16] The first line describes the psychological state philo-

---

[13]Dickinson herself lived a life of self-imposed separation and enclosure in which she explored these new relationships between words.

[14]Charles F. Meyer, *A Linguistic Study of American Punctuation* (New York: Peter Lang, 1987), 4.

[15]William Livingston Klein, *Why We Punctuate; or Reason versus Rule in the Use of Marks* (Minneapolis: Lancet, 1916), 8.

[16]Lineation and meter also contribute to the ensuing fragmentation and disruption: the second stanza expands to five lines, and the poem oscillates between iambic pentameter, ballad meter, and tetrameter.

sophically, the second describes it imagistically, and the two make an impressive epigram. But Dickinson is not content to end the poem there: she must explore the state from a more intimate and vulnerable standpoint. She is not content to recollect emotion in tranquillity, nor to describe it in eloquent, complete sentences. The introduction of the subject, "He," causes the clear ideas and images of the first two lines to crumble into disconnected images and fragmented phrases. The comma that follows the word, "He," is the first signal of the breakdown in the syntax, separating predicate nominative from its relative pronoun and verb, and person from action. The disruptive comma also creates a temporal dislocation that permeates the poem: the present thought is not completed (the object of "bore" is lacking), as the speaker unsuccessfully seeks to locate the incomplete action in past time. The present experience described in the second stanza is a mechanical, cyclical treadmill, while the past of the first stanza stretches out vaguely and endlessly. In the final stanza, past and present are confused in the line, "Freezing persons, recollect the Snow." The present participle evokes a present condition, but the snow that is causing the freezing is disconcertingly thrown into the chasm of the past by the verb, "recollect." The experience of freezing is so intensely present that even the snow that causes it, like the "He" who bore the pain, seems to belong in the past.

Temporal dislocation in the content of the poem is integrally related to its syntactic and metrical form. Generally, the order of words in temporal sequence establishes linguistic relationships from which meanings emerge. In this poem, the temporal disruption of the speaker's psyche extends to the syntax and meter, with incomplete sentences and sudden shifts from pentameter to tetrameter to trimeter to dimeter and back. Other phrases in the poem initially seem to form complete sentences but then unravel in subsequent lines that confuse the original meaning, as in the last stanza. There are no periods to mark off any thought as complete, nor even to mark the poem as a complete thought: the final sentence is completely fragmented by dashes. Alan Helms, in his incisive reading of the punctuation in this poem, says that the dashes in the last line approximate the experience of freezing by slowing down the tempo.[17] The final verb, "letting go," is followed by a dash that hangs the poem and the experience described in the poem over a visual and aural precipice of frozen silence. Were the sentences to be made complete and the poem conventionally punctuated, the essence of the experience it describes would be lost. Clearly, much of Dickinson's power in evoking psychological states lies in her disregard for conventional rules of grammar and punctuation, as well as conventional rules of poetic meter, line, and rhyme.

Such disregard inevitably evoked editorial correction and critical comment. Dickinson's belatedly revealed punctuation in Johnson's 1955 variorium edition caused a critical furor in which R. W. Franklin has had the last word. He roundly attacks all theories giving significance to Dickinson's punctuation in musical, mythopoetic, elocutionary, or any other terms: "Familiarity with the manuscripts should show that the capitals and dashes were merely a habit of handwriting and

[17]Alan Helms, "The Sense of Punctuation," *The Yale Review* 69.2 (1980): 188–189.

that Emily Dickinson used them inconsistently, without system . . . without special significance." To support his argument, he shows how Dickinson used the
same style of capitalization and punctuation in letters, in copying excerpts from
books, and in handwritten recipes. He then ridicules theories of Dickinson's
punctuation by applying them to a recipe for Cocoa Nut Cake that Dickinson
penned in 1881:

> If we follow John Crowe Ransom's theory, the capitals are Emily's "way of conferring
> dignity" upon the ingredients of Mrs. Carmichael's cake, or are her "mythopoetic
> device" for pushing Butter, Flour, 6 Eggs, and a Cocoa Nut (grated) into "the fertile
> domain of myth." At the same time, according to Charles R. Anderson, we are asked to
> use the punctuation here as "a new system of musical notation for reading" the recipe.
> Or, applying Miss Stamm's theory, Emily Dickinson has not only got the recipe, but
> has indicated how one is to declaim it.[18]

But Dickinson's single comment about punctuation can provide a baseline theory
that will satisfy even the rigorous critical demands of Mrs. Carmichael's recipe. In
her comment on the publication of "The Snake," Dickinson says that words not
separated by punctuation are "one." Dickinson used punctuation to create units of
words, words that were one, enclosed within marks of punctuation and separated
from other words by these marks. These units were not immutable, as is clear from
the differing punctuation in various extant versions of the same poems.
Dickinson's manuscripts show that she grouped and regrouped her units of
speech, never allowing words to remain static or in static relationship to other
words. The reasons that words belong together are multiple. Words can be uncon-
ventionally joined to disrupt conventional patterns and meaning or separated
against grammatical convention to explore the inherent dissociation and ambiguous nature of language. Word groupings can communicate heightened tone and
emotional force, as in the highly charged poems of 1861, written with more disrupting dashes than in any other year. Rhythmic, tonal, imagistic, or aural
demands of the poetry can require unconventional groupings. Or words can simply be the ingredients of a cocoa nut cake, separated in order to be gathered, broken, beaten, combined, and baked in order to create a new whole. The recipe is
not such a ridiculous analogy after all.

In this constant process of separation and recombination, Dickinson not only
subverted conventional language through punctuation, she continually submitted
her own language to the same disruptive process. She was her own rigorous, if
unconventional editor. Critics have been reluctant to see changes in Dickinson's
poetry over time, generally claiming that Dickinson's style is static. As Timothy
Morris says: "It has become a given of Dickinson criticism that the poet's style
never changed."[19] For example, Sharon Cameron writes: "If we could observe
changes in the style of the poems, it might be easier to arrive at textual decisions.

---

[18]Franklin, *Editing*, 120–121.
[19]Timothy Morris, "The Development of Dickinson's Style," *American Literature* 60.1 (1988):
26–41.

But, in fact, as most critics agree, there is no development in the canon of poems. The experiences recorded by these poems are insular ones, subject to endless repetition."[20] Morris, however, goes on to challenge this idea in relation to Dickinson's use of enjambment and rhyme. A study of the patterns of punctuation in Dickinson's poetry over time also reveals a practice that was far from static.[21] Dickinson's exploration of language took her from conventional punctuation in the earliest poems through a prolific period where punctuation pulled apart every normal relationship of the parts of speech, to a time of grim redefinition punctuated by weighty periods, on to a final stage where language and punctuation are minimal but intensely powerful.[22]

While the themes of Dickinson's poems remained constant throughout her life—love, death, nature, and religion—the variations in punctuation over time create a marked difference in the tone of the poems. Punctuation not only guides meaning, it adds expression and affect to language. William Livingston Klein illustrates:

John has gone home.
John has gone home?
John has gone home![23]

Here, variant punctuation of identical words evokes three entirely different speakers, and even three different interpretations of the sentence. The first statement simply informs us that John has gone home; the second indicates doubt regarding the statement; and the third expresses strong emotion regarding John's departure—-but whether the emotion is one of surprise, disapproval, horror, triumph, fear, joy, or grief cannot be determined apart from a larger context.

While Dickinson's earliest poetry was conventionally punctuated, by 1858 she is consistently using highly individualized punctuation to create an intensity of tone in her poems. The overuse of the exclamation mark is the most pronounced punctuation feature of this period and occurs in letters as well as in poems. Describing a scene to Dr. and Mrs. J. G. Holland, Dickinson writes: "My window overlooks the wharf! One yacht, and a man-of-war; two brigs and a schooner!" (L

---

[20]Sharon Cameron, *Lyric Time: Dickinson and the Limits of Genre* (Baltimore: Johns Hopkins UP, 1979), 14.

[21]Issues of dating are crucial for an argument such as this one. The objection may be raised that the date of packet copies does not necessarily coincide with the date of composition. However, from the point of view of punctuation, this does not matter. Dickinson's punctuation evolved as an integral part of her writing, and poems composed earlier and copied later are copied using the punctuation characteristic at the time of copying, not at the time of composition. Poem 174, for example, has extant manuscripts in the handwriting of 1860 and 1862. In the former, there are many more exclamation marks. In the latter, dashes predominate, replacing commas and all exclamation marks but one, and appearing as well in places where there was no punctuation in the earlier version.

[22]In light of attempts to dismiss Dickinson's unusual use of punctuation as idiosyncratic or a mere habit, one cannot stress sufficiently how completely conventional she was in her earliest poetic punctuation. Poem 1, written in 1850, contains only two of the dashes for which she was to become (in)famous; it has five semi-colons and one colon (as many as she used in the entire future course of her poetic career after 1853), and fifty-nine commas.

[23]Klein, 2.

195). Here, she communicates her enthusiasm for her surroundings through punctuation alone. Poem 92 provides a brief example of the same overuse:

My friend must be a Bird—
Because it flies!
Mortal, my friend must be,
Because it dies!
Barbs has it, like a Bee!
Ah, curious friend!
Thou puzzlest me!

The general mood in 1858—1859 is one of intensity, whether arising from joy, pain, playful satire, or exultant discovery, and Dickinson relies heavily on the exclamation mark to create this mood. The exclamation mark is a vertical, phallic figure, connected with the certainty of "Eureka!" and with erections, steeples, and religious faith. The verb, "exclaim," from which the mark derives its name, has various meanings. According to the *OED*, it signifies "the act of exclaiming or crying out; the loud articulate expression of pain, anger, surprise, etc.; clamour, vociferation; an emphatic or vehement speech or sentence; the action of loudly complaining or protesting."[24] Dickinson's early poetry is certainly filled with exclamations of pain and protest, as well as moments of surprise and exultation. There is also a sense of dramatic intention and control in these early poems: so many final exclamatory lines come like the unveiling of a surprise that the author has known from the start.

By contrast, the poems of 1860–1863 are less controlled and directed, as the punctuation indicates. By 1862, the exclamation mark is increasingly rare. In this period, Dickinson becomes anarchic in her use of the dash, both in terms of its replacement of almost every other mark of punctuation and in its placement between almost every one of the parts of speech, as the following poems illustrate:

If *He Dissolve*—then—there is *nothing—more—*
Eclipse—at *Midnight*—
It was *dark—before*—
                              (P 236, ca. 1861)

Read—Sweet—how others—strove—
Till we—are stouter—
What they—renounced—
Till we—-are less afraid—
                              (P 260, ca, 1861)

This anarchic practice occurs in letters as well as poems. A letter written to Samuel Bowles about February 1861 reads: "To count you as ourselves—except sometimes more tenderly—as now—when you are ill—and we—the haler of the two—

---

[24]*OED*, 5: 507–508.

and so I bring the Bond—we sign so many times—for you to read, when Chaos comes—or Treason—or Decay—still witnessing for Morning" (L 229).

Unlike the exclamation mark, the dash that dominates the prolific period is a horizontal stroke, on the level of this world. It both reaches out and holds at bay. Its origins in ellipsis connect it semantically to planets and cycles (rather than linear time and sequential grammatical progression), as well as to silence and the unexpressed. But to dash is also "to strike with violence so as to break into fragments; to drive impetuously forth or out, cause to rush together; to affect or qualify with an element of a different strain thrown into it; to destroy, ruin, confound, bring to nothing, frustrate, spoil; to put down on paper, throw off, or sketch, with hasty and unpremeditated vigour; to draw a pen vigorously through writing so as to erase it; [is] used as a euphemism for 'damn,' or as a kind of verbal imprecation; [or is] one of the two signals (the other being the dot) which in various combinations make up the letters of the Morse alphabet."[25] Dickinson uses the dash to fragment language and to cause unrelated words to rush together; she qualifies conventional language with her own different strains; and she confounds editorial attempts to reduce her "dashed off" jottings to a "final" version. Not only does she draw lines through her own drafts but also through the linguistic conventions of her society, and her challenges to God are euphemistic imprecations against conventional religion. Even the allusion to the Morse alphabet is not entirely irrelevant: through her unconventional use of punctuation, particularly the dash, Dickinson creates a poetry whose interpretation becomes a process of decoding the way each fragment signals meaning.

Dickinson's transition from a dominant use of the exclamation mark to a preference for the dash accompanied her shift from ejaculatory poems, which seem outcries aimed with considerable dramatic effect at God or others, to poems where the energies exist more in the relationships between words and between the poet and her words. In this intensely prolific period, Dickinson's excessive use of dashes has been interpreted variously as the result of great stress and intense emotion,[26] as the indication of a mental breakdown,[27] and as a mere idiosyncratic, female habit.[28] Though these speculations are all subject to debate, it is clear that in the early 1860s Dickinson conducted her most intense exploration of language and used punctuation to disrupt conventional linguistic relations, whether in an attempt to express inexpressible psychological states or purely to vivify language.

Whatever Dickinson's motivation may have been, readers have found her excessive use of dashes in the poems of this period somewhat jarring. Critics who complain of Dickinson's punctuation and those who defend it alike remark on its aural and rhythmic effects. Alan Helms likens the dynamic interplay of music and

---

[25]*OED*, 4: 257–259.

[26]Theodora Ward, "Poetry and Punctuation," Letters to the Editor, *Saturday Review* (1963) 46: 25.

[27]John Cody, *After Great Pain: The Inner Life of Emily Dickinson* (Cambridge, MA: Belknap P of the Harvard UP, 1971), 291–355. Although Cody does not refer explicitly to the punctuation, he regards the disintegration of Dickinson's language as indicative of her psychosis.

[28]Franklin, 124.

silence to poetry and punctuation.[29] Given the rhythmic function of punctuation in poetry, it is not surprising that so many critics have posited a musical theory of Dickinson's punctuation. Whereas Dickinson certainly characterizes her writing in volcanic terms, more often she . . . equates her poetry with music, identifying herself as a singer and a robin ("I shall keep singing! / . . . I—with my Redbreast—/ And my Rhymes—" P 250). Although the two images seem quite disparate, in poem 861 they connect:

> Split the Lark—and you'll find the Music—
> Bulb after Bulb, in Silver rolled—
> Scantily dealt to the Summer Morning
> Saved for your Ear when Lutes be old.
>
> Loose the Flood—you shall find it patent—
> Gush after Gush, reserved for you—
> Scarlet Experiment! Sceptic Thomas!
> Now, do you doubt that your Bird was true?

Like volcanic lava or the waters of a flood, the music of the bird resides within, and its expression is an overflowing of inner essence. But whereas volcanic fire supplants existing structures only on rare occasions, and then on a grand scale, the bird's "silver Principle / Supplant[s] all the rest" on a smaller, daily scale (P 1084).

It is important to note that Dickinson is not a musical poet in the purely lyrical sense of the word: she saw herself as a translator of music into language:

> Better—than Music! For I—who heard it—
> I was used—to the Birds—before—
> This—was different—'Twas Translation—
> Of all tunes I knew—and more—
>
> 'Twas'nt contained—like other stanza—
> No one could play it—the second time—
> But the Composer—perfect Mozart—
> Perish with him—that Keyless Rhyme!
> .   .   .   .
> But—I was telling a Tune—I heard—
>
> Not such a strain—the Church—baptizes—
> When the last Saint—goes up the Aisles—
> Not such a stanza splits the silence—
> When the Redemption strikes her Bells—
>
> Let me not spill—it's smallest cadence—
> Humming—for promise—-when alone—
> Humming—until my faint Rehearsal—
> Drop into tune—around the Throne—
>
> (P 503)

[29]Helms, 177.

In songs, music expands the space and pitch in which words are uttered; it lends affect and emphasis to language; it can undercut or underline the words it accompanies; it can blend words or dislocate them from their context. Clearly, it functions in much the same way as punctuation in Dickinson's poetry. To look at Dickinson's punctuation purely as a disruption of language, then, is to miss this musical dimension, where the semantic and rhythmic disruptions are smoothed through an implied melody.

Given the limited form of the hymn or ballad stanza, punctuation provides an important temporal variation within the relentless rhythms of the meter, but it is often a variation that readers find disruptive or jarring. Critics are fond of pointing out how Dickinson went beyond the hymnody and ballads of the period in her use of common meter, but a look at the music of nineteenth-century hymns is eluci- dating with regard to her punctuation. Her meter, used in the ballads, hymns, and nursery rhymes of the period, is essentially a musical one. Dickinson's meter is all too often connected to hymns and then divorced from the music that would have accompanied those hymns. Any nineteenth-century ballad meter hymn read as a poem sounds monotonous, mechanical, and trite. But when it is sung, the music temporally expands the words, often allotting several notes to a single word; and it adds texture through variations in tone and pitch. The four-part harmonies deepen this texture and create multiple ways of singing and experiencing the words through music.

When sung to any of the tunes that accompanied the hymns of Isaac Watts and John Newton (such as Handel's music for "Joy to the World" or Haydn's for "Glorious Things of Thee Are Spoken"), Dickinson's poems take on a completely different texture, so that the punctuation works with, not against, the meter. A similar effect is produced by the application of nineteenth-century ballad tunes to Dickinson's poems.[30] All too often, Dickinson scholars read the poems in silence or aloud at the speed of nursery rhymes, rather than in the musical context that liber- ates common meter from the mechanical and the banal. Read quickly, the poems seem metrically disrupted by the punctuation. But when the poems are read at the tempo at which metrically similar hymns would have been sung, the rhythmic dis- ruption vanishes. While there is no evidence that Dickinson had contemporary music in mind when she wrote her poems, her repeated references to herself as a singer and the hymns in which her culture was steeped mean that this possibility cannot be excluded. Since the publication of her poems at the end of the nine- teenth century, composers have been fully aware of the musical potential of her poetry, as evinced by the frequency with which her poems have been set to music.[31]

---

[30]Since this is an aural argument, the only proof I can suggest is for the reader to test the theory vocally.

[31]Aaron Copland (*Eight Poems of Emily Dickinson for Voice and Chamber*, 1981), John Adams (*Harmonium for Chorus and Orchestra*, 1988), George Walker (Emily Dickinson Songs, 1986), and Ernst Bacon (*O Friend*, 1946) are examples of those who have set Dickinson's poetry to various forms of music.

In musical terms, one could say that after 1863, Dickinson's poetry moves from *allegro* to *andante,* for there is a distinct shift in the diction, tone, and punctuation of these later poems. Images of spring, summer, birds, and flowers are largely replaced by wintry images of wind, thunder, lightning, clouds, and frost. Instead of views toward a limitless future, there is a distinct sense of loss and bitter nostalgia (see, for example, poems 744, 755, and 753). In this period, Dickinson's assault on language takes the form of redefining words rather than the disruption of syntax through punctuation. Many poems fall under the rubric of definitional poems, beginning, for example, with the words "Love is," "Time is," "Power is," or "Risk is."[32] The more sober mood is marked by sparser and heavier punctuation: periods begin to settle at the end of poems, while dashes are sparingly used. Though Dickinson still grapples with themes of love, death, and separation, she is now more concerned in this enterprise with generalities and universals. The poetry of the "I" has become the poetry of the "we."[33]

From 1870 on, a number of poems have no punctuation at all. But the absence as well as the presence of punctuation is significant. In this period, Dickinson seems to be thinking increasingly in ballad meter, creating word groupings based on the metrics of trimeter and tetrametor. When a phrase is not contained by the meter, she uses punctuation to indicate grouping, but almost as often she adds a line break instead of punctuation to separate words. Clearly, punctuation is not an indispensable part of composition at this stage, though it is still an ingredient. But even in this partial abandon of punctuation, Dickinson continues to be unconventional, resisting as always the containment and closure inherent in rules of punctuation.

With the diminishing use of punctuation there is also a decrease in the number of words in poems and letters. Dickinson herself explains: "I hesitate which word to take, as I can take but few and each must be the chiefest, but recall that Earth's most graphic transaction is placed within a syllable, nay, even a gaze—" (L 873, 1880). In her writing, one might say Dickinson moves increasingly towards silence, a quality she affirms throughout her poetry and letters. In part, this move indicates a rejection of her highly verbal society. Dickinson explains her social withdrawal in terms of avoiding discourse: "Of 'shunning Men and Women'—they talk of Hallowed things, aloud—and embarrass my Dog—He and I dont object to them, if they'll exist their side" (L 271). Poem 1159 places her value of silence in an even more anti-cultural context:

---

[32]See, for example, poems 1238, 1239, 1241, 1251, 1255, 1292, 1306, 1316, 1329, 1331, 1340, 1347, 1350, 1354, 1356, 1372, 1376, 1385, 1392, 1412, 1416, 1417, 1445, 1455, 1474, 1475, 1482, 1491, 1506, 1508, 1530, 1547, 1563, 1575. Though Johnson chose to date poems by concrete historical evidence and by the handwriting, several poems not dated by Johnson in the absence of manuscripts or historical data could reasonably be assigned to this period by the diction, tone, and style (for example, poems 1652, 1657, 1654, 1660, 1716, 1763).

[33]See, for example, poems 1157, 1165, 1172, 1214, 1235, 1240, 1242, 1375, 1452, 1496, 1505, 1507, 1589.

Great Streets of silence led away
To Neighborhoods of Pause—
Here was no Notice—no Dissent
No Universe—no Laws—

By Clocks, 'twas Morning, and for Night
The Bells at Distance called—
But Epoch had no basis here
For Period exhaled.

(ca. 1870)

In Dickinson's imagined locale, which may be her vision of eternity in contrast to the Christian one, language is absent, but more significant are its concomitant absences: attention, disagreement, the universe with its universal laws, linear time, and "Period." In the last, Dickinson plays on the temporal and punctuational definitions of the word by refusing to give it an article or any other definition, glibly placing a period after it in one extant version of the poem and letting it exhale in a dash in the other. Though the poem primarily refers to absent items, the things that are present in the poem are revealing. Dickinson's silence is not a total one, but one filled with rhythm and wordless music in the ticking clocks and tolling bells. Linear time is replaced by cyclical time in the clocks, which are visual symbols of endlessly repeating points in the units of time. The tolling of bells, which traditionally marks significant points in the life cycle and the liturgical cycle, contributes to the erosion of linear time and the affirmation of the recurring. In the exhaling period, Dickinson points to a silence and a pause not only beyond language but beyond punctuation.

But despite her visionary foray beyond society, language, and punctuation, the poem that describes the "Neighborhoods of Pause" is written in words, and it is punctuated. Punctuation not only groups words, indicates tone, and marks rhythms, it creates places of silence in the pauses between words, a function that Dickinson utilized fully. In her earlier poems, dashes create disruptive and lingering pauses beyond anything required by conventional rules of punctuation. The following poem illustrates this practice:

Going—to—Her!
Happy—Letter! Tell Her—
Tell Her—the page I never wrote!
Tell Her, I only said—the Syntax—
And left the Verb and the Pronoun—out!
·   ·   ·   ·   ·   ·   ·   ·   ·   ·   ·
Tell Her—it was'nt a practised writer—
You guessed—
From the way the sentence—toiled—
You could hear the Boddice—-tug—behind you—
As if it held but the might of a child!

You almost pitied—it—you—it worked so—
Tell Her—No—you may quibble—there—
For it would split Her Heart—to know it—
And then—you and I—were silenter!
                    (P 494, ca. 1862)

The punctuation and syntax create a halting but emotionally charged tone and
mark the silent places where the speaker either cannot or dares not write. The
image used to express this inability to communicate is, appropriately, grammatical: the writer announces that the verb and the pronoun, the active and personally indicative parts of the "sentence" that stands for her inner thought, have
been omitted. But the breakdown of grammar is not merely an image for the
unutterable: it occurs in the form of the poem as well, as in the lines, "You
almost pitied—it—you—it worked so— / Tell Her—No—you may quibble—
there—." The stretching stitches of the tugging bodice and the erratic beat of
the speaker's bursting heart are visually and aurally represented by the stitch-
like, pulsing dashes of the poem. Like the heartbeat of a tremulous person, they
create an irregular rhythm that also disrupts the smooth flow of grammar in the
poem.

   By contrast, Dickinson's later poems contain little or no punctuation; yet they
are shorter and fewer, indicating that if the poet continues to ponder the silent and
the wordless, she does so by being more sparing of words:

By homely gift and hindered Words
The human heart is told
Of Nothing—
"Nothing" is the force
That renovates the World—
                    (P 1563, 1883)

Here, the hindered, halting words of the earlier poem are condensed into a minimally punctuated poem of far fewer words. The unutterable behind the hindered words is no longer an unexpressed thought that the speaker fears to communicate; it is rather a formless, renovating force that exists not so much behind
language as in spite of language. Again, the form of the poem reinforces its content: it cuts itself down to the fragment, "Of Nothing," from which it then
reasserts itself to complete the ballad rhythm set up at the beginning, adding an
off-rhyme for a further sense of resolution. But as in many of her poems, the
dash at the end leaves the poem open, pointing towards the silence, the nothing
that renews and renovates not only the world, but the words that create and
express it.

   Silence provides not only the time and space in which words can be uttered and
heard but is for Dickinson a generating source of language: "The Lassitudes of
Contemplation / Beget a force" (P 1592). Silence is not a void but rather a fullness
from which the most powerful language emerges:

Declaiming Waters none may dread—
But Waters that are still

Are so for that most fatal cause
In Nature—they are full—

(P 1595)[34]

The silence preceding a flood, like poetic silence, is pregnant with lethal power.

For all her interest in words and their arrangements, Dickinson was profoundly drawn to silence and the nonverbal. Dickinson was convinced that the greatest things impress their presence without words:

By intuition, Mightiest Things
Assert themselves—and not by terms—
"I'm Midnight"—need the Midnight say—
"I'm Sunrise"—Need the Majesty?

Omnipotence—had not a Tongue—
His lisp—is Lightning—-and the Sun—
His conversation—with the Sea—
"How shall you know?"
Consult your Eye!

(P 420)

Her poems often celebrate mute, natural beauty at the expense of her own language. With a flower, she sent the following poem:

All the letters I can write
Are not fair as this—
Syllables of Velvet—
Sentences of Plush

(P 334)

The Dickinson poem is thus paradoxically anti-poetry: "True Poems flee" like a summer sky (P 1472). Yet the paradox circles and reverberates endlessly, for this observation is expressed in a poem. Dickinson turns the silent and the nonverbal into language: "There's a noiseless noise in the Orchard—that I let persons hear" (L 271). She thus becomes a translator of silence as well as of music into language.

Nowhere is this more apparent than in her latest poetry. In the 1880s, there is a quiet exultation in the inner life, in transcendence, in mystery, and in what cannot be expressed through language, despite the many elegiac poems of the period. Dickinson's last poems represent the brief and compressed poetry that she had spent her life preparing to write and deserve much more critical attention than they have received. Towards the end of her life, she described the process by which one moves from propped up dependence to mature self-sufficiency:

The Props assist the House
Until the House is built
And then the Props withdraw

[34]Another fair copy reads "mighty cause": the two adjectives combined evoke the deadly power of the volcano, Dickinson's "explosive force."

And adequate, erect,
The House support itself
And cease to recollect
The Augur and the Carpenter—
Just such a retrospect
Hath the perfected Life—
A past of Plank and Nail
And slowness—-then the Scaffolds drop
Affirming it a Soul.

(P 1142)

The same claim might be made for the perfected poem. Among the props that Dickinson used to build her poems are marks of anguished and exultant exclamation, defiant and playful questioning, hesitant and tantalizing pauses, and disruptive, musical, elliptic dashes. At the end of her life, these marks increasingly fall away, leaving words and lines of poetry largely undirected and uncontrolled by the restrictions of punctuation.

Like the robin to which she so often compared herself, Dickinson was "a Gabriel / In humble circumstances," a member of "Transport's Working Classes," writing with an "oblique integrity," "As covert[ly] as a Fugitive, / Cajoling [the] Consternation" of readers, editors, and critics "By Ditties to the Enemy / And Sylvan Punctuation" (P 1483). Dickinson uses the syntactic, affective, rhythmic, and tonal functions of punctuation with great innovation and effect, disrupting the reader's syntactic expectations and charging her poetry with intensity. Concomitantly she soothes these disruptions and eruptions with musical rhythms and long pauses which point to silence.

"Sylvan Punctuation" evokes the symbolic and mythical associations of the woods, which Marie Louise von Franz has described in her *Interpretation of Fairy Tales:* "A wood is a region where visibility is limited, where one loses one's way, where wild animals and unexpected dangers may be present, and therefore, like the sea, it is a symbol of the unconscious. . . . Aside from this, wood is vegetable life, an organic form that draws life directly from the earth and transforms the soil. Through plants inorganic matter becomes living."[35] The robin's punctuation, the devices used to shape and guide its music, has been learned in the woods, in a mythical and unconscious place apart from society. Dickinson's "Sylvan Punctuation," learned from the robin who is her "Criterion for Tune— / Because I grow—where Robins do—" (P 285) in a self-imposed exile from society, is consequently mystifying, circular, elusive, full of unexpected turns that cause readers to lose their way. It lies outside the orderly structures of her society and ours, is closely connected to the unconscious, nonverbal aspects of the human psyche and of music, and is one of the ways in which she makes the inorganic matter of language into living poetry. Dickinson's woods are even more pregnant and threatening than the woods of myths and fairy tales, for they grow on a volcano:

[35]Marie Louise von Franz, *Interpretation of Fairy Tales* (Dallas: Spring Publications, 1970), 93. Besides her identification with robins, Dickinson also claimed, "I lived in the Sea always" (L 306).

On my volcano grows the Grass
A meditative spot—
An acre for a Bird to choose
Would be the General thought—
How red the Fire rocks below
How insecure the sod
Did I disclose
Would populate with awe my solitude
　　　　　　　(P 1677)

Works Cited

Anderson, Charles R. *Emily Dickinson's Poetry: Stairway of Surprise*. New York: Holt, Rinehart, and Winston, 1960.

Bingham, Millicent Todd. *Ancestors' Brocades: The Literary Debut of Emily Dickinson*. New York: Harper, 1945.

Cameron, Sharon. *Lyric Time: Dickinson and the Limits of Genre*. Baltimore: Johns Hopkins UP, 1979.

Cody, John. *After Great Pain: The Inner Life of Emily Dickinson*. Cambridge, MA: Belknap P of Harvard UP, 1971.

Dickinson, Emily. *The Poems of Emily Dickinson*. Ed. Thomas H. Johnson. 3 vols. Cambridge, MA: Belknap P of Harvard UP, 1955.

———. *The Letters of Emily Dickinson*. Eds. Thomas Johnson and Theodora Ward. 3 vols. Cambridge: Belknap P of the Harvard UP, 1958.

Emerson, Ralph Waldo. "The American Scholar." *Selections from Ralph Waldo Emerson: An Organic Anthology*. Ed. Stephen E. Whicher. Boston: Houghton Mifflin Co., 1960. 53–71.

Franklin, R. W. *The Editing of Emily Dickinson: A Reconsideration*. Madison: U Wisconsin P, 1967.

———. *The Manuscript Books of Emily Dickinson*. Cambridge, MA: Belknap P of Harvard UP, 1981.

Helms, Alan. "The Sense of Punctuation." *The Yale Review* 69.2 (1980): 177–196.

Honan, Park. "Eighteenth and Nineteenth Century English Punctuation Theory." *English Studies* 45.2 (1960): 92–102.

Klein, William Livingston. *Why We Punctuate; or Reason versus Rule in the Use of Marks*. Minneapolis: Lancet, 1916.

Lindberg-Seyersted, Brita. *The Voice of the Poet: Aspects of Style in the Poetry of Emily Dickinson*. Acta Universitas Upsaliensis, Studia Anglistica Upsaliensia 6. Upsala: Almqvist & Wiksells Boktryckeri, 1968. [Also Cambridge, Mass.: Harvard UP, 1968.—Ed.]

Meyer, Charles F. *A Linguistic Study of American Punctuation*. New York: Peter Lang, 1987.

Miller, Cristanne. *Emily Dickinson: A Poet's Grammar*. Cambridge, MA: Harvard UP, 1987.

Morris, Timothy. "The Development of Dickinson's Style." *American Literature* 60.1 (1988): 26–41.

Simpson, J. A., and E.S.C. Weiner, eds. *Oxford English Dictionary*. 2nd ed. 20 vols. Oxford: Clarendon P, 1989.

Turner, Joseph A. *A Handbook of Punctuation*. Philadelphia: J. B. Lippincott & Co., 1876.

Von Franz, Marie Louise. *Interpretation of Fairy Tales*. Dallas: Spring Publications, 1970.

Ward, Theodora. "Poetry and Punctuation." Letters to the Editor. *Saturday Review* (1963) 46: 25

A Musical Aesthetic

Judy Jo Small

As a teenager, Dickinson wrote to a friend, "you know how I hate to be common" (L 5). The statement is a telling one, for it marks a trait in her temperament that proved to be permanent: cultivation of an elite self defiant of conventional authority. Her deliberate separation from the common would extend to stylistic revision of traditional practices of the literary establishment. Her peculiar rhymes in particular are part of a "fuller tune" that she set out to give to the sounds of poetry.

> I shall keep singing!
> Birds will pass me
> On their way to Yellower Climes—
> Each—with a Robin's expectation—
> I—with my Redbreast—
> And my Rhymes—
>
> Late—when I take my place in summer—
> But—I shall bring a fuller tune—
> Vespers—are sweeter than Matins—Signor—
> Morning—only the seed of Noon—
>
> (P 250)

This poem is something of a poetic manifesto, and its phrasing emphasizes the poet's awareness of herself as belated, part of a poetic process active long before her arrival. Whatever anxiety she may have felt with regard to her precursor poets, however, the tone here betrays no sense of impotence; on the contrary, with a mock-deferential bow to "Signor," she expresses confident assurance that she will bring a superior fullness to the tradition. Significantly, as she does again and again, she speaks of poetry as music, as song, and she expresses her revisionary intent in musical terms.

Much has been written about Emily Dickinson's visual and visionary power; the power of her auditory imagination, however, has been relatively neglected. The prominence in her poetry of sound and music, both as content and as acoustic texture, merits far more attention. Her poems often rely on auditory images and aural figures referring to metaphysical concepts. She writes repeatedly about the

Reprinted from *Positive as Sound* (1990) by permission of the author and the University of Georgia Press.

effects of sound on the hearer. And her poems and letters indicate not only that she had a keen auditory sensitivity but also that she had given thought to the ways sound conveys meaning. Her ideas about sound and about music hold implications relevant to her handling of sound devices in poetry and specifically to her uncommon handling of rhyme.

"*My* business is to *sing*," she wrote to her friends the Hollands (L 269). In the context of her letter, the statement, attributed to a bird that has been singing in her garden, stands as part of a parable with meaning immediately applicable to her writing a second letter when her previous one had received no answer. Her statement also must have had, at least for Dickinson, meaning applicable to her dedication to a poetic career, particularly since she wrote the letter some time in or around 1862, at about the same time she wrote to Higginson the more famous and cryptic statement "My Business is Circumference" (L 268). Much earlier, in 1850, struggling with a temptation that seemed irreligious, she had written to Jane Humphrey: "The path of duty looks very ugly indeed—and the place where *I* want to go more amiable—a great deal—it is so much easier to do wrong than right—so much pleasanter to be evil than good, I dont wonder that good angels weep—and bad ones sing songs" (L 30). Even then, she seems to have been thinking of her real vocation as a kind of singing.

Writing to Higginson for artistic guidance, she wonders, "Could you tell me how to grow—or is it unconveyed—like Melody—or Witchcraft?" (L 261). In the same letter, she confesses, "I had a terror—since September—I could tell to none—and so I sing, as the Boy does by the Burying Ground—because I am afraid—." To her Norcross cousins she writes some time after the death of Elizabeth Barrett Browning, "I noticed that Robert Browning had made another poem, and was astonished—till I remembered that I, myself, in my smaller way, sang off charnel steps" (L 298). She asks in one poem,

> Why—do they shut Me out of Heaven?
> Did I sing—too loud?
>
> (P 248)

She thought of herself as a singer, and it is no coincidence that her poetry is full of singing birds, which often carry metaphorical value relevant to artistic expression. She frequently describes herself as like a bird—a wren (L 268), a phoebe (P 1009), a bobolink (L 223), or, as in "I shall keep singing," quoted above, a robin.

In depicting herself as a songbird, Dickinson is aligning herself with the contemporary female poets, who were commonly referred to as little birds sweetly chirping spontaneous lays.[1] Not only female poets were regarded as singers—the metaphor is an ancient one, of course, and derives from the time when poetry and song were in fact one art. Dickinson's linking of herself and Robert Browning as

---

[1] For this idea I am indebted to Mary G. DeJong and her paper "Frances Osgood, Sara Helen Whitman, and 'The Poetess.' "

singers makes it clear that she by no means considered herself as part of an exclusively female tradition. Nevertheless, when she adopts the stance of a simple songbird singing either sweetly or "too loud," she evokes the standard image of the nineteenth-century poetess, a distorted image with which Dickinson has often been mistakenly identified. Though indeed her writing should be viewed in the context of a flourishing subculture of women writing and publishing popular lyrics, it is important not to lose sight of the fact that Dickinson's uses of gender stereotypes are frequently subversive.

Caroline May's *The American Female Poets* (1869) is a representative treasury of the clichés current about women who wrote poetry and thus of what might be called "the songbird tradition." In the preface, May says appreciatively, "poetry, which is the language of the affections, has been freely employed among us to express the emotions of woman's heart." The profusion of women's verse in periodical literature, she says, unwittingly deprecating the product she praises, "has led many to underrate the genuine value, which upon closer examination will be found appertaining to these *snatches* of American song" (v) [emphasis added]. Of Caroline Gilman she writes: "Her poems are unaffected and sprightly; inspired by warm domestic affection, and pure religious feeling" (115). Of Sarah Louisa P. Smith: "The qualities of her heart were superior to those of her head; and bright as the shining intellect was, the lustre of her love and truth and purity far outshone it . . . ; and when we are assured that to beauty, genius, and amiability, there was added the most ardent and unaffected piety, we may well believe that she was fitted while on earth for singing among the seraphs in heaven" (298). Of Lydia Jane Peirson: "Her privations and inconveniences were many, and her sorrows, too; but she poured out her soul in song, and found—to use her own words—that her 'converse with poetry, wild-flowers, and singing birds, was nearly all that made life endurable' " (303). Of Catherine H. Esling: "Her poems are smoothly and gracefully written; always pleasing, from the deep and pure affection they display. . . . [She never] left her home for a greater distance than forty miles, or for a longer period than forty-eight hours. Well may such a nestling bird sing sweetly of home's quiet joys!" (328). And of Amelia B. Welby: "her rhythm is always correct, and always full of melody, worthy of expressing the ardent impulses of a true and guileless heart. Pure friendship, undivided admiration for the beautiful, and ever-gushing love for the gifts of loving Nature, seem to be the chief incentives to her song" (471). The composite picture of these poets is indistinguishable from that offered by Henry Coppee in his introduction to *A Gallery of Distinguished English and American Female Poets* (1860): ". . . from secluded homes, from the midst of household duties,—woman's truest *profession*,—the daughters of song send forth, bird-like, sweet heart-melodies, which can no more be restrained than the voice of the morning lark, or the plaintive sounds of the nightingale" (xv). Obviously, the image of Dickinson in legend and in popular perception bears more than a passing resemblance to the nineteenth-century idea of the "female poet."

The disparity between this debased image of the woman poet and the real lives of women who wrote and struggled to have their works regarded seriously has become increasingly evident through feminist scholarship in recent years.[2] Dickinson was influenced by the writings of female poets, but she appropriated the stereotyped image of the female poet for her own ends. In her study of American women's poetry, *Nightingale's Burden*, Cheryl Walker has identified a number of poetic subjects that Dickinson derived from that women's tradition— "the concern with intense feeling, the ambivalence toward power, the fascination with death, the forbidden lover and secret sorrow" (116). She might have added, as her title implies, the sweet bird pouring out her heart's joys and pains in melody. For Walker shrewdly observes that Dickinson "toyed in her poems with that stock character the poetess, craftily using the conventions of the role to serve her own purposes and then rewriting the part to suit herself" (87). That is precisely what happens when Dickinson takes up the role of the songbird.

In that role, as so often happens in her self-presentations, "what looks like demurral, reticence, and self-abnegation can also be interpreted as a stubborn assertion of self-importance" (Juhasz 35). While the songbird metaphor types the woman writer as guileless, instinctive, scarcely conscious of matters of art (except, perhaps, correctness of rhythm), Dickinson is only *apparently* the guileless warbler, pouring forth her soul artlessly. She is, at least in part, posing. When she writes of the motives for song, she is drawing upon the tradition: sometimes a song is a way to use the idle time of life's waiting and "To Keep the Dark away" (P 850), sometimes it is a remedy for pain (P 755), and sometimes it is just "For Extasy—of it" (P 653) or "for joy to Nobody" but one's own "seraphic self" (P 1465). Elsewhere, when she ponders *why* a bird sings—"to earn the Crumb" (P 880) or not to earn the crumb (P 864), she makes more original use of the conventional subjects but remains within the tradition; the actual question, surely, is whether public recognition and remuneration should or should not be part of a poet's aim, an issue of considerable concern to women writers, who were not supposed to care about such things. But when she sings too loud and with mock remorse offers to sing "a little 'Minor' / Timid as a Bird" (P 248), she is standing the tradition on its head, parodically offering to mimic the timid little songs of timid little poetesses who do their best not to trouble the gentlemen who control the gateways to power. And when she decides (P 324) to "keep the Sabbath" not at church but in her own backyard "With a Bobolink for a Chorister" and another little bird for a "Sexton," she uses the conventional role of the female poet as home-loving and sensitive to nature while at the same time flouting the sentimental piety conventionally associated with the role. When she, artfully artless, daringly constructs irregular rhythms and eccentric rhymes that seem to have gushed willy-nilly from a simple heart, she reshapes the whole idea of verse melodies, bringing in fact "a fuller tune."

---

[2]Ann D. Wood, considering the "scribbling women" of the nineteenth century, discusses the popular descriptions of women writing "heedless of any sense of literary form," from "instinctive womanly nature," "because they cannot help it." At the origin of such descriptions, she explains, was a taboo against competition by women, especially economic competition in the marketplace: "women's motives in writing are being stripped [by these descriptions] of all aggressive content" (18–19).

Lydia Huntley Sigourney was known as the "Sweet Singer of Hartford." Lydia Jane Peirson was called "the forest minstrel." Dickinson too set out to be a singer, but—hating to be common—a singer of a superior sort. In "I cannot dance upon my Toes," she exults in her ability as poet-musician.

> I cannot dance upon my Toes—
> No Man instructed me—
> But oftentimes, among my mind,
> A Glee possesseth me,
>
> That had I Ballet knowledge—
> Would put itself abroad
> In Pirouette to blanch a Troupe—
> Or lay a Prima, mad,
>
> And though I had no Gown of Gauze—
> No Ringlet, to my Hair,
> Nor hopped for Audiences—like Birds,
> One Claw upon the Air,
>
> Nor tossed my shape in Eider Balls,
> Nor rolled on wheels of snow
> Till I was out of sight, in sound,
> The House encore me so—
>
> Nor any know I know the Art
> I mention—easy—Here—
> Nor any Placard boast me—
> It's full as Opera—
>
>   (P 326)

As [Charles R.] Anderson points out, the phrase "A Glee possesseth me" refers to minstrelsy and hence to bardic inspiration (23). More immediate to Dickinson's experience, though, were popular songs called "glees" and the glee clubs, popular in towns throughout America, such as existed at Amherst College. In this poem, all the balletic details are a surface decoration deflecting attention, like an epic simile, from the poem's main concern, for she says this "Glee," that is, this song in her mind that is also her joy, *would* express itself in ballet but *does* not because she has no gown, no ballet steps, no ballet knowledge—we may remark the string of negatives. The "Art" she knows and practices "out of sight, in sound" (and why else would she use this phrase?) is the "Glee," the art of poetic song, and at this art she is a virtuoso and knows it, proclaiming "gleefully," "It's full as Opera."

As a singer of glees, as bobolink, as robin, as wren, Dickinson exploits the song-bird convention of contemporary female poetry, then, but her references to song and music should be seen in relation to a broader historical context as well, the general interest of the nineteenth century in the music of poetry. Of Dickinson's immediate forebear[s], Edgar Allan Poe had focused attention on the musical aspect of poetry; in the preface to his *Poems* of 1831, he argued that the object of poetry is "an *indefinite* instead of a *definite* pleasure . . . to which end music is an *essential*, since the comprehension of sweet sound is our most indefinite conception. Music, when combined with a pleasurable idea, is poetry . . ." ("Letter" 17). Poe's theories were to influence the French symbolist poets, whose aesthetic stressed the suggestive nuance, the melody of language: "De la musique avant toute chose," Verlaine's "Art poétique" declared (326)—"Music before everything." Emerson's essay "The Poet" claimed that "whenever we are so finely organized that we can penetrate into that region where the air is music, we hear those primal warblings and attempt to write them down . . ." (5–6). Earlier, Thomas Carlyle (whose portrait Dickinson kept on her wall) had written in his discussion of the hero as poet, "A *musical* thought is one spoken by a mind that has penetrated into the inmost heart of the thing; detected the inmost mystery of it, namely the *melody* that lies hidden in it; the inward harmony of coherence which is its soul . . . (108–9). See deep enough, and you see musically, the heart of Nature *being* everywhere music, if you can only reach it. . . ." Sidney Lanier wrote a treatise probing the links between verse and music, *The Science of English Verse*. Walt Whitman found poetic inspiration in the opera. The association of music with sublimity permeated the age. Music, as Joseph Kerman says, "became the paradigmatic art for the Romantics because it was the freest, the least tied down to earthly manifestations such as representation in painting and denotation in literature" (65). Walter Pater's pronouncement in *The Renaissance* that "[a]ll art constantly aspires towards the condition of music" (106) must not be thought extravagant: it merely articulates an aesthetic belief then very widely held.[3]

Twentieth-century theorists have tended to recoil from the Romantic fascination with the music of poetry. When Irving Babbitt discussed the turning away of Romantic poets from the classical doctrine of *ut pictura poesis* towards musical suggestiveness, his essay became a diatribe against confusion of the arts, warning that "The constant menace that hangs over the whole ultra-impressionistic school is an incomprehensible symbolism" (185, 169). Such criticism has been profoundly influential, to the extent that many students of literature have become contemptuous of discussions of the "music of poetry" and uncomfortable even with discussions of the sound of poetry, which can seem all too subjective. The relationship of sound and meaning is admittedly a murky area. It is not yet clear to what extent the mere sound of a word, beyond the level of onomatopoeia, can be said to convey meaning at all. Since sounds do not have correspondent meanings in any universal system of signification, either musical or linguistic, talk about "the music of poetry," based on a dubious analogy, is unscientific and can indeed seem impressionistic. René Wellek and Austin Warren have held that "[t]he term 'musicality' (or 'melody') of verse should be dropped as misleading. The phenomena we are identifying are not parallel to musical 'melody' at all . . ." (159).

---

[3]M. H. Abrams discusses the importance of music in the expressive theory of aesthetics in *The Mirror and the Lamp*, 91–94.

Still, I would like to urge, Dickinson shared the Romantic concern with the ineffable power of music; further, it is precisely because music and sound generally are so indefinite in their suggestiveness, so resistant to analysis, that she found them appealing. Music, she wrote, "suggests to our Faith" rather than to "our Sight," which must be "put away" (P 797).[4] Like other Romantic writers, she criticized the cast of mind that, demanding certainty, is stupidly insensitive to sublimity. Logical analysis quickly becomes a murderous dissection, for example, in this satirical poem:

> Split the Lark—and you'll find the Music—
> Bulb after Bulb, in Silver rolled—
> Scantily dealt to the Summer Morning
> Saved for your Ear when Lutes be old.
>
> Loose the Flood—you shall find it patent—
> Gush after Gush, reserved for you—
> Scarlet Experiment! Sceptic Thomas!
> Now, do you doubt that your Bird was true?
>   (P 861)

As it so often does in her poetry, "Music" here represents the elusive sublime. The "Sceptic," whose doubt in the presence of the miraculous links him in shame with the disciple who demanded to touch the wounds of the resurrected Christ, is determined to probe and pry until he locates the song of the lark. The song, though, is impalpable, not contained in the physical mechanism of the bird's body, and it cannot be separated from the secret of its life. Remembering Dickinson's frequent presentations of herself as a poetic songbird, the analyst of her poetry may find in this poem a warning against improper skepticism. Her first letter to Higginson besought him to tell her if her poetry was "alive," if it "breathed." Together, the abundance of her musical references and the persistence of her uncommon phonetic practices argue that she knew that "Music" was part of the vital life of her poetry.

The epistemological question latent in "Split the Lark" is answered in poem 1279, which opens with these lines:

> The Way to know the Bobolink
> From every other Bird
> Precisely as the Joy of him—
> Obliged to be inferred.

Only through inference from the sound of the song, that is, however elusive that sound may seem, can one hope to gain true knowledge of the bird. That this poem is at one level self-referential becomes clear in the second and third stanzas:

---

[4]This poem, about the pine at her window which the wind rushes through, ends "Apprehensions— are God's introductions— / To be hallowed—accordingly." The poem may owe something to Emerson's "Woodnotes," which also associates the wind with the breath of the primal mind.

> Of impudent Habiliment
> Attired to defy,
> Impertinence subordinate
> At times to Majesty.
>
> Of sentiments seditious
> Amenable to Law—
> As Heresies of Transport
> Or Puck's Apostacy.

She, too, could be "Amenable to Law" but was more frequently "impudent," "seditious," puckish, or defiant as she manipulated her language to give it an uncommon, individual voice. Indeed, we know her by her distinctive music. As she wrote of the robin, we "know Her—by Her Voice" (P 634).

Other poets of the era experimented with verse-music quite deliberately. Poe, Lanier, Tennyson, and Swinburne lavished [musical effects on] their poetry . . . Though they tended to the mellifluous, others broke away from lushness of sound in a variety of ways. Hopkins's experiments with word-sounds, rhythms, and rhymes are distantly akin to Dickinson's, though the two poets worked in ignorance of each other. Emerson may have been a direct influence; his dicta encouraged disregarding the rules of prosody when they cramped lofty thought. His ideas are put forth most clearly in "Merlin":

> No jingling serenader's art,
> Nor tinkle of piano strings,
> Can make the wild blood start
> In its mystic springs.
> The kingly bard
> Must smite the chords rudely and hard,
> That they may render back
> Artful thunder, . . .
>
> He shall not his brain encumber
> With the coil of rhythm and number;
> But, leaving rule and pale forethought,
> He shall aye climb
> For his rhyme.
>
> (120–21)

Emerson's verse is correspondingly jagged, not infrequently reckless of rhythm and rhyme, because he was convinced of the primacy of poetic *thought*. "For it is not meters, but meter-making argument that makes a poem," he said in his essay "The Poet" (6). Influenced by Emerson, of course, Whitman developed free verse; but, whereas Emerson, cultivating impulsiveness, was inclined simply to ignore conventional notions of verse-music when they got in the way of expression, Whitman more consciously developed the musical aspect of his poetic language as he tried to shape it into a grander, freer music. Robert Browning experimented with roughened diction and rhythm in poems where it seemed thematically appropriate. And Elizabeth Barrett Browning, whom Dickinson ardently admired, deliberately introduced into some of her poems rhymes she knew critics would complain of as incorrect, evidently aiming for expressive effect in contexts where some disharmony is the poem's subject—"The Cry of the Children," for example, and "The Death of Pan."[5] But the departures that Dickinson makes from full rhyme, except in the fact that they *are* departures, are not like Barrett Browning's. Barrett Browning uses a greater variety of verse forms, abundant double—or "feminine"—rhymes (while Dickinson uses almost none), and few consonantal rhymes (which make up most of Dickinson's unconventional rhymes). Emerson's nonstandard rhymes (including *foot/fruit, once/bones, horse/purse, solitudes/ woods, wreath/breath*) are more like Dickinson's in kind than Browning's (including *faces/presses, children/bewildering, shower/know her, mouth/youth, silence/ islands, Aethiopia/mandragora, driven/heaving, from/storm, benches/influences*), but Browning and Dickinson both seem to use deviant rhymes toward more specific aesthetic and semantic purposes than Emerson usually did.[6]

Isaac Watts is the predecessor who is ordinarily assumed to be the greatest influence on Dickinson's prosody. Though Watts indeed wrote hymns with deviant rhymes, the narrow linking of her forms with his is erroneous. The notion of her reliance on the verse structures of English hymnody and particularly on those of Watts is so pervasive in commentary on her work that the issue needs to be addressed at some length. Gay Wilson Allen had already pointed out in 1935 in his *American Prosody* (312–14) the fundamental similarity of most of her rhythms to those of traditional ballad quatrains, when Whicher noted the similarity of her meters to those in the hymnals available in her family library (240). Ever since Johnson worked out this insight in detail in his interpretive biography (84–86), commentators have tended to accept it as the central, incontrovertible fact of her poetics. Some have viewed her use of hymn meters in a derogatory light, considering it an index of her provincialism and aesthetic naïveté, if not downright laxness (Walsh 136; Porter, *Idiom* 99, 106, 137). Others have praised her handling of the meters, seeing them as ironically poised against the subject matter of her poems, which is frequently skeptical, sometimes even blasphemous, and generally subversive of the simple religious piety associated with hymns and supposedly "echoing" in the meters (England 120; Porter, *Early* 68, 74; Wolosky 14–16, 118). She can hardly have used the hymn meters for *both* reasons—because that form was at hand in Amherst for a poet who lacked the sophistication to handle more complex forms *and* because she was expertly manipulating and

---

[5]In a letter to H. S. Boyd, postmarked August 13, 1884, Browning wrote: "And now I must explain to you that most of the 'incorrectnesses' you speak of may be 'incorrectnesses,' but are not *negligences*."

[6]The Earth-Song in "Hamatreya" is an instance where Emerson's deviation is functional; as Hyatt Waggoner puts it, "The free use, and breaking, of traditional verse forms is as effective in 'Hamatreya' as in any poem Emerson ever wrote" (153). But complaints about Emerson's "ear," his carelessness of prosody, are valid, I think. Similar complaints about Dickinson are not.

deviating from those forms to criticize religious pieties. All in all, the influence of the hymn form on her prosody has been greatly exaggerated.

Her partial rhymes do bear some resemblance to those of Watts, Wesley, and other hymnodists. Her familiarity with hymns may have encouraged her in the use of such rhymes, as James Davidson, Martha England, and others have indicated. It is unwarranted, though, to suppose that her departures from conventional rhyme offer an oblique, ironic commentary on the hymn by providing "a counterpoint of worldliness to the tonal connotations of the ideal associated with the hymn form" (Porter, *Early* 120) or, on the other hand, that her rhymes are naïvely copied from hymns (Porter, *Idiom* 100). Again, the connection of her rhymes to hymns cannot operate in both ways. The fact is that it scarcely operates either way.

Notably, the actual number of poems that have been shown to refer directly to any particular hymn is extremely small. In an early and frivolous Valentine poem (P 3, not included in any of the fascicles) Dickinson does quote (not quite exactly) a line from Watts's "How doth the little busy bee" and (exactly) part of a line from his "There is a land of pure delight," as England has pointed out (122-23). Less convincing, though, is her contention that the numerous bees throughout Dickinson's poetry provide "a defiant counter-emblem" to Watts's industrious bee (122); these bees frequently are, as England says, idle and irresponsible, "seducers, traitors, buccaneers, given over to apostacy [*sic*] and heresies," but in most of the bee poems Watts seems much too far in the background for any but the faintest of overtones. Similarly, though the poet's allusion to Moses' vision of the promised land in Watts's "There is a land of pure delight" in poem 3 and again in poem 112 is indisputable, it does not seem likely that the references to Moses in poems 168 and 597 represent any attempt "to turn Watts' leading character against Watts" (England 123). Metrically the poems do not parallel the Watts hymn, and generally they seem aimed in other directions.[7] St. Armand (159) suggests three additional hymns that he thinks are "mocked" by Dickinson's "Safe in their Alabaster Chambers" (P 216), "I heard a Fly buzz—when I died—" (P 465), and "I cannot live with You" (P 640), but, though the subjects are similar, there are no parallel phrases and the meters are different in two of the instances. It seems more likely that the mockery of the poems is directed towards broad conceptions than towards any specific hymns.[8]

---

[7]England is not mistaken in noticing an allusion. Watts's hymn speaks of seeing "the Canaan that we love, / With unbeclouded eyes!" while in P 168 Dickinson also refers to Moses, to Canaan, and "beclouded Eyes." But her poem shows no intent to parody or criticize Watts's. Further, his poem is in common meter, whereas hers is in trochaic eights and fives. It is nearly as plausible to emphasize the parallel with Burns's "Comin' through the Rye," which is in the same meter and works with the same "If"-this-happens-"Need"-this-happen structure.

[8]Wolosky asserts that P 1491 is a parody of Watts' Hymn 158, "Broad Is the Road that Leads to Death" (76). Again, the irregular short lines of Dickinson's poem are sharply divergent from the long meter of Watts's poem, and there is no common phraseology in the two poems; consequently, the connection seems too remote to be called parody. I would agree with Timothy Morris that "Far from being constrained by her form or immured within the tradition of the hymn, she escaped that tradition completely, to the point where most of her poems no longer bear even a parodic or contrasting relationship to hymns (27) . . ."

Moreover, the use of the word "hymn" in the poems shows no trace of ironic intent. It appears eight times, in poems 157, 196, 260, 616 (twice), 746, 944, and 1177. Sometimes it refers to a song that offers spiritual strength, but she also speaks of a "Biscayan Hymn" (P 746) and a "Bailiff's Hymn" (P 1177), both clearly secular. A "Bailiff's Hymn," presumably, is simply the cry "Oyez, Oyez" with which an official silences the court; she compares it to a bluejay in boldness. "Biscayan Hymn" refers to a rousing song about a shipwreck, a popular favorite in Dickinson's day, "The Bay of Biscay."[9] In her letters she uses the word "hymn" in the broadest possible way, including reference to secular poems and even to birdsong. The early letter, L 110, where she teases Austin for having written a pious poem and offers to send him "Village Hymns" is an exception. Elsewhere, she refers to Higginson's poem "Decoration" as a "beautiful Hymn" (L 418). And when she solicits Higginson's advice about poems she is planning to give to a charitable organization to "aid unfortunate Children," she calls these poems "Hymns" (L 676, L 674). The four poems she encloses for his approval (having promised three to the charity and evidently intending with his help to select three from these four) seem surprisingly unhymnlike by today's definition in subject, in diction, in cadence, and in tone: the group consists not only of the Christmas poem she entitles "Christ's Birthday" (P 1487), but also of a homily on anger she calls "Cupid's Sermon" (P 1509), the patriotic poem "My Country's Wardrobe" (P 1511), and the famous "A Hummingbird" (P 1463), now generally known by its first line as "A Route of Evanescence" (L 675).

The assertion that a "hymn vocabulary" impregnated hers (England 119) amounts to little more than a recognition of her use of a generalized religious vocabulary not specific to hymns. Then, too, so many poems depart so widely from hymn meters and hymn vocabulary that any relation is too tenuous even to be ironic.[10] In fact, the two meters most frequent in Dickinson's verse after common meter—sevens and sixes (7-6-7-6) and common particular meter (8-8-6-8-8-6)—are not used by Watts, whose rhythms supposedly permeated her thoughts (Lindberg-Seyersted 130); they do appear in the work of other hymn writers but may be found in a great many secular poems as well.

---

[9]The song lyrics, by Andrew Cherry, with accompanying tune by John Davy, first appeared in the ballad-opera *Spanish Dollars* in 1805. The refrain is included as an epigraph to a chapter in James Fenimore Cooper's *The Pioneers*. Interestingly, in that novel, Marmaduke Temple speaks with amusement of his domestic servant, who loves to brag of his adventures on the high seas and who loves to sing that song, as having sung "part of it" at an evening church service, whereupon another character launches pompously into a "dissertation . . . on the subject of psalmody, which he closed by a violent eulogium on the air of the 'Bay of Biscay, O.' . . ." The episode underlines the interrelationship of hymn-meters and the meters of popular songs and dances. The Puritans appropriated secular tunes to sacred words for psalms and hymns, with the result that, in the early days, some people cried out against hearing profane ballad and dance tunes in church. The music accompanying the first half of each stanza in "The Bay of Biscay" has a hymn-like cadence, but the latter half is pure music-hall material. Sigmund Spaeth reports that Davy "is said to have taken" the melody "from some Negro sailors in London" (51).

[10]Margaret Freeman, who has conducted an extended study of Dickinson's metrics, writes: "The poems have usually been categorised in terms of the forms found in hymnody, also according to the number of syllables per line. The limitation of grouping the poems by syllable number alone, however, is that it becomes only a rough approximation for many of the poems that bear little, if any, resemblance to the strict forms of hymn metre. . . .

Attention to Dickinson's debt to hymn forms has tended to obscure the fact that these stanzaic patterns are by no means exclusive to hymnody. Long meter is a pattern fundamental throughout Indo-European literature. Common meter is the same as ballad meter and apparently derives from seven-stress couplets ("fourteeners") rearranged in quatrain form. Short meter is the poulter's measure (alexandrine plus fourteener) arranged as four lines instead of two. Common particular meter is the same as the romance-six. These stanzas and numerous variants of them have long been abundant in English lyric poetry, especially in the fifteenth to seventeenth centuries. They have always been the mainstay of popular poetic forms including songs and hymns. They regained their importance to the poetry of high culture in the late eighteenth century, after the ballad revival. It is noteworthy that the common meter stanza and variations on it occur more frequently than any other in Wordsworth's poetry, followed only by the common particular meter (O'Donnell 16). Coleridge wrote *The Rime of the Ancient Mariner* in common meter, freely extended. Blake's *Poetical Sketches* and *Songs of Innocence and of Experience* show his fondness for long meter and common meter.[11] Whittier's most frequently used measures are long meter and common meter (Allen 131, 139). And a great deal of the poetry in the magazines and newspapers of Dickinson's day, was composed in these meters.

The *Odeon*, a collection of secular songs available at Mount Holyoke when Dickinson was a student there, contains a dozen lyrics in common meter, including "Hark! the Lark" from Shakespeare's *Cymbeline*, "The Harp, that once through Tara's Halls" by Thomas Moore, and a lyric called "County Guy" by Sir Walter Scott to the tune most of us associate with (and in the meter of) Ben Jonson's "Drink to Me Only with thine Eyes"; there are more than a dozen in long meter, including Robert Burns's popular Scottish lyric "Bonnie Doon," to which Dickinson refers in the same early Valentine poem (P 3) that quotes Isaac Watts. It also includes "My Country, 'tis of Thee," which except for an additional line is in the same stanza pattern as Dickinson's poem beginning "An antiquated Grace" (P 1345). Other collections of secular lyrics available in her day reveal similar metric patterns. Hence, we should be leery of the kind of criticism that makes much of the fact that a certain poem can be sung to the tune of "Oh God Our Help in Ages Past"; we should remember that it can also be sung to the tune of "Auld Lang Syne," which Dickinson also knew and played on the piano.

It is probably appropriate to hear a hymn resonance in such poems as the famous "I never saw a Moor" (P 1052), which Davidson likens to these lines by Watts:

> My gracious God, how plain
>   Are thy directions giv'n!
> O may I never read in vain
>   But find the path to heaven
>   (144)

---

[11]Scholars have remarked the influence on Blake of Protestant hymns, particularly those of Charles Wesley and Isaac Watts (See England 43–112 and Saintsbury 3:14). It is worth remembering, though, that Blake was familiar with literary ballads and enjoyed ballads as song, too, as B. H. Fairchild explains (3).

But many other poems, especially those with a narrative element, are more closely kin to ballads—"I started Early—Took my Dog / And visited the Sea" (P 520), for example, or "My Life had stood—a Loaded Gun—" (P 754). Some have an element that aligns them partly with children's verse or nursery rhyme, as several critics have noted. "The Mushroom is the Elf of Plants" (P 1298) is one such example, as is this fanciful poem:

> Did the Harebell loose her girdle
> To the lover Bee
> Would the Bee the Harebell *hallow*
> Much as formerly?
>
> Did the "Paradise"—persuaded—
> Yield her moat of pearl—
> Would the Eden *be* an Eden,
> Or the Earl—an *Earl?*
>
> (P 213)

Though Dickinson may not have known the jingle "How much wood would a wood-chuck chuck," the harebell poem has a similar tongue-twister quality and a similar delight in preposterousness; its jingling trochaic rhythm and its chimey rhyme are resonant of Mother Goose rather than of Isaac Watts, in spite of the reference to "Eden." Sober analyses that meditate on the revelation in this poem of the poet's psychosexual anxieties overlook both its whimsical treatment of a poetic subject at least as old as the Wife of Bath and its generic alliance with such poems as Thomas Moore's "What the Bee is to the Floweret," a dialogue including these verses:

> HE: What the bee is to the floweret,
>   When he looks for honey-dew,
>   Through the leaves that close embower it,
>   That, my love, I'll be to you.
>
> SHE: What the bank, with verdure glowing,
>   Is to waves that wander near,
>   Whispering kisses, while they're, going,
>   That I'll be to you, my dear.
>   But they say, the bee's a rover,
>   Who will fly when sweets are gone;
>   And, when once the kiss is over,
>   Faithless brooks will wander on.
>
> (57–58)

Though both may be traceable to the same origins, these owe practically nothing to the hymn genre. Likewise, a number of the poems belong to the genre of the epi-taph, and some to that of the gift-card. But most are varieties of lyric too diverse to categorize—love poems, nature poems, meditations, riddles, and so forth.[12]

---

[12]For examples of each, see "If you were coming in the Fall" (P 511), "A Light exists in Spring" (P 812), "A Prison gets to be a friend" (P 652), or "It was not Death, for I stood up" (P 510), and "Pink—small—and punctual—" (P 1332). In these, and indeed in most of her poems, Dickinson is operating out of a lyric tradition broader than that of the hymn.

Certainly, Dickinson uses traditional stanza patterns as the basis of her poetic structure and she did not compose sonnets or odes or villanelles, but Anthony Hecht is surely right when he asserts his conviction that "one of the commonplaces that is due for serious revision is her supposedly narrow indebtedness to the hymnals, and to Dr. Watts in particular."[13] For Wordsworth and Coleridge, who sought an alternative to Augustan form, "Ballads afforded a model of prosodic innocence" (Wesling, *New Poetries* 30). Similarly, I believe, Dickinson chose her stanza forms because of their apparent simplicity and because of their connection with the roots of lyric poetry. It was a choice: her knowledge of poetry was broad, and she undoubtedly *could* have written sonnets had she wanted to. It was, moreover, a significant gesture; she wrote not in the pentameters of a predominantly patriarchal tradition but in the simplest and commonest of song forms, from which she made melodies uncommonly fine.

As for rhyme, it is quite true that Dickinson's rhymes bear some similarity to Watts's, but her practice is considerably more radical.[14] Moreover, many of the simple consonantal rhymes found in Watts's hymns (*abode/God* and *obey/sea* for example) are by no means exclusive to Watts or to hymns but have come down through centuries of work by other poets (to some of whom, once, such pairs had been full rhymes and to the later of whom such pairs had become traditional). As pronunciations change, once-full rhymes alter in character. By Dickinson's time, readers accepted as a matter of course a few consonantal and unaccented rhymes in all kinds of poetry. In hymns and ballads they accepted a great many more consonantal rhymes. It may be that Dickinson heard in the nonmatching rhymes of poetry she knew a potential she might exploit to a fuller poetic effect. But the example of none of her precursors can encompass, or account for, the radical nature of her prosodic rebellion. They may have offered an impetus, but she had no models.

It is worth remembering that Dickinson had a fairly extensive musical experience—not just in church, where she heard and sang hymns, but beyond that as well. Her aunt Lavinia fondly describes Emily at age two and a half playing the piano and talking about the "moosic" (L 11, editor's note). More important is the fact that she studied voice at Mr. Woodman's singing school in Amherst (L, 5, L

---

[13]Cf. Hecht, "The Riddles of Emily Dickinson," 149–162.—Ed.

[14]Consonantal rhymes are frequent in Watts's psalms and hymns, not only eye rhymes such as *good/food*, *gone/atone*, *have/grave*, and *Lord/word*, but also (and more frequently) such consonantal rhymes as *blood/God*, *sin/clean*, *Lamb/name*, *adore/power*, *Son/down*, *known/Son*, *tombs/comes*, *cup/hope*, *maladies/arise*, *lost/dust*, and *tread/exceed*. Dickinson has a great many rhymes of the same type. Extremely rare in hymns are any combinations involving a final consonant blend rhymed with a non-identical consonant blend or a single consonant (*thoughts/faults* is a rare instance in Watts); she, on the other hand, frequently pairs such words as *rides* and *is*, *around* and *Head*, or *endured* and *Beloved*, and even sometimes such remote pairs as *Death* and *enough* (in this case, both end in fricatives) or *Equinox/intercourse*. Rhymes including an accented syllable with metric promotion such as *thee/immortality* or *eyes/vanities* are infrequent in Watts's practice and abundant in Dickinson's—pushed to such further lengths as *beyond/satisfied*, *extinct/thanked/Retrospect*, *woe/Italy*, *Flail/burial*, *gash/Countenance*, or (doubled) *Melody/Eternally*, *privacy/infinity*, *Brigadier/Troubadour*, or (tripled) *Immortality/Strategy/Physiognomy*. Other more experimental rhymes she used, such as rich consonance (*Birds/Bards*) and identical rhymes (*Sow/so*), are practically non-existent in hymnody.

6)[15] and that she studied piano, beginning in 1845 when her father purchased one, as a student of her Aunt Selby (L 7). She wrote to her friend Abiah Root about her piano-playing with great enthusiasm, and she evidently practiced two hours a day up until the time she entered Mount Holyoke (L 8, L 9, L 12, L 14). It is not clear that there was any teacher of piano at Mount Holyoke, but she writes that she was practicing an hour every afternoon there (L 18). A classmate recounts a peculiar episode from this year. She begins her story in a visionary vein, then subsides into ordinary remembrance:

> Again we see them, a flock of new-comers, as they crowd into the hall for the opening exercises, some comely and graceful, and some destined to win admiration by their shining virtues and talents. We mark one modest, palefaced maiden crowned with a wealth of auburn hair. Who could have divined that Emily Dickinson's brain teemed with rare notes that would ring through the land? . . . E. was my friend and schoolmate in early youth and together we entered the junior class [the first-year class] at Mount Holyoke Seminary. After our novitiate, and before our studies had become of engrossing interest, we began to feel our limitations and fear lest "in many things we offend all". The dignity of our senior room-mates was a restraint upon us. We had been singers in our respective churches at home, and now were pining for our choir-mates and rehearsals.
>
> One day E. came to my room, singing-book in hand. "I can stand it no longer," she said. "Come with me." We took the road to the ferry as the most sequestered, and having walked our required distance, we ventured to delay in the spaceway—the broad spaceway bounded by the horizon. Then, perched upon the topmost rail of a fence, we opened the book and our mouths, drew the diapason stops of our vocal organs, and sang tune after tune,—long metres, short metres, hallelujah metres, *et id omne genus*,— chants, rounds, fugues, anthems, etc., etc., carrying two parts, and by snatches three or four, as the score demanded. We sang and sang till the valley rang "with our hymns of lofty cheer." Our only visible auditors were two or three cows that had been quietly feeding in a pasture near. They were too well-bred to obtrude with double-base bellowing or with horn accompaniment, but they ceased their cropping and stood in silent amazement at the unusual sight and sound. We needed no plaudits, for we were a joy to ourselves. We had found a remedy for depression, repression, suppression and oppression, and no two maidens returned that day from open-air exercises more exhilarated than we. The seminary choirs were ere long arranged for regular practise, which was the tonic and safety-valve we needed.[16]

[15]George Sullivan Woodman was a student at Amherst College who later received an M.D. from Harvard. He had studied with Lowell Mason, the president of the Handel and Haydn Society in Boston and the major organizer in the U.S. of music instruction for schoolchildren and their teachers. Mason published dozens of songbooks for children (beginning with *The Juvenile Lyre* in 1831) as well as for adult choirs. Singing schools, "common in New England before the end of the eighteenth century," taught a variety of music, such songs as "Old Hundred," "Indian Converts," "Romish Lady," or "Captain Kidd," and "[t]he line between religious and secular music was tenuous," according to Irving Sablosky (*American* 67).

[16]From a volume of recollections, entitled "Memorabilia of Mary Lyon," found in the archives of Mount Holyoke College, this excerpt is by Amelia D. Jones, class of 1849. Her comments indicate something about the breadth of musical kinds sung in the singing schools.

Mount Holyoke did have an instructor of vocal music, Harriet Hawes, and Dickinson sang for a half hour each day in Seminary Hall, probably with all or most of the student body (L 18).[17]

Though there is no evidence of any formal musical instruction afterward, music certainly played a large role in the parlor entertainments and in the Amherst College ceremonies attended by the poet in her youth.[18] A volume of Dickinson's collected sheet music (preserved at the Houghton Library, along with her piano) shows her familiarity with a large range of popular songs, waltzes, marches, and quicksteps, extending from adaptations of Beethoven to "Ethiopian Melodies," with lyrics in dialect, from contemporary minstrel shows. The difficulty of the selections indicates that she must have been a moderately accomplished pianist.

As provincial as she was—and she admits "I see . . . Provincially" (P 285), she managed to come in contact with some of the leading musical developments of her time, in addition to participating in the singing-school movement and the genteel growth of piano-playing. She probably heard at Mount Holyoke a performance by the most popular of the touring family singing groups, the Hutchinson Family, "whose programs included sentimental songs along with folk hymns and often temperance and abolition songs" (Sablosky, *American* 59), and two of whose songs are in her collected sheet music. She went to two concerts in Boston in 1846, which she mentions in a letter of September 8; Leyda indicates that these were a program "of secular music and songs" presented by the "Teachers' Class of the Boston Academy" and a performance of Haydn's oratorio "The Creation" (Leyda 1: 112). She attended concerts by the celebrated Jenny Lind, whom Dwight's Journal called "the dear and sovereign Queen of Song" (Sablosky, *What* 25), and by the Germania Musical Society, a touring band of about twenty players, based in Boston, with a repertoire including symphonic works by Mozart, Beethoven, Hayden, Mendelssohn, Weber, Schumann, and Rossini (Sablosky, *What* 17–21).[19]

---

[17]Harriet Hawes is listed in the *Annual Catalogue of the Mount Holyoke Female Seminary* for 1847–48 (Amherst: J. S. and C. Adams, 1848).

[18]Susan Dickinson's sketch "Two Generations of Amherst Society," written before her death in 1913, recalls the Senior Levee given annually by the president of Amherst College: "There was music, with the piano," and she mentions women singing there such songs as "O Summer Night!" and "Wert thou in the cauld blast." She tells, too, of a typical party at the Sweetsers, where "voices somewhat decadent sang sweetly though with a timid tremulo, 'Are we almost there? Said the dying girl,' 'Coming Through the Rye,' etc., or a resident basso of solemn mien, with a tone really below any pitch known to musical necessity, was prevailed upon after the habitual prolonged urging to give us, 'Rocked in the Cradle of the Deep,' the refrain being held with such sustained power I am sure the glasses in the corner cupboards tinkled from the jar. By this time music was in the air, and aroused to an almost vivacious gaiety, all stood about the piano and sang together, 'Lest auld acquaintance be forgot,' 'America,' and 'Scotland's burning!' " (171, 176). (Martha Dickinson Bianchi's version of this sketch identifies the voice singing "Are we almost there?" as Lavinia Dickinson's, but without reference to either sweetness or decadence [35–38].)

[19]Referring to the performance of Jenny Lind in a letter, Dickinson's rhetoric stands in sharp contrast to the inflated praise of Dwight (and most of the American public), but she does admit to being impressed by "some notes from her 'Echo [Song]'—the Bird sounds from the 'Bird Song' and some of her curious trills" (L 46). Of the Germania Orchestra, she said, "I never heard [such] *sounds* before" (L 118); that sentence has a more Dickinsonian ring and probably conveys her meaning better without Johnson's bracketed editorial insertion.

As is well known, one of the delights of her later years of seclusion was to have visitors play and sing for her. A curious reminiscence of one of these occasions is that of Clara Bellinger Green, who recounts a visit made in 1877 after Dickinson asked to hear Clara's sister Nora sing a solo version of the Twenty-third Psalm as she had sung it earlier in the village church; the poet listened from upstairs, then came down to meet the two sisters and their brother in the library and to express her pleasure:

> "Except for the birds," she said, "yours is the first song I have heard for many years. I have long been familiar with the voice and the laugh of each one of you, and I know, too, your brother's whistle as he trudges by the house." . . . She told us of her early love for the piano and confided that, after hearing Rubinstein [?]—I believe it was Rubinstein— play in Boston, she had become convinced that she could never master the art and had forthwith abandoned it once and for all, giving herself up then wholly to literature.[20]

This recollection suggests two rather remarkable things: first, that Dickinson may once have had serious musical ambitions that she relinquished for poetry, and second, that she had an auditory relationship to a town and its people that she had closed out of her sight.[21] What part her persistent eye problems may have played in magnifying the importance of her hearing one can only guess.

Other friends recall her piano playing. Kate Scott Anthon, for example, remembers Emily Dickinson "playing weird and beautiful melodies, all from her own inspiration . . ." (Leyda, 1: 367). Writing to her friend John Graves in 1856, Dickinson reminds him of old times together and remarks, "I play the old, odd tunes yet, which used to flit about your head after honest hours—and wake dear Sue, and madden me, with their grief and fun . . ." (L 184). Richard Sewall, her biographer, writes, "Her particular talent, it seems, was for improvising"; implicit in his statement is a surmise that she may have experimented with extending the conventional range of music as she extended the conventions of poetry (407). The suggestion is intriguing, particularly if we think of her main extension of the phonic conventions of poetry—her "weird" rhymes. . . .

[20]Leyda 272–73. Leyda dates this event in June 1877. He takes his account from Green's article in *The Bookman* 60 (Nov. 1924). Dickinson mentions hearing the song in a letter to Higginson in January 1878 (L 533).

[21]Green was right in expressing doubt about whether it was Anton Rubinstein the poet had heard. Dickinson *was* deeply impressed with the celebrated composer and performer; in a letter of 1873 she wrote to Frances Norcross, "Glad you heard Rubinstein. . . . He makes me think of polar nights Captain Hall could tell! Going from ice to ice! What an exchange of awe!" (L 390). (Hall was an explorer who died in the Arctic in 1871.) But she could not have heard Rubinstein perform. He did not come to the United States until 1872, after she had ceased to leave Amherst. It is not clear what pianist she might have mentioned to Green. She may have attended concerts during other trips to Boston; few letters survive from the months she spent in Boston in 1864 and 1865. In any case, her extravagant praise of Rubinstein indicates that she maintained a vivid interest in the musical life beyond her seclusion. (See also L 907, where she asks to know what tunes please her cousin.)

Works Cited

Abrams M. H. *The Mirror and the Lamp: Romantic Theory and the Critical Tradition.* New York: Norton, 1958.

Allen, Gay Wilson. *American Prosody.* New York: American Book, 1935.

Amherst College Biographical Record of the Graduates and Non-Graduates, Class of 1846. Amherst, Mass., 1927.

Anderson, Charles R. *Emily Dickinson's Poetry: Stairway of Surprise.* New York: Holt, 1960.

Annual Catalogue of the Mount Holyoke Female Seminary. Amherst: J. C. and C. Adams, 1848.

Babbitt, Irving. *The New Laokoon.* Boston: Houghton, 1910.

Browning, Elizabeth Barrett. *Aurora Leigh.* New York: C. S. Francis, 1859.

———. *The Letters.* Ed. Frederic G. Kenyon. Vol. 1. London: John Murray, 1898.

———. *The Poems.* 2 vols. New York: C. S. Francis, 1852.

Carlyle, Thomas. *On Heroes, Hero-Worship and the Heroic in History.* Oxford: Geoffrey Cumberlege, 1904.

Coppee, Henry. *A Gallery of Distinguished English and American Female Poets.* Philadelphia: E. H. Butler, 1860.

Davidson, James. "Emily Dickinson and Isaac Watts," *Boston Public Library Quarterly* 6 (July 1954), 141–49.

De Jong, Mary G. "Frances Osgood, Sara Helen Whitman, and the 'Poetess.' " Meeting of the Philological Association of the Carolinas, Greensboro, N.C., March 13, 1987.

Dickinson, Emily. *The Letters.* Ed. Thomas H. Johnson and Theodora Van Wagenen Ward. 3 vols. Cambridge, Mass.: Belknap Press of Harvard University Press, 1958.

———. *The Poems: Including Variant Readings Critically Compared with All Known Manuscripts.* Ed. Thomas H. Johnson. 3 vols. Cambridge, Mass.: Belknap Press of Harvard University Press, 1955.

Dickinson, Susan. "Two Generations of Amherst Society." In *Essays on Amherst's History*, ed. Theodore P. Greene, 168–88. Amherst: Vista Trust, 1978.

Emerson, Ralph Waldo. "Merlin." In *Poems*, Vol. 9 of *The Complete Works.*, ed. Edward Waldo Emerson, 120–24. Boston: Houghton, 1903–4. 12 vols.

England, Martha Winburn and John Sparrow. *Hymns Unbidden: Donne, Herbert, Blake, Emily Dickinson and the Hymnographers.* New York: New York Public Library, 1966.

Fairchild, B. H. *Such Holy Song.* Kent: Kent State University Press, 1980.

Freeman, Margaret Helen. "Emily Dickinson's Prosody: A Study in Metrics." Dissertation, University of Massachusetts, 1972.

Hecht, Anthony. "The Riddles of Emily Dickinson." *New England Review* 1 (1978), 1–24.

Johnson, Thomas H. *Emily Dickinson: An Interpretive Biography.* Cambridge, Mass.: Harvard University Press, 1955.

Jones, Amelia D. "Memorabilia of Mary Lyon." Archives of Mount Holyoke College.

Juhasz, Suzanne. *The Undiscovered Continent: Emily Dickinson and the Space of the Mind.* Bloomington: Indiana University Press, 1983.

Kerman, Joseph. *Contemplating Music.* Cambridge, Mass.: Harvard University Press, 1985.

Lanier, Sidney. *The Science of English Verse.* New York: Scribner, 1880.

Leyda, Jay. *The Years and Hours of Emily Dickinson.* 2 vols. New Haven, Conn.: Yale University Press, 1960.

Lindberg-Seyersted, Brita. *The Voice of the Poet: Aspects of Style in the Poetry of Emily Dickinson.* Cambridge, Mass.: Harvard University Press, 1968.

May, Caroline. *The American Female Poets: with Biographical and Critical Notices.* New York: Leavitt and Allen, 1869.

Moore, Thomas. "What the Bee is to the Floweret." In *Irish Melodies*, 57–58. Philadelphia: E. H. Butler, 1865.

O'Donnell, Brennan P. "Wordsworth's Verse Forms: A Descriptive Catalogue." M.A. Thesis, University of North Carolina at Chapel Hill, 1983.

Pater, Walter. *The Renaissance: Studies in Art and Poetry. The 1893 Text,* ed. Donald L. Hill. Berkeley: University of California Press, 1980.

Poe, Edgar A. "Letter to Mr. _____." In *Edgar Allan Poe: Poetry and Tales*, 10–17. Library of America Series 19, 1984.

Porter, David T. *The Art of Emily Dickinson's Early Poetry.* Cambridge, Mass.: Harvard University Press, 1966.

———. *Dickinson: The Modern Idiom.* Cambridge, Mass.: Harvard University Press, 1981.

Sablosky, Irving. *American Music.* Chicago: University of Chicago Press, 1969.

———. *What They Have Heard: Music in America 1852–1881; From the Pages of "Dwight's Journal of Music."* Baton Rouge: Louisiana State University Press, 1985.

Saintsbury, George. *A History of English Prosody.* 3 vols. London: Macmilan, 1908.

Sewall, Richard B. *The Life of Emily Dickinson.* New York: Farrar, Straus, and Giroux, 1974.

Spaeth, Sigmund. *A History of Popular Music in America.* New York: Random House, 1948.

St. Armand, Barton Levi. *Emily Dickinson and Her Culture: The Soul's Society.* Cambridge: Cambridge University Press, 1984.

Verlaine, [Paul Marie]. "Art poetique." In *Oeuvres Poetiques Completes*, ed. Jacque Borel, 326. Paris: Gallimard, 1962.

Waggoner, Hyat H. *Emerson as Poet.* Princeton, NJ.: Princeton University Press, 1974.

Walker, Cheryl. *The Nightingale's Burden: Women Poets and American Culture before 1900.* Bloomington: Indiana University Press, 1982.

Walsh, John Evangelist. *The Hidden Life of Emily Dickinson.* New York: Simon and Schuster, 1971.

Watts, Isaac. *The Psalms, Hymns, and Spiritual Songs, of the Rev. Isaac Watts D.D.: To Which are Added Select Hymns from Other Authors; and Directions for Musical Expression.* Ed. Samuel Worcester. Boston: Crocker and Brewster, 1834. (Owned by Emily Dickinson's father.)

Wellek, René, and Austin Warren. "Euphony, Rhythm, and Meter," 158–73. In *Theory of Literature*. New York: Starcourt, 1956.

Wesling, Donald. *The Chances of Rhyme: Device and Modernity*. Berkeley: University of California Press, 1980.

———. *The New Poetries.* Lewisburg, Pa.: Bucknell University Press, 1985.

Wolosky, Shira. *Emily Dickinson. A Voice of War.* New Haven, Conn.: Yale University Press, 1984.

Wood, Ann D. "The 'Scribbling Women' and Fanny Fern: Why Women Wrote." *American Quarterly* 23 (1971), 3–24.

The Poet as Cartoonist:
Pictures Sewed to Words

Martha Nell Smith

Upon the publication of *Poems by Emily Dickinson* in 1890, Susan Dickinson lamented to William Hayes Ward, editor of the *Independent*, "I have a little article in mind, with illustrations of [Emily's] own, showing her witty humorous side, which has all been left out of [Lavinia's] vol. [as Sue chose to call that first edition produced by Higginson and Mabel Loomis Todd]" (H Lowell Autograph).[1] Dickinson's most constant audience, Sue recognized the importance of drawings and cartooning paste-ups to her sister-in-law's artistic objectives. With the exception of a sketch to her brother Austin, all the layouts under study in this section were sent to Sue. In these, Dickinson appears to interrogate the ideology of individual authorship in several ways. At the very least, all of these, like Dickinson's ellipses or gaps in expression, require a reader's collaboration to produce and reproduce meaningful texts, and, with increasing numbers of Dickinson critics, I concur that this strategy is not simply technique, but is also philosophical statement. And I will add that it is one to which Sue was privy. Recognizing that they are bound to arouse audience interest, biographers Martha Dickinson Bianchi and Richard Sewall have printed photographs of her sketches. Many will remember Sewall's reproduction of Dickinson's sketch to John Graves—two tombstones with the caption "In memory of AEolus," the invisible but powerful (and masculine) wind (Sewall 374). Sewall does not comment much on the sketch, calling it Dickinsoniana, but in the context of lifelong poetic production and dedication to her art, perhaps this is a caricature of the dire circumstance, writer's block, and "in memory of poetic inspiration." Or, in a time when male anxiety ran at a feverish pitch worrying about that "damned mob of scribbling women," and when men of letters more sympathetic to women writers like Higginson observed that "during the last half century more books have been written by women and about women than during all the previous uncounted ages" and that the "yearning for a literary career is now almost greater among women than

Reprinted from *Comic Power in Emily Dickinson* by Suzanne Juhasz, Christanne Miller, and Martha Nell Smith. Copyright © 1993. By permission of the author and the University of Texas Press.

[1]March 23, 1891, letter, quoted by Millicent Todd Bingham (*Ancestors' Brocades* 118). Manuscripts at the Houghton Library, Harvard University, will be indicated by the initial "H" and the library catalog letter and/or number.

among men" (*Women and the Alphabet* 5, 232), perhaps it burlesques the death of the male possession of literature; or, during a time when influential figures like Higginson anxiously observed the "American style of execution, in all high arts" to be "yet hasty and superficial" and exclaimed that Americans needed "the opportunity of high culture somewhere," perhaps the sketch satirizes conventional hierarchies between lofty and low art (Levine 213).[2]

However liberal suffragist Higginson may have been, his ideas about what constitutes important literature were quite conventional and did not extend to concur with Sue that Dickinson's humorous sketches and layouts were significant. His history of American literature, produced after the three volumes of Dickinson's poetry, reveals his staunch beliefs about major and minor literature, high and low culture. There he writes of "concentrating attention on leading figures, instead of burdening the memory with a great many minor names and data," of "pure literature," and of "the highest" and "important" literature and authors (Higginson and Boynton iii, 123).[3] This is important for understanding why he would have deemed Dickinson's cartoons unsuitable for inclusion in the volumes featuring her literature. Since he regarded them as ephemeral products of "feminine" popular culture, Higginson could not imagine how they might serve his presentation of a woman poet concerned with essential truths, sentiments, and finer feelings. For him they would exemplify the "epistolary brilliancy" he readily attributed to women's letters and which he proclaimed must be worked over much more thoroughly in order to be converted "into literature." "The trouble is," Higginson argued, "that into the new [literary] work upon which they [women] are just entering they have not yet brought their thoroughness to bear." Undoubtedly he would argue that, like the poetry collected by Rufus Griswold in *Female Poets of America*, Dickinson's handwritten productions would best be "utterly forgotten" because, presumably dashed off and lacking thoroughness, they have "no root." Though they most assuredly would demonstrate her "cleverness," he would not recognize that such humorous endeavors might teach readers something about the higher aims of her art (*Women and the Alphabet* 229–231).[4] Searching Dickinson's works for the topics contemporarily considered both most important and most marketable—Life, Love, Nature, Time and Eternity—and organizing her lyrics accordingly, these first editors of *Poems by Emily Dickinson* share some assumptions with "serious" critics who devalue and marginalize popular culture.

---

[2]A frequent essayist in periodicals like the *Atlantic Monthly* and the *Woman's Journal*, Higginson wrote extensively on American culture, abolition, women writers, and women's rights. The first quotation here is from his 1859 *Atlantic Monthly* essay "Ought Women to Learn the Alphabet," the second from "Study and Work," both of which are reprinted in *Women and the Alphabet*. Lawrence W. Levine both quotes from Higginson's 1866 *Atlantic Monthly* essay "A Plea for Culture" and points out that Higginson defines culture in a "resolutely classical and European-oriented manner" and often appends the term with the adjective "high."

[3]In a section on "minor" women writers, Higginson describes Emily Dickinson in a paragraph and reproduces a facsimile of his copy of "Safe in their Alabaster Chambers" (Higginson and Boynton 130–131).

[4]Of women writers and poets like those presented by Griswold, Higginson says, "Young girls appear one after another: each writes a single clever story or single sweet poem, and then disappears forever. . . . Nobody doubts that women have cleverness enough" (*Women and the Alphabet* 231).

Analyzing the relative insignificance with which the reproductions of popular culture have been regarded, Andreas Huyssen reminds us of "the notion which gained ground during the nineteenth century that mass culture is somehow associated with women while real, authentic culture remains the prerogative of men" (47).[5] By editing her poetry and imposing a conventional notion of thoroughness on her work, Higginson and Loomis Todd in one sense sought to elevate the status of the woman poet Dickinson as a producer of lasting culture with roots. However, by grouping her lyrics into topics highlighted in the widely read anthologies of female poetry edited by Rufus Griswold, Caroline May, and Thomas Buchanan Read, Higginson and Loomis Todd also produced a poet more readily bought and sold. But their editions were commodities with pretensions to a cultivated seriousness that inclusion of Dickinson's humorous illustrations might call into question. To take Sue's suggestions and make less conventional editions of her poetry "showing her witty humorous side" would have meant including items believed to be products of "low," dispensable, parlor culture inconsequential to weighty literary objectives. In contrast to their opinion, Sue apparently judged the distinction between "high" and "low" invidious, as do feminists and many other critics today. In fact, her brief critique is a precursor of Barton St. Armand's recent assertion that the "art of assemblage" or " 'quilting' of elite and popular ideas onto a sturdy folk form, frame, or fabric" is paradigmatical for Dickinson's poetic designs and the range of her comic expressions (9–10).

Since the layouts and sketches, handmade greeting cards, scrapbooks, and herbariums (collections or "books" of dried plant specimens mounted and systematically arranged for reference) fashioned by so many women of Dickinson's class were regarded by editors like Higginson as clever products hastily made and not as items for serious study, they were treated as if they would undermine important critical goals.[6] Of course the threat of mass culture, "against which high art has to shore up its terrain," is that one will be seduced into enacting Marx's nightmare, lose oneself in delusions and daydreams, and thus become primarily a passive consumer and not an active producer involved with the complex pleasures offered by "high" art (Huyssen 56).[7] Similarly, the detraction from deliberative study that Higginson surely assumed the layouts and sketches posed is that they offer merely an occasion for consumption but not for critical engagement, that they tell us a bit about Dickinson's personal pleasures but very little about her artistic designs and literary processes. That miscalculation proved profound, for writerly participations on the part of readers are precisely what they require.

---

[5]Critical treatment of *Uncle Tom's Cabin*, nineteenth-century America's best seller, provides a perfect literary example of how popular literature has traditionally been devalued in the academy as second-rate. See Jane Tompkins, "Sentimental Power" (122–146).

[6]For discussion of the cultivations common for women of Dickinson's class (like tending a conservatory with a wide range of flowers, ferns, and exotic plants and making herbariums), see Jean McClure Mudge, *Emily Dickinson and the Image of Home* (esp. 145–172), and St. Armand's presentation of Martha Dickinson Bianchi's unfinished essay, "Emily Dickinson's Garden" in *Emily Dickinson International Society Bulletin*.

[7]As Huyssen points out, Tania Modleski analyzes the relationship of the production/consumption paradigm in "Femininity as Mas(s)querade: A Feminist Approach to Mass Culture." For a complementary analysis of the threat to the pretensions of "high" art raised by late twentieth-century popular culture, see Martha Nell Smith, "Sexual Mobilities in Bruce Springsteen: Performance as Commentary."

When Dickinson produced her cutouts, she did not turn to shopping catalogs and popular magazines so much as she turned to her Bible, her *New England Primer*, and her father's Dickens, texts considered on the one hand sacred and, on the other, inviolable as literary entertainment and guides to proper speech. To observe only that these mutilations of her Bible or of Dickens or of a guide for using language properly are irreverent misses the more important points to be made about them, for these manipulations of texts are transformations, opportunities for Emily Dickinson and her readers to exert control over expression by remaking supposedly fixed utterances and thereby challenge conventional authorities in a constructive way. By manipulating the material embodiments of texts, Dickinson clowns and toys with convention, and thereby overturns the dicta of her day. Careful examination of four layouts and sketches reveals how she critically exposes five different types of cultural authority by "cartooning": that of poetic tradition, that of patriotism, that of romantic thralldom, that of the patriarchal family, and that established by the rigidities of the printing press.

The first layout to consider is also the simplest: atop "Whose cheek is this?" (H B 186; P 82), Dickinson attached a cutout of a robin from her *New England Primer*. The poem reads:

> Whose cheek is this?
> What rosy face
> Has lost a blush today?
> I found her, 'pleiad', in the woods
> And bore her safe away.
>
> Robins, in the tradition
> Did cover such with leaves,
> But which the Cheek—
> And which the pall
> *My* scrutiny deceives

When she sent this poem to Sue, Dickinson sewed or pinned a flower just to the right of the cutout of the robin glued onto this page (or leaf), and the questions comprising the first three lines of the poem refer to that wilting token. The "rescue" of this little star of the woods is to a "safety" of death; it will be preserved, but not as ebullient, colorful, and full of life. In preservation the flower "Has lost a blush," is dried and withered in decease. The robins "in the tradition" are the versifying multitudes covering real life by writing the many "leaves," pages upon pages, about nature, love, life, God, time and eternity, the popular topics for last century's American poetry. Especially when one keeps in mind the wide circulation of Fanny Fern's *Fern Leaves from Fanny's Portfolio* (1853) and its probable influence on Whitman's producing *Leaves of Grass* (1855), Dickinson's pun is obvious.[8] The

---

[8]In an 1853 letter to Austin, Lavinia mentions reading Fanny Fern's work to their father: "Father was *thoughtful* enough to spend last evening with us *socially* & as he seemed rather dull, I endeavored to entertain him by reading spicey passages from Fern leaves, where upon he brightened up sufficiently to correct me as I went along, advising me to put in all the little words as they would'nt hurt me &c. You can imagine the rest as you have heard such like before" (Bingham *Home* 312).

Copy of "Whose cheek is this?" sent to Sue. By permission of the Houghton Library, Harvard University.

query of the last three lines—is poetry killing life into art or giving some semblance of life a new lease on existence—either deceives the speaker or is a question the speaker scrutinizes and regards, perhaps because of its overly simple dichotomies, as deceptive. Like the flower attached to the page, poems idolized wither and die.

Why are the visual props important, and what purpose do they serve? The dying flower makes a three-dimensional cartoon as it helps to clarify the reference of the pronoun "this." The cutout of the robin seems superfluous, yet its significations are not merely decorative. Most likely, Sue would have recognized the snippet as one from the *New England Primer*. Importantly, Dickinson situates the grammar book cutout so the robin faces the flower or pleiad. Since "pleiad" may also refer to the seven tragic poets of Alexandria, perhaps the lyric with layout is designed to suggest that the robins "in the tradition," or the poetesses "extricating humanity from some hopeless ditch" (L 380), make elementary or grammar book sense of tragic poetry. Clearly the layout and attachment function as commentary on the poem, and the reader must develop their intertextual connotations. Doing so, one cannot help but recognize nor resist being amused by Dickinson's caricature of nineteenth-century popular poetry. Dressed up with a souvenir from nature's bounty and a woodcut of a warbling thrush commonly associated with merry times, what appears to be a relatively insignificant ditty of a lyric in fact mirthfully interrogates common poetic praxis.

Such implicit demands on the reader are evident in her other illustrations. A sketch incorporated into a letter to her brother in the early 1850s lampoons Congress, particularly the Whigs (her father's party), hence privately to Austin pasquinades patriotic duty. The rather conservative Edward Dickinson was a member of the House of Representatives, but his eldest daughter used his official stationery liberally when she wrote her brother. The poet draws around the diminutive embossed likeness of the U.S. Capitol building, adding a smokestack to its dome and, on its left, a little stick figure shuffling along. Beneath the cartoon is the caption, "Member from 10*th!*" Thomas H. Johnson describes this sketch in a brief editorial note, interpreting it as "a striding Indian" in feathered headdress approaching the smoking dome. Indeed, the little figure has something sticking straight up off his head, but it is not plainly a headdress. Since he was a Whig (and it was a dying party), and since his frustrations with Washington were no secret, Dickinson might well be depicting her exasperated father with his hair standing on end—or "flipping his wig"—as he approaches the house of government. Whatever one's interpretation, her humor is obvious. As Katharine Zadravec has noted, the poet "is satirizing her congressman father's arrival in Washington" (27).

This is very much in keeping with and lends credibility to a story her niece told about Aunt Emily's visit to Washington while her father served in Congress:

> She had a keen scent for the meanings hid beneath the goodly outside of diplomacy and watched for developments in home and foreign policies with surprising acumen. The winter she was at Willard's, during her Father's congressional career, she is said to have astonished his political friends by her insight and created quite a sensation by her wit, though the only story I recall now was of her saying to a prim old Chief Justice of the

Enlargement of stick figure.

(A 617; L 144)[9]

Copy of cartoon satirizing their congressman father's arrival in Washington sent to Austin. By permission of the Trustees of Amherst College.

Supremest sort, when the plum pudding on fire was offered—"Oh Sir, may one eat of hell fire with impunity here?" (Bianchi xiii–xiv)

The wry query reflects a sensibility similar to that evident in the presumably shocked figure approaching the smokestack-adorned capitol. Sister Lavinia's somewhat lighthearted account of Mr. Dickinson's arrival in Washington complements Emily's sketch. According to Vinnie, a man accustomed to enjoying power over almost all of his neighbors in Amherst felt a little intimidated in the halls of Congress: "He told us in his last letter, that he had been sending out his cards to various persons of rank. He says he dont know much about etiquet but is trying to learn [*sic*]" (Bingham, *Home* 329). Both Emily's drawing and the anecdote about her visit to the District of Columbia evince efforts on the daughter's part to put a humorous spin on what were by all accounts frustrating times for her father and anxious times for a family concerned for him. What could have been dreary concerned responses are instead comically deflating jabs at pompous politicos. By engaging in these kinds of epistolary and dinnertime repartee, she challenges blind belief in and obeisance to provincial institutions like the government of these United States.

Twenty-five years later Dickinson was breezy but unequivocal when to Abigail Cooper she remarked upon her alienation from the officially delineated nation:

"My Country, 'tis of thee," has always meant the Woods—to me—
"Sweet Land of Liberty," I trust is your own—

(L 509, about 1877)

---

[9]Manuscripts at Amherst College will be indicated by the initial "A" and the library catalog number.

A few years after that irreverent note, she, with considerable levity, was even more forthright about her feeling for patriotism and Fatherland in a letter to Elizabeth Holland:

> "George Washington was the Father of his Country"—"George Who?"
> That sums all Politics to me—but then I love the Drums, and they are busy now—
> (L 950, late autumn 1884)

The United States is "their" and "his" country, never Dickinson's, and it is the sound of patriotic pageantry, of men in unison, not its sense, that amuses and/or attracts her. Likewise, July 4th is a holiday when "Little Boys are commemorating the advent of their Country" (L 650, July 1880). As she had more than twenty years earlier, through ironic deflation, Dickinson mocks the heromaking institutions of men, governments, and their armies. These sociopolitical commentaries are all the more startling to today's reader since they come from a poet about whom it is a commonplace to say that "she all but ignored the stirring events of her time," that she cared not a whit for national causes, and was "never discursive on historical matters" (Sewall 535, 445). Through these comic portrayals readers can clearly see that Dickinson had not just a moment's but several decades worth of doubts about the American democratic process. But as Nancy Walker observes, for Dickinson, "the expression of freedom was laughter" and wit "provides the detachment from convention which allows her an identity separate" from that which customary religious, social, and political commitments "would demand" ("Emily Dickinson and the Self" 63). Whether because the received biographies render her as apolitical, or because she has been considered more witty and ironic than boldly humorous and comic, or for some other reason distorting literary historiography, her challenges to the official political institutions of her time have not been descried. When the point of Dickinson's humor, "her usual means of declaring independence," has been similarly overlooked or her topic misconstrued, her interrogation of other powerful cultural or social institutions has likewise hardly been noticed (Walker, "Emily Dickinson and the Self" 63).

Interpreting "A poor—torn Heart—a tattered heart— / That sat it down to rest," (H B 175; P 78), some have argued that this poem was written about the same time as the infamous "Master" letters, and so is yet another testament to Dickinson's unrequited dejection and thralldom to romantic love and her desire to join the ranks of those ensconced in the institution of marriage. Indeed, the handwriting does match that of the penciled "Master" draft beginning "Oh' did I offend it" (A 829, 829a; L 248).[10] Yet the two pictures Dickinson clipped from her father's copy of Dickens' *The Old Curiosity Shop* suggest anything but interpretation without irony. In fact, by making a "cartoon" of what has been judged to be one of her most sentimental lyrics, she arguably critiques the one-dimensional, cartoon-like

---

[10]To compare handwriting, readers should consult Franklin's facsimile reproduction of *The Master Letters of Emily Dickinson* (esp. 21–29). In *Rowing in Eden*, I examine this cartoon specifically in relation to the "Master" letters.

Copy of "A poor—torn Heart" sent to Sue. By permission of the Houghton Library, Harvard University.

quality of nineteenth-century notions relegating women to a "separate sexual caste" and defining females exclusively by their relationships to love.[11] If the speaker voices her grief, she has become able to joke about it, is in control, not driven out of control and into effusive, unreflective expression.

The poem reads:

A poor—torn Heart—a tattered heart,
That sat it down to rest,
Nor noticed that the Ebbing Day
Flowed silver to the West,

[11]Various impacts of the nineteenth-century notions and theories of separate spheres for male and female have been studied by a wide variety of critics. One of the most influential has been Nancy Cott's *The Bonds of Womanhood: "Woman's Sphere" in New England, 1780–1835.* For commentary attending specifically to American women poets, see Cheryl Walker, *The Nightingale's Burden: Women Poets and American Culture before 1900* (esp. 21–58).

Nor noticed night did soft descend,
Nor Constellation burn╲
Intent upon a vision
Of Latitudes unknown╲

The Angels, happening that way
This dusty heart espied╲
Tenderly took it up from toil,
And carried it to God╲
There—Sandals for the Barefoot╲
There—gathered from the gales
Do the blue Havens by the hand
Lead the wandering sails.

When Dickinson sent this poem next door to her sister-in-law, she appended a picture of Little Nell being comforted by her grandfather to the top of the poem with pink thread; then, also with pink thread, she bound a cutout of Nell being ferried to heaven by a host of angels to the bottom of the poem. This appears to have been attached in such a way so that when the missive was unfolded, the bottom picture of Little Nell among the seraphs popped up—like a pop-up greeting card—to the reader. In this context calling attention to her appropriation of Dickens' work and the poem's hyperbolic overstatement, a lyric that might be either disregarded or read earnestly as religious or romantic sentiment becomes the cartooning play of one writer responding to another.[12] The fact that her own surname christened her "Dickens' son" was surely not lost on this writer so given to puns and verbal play. What is also clear from Dickinson making this poem in direct response to Dickens and then sending it to Sue is the women's communion and mutual play as readers, kinds of interpretive interaction common among America's literate classes.

As Cathy Davidson has pointed out after examining the responses of earlier nineteenth-century American readers, in their "inscriptions, the marginalia, and even the physical condition of surviving copies of early American novels" twentieth-century readers encounter century-old, seemingly extemporaneous poems written to instruct borrowers about how to treat a particular copy of a book, poems of reverie about a novel's character, and poems inscribed in response to a novel's especially emotional passages. Commentaries on a novel's moral or entertainment value are also evident, and in a copy of *Charlotte Temple* one reader even doodled a rendition of the heroine. Besides revealing "a surprising range of reader response" and books prized for decades by the same reader or group of readers, some names and inscriptions in books begin "to suggest the outlines of a contemporaneous interpretive community"— books passed back and forth between siblings, friends, acquaintances, and be-

---

[12]For example, Mary Ann C. McGuire overlooks the ironies suggested by this poem in "A Metaphorical Pattern in Emily Dickinson." Jack L. Capps also appears to read the poem as an uncritical response to "the image of Little Nell's mourning grandfather" (97–98).

queathed to subsequent generations (75–79). Dickinson's production of "A poor—torn Heart—a tattered heart" for Sue is part of that genteel world of reader response.

Dickinson's cartooning cutout works to undercut any culturally predetermined insistence that hers is simply a reiterative poem articulating Little Nell's miserable flight into angelic rescue. What might be read all too solemnly when divorced from the illustrations Dickinson attached cannot be read without humor with her original context restored. What is unusual about Emily Dickinson's act is that she does not limit herself to the borders of leaves or back pages of *The Old Curiosity Shop* itself as do the readers of Susanna Rowson's *Charlotte Temple, A Spelling Dictionary,* and Samuel Relf's *Infidelity, or the Victims of Sentiment* whom Davidson describes. Instead of situating her poetic commentary on the Dickensian scenes so that it is marginal, Dickinson scissors illustrations originally bound into the novel and, by attaching them to her poem, subordinates the printed text to her holographic response. The poet's production invites readers to peruse both the poem and Dickens' story again, reading them "backward," against conventional instructions, lest "the plunge from the front overturn" sense (PF 30).[13] Reading straightforwardly, without admitting any role for a sense of humor, produces a kind of nonsense by consigning Little Nell and female characters similarly fated to only one sort of fortune and their readers to facile responses that either mawkishly identify with or cynically explain away such scenes. In this conventional scheme of things, failures of authorial and readerly imaginations prevail.

Dickinson's reformulation, on the other hand, both evinces and demands imaginative interpretation. By cutting up Dickens' novel, Dickinson demonstrates that no plot is fixed. By attaching illustrations included in *The Old Curiosity Shop* to a poem superficially reiterative of the novel's sentiments, she invites readers to consider how heavy-handed and gratuitous Dickens and/or his publisher chose to be. Most important, by removing the illustrations from the context of the novel itself and attaching them to a seemingly simple lyric in which the rhythms and rhymes are subtly unsettled, Dickinson encourages readers to peruse beyond the predictable responses. Scanning the poem, a reader's conventional expectations for an iambic tetrameter line are immediately disrupted by a spondaic second foot in the first line. To begin the poem with such heavy syllabic emphasis ironically attentuates any straightforward tone by overstressing both the pathetic singularity of and the rending infliction to "A poor—torn Heart." More suggestively, the first stanza's regularly alternating tetrameter, trimeter iambic lines are broken in the seventh by the three-and-a-half-foot "Intent upon a vision," unless, of course, the reader enunciates the last word out of its two-syllable modern English—*vizh-ən*—and back into some bastardized three-syllable rendition—*vizh-e-ən*—pretentiously informed by its Middle English and Old

---

[13]References to Dickinson's prose fragments reproduced in Johnson and Ward's edition of her letters will use "PF" and give the number assigned by Johnson.

French origins. In the second stanza, a three-and-a-half-foot fifth line appears where one expects a four foot line in "There—Sandals for the Barefoot." Amusingly, the extra syllable is "-foot," left bare of its iambic companion. As Paul Fussell has observed, "poetic meter is a prime physical and emotional constituent of poetic meaning (13)."[14] By over- and understating meter, then, Dickinson urges her readers to inflect the poem with far more than sentimentally sober-minded tones. The death of Little Nell also prompted Oscar Wilde, half a century later, to encourage readers to interpret imaginatively and well beyond convention when he remarked that one must have a heart of stone to read about it without bursting out laughing.

The special effects of Dickinson's cartooning strategies here are not those of an elitism that would belittle readers moved by such scenes as the death of Little Nell. Instead, by mixing media—illustrations from a popular novel with linguistic descriptions of brokenhearted, barefooted, and angelic figures common in popular poetry—Dickinson also mixes tones and in doing so reminds audiences that no singleminded or singlehearted response to a subject is enough. Dickinson's strength as an artist in this instance is akin to the important service Richard Poirier ascribed to the work of the Beatles: "they locate the beauty and pathos of commonplace feelings even while they work havoc with fashionable or tiresome expressions of these feelings" (124). Dickinson's ironic commentary simultaneously remarks upon reading her lyric, Dickens' novel, and the myriad lyrics of "secret sorrow" permeating her culture, as well as upon critical attitudes that would dismiss them all in the name of a hierarchy of proper interests. Implicitly the poem as Dickinson wrote and presented it to Sue challenges the literary cliché of the lovelorn lady, as represented in forms as diverse as Clarissa Harlowe to Emmy pining for Captain Dobbin to Higginson's "virgin recluse." Thus challenging the preconceptions of literary institutions, she eludes a critical control that would classify her as a particular kind of poet; similarly, her works complicated the categorizations of Higginson and Loomis Todd and had to be pruned and rearranged, sometimes dramatically, to fit into them, as when they scissored away the last two stanzas of Dickinson's sardonically bold "A solemn thing—it was— / I said— / A woman— white—to be" (F 14; P 271) to produce a conventionally celebratory bridal tribute, "Wedded."[15]

Apparently, Dickinson also eluded the controlling designs of her father. When she stays too late next door at an Evergreens' fete, she pokes fun at his reprimand by sending a cartooning cutout over to Sue the next morning.

---

[14]Interpreting Dickinson's strategies to impel the reader beyond conventional endings, I am consciously echoing Rachel Blau DuPlessis' examinations of women writers' strategies, though I argue that these tactics appear in women's works long before 1900 and, for that matter, long before Dickinson; see *Writing beyond the Ending: Narrative Strategies of Twentieth-Century Women Writers*.

[15]I discuss the editing of this poem at length in both *Rowing in Eden* and "Gender Issues in Textual Editing of Emily Dickinson."

The text of the note is as follows:

> My "position"!
> Cole⸝

> P.S. — Lest you misapprehend,
> the unfortunate insect upon
> the *left* is Myself, while the
> Reptile upon the *right⸝* is my
> more immediate friends, and
> connections.
>
>   As Ever⸝
>   Cole⸝

Clipped from her *New England Primer* is the illustration for the moral lesson "Young Timothy / Learnt sin to fly." The cartoon "shows a youth pursued by an upright wolf" or dragon-like "creature with forked tail," and is signed "Cole" (H B 114; L 214). "To the note" Thomas Johnson found "another attached by Mrs.

Copy of "My 'position'!" sent to Sue. By permission of the Houghton Library, Harvard University.

Bianchi: 'Sent over the morning after a revel—when my Grandfather with his lantern appeared suddenly to take Emily home the hour nearing indecent midnight'" (L 214 n.; see also Bianchi, *Life and Letters* 156). Most likely this signature refers to the English painter of American landscapes, Thomas Cole, and more specifically to Bryant's poem, "To Cole, the Painter, Departing for Europe," which beseeches Cole to carry a "living image" of America with him. The poem concludes: "Keep that earlier, wilder image [of America] bright." Dickinson's recollection of the revel the night before is certainly "wilder" than the company of her father. By naming herself Cole and subtly alluding to Bryant, Dickinson both authorizes her complaint by aligning herself and her friends with some of the most respected figures of the day and demonstrates her good-humored reception of her father's overbearing reprimand through the jollity conveyed by such a ludicrous comparison. In light of her father's disapproval, her lighthearted sanguine response is further conveyed by the fact that she represents herself as one of the little beasts almost universally received as pests and depicts her friends as mythical reptilian creatures frequently associated with obstacles to be battled and overcome to complete successful quests. Her father's retrieval of his eldest daughter from an evening of sociability and fun is thus compared to a heroic venture in this clipping and note that form a cartoon both to make light of his scolding and simultaneously to proclaim Dickinson's affection for the revelers. This playful challenge to patriarchal authority that seems too possessive is not bitter or spiteful, but "makes room for Daddy"; she pokes fun at prim and conventional manners which leave little room for spontaneity, but she does so without acrimony.

There was much that Dickinson could not command about her situation, but she could and did govern her outlook. Recognizing the bold cartooning humor of a woman whose wit has been characterized as understated shakes up assumptions about how precisely literary history has rendered Emily Dickinson. Her privatized role and productions as cartoonist raise many questions about genre, about editing as interpretation and the role of textual reproduction in shaping an author's biography, and about the critical relation of these editorially obscured documents to her poems, letters, and letter-poems, as well as to literature and texts in general. What is plain is that Dickinson takes often empty social forms—the role of friendly neighbor forwarding a flower, the role of fellow reader sharing a ditty about a sobbing character, [and] the role of satisfied guest sending a thank-you note for a riotous evening the night before . . . —and rescues these from the banal by turning them into artistic performances, occasions for displaying her warmth, her wit, her respect for and encouragement of readers. . . .

Works Cited

Bianchi, Martha Dickinson. *The Life and Letters of Emily Dickinson*. Boston and New York: Houghton Mifflin, 1924.

Bingham, Millicent Todd. *Ancestors' Brocades: The Literary Debut of Emily Dickinson*. New York: Harper and Brothers Publishers, 1945.

————. *Emily Dickinson's Home: Letters of Edward Dickinson and His Family*. New York: Harper and Brothers Publishers, 1955.

Capps, Jack L. *Emily Dickinson's Reading, 1836–1886*. Cambridge, Mass.: Harvard University Press, 1966.

Cott, Nancy. *The Bonds of Womanhood: "Woman's Sphere" in New England, 1780–1835*. New Haven and London: Yale University Press, 1977.

Davidson, Cathy N. *Revolution and the Word: The Rise of the Novel in America*. New York and Oxford: Oxford University Press, 1986.

Du Plessis, Rachel Blau. *Writing beyond the Ending: Narrative Strategies of Twentieth Century Women Writers*. Bloomington: Indiana University Press, 1985.

Fussell, Paul. *Poetic Meter and Poetic Form*. New York: Random House, 1965.

Griswold, Rufus, ed. *The Female Poets of America*. Philadelphia: Carey and Hart, 1849.

Higginson, Thomas Wentworth. *Women and the Alphabet: A Series of Essays*. Boston and New York: Houghton Mifflin Co., 1900.

————, and Henry Walcott Boynton. *A Reader's History of American Literature*. Boston, New York, and Chicago: Houghton, Mifflin and Company, 1903.

Huyssen, Andreas. "Mass Culture as Woman: Modernism's Other." In *After the Great Divide: Modernism, Mass Culture, Postmodernism*, 44–62. Bloomington and Indianapolis: Indiana University Press, 1986.

Levine, Lawrence W. *Highbrow/Lowbrow: The Emergence of Cultural Hierarchy in America*. Cambridge, Mass.: Harvard University Press, 1988.

McGuire, Mary Ann C. "A Metaphorical Pattern in Emily Dickinson." *American Transcendental Quarterly* 29 (Winter 1976), 83–85.

Mudge, Jean McClure. *Emily Dickinson and the Image of Home*. Amherst: University of Massachusetts Press, 1974.

Poirier, Richard. *The Performing Self: Compositions and Decompositions in the Languages of Contemporary Life*. New York: Oxford University Press, 1971.

St. Armand, Barton Levi. *The Soul's Society: Emily Dickinson and Her Culture*. Cambridge and New York: Cambridge University Press, 1984.

Sewall, Richard B. *The Life of Emily Dickinson*. New York: Farrar, Straus, & Giroux, 1974.

Smith, Martha Nell. "Gender Issues in Textual Editing of Emily Dickinson." *Women's Studies Quarterly* 19 (Fall/Winter 1991), 78–111.

————. "Sexual Mobilities in Bruce Springsteen: Performance as Commentary." *South Atlantic Quarterly* 90 (Fall 1991), 833–854.

————. *Rowing in Eden: Rereading Emily Dickinson*. Austin: University of Texas Press, 1992.

Tompkins, Jane. "Sentimental Power: *Uncle Tom's Cabin* and the Politics of Literary History." In *Sentimental Designs: The Cultural Work of American Fiction*, 122–146. New York and Oxford: Oxford University Press, 1985.

Walker, Cheryl. *The Nightingale's Burden: Women Poets and American Culture before 1900*. Bloomington: Indiana University Press, 1982.

Walker, Nancy. "Emily Dickinson and the Self: Humor as Identity." *Tulsa Studies in Women's Literature* 2, no. 1 (Spring 1983) 57–68.

Zadravec, Katharine. "Emily Dickinson: A Capital Visitor." In *Emily Dickinson: Letter to the World*, ed. Katharine Zadravec, 26–33. Washington, D.C.: The Folger Shakespeare Library, 1986.

Amplified Contexts: Emily Dickinson and the Fascicles

Sharon Cameron

Why didn't Dickinson publish? There are at least three ways of answering that question: She couldn't publish. She chose not to. Or she *couldn't* choose—that is, she couldn't choose how to publish her poems.

To amplify, briefly, each of these alternatives: She couldn't publish. Because "portfolio" poetry, as Emerson and, after him, Higginson, called it, was not traditional poetry, the fascicles could be considered a solution to a set of cultural prohibitions, or rather cultural prescriptions, which delineate certain features poems should have. Dickinson published her poems in manuscript rather than in print because in the case of those few poems that were printed in her lifetime, as well as of those of her poems which were printed posthumously, the conventions of print, reflecting the traditions of established poetry, violated the characteristics of *Dickinson's* poetry—its grammar, its syntax, its style, its capitalization, its variants, its insistent absence of titles. The handful of poems published in Dickinson's lifetime had their essential features altered. In the face of these constraints and violations, there is no way Dickinson could have printed her poetry in its uniqueness.

A second answer to the question, however, is not that Dickinson couldn't publish, but rather that, like Bradstreet and Taylor, she chose not to. "If fame belonged to me, I could not escape her," a letter written on June 7, 1862, to Higginson explains, obliquely addressing the issue. Earlier in the same letter she archly comments: "I smile when you say that I delay 'to publish'—that being foreign to my thought, as Firmament to Fin—."[1] Therefore she collected her poems privately. Her defiant letters to Higginson, in which she solicited his opinion only to challenge it, to argue with the literary conventions she claimed she wanted to learn, make it possible to suppose that her alternative way of writing poetry required a private space in which conventions could be revised without the revision's being contested.

Reprinted from Sharon Cameron, *Choosing not Choosing* (1992) by permission of the author and the University of Chicago Press.

[1]*The Letters of Emily Dickinson*, ed. Thomas H. Johnson (Cambridge, Mass.: Harvard University Press, 1958), II:408.

In fact, one feature that distinguishes Dickinson's poetry is the way in which the notion of (anyone's) poetic sequences, with their attendant irregularities, is complicated by Dickinson's irregular and fractured notions of form. Dickinson, for example, is not writing sonnets. Her metrics are not standard, nor are her punctuation and rhyme. It may be, then, that formal inventiveness is something that writing in private allowed Dickinson to develop. For Dickinson the process of writing the manuscripts without circulating them opened the space of writing to incorporate the social into the private sphere. Or rather it resituated the social in a liminal space: readers, or potential readers, were established at the edge of the private. They were able to look at the fact of her writing, forced to look at it, while being essentially prevented from looking *into* it. For it was a well-known fact—well known to all who knew Dickinson—that Dickinson was a writer. Thus Dickinson created the public spectre of herself as a writer. But in not publishing her poems, and in not circulating her manuscripts, with the exception of certain lyrics, she achieved the particular feat of writing in public while effectively exempting her writing from public legislation.

But there is also a third way of understanding the packets discovered in the bureau drawer. It is not that Dickinson couldn't publish, or that she chose not to. It is rather that she couldn't choose how to do so. She could not decide whether to publish her poems in sequences or as lyrics, just as where there were variants she could not choose among them. Moreover, at the level of whole poems Dickinson herself treated her manuscripts as versions of each other. She copied them as sequences in the fascicles while sending them as single lyrics to friends—a not exceptional practice among poets writing sequences, although most of the poets who circulated poems as single entities (Gray or Pope, for instance) subsequently published them in sequence. It may well have been the case that Dickinson did not publish her poems because she literally did not know whether to publish them as a sequence or as single lyrics. Or because she could not publish them in both forms at once.

In fact, were there an exceptionalist case to be made with respect to Dickinson, it might be founded on the unprecedented degree to which the formal and the professional are made inseparable in this poetry. Dickinson redefined the profession of the writer to just the extent that she redefined the non-exclusive relation among competing poetic forms. So doing, she misleadingly appeared to stand outside the profession, cherishing instead her vocation. The true writer, or rather the poet, then, was she who invited the comments about form which subsequent poetic form never registered. Dickinson's lyrics evaded the formal conventions Higginson would have imposed on them, and the form of the lyric was itself evaded by the fascicles' restructuring of relations among lyrics. And this defiant originality, this refusal to allow the original to be shaped by the conventional, could be seen to have depended *ultimately,* however negligibly it depended *initially,* on the principled refusal to publish. Thus Dickinson s poetry might be discovered to immortality rather than to the imperfect "professional" readers (Higginson, Samuel Bowles) whose friendship she welcomed but whose literary advice she ignored. In one of her celebrated lyrics on poetry Dickinson designates the poet as "Exterior—to Time—" (P 448). There are poems . . . that confidently predict this outcome for her own work.

Even if there were no exceptionalist case, reading the fascicles in the context of other poetic sequences would clarify important features of Dickinson's fascicles. The critical problems raised by reading Dickinson's poems are of course not unlike the problems raised by reading the poems of Whitman, Herbert, Shakespeare. In this respect, my attempt to recontextualize Dickinson's lyrics is on one level formal. But to say that the attempt is formal is not to say that it is simple. Nor is it to say that what would count as formal is clear.[2] One can, for example, ask about how the narrative told by Dickinson's fascicles is related to other narrative groupings, such as Herbert's or Shakespeare's, which she can be presumed to have read. Such sequences tell similar stories about wooing and not getting. In distinction, however, as I shall elaborate, Dickinson likes to return to a situation in which a lover is dead, and she wishes that he weren't, or to a situation in which she finds a means to negate the consequences of the death. But, one is led to ask, is that the same kind of story—and is it even a story—as the one told in Shakespeare's sonnets?

To amplify the comparison: In a sonnet sequence there are stages, and the end is known. With Shakespeare, however tenuously, the grouping relates to the narrative, and there is a narrative structure. With Herbert, on the other hand, it is hard to claim a narrative even if there is an ending. Perhaps one should ask whether apparent fascicle sequences are more like sonnet sequences or devotional sequences. Such a distinction is suggested because, on the one hand, the speaker in Dickinson has lost the lover, as in many of Shakespeare's sonnets; on the other hand, she has not yet had the lover, but awaits precisely that union, as in Herbert's poems. In this respect the erotic dimensions of the love poem and the spiritual dimensions of the religious poem come together in Dickinson's fascicles because the erotic moment has been *de*-theologized or re-theologized. Even if such contextualizations suggest that Dickinson's groupings are more than chronological, it is important to consider why we should pay more attention to Dickinson's groupings than to those of other poets who reorder single lyrics—more attention to Dickinson groupings than to regroupings of lyric poems by Whitman, Stevens, Yeats, Marianne Moore, or Williams, for instance.

One way of formulating a distinction between Dickinson's fascicles and other sequences is to say that what binds them together is not only or primarily chronology and theme, but rather a structural element. To begin to describe this element is to see something so idiosyncratic that it appears almost unprecedented in nineteenth-century American poetry. For if in Dickinson's fascicles there is a moment that obsessively occurs, the recurrence of this single moment raises the question of

---

[2]In fact, an adequate account of relations among poems would require an edition of them like Stephen Booth's edition of Shakespeare's sonnets, with its accompanying commentary. [Stephen Booth, *Shakespeare's Sonnets*, New Haven, Conn.: Yale University Press, 1978.—Ed.]

whether there is a narrative or whether narrative structures are invoked only inter-
mittently. The moment obsessively returned to might operate more in the manner
of a variant, a phenomenon I shall examine specifically with respect to Fascicle 20.
It will further be seen that if there is a story in the fascicles, it is told discontinu-
ously. In addition, because the poems that do not adhere to this story seem themselves amorphous in topic, the poems that *do* tell the story appear to dominate the
fascicles. Yet since the story is also itself disrupted in the telling, even *by* the
telling, it does not, I shall argue, function as a story. Rather, as suggested, these
"returned to" moments function as variants of something, though what is being
returned to and departed from is never, within the limits of one lyric entity, fully in
view. The story is not fully in view precisely because there is no narrative structure
that would sustain it from without, and also because as the speaker tells the story,
she deflects from and subverts the story being told. Thus the discontinuity exists
along the lines of a narrative that is broken from outside, or rather that is never
fully established. But discontinuity also exists by virtue of the fact that the narrative is disrupted from the inside. Although the binding of the fascicles seems to
promise continuity, seems to promise moments that are either connected or
returned to, in Dickinson's fascicles these reiterated moments are not the same.
But they are also not fully differentiated. Hence there is an apparent self-contra-
diction from "inside" the lyrics, which, I shall argue, must be understood in terms
of the structure of the "variant." It is this combination of narrative discontinuity
and displacement of narrative structures by variants which sets apart the kind of
connections that link Dickinson's poems in the fascicles. They are thus distinguished from the connections made by Shakespeare on the one hand and Herbert
on the other, even as the structure of the variant links the poems in the fascicles
more than poems are linked in "books" by Stevens, Yeats, or even Whitman.

One might further ask how in Dickinson's sequences relations named as "anti-
thetical" and "complementary," which function like variants, structure ostensibly
discrete entities. Perhaps the relation between words in Dickinson's poems, as
emblematized by the dash, is like the relation between poems—not unfigurable,
but oppositely figurable: "I saw no Way—The Heavens were stitched—"/ "I saw
no Way the Heavens were stitched—." The double grammar of the poem's first
line exemplifies at the smallest unit the undecidable meaning generated by the
poem's internal relations as well as by its ambiguous relations to the surrounding
poems in the bifolium. At a different level of formal connection, one might ask
how the variants not only associate words within a poem, but also create antitheti-
cal and complementary associations between poems in the same fascicle, even
when the poems are not placed in proximity. For example, in Fascicle 20, "Dare
you see a soul at the 'White Heat'?" (P 365) and "One need not be a Chamber—to
be Haunted—" (P 670) are connected by the first line of one poem and a variant of
a line of the second poem. The "White Heat" in one poem, a metaphor for passion
ostensibly refined, even purified, then repudiated by death, when encountered in
the variant of the second poem as a specter called "That Whiter Host," inevitably,
if subterraneanly, links the two poems, suggesting that the ghost who is feared is

not generalized at all, but is rather some embodied vestige of a once familiar, now concealed, but still embodied, passion. . . .

We may see [Dickinson's] variants as raising not only a textual question but a question that is other than textual, and so not resolved by determining which edition one reads, because it has to do with the nonidenticality of poem and text. For . . . one can read the Franklin text, but where variants exist, the issue of how to choose among them is still unresolved. We may also see variants in an amplified context: displacing narrative structures as a means of connecting ostensibly discrete poems. We should, in addition, see the variants as raising a fourth concern, asking us to deliberate what not choosing means. For example, it would be interesting to ask whether the thematic problem of not being able to choose a single topic (to choose the lover, vision, death, as exemplified in Fascicles 15 and 16)—or a single relation to any of these topics—is connected to the textual problem of not being able to choose among the variants. Here the undecidability in the content of the poems could be seen to have consequences for their form. In these fascicles choice is being thematized, but it is also being superadded and embodied in the poem's textual manifestations. Thus the question of choice seems not just thematized but also formalized, although by broken form. And since alternatives to words are not treated as other than those words, the existence of multiple variants may indicate how Dickinson might have regarded revision, as deflecting the necessity of choice; how she might have regarded revision in terms of amplification rather than of substitution, equivocation being played out in corollary thematic and formal terms.

Another issue raised by the fascicles is the way in which economy and gender are related to each other. As noted in the previous chapter, measurement is one of the ways in which Dickinson thinks of her project. She is asking: What is small and what is large, and how is the small unexpectedly potent? Dickinson may be raising these questions in a private space because there is no room to raise them in a public space. Transacted in this private space is a renegotiation of gender definitions as well as of poetic definitions. For not only are representations of women redefined in poems like "Title divine—is mine!" (P 1072) but perhaps also, albeit obliquely, is the representation of women poets, as in "I would not paint—a picture—" (P 505), where poetry and the speaker's relation to poetry are explicitly reconstrued. Since this poem redefines the relation of passivity and power, witnessing and creation, it also implicitly redefines whether the choice not to write poetry may be discovered—as in this poem—to be a subverted choice. I take such a subversion, in which choosing not to create is itself negated as a choice (since the poem that would not be written already *has* been) to be implicitly connected to the question of *who* can create (in the poem's last stanza, the question of who can write poetry), and, given the way in which poetry is shown to be received, also connected to the question of *how* poems may be written. Thus in "I would not paint—a picture—," . . . the poem that is almost unrecognized by its author may be the poem that is almost unrecognizable, at least according to the conventions of how poems may be written. Poems like P 505 may implicitly redefine the kind of poetry that women may write. "Women's poetry" could in fact be published in the 1860s. Periodicals are filled with it. Such poetry is explicitly what Dickinson is not writing.[3]

In addition, albeit put too generally: In the nineteenth century structures, and not only poetic structures, are subject to construction. Consider Poe's *Eureka,* for instance; Melville's last three novels; Thoreau's *A Week on the Concord and Merrimack Rivers;* and Poe's "The Philosophy of Poetic Composition," a document that theorizes how the lyric should be structured. In Whitman's and Dickinson's cases poetic structures lie outside of the province of conventional genres. In the American nineteenth century, moreover, the cultural and the intertextual come together because American ways of addressing the problem of poetic structure seem to depend on models of federation. Ostensibly discrete poetic entities are at once independent and united. Though such a political model would more evidently pertain to Whitman than to Dickinson, the vexed connection between autonomous structures and dependent structures is analogously visible in the fascicles. And although the relation of single poems to the plurality of other poems is a specific problem with which all poets must contend, Whitman and Dickinson deal with this problem in a particularly repetitive way. Both of them, albeit differently, write new poems by rewriting the old ones, and they formulate the relation between old and new, different and same, private and public, in terms of generic inventions that simultaneously isolate and unite entities. Hence Whitman's invention of poetic clusters, which are defined in that they are titled but amorphous, for the lyrics assigned to each cluster shift with successive editions and his reinvention of the so-called same poem. Hence Dickinson's fascicle struc-

---

[3]See, for example, Richard Sewall's Appendix IV, "Popular Poetry from the *Springfield Republican,* 1858–62" in vol. II of *The Life of Emily Dickinson* (New York: Farrar, Straus and Giroux, 1974), pp. 742–50. The sample of sentimental poems provided by Sewall is written by both men and women. But Dickinson would also have read anthologies like Rufus Griswold's 1840 *American Women Poets.* For a discussion of poets Dickinson would likely have read, see also Cheryl Walker, *The Nightingale's Burden: Women Poets and American Culture Before 1900* (Bloomington: Indiana University Press, 1982). Walker argues that, in addition to Helen Hunt Jackson and Elizabeth Barrett Browning, mentioned by Dickinson in her letters, Dickinson was probably acquainted with the poetry of Maria Gowan Brooks, Lydia Sigourney, Maria Lowell, Caroline Gilman, and Amelia Welby. She had surely seen copies of magazines like *Godey's Lady's Book.* Walker writes: "At the age of fourteen, [Dickinson] mocks her tendency to become 'poetical' . . . 'you know that is what young ladies aim to be now-a-days.' For the rest of her life, [Dickinson] toyed in her poems with that stock character, the poetess, craftily using the conventions of the role to serve her own purposes and then rewriting the part to suit herself" (p. 87).

The topic of "secret sorrow" was, Walker argues, a convention of women's poetry that Dickinson adopted and transformed. I would specify the transformation to which Walker alludes as follows: Dickinson *celebrated* sorrow when it defied hypocritical secrecy, as in "I like a look of Agony, / Because I know it's true—" (P 241). But celebrating the sorrow in Dickinson's poems is often a prelude to *contesting* the sorrow. (At the end of P 463, in which a speaker lives with the memory of a lover rather than with the lover, the summary personal assessment renders all but gratuitous the conventional theological one, claiming "That Life like This—is stopless— / Be Judgment—what it may—.") In these two ways—celebrating the sorrow and contesting the sorrow—the convention of women's poetry is unabashedly reversed.

tures, which seem alternative to wholly individuated lyric structures but are not in fact alternative.

Alternatives that are not exactly alternative can be viewed in the contents page of the deathbed edition of Whitman's *Leaves of Grass,* which provides titles for poems that lack them in the 1855 edition. Poems are in some cases differently titled in intermediate editions. Thus "Sun-Down Poem" of the 1856 or second edition becomes "Crossing Brooklyn Ferry" of the 1860 or third edition. "Repeated" poems are often reordered in successive editions. "There Was a Child Went Forth," the tenth poem of the 1855 edition, is ultimately placed in the cluster of poems titled *Autumn Rivulets,* even as poems in some editions (for instance, "By Blue Ontario's Shore") derive from the prose of other editions—in this case from the "Preface" to the 1855 edition, from which it takes more than sixty of its lines. Such equivocation about what a poetic entity "is," such reconstitution of the entity by virtue of its placement in a larger structure, so that the poem is not simply subordinated to other poems in the structure—in Whitman's clusters, in Dickinson's fascicles—but reformed as a different, dependent entity, is to be remarked upon. For by virtue of rearrangement the poem as delimited text is deprived of stable integrity.

The textual instability shared by Whitman and Dickinson—the way in which their poetic structures derive their elements simultaneously from variation and repetition, subordination and autonomy—is only one of many crucial features that draw the two poets together, despite the propensity of literary criticism to celebrate their differences. For instance, Whitman is understood to illustrate the inclusiveness of emotion, its embrace of everyone. Dickinson is understood to illustrate the exclusiveness of emotion, its singular choice of object and its pervasive rejections. In Sandra Gilbert's "The American Sexual Poetics of Walt Whitman and Emily Dickinson,"[4] characterizations like these are seen to typify the difference between "men's poetry" and "women's poetry," resulting even in the two poets' preferences for their respective genres. Yet the poetic features thus characterized as opposite are not in a most significant context opposite at all, because Whitman's fiction of nonexclusivity and Dickinson's of complete exclusivity equally exaggerate, albeit in different directions, sentiments that cannot possibly be either all-inclusive or all-exclusive. In this respect the two poets are alike. Each espouses an opposite fantasy of self-conversion: completely to exclude the world, completely to incorporate it. Moreover, the two poets similarly imagine that the redeterminations of the boundaries of a poem could be made analogous to the redetermination of the boundaries of a self. In Dickinson's case, such redeterminations revolve around impossible partializations—of the self, of the poem—employed to make visible something like identity or essence. In Whitman's case, such redeterminations revolve around impossible totalizations—of the self, of the poem—also employed to make visible something like identity or essence. Thus to see beyond the conventional construc-

---

[4] In *Reconstructing American Literary History*, ed. Sacvan Bercovitch (Cambridge, Mass.: Harvard University Press, 1986), pp. 123–54.

tion of the two poets is inevitably to observe that in each case similar choices appear to be made—and, consequently, structures to be respectively fractured and compounded—that "cannot" be real choices.

Finally, in one important sense, as Whitman does not choose—as the thematic principle of *Song of Myself* is one of inclusion, and the principle of successive editions is one of textual variation—so the identity of Whitman's texts, much like that of Dickinson's, must be understood in terms of those textual variants. Variants and variation are strategies for redefining the boundaries of a Whitmanian as well as of a Dickinsonian text. They seem strategies for making unresolvable the question of what lies outside the text. In Whitman's poetry, however, although unboundedness is thematized, although choices in the poems are explicitly declined, and although textual rearrangements of the ostensibly "same" poem seem continuously renegotiated, ultimately there is a terminus to the oscillations enacted by Whitman's successive editions of *Leaves of Grass*. For in the last of the editions overseen by Whitman, the borders of Whitman's texts, in some ways always fluid, in other ways are stabilized, even definitively fixed.

In distinction, Dickinson's texts remain permeable. [We] turn to the fascicle texts to consider questions of permeability in relation to questions of choice—as choice is formalized in the variants, as it is thematized in the fascicles, as it unfolds in other contexts in which something (a person, a desire, an ability, even a second poem) appears to be eschewed and excluded, even as that thing is discovered to be included and incorporated in, sometimes even intrinsic to, the entity from which it was deceptively set apart. [We must] consider, first, how we read the variants, proximate words that do not in fact displace each other; second, how we read poems that are proximate to each other; third, how we read connections among poems not proximate but in the same fascicle; and, fourth, how we must differently read single fascicles (16 and 20). . . . For the problems of reading and the problems of choice are in this poetry inseparable.

Emily Dickinson's Visible Language

Jerome McGann

The argument of my essay is straightforward.[1] I mean to unpack the deep truth of the following prescription, which you may take as my epigraph:

"Poems will be called letters and letters will be called poems."[2]

A dramatic shift of style divides the texts of fascicles 1–8 from the texts of all other fascicles (as well as all the so-called "sets" of poems, and most of Dickinson's loose poems as well). If, for example, we compare the first poem of fascicle 8 ("A Wounded deer leaps highest," J165) with the first of fascicle 9 ("What shall I do— it / Whimpers so," J186) the difference is clear. Whereas in the first text the linear metrical units correspond to their scriptural presentation, the second text skews this correspondence. Metrical lines are now distributed over two scriptural lines. So while the fascicle 9 poem is metrically a work of three quatrains (twelve lines altogether—if it were printed or written according to its normative metrical scheme), it is scripturally a much different work. It has nineteen lines, it isn't ordered in quatrains, and the metrical scheme is drastically altered from the metrical norm that we (as it were) *un*hear below Dickinson's visible language.

Susan Howe was the first person to recognize this scriptural change in the fascicles as a crucial event in the history of modern poetry. Emily Dickinson's importance as a poetic innovator, and perhaps even her true greatness, is marked by what might appear to be a mere shift in her handwriting or in her copying habits. In fact, the change represents something far more radical, far more significant.

At some point—I believe it might have been during the winter of 1861— Dickinson decided to use her textpage as a scene for dramatic interplays between a poetics of the eye and a poetics of the ear. Eventually she would elaborate a complex set of writing tactics from this elementary textual move. In a very real

Reprinted from *The Emily Dickinson Journal*, Vol. II, No. 2, 1993 by permission of the editors and the author.

[1]This paper requires two initial acknowledgements: first, to R. W. Franklin, whose edition of the *Manuscript Books of Emily Dickinson* has set Dickinson studies on a whole new footing; and second to the work of Susan Howe, whose poet's eye discerned the radical significance of what Franklin's editorial labors had implicitly revealed. My argument in this essay should be compared with the similar ideas developed so brilliantly by Paula Bennett in " 'By a Mouth that Cannot Speak': Spectral Presence in Emily Dickinson's Letters." *The Emily Dickinson Journal* Vol. I, No. 2, pp. 76–99.

[2]Susan Howe, *Sulfur* 28 (Spring 1991), 142.

sense, Modernism's subsequent experiments with its many "visible languages" are forecast in the textual ventures of Emily Dickinson.

From the beginning, however, Dickinson's editors have erased the evidence of these experiments. Johnson's now standard edition regularly elides Dickinson's irregularities. Dickinson's first editors did much the same thing, only they followed late nineteenth-century popular conventions of text presentation, whereas Johnson followed twentieth-century scholarly conventions. Besides, Todd and Higginson were well aware that they were changing her poems. They called it "creative editing." They thought the late nineteenth-century reader could not bear too much of Dickinson's poetic realities. By contrast, Johnson believed he was *un*doing those initial bowdlerizations, believed he was restoring the pristine originals in an equivalent bibliographical form. In this illusion his work obscured Dickinson's poetic practices perhaps even more deeply than those much maligned early editors.

It would not be difficult to generate an "interpretation" of fascicle 9's first poem that would take account of its textual irregularities. For example, if we simply restore the first line from what we have been led to read—"What shall I do—it whimpers so"—to what we actually have in the fascicle—"What shall I do—it," we realize that the lineation opens the text to several syntactic options—several "readings"—that the normalized line closes down. Similarly, it makes a great deal of difference if we read the text this way:

All day and night—with bark and start

or this way:

All day and night—with bark
And start

In this last case, Dickinson's scriptural moves call attention to the self-referential act of the poem. Its "subject" is Dickinson's dog Carlo, who is named in the final line of the poem: "Tell Carlo—He'll tell me!" But the third line of the first stanza emphasizes the metaphoric character of the ostensible subject:

This little Hound within the Heart[.]

The initial irregularities dramatize the poem's selfconsciousness, which is playing with its own textuality. Playing with Carlo is a poetic figure: that event in time has as it were a transcendental equivalent, which is literalized in Dickinson's text. Thus, lines two and five of the first stanza—the fragments "Whimpers so" and "And start"—comprise a kind of syntactic and metrical onomatopeia: not so much equivalents of the actual dog Carlo's whimpers and starts as the literal appearance of the poetical events, the life of the Hound within Dickinson's Heart, the visible acts of her artistic imagination.

What I am talking about here are Dickinson's experiments with a certain kind of what used to be called "free verse." These experiments emerge from an initial decision to forego a long-established convention governing the bibliographical presentation of poetry. The textual condition of almost all the poems copied in fascicles 1–8 represents Dickinson adhering to that convention: as she copies her poems out, she arranges the lines as they would be expected to appear in a printed book.[3] These texts are being copied to imitate, at their basic scriptural level, the formalities of print. Though handwritten, these are poems that have been imagined under a horizon of publication.

Permit me a digression before I turn to another—and finally a more important—aspect of Dickinson's textual condition. There is a long-standing debate among Dickinson scholars about whether or not she wanted to be published. Some say yes, some no, others see her as vacillating on the matter. Among the last group, many think that Dickinson finally abandoned the desire for publication in face of the puzzled "what?" that her writing so commonly provoked even among the small circle who read her things.

For myself, I prefer to approach this problem as an issue of writing rather than an issue of psychology. So I make a distinction between Dickinson's efforts to extend the circle of her readership and her reluctance to enter the marketplace of publication. If the question has to be put in psychological terms I should say this: while Dickinson wanted readers, and while she was even ambitious of fame as a poet, she rejected the traditional (early capitalist) institution for achieving those ends. I believe she made this rejection not because of some large cultural or political sense of the limits of the "auction" of publishing—though she was certainly aware of those limits. Rather, I think she rejected a market-model of publishing, with its medium of print, because she came to see how restrictive and conventional that medium had become. What Emily Dickinson was doing in her private writing between 1860 and her death would itself become a type of the formal options opened up by the publishing institutions that were soon to emerge in and through the Modernist movement.

Dickinson's innovations appear if we recall how this intense and reclusive woman made contact with others. It came by writing—more particularly, by writing letters. If we choose to communicate with written language, we may connect with others through the commerce of publication or through the intercourse of correspondence. Dickinson wrote a great many poems, and most of them were

---

[3]Susan Howe says that "Around fascicles #6–12 . . . [Dickinson] begins to break her lines a new way" (ibid., 152n). It is possible to be more precise. In fact, the first experimental moment comes in fascicle 1, poem no. 31 ["Summer for thee, grant I may be"]. Normatively a poem of two quatrains, it has a second quatrain of five lines, and the crucial word "Anemone" appears by itself, in the penultimate position. Fascicle 3 has one irregular text (in the second stanza of no. 11 ["I never told the buried gold"]). The next irregular text comes in fascicle 4, no. 136 ["Have you got a Brook in your / little heart"]: this poem is the first to make its scriptural irregularities a regular feature of the entire work, rather than an isolated scriptural moment. Fascicle 5 has two irregular texts, nos. 111 ["The Bee is not afraid of me"] and 70 [" 'Arcturus' is his other name"]. Fascicle 6 has one, poem no. 132 ["I bring an unaccustomed wine"]. In fascicle 7 there are two irregular texts, nos. 148 ["All overgrown by cunning moss"] and 61 ["Papa above"]. In fascicle 8 we find three irregular texts, nos. 174 ["At last to be identified"], 177 ["Ah! Necromancy Sweet!"], and 179 ["If I could bribe them by a rose"].

In fascicle 9 these testing moves toward a practise of regular irregularity overwhelm the entirety of the writing.

never included in letters—all those poems in the fascicles and the sets, for instance, which she kept in her desk. But from the moment she began copying fascicle 9, Dickinson clearly began to construct her poetry within writing conventions permitted and encouraged in the textuality of personal correspondence.

What a difference this makes to the writing appears dramatically in the following example. Here are two "copies" that Dickinson made of "the same" poem (J323: "As if I asked a common Alms"):

As if I asked a common alms,
And in my wondering hand,
A Stranger pressed a kingdom
And I bewildered stand—
As if I asked the Orient
Had it for me a morn?
And it should lift it's purple dikes
And flood me with the Dawn! [fascicle 1]

As if I asked a
common Alms,
And in my wondering
hand
A Stranger pressed
a Kingdom,
And I bewildered
 stand—
As if I asked the
 Orient
Had it for me
A Morn
And it should lift
it's purple Dikes
And shatter Me
with Dawn!
  [letter to Higginson, 7 June 1862][4]

The text in fascicle 1 is copied out according to the conventions of the medium of print. In the letter to Higginson, on the other hand, the poem is copied according to what Higginson himself called "the habit of freedom and the unconventional utterance of daring thoughts."[5] In truth, however, Dickinson's text in the letter is by no means "unconventional." Rather, it is a poetical text that exploits the writing resources—the conventions—of epistolary intercourse. So when Higginson speaks of her writing as "Wayward and unconventional in the last degree; defiant of form,

---

[4]The first text is taken from Franklin, p. 10. The second is letter 265 in Johnson's edition of *The Letters of Emily Dickinson* (Cambridge: Harvard UP, 1958).

[5]Quoted from *The Recognition of Emily Dickinson*, ed. Caesar R. Blake and Carlton F. Wells (Ann Arbor: U of Michigan Press, 1968), 10.

measure, rhyme, and even grammar" (ibid.), his judgment reflects his expectations about the appropriate "conventions" that should govern a poet's work.

Following Emerson, Higginson classified Dickinson's work as "The Poetry of the Portfolio": private writing "not meant for publication" (ibid., 3). This judgment seems to me exact if we understand the specific historicality of Higginson's remark; if we understand that in the late nineteenth-century "publication" only came when a poet followed certain textual conventions. These conventions—they are strictly bibliographical rather than more broadly formal—were so dominant that most poets and readers could not imagine poetry without them. (Tennyson and D. G. Rossetti, for example, both said that they could not really begin to see their own poetry until it was put into print!) Higginson's response to Dickinson's writing as "spasmodic" and "uncontrolled" reflects these habits of thought.

But the writing is not spasmodic or uncontrolled or defiant of form. It has instead chosen to draw its elementary rules of form by an analogy to the writing conventions of personal correspondence rather than to the conventions of the printed text.

Up to now Dickinson's editors, as well as the vast majority of her readers, have not understood this crucial formality of her work. The poem Dickinson sent to Higginson in her letter of 7 June 1862 is run into the text of the "prose." In Johnson, this scene of writing is bibliographically translated. For the poem, Johnson's edition of the *Letters* puts into print an equivalent of the text Dickinson wrote in fascicle 1. In the letter she rewrites her earlier text—the fascicle text Higginson hadn't seen—by following the options released through a scriptural and epistolary environment rather than a publishing and bibliographical one. No doubt Higginson would have approved the fascicle 1 text: after Dickinson's death, when he first saw the fascicles, he was surprised (he said) to find that so many of the poems "have *form* beyond most of those I have seen before." He says this because what he had "seen before"[6]—the poems she sent to him in her letters—were all organized scripturally rather than bibliographically.

The poem in this letter is particularly important because the letter famously addresses the issue of publication. "I smile when you suggest that I delay 'to publish'—that being foreign to my thought, as Firmament to Fin" (*Letters* II.408). Dickinson is not writing to ask Higginson for professional help or for schooling in formal proprieties. She is aware that she has undertaken an unusual approach to poetical writing. The question she wants to ask him is different: given the choice she has made, is her work "clear?"

The answer she received was "yes," as we know from the continuation of their correspondence. Higginson understood, and his understanding is measured as much by his admiration for the force of her writing as it is by his dismay at her incorrigible incorrectnesses. So far as Dickinson was concerned, that doubled understanding—Higginson's blindness and insight alike—proved equally important to her life as a writer.

---

[6]See Millicent Todd Bingham, *Ancestors' Brocades. The Literary Debut of Emily Dickinson* (New York: Harper and Brothers, 1945), 34.

Let me make one further comment on his famous letter. The text of "As if I asked a / common Alms" is introduced by a series of apparitionally "prose" texts. As so often in her letters, however, these passages run along evident metrical feet. Johnson's edition of the *Letters* assumes a sharp division between the formalities of verse and prose, so he prints the metrical prose margin-to-margin and the spatially disordered verse in "correct" metrical lines. But a typographical translation of this extraordinary text of Dickinson's might just as well reverse Johnson's method in order to reveal what Johnson's translation overrides: the metrical subtext of the prose, and the prosy surface of the verse. So instead of Johnson's margin-to-margin prose text we might print the following:

> You think my gait "spasmodic"—
> I am in danger—Sir—
> You think me "uncontrolled"—
> I have no Tribunal.
> Would you have time to be the "friend"
> You should think I need?
> I have a little shape—
> it would not crowd your Desk—
> nor make much Racket as the Mouse,
> that dents your Galleries—
> If I might bring you what I do—
> Not so frequent to trouble you—
> and ask you if I told it clear—
> 'twould be control to me—
> The Sailor cannot see the North—
> but knows the Needle can—
> The "hand you stretch me in the Dark,"
> I put mine in, and turn away—
> I have no Saxon now—
> As if I asked a
> common Alms, . . .

My translation is of course a travesty of Dickinson's text, because it turns the writing into doggerel by forcing one of its musical features into an excessively straightened form. It is exactly the loose "prose" arrangement of the words on the page that allows the language to transcend the metronome. I give the translation only because it throws into relief the innovative character of Dickinson's writing, and the crucial significance of her original scripted pages.

In editing Dickinson, the scripts must be faithfully followed, whether the visible language of the texts appears to us as "prose" or as "poetry." They must be followed because Dickinson's writing, particularly in the letters, continually erodes the distinction between those two ancient textual formalities. So if Johnson's edition of the *Letters* did right to follow Dickinson in presenting the above passage as prose, he did wrong when he departed from Dickinson in his textual presentation of the letter's "poem." By normalizing Dickinson's letter-poem, Johnson shows that he thinks about her poetry the way

Higginson was thinking at the end of the nineteenth century: he is thinking that when poetry is put into print, it must conform to certain received typographical conventions. But Dickinson's work is precisely characterized by her refusal to submit to those conventions and forms. By avoiding the auction of publication, along with its specialized and restricted norms for text presentation, Dickinson began to exploit new technical ranges for imaginative writing—quite literally, a whole new space/time continuum for the material texts of poetry.

When scriptural texts are not shaped to the fit model of printed texts, they free up the more formal expectations of the latter. In that freedom Dickinson discovered a world of surprising [sic] new poetical formalities. The final line of "What shall I do—it" exemplifies what Dickinson was discovering through her experiments with the scripted medium. Because the final line appears only when the page is turned, it comes upon one with a special kind of dramatic suddenness. Dickinson would later resort to that trick of style a number of times—not least memorably in the poem known as "September's Baccalaureate" (J1271; Franklin Set 15), where the final two lines (the final metrical unit) appear only when the page is turned. The point of the device is clear if we simply recall the closing passage:[7]

> That hints
> without assuming
> an Innuendo
> sear
> that makes the
> heart put up its
> fun
>   [and then on the verso]
> and turn
> Philosopher

This type of move has many variations: for example, in the poem commonly called "Pain—has an element of—Blank" (J650). Dickinson's poem is scripted very differently from the Johnson printed text:

> Pain—has an Element—
> of Blank—
> It cannot recollect
> When it began—or if
> there were
> A time when it was not—

---

[7]This example was first brought to my attention by Susan Howe, in a lecture she delivered at U of Virginia in 1991 on the texts of Dickinson.

Here the blank space of the page is made to serve the argument of the writing. As in the previous example, the medium of the text is not simply taken as a given, something to be worked *within*; the medium is part of the imagination's subject.

The same is true in this example from "Many a phrase has the English language" (J276; see illustration 1). When Dickinson's line literally "breaks" into its "bright Orthogra/phy," this is more than a trick of style. The whole poem is a conscious meditation on the nature of language—and not language in some general and abstract sense, but *language* as she received it through the formalities of her copy of Webster's American dictionary. The textual play with the word "Orthogra/phy" rhymes with the poem's many similar wordplays—for example, with the specific spelling she gives to that most American of birds, the "Whippowil." About that word and that bird, Dickinson's *Webster's* has much to say, not least in distinguishing the American bird from the English by drawing an important orthographic distinction between the English word ("whipoorwill") and the American ("whippowil"). The different words mark out different languages

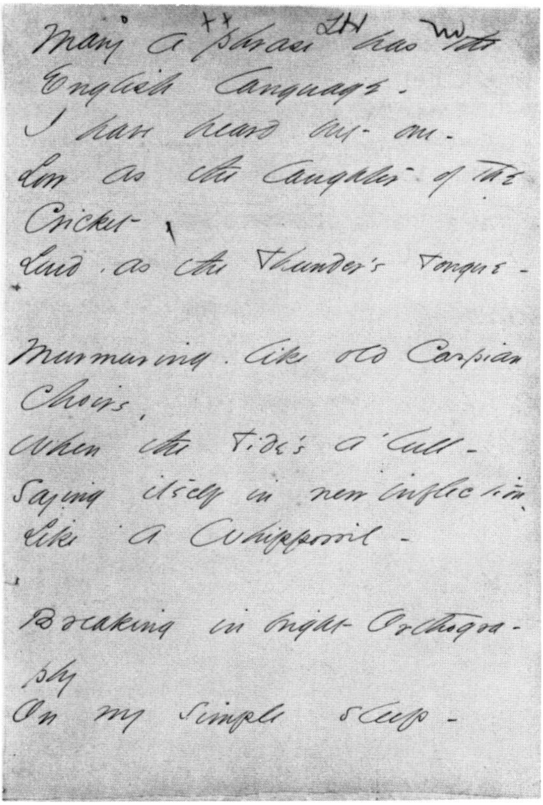

Illustration 1.

that comprise as well entirely different worlds: different worlds of speech patterns, different etymologies, different birds.

Even more complex are the many experiments Dickinson made with texts that had generated variant readings. The print convention she inherited would organize such variants at the foot of the page, in what scholars call an "apparatus." Many of her own poems exploit that convention, but Dickinson also habitually threw her "variants" all over the space of her pages—interlinearly, in both margins (sometimes written up and sometimes down), and within the area of "the line itself," the so-called "superior text." The whole space of the page was open to these add-on, sometimes freefloating, textual events.

Because she approaches this feature of her writing so freely, she is able to produce remarkable effects even when she appears to be following the manner of the received convention—as we can see in the poem "I took my Power in my Hand" [J540; Franklin Fascicle 30, p. 719]. In the fascicle the variants enter the text not as a simple set of alternate readings, but as a last unrhymed shard of verse—as it were the poem's final collapsing gloss on itself.

Equally remarkable are the numerous poems where textual invasions appear in the work's metrical units and spatial lineations. Dickinson will so imbed her "variant readings" as to derange the conventional expectations of text presentation. Here is a typical instance (this is J939; Franklin, p. 1014; see illustration 2). Part of this text's poetical effect comes from the reading contradictions it generates. The placement of the "variants" along the lines of the text forces the reader to make a

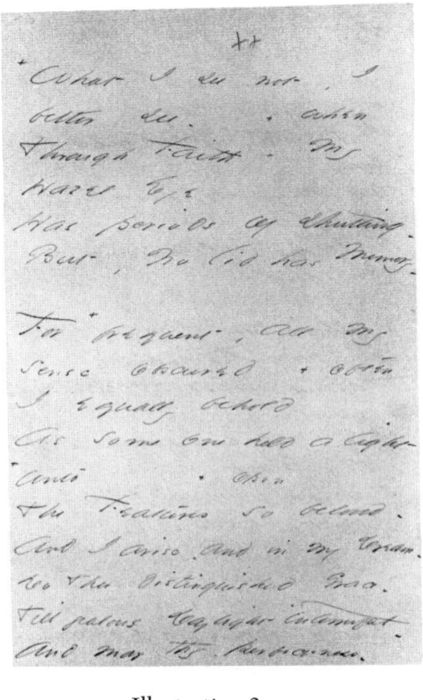

Illustration 2.

series of recursive shifts in the course of reading. We keep turning back to re-read and reconsider the textual options—to "better see" what the print conventions of poetry work to keep us from seeing.

Hidden in this text is a relatively conventional three-quatrain lyric with three simple variant readings (the words "when" [1.2] "often" [1.8], and "upon" [1.11]). That is the work Johnson reconstructed and called poem 939. J939 is one face, as it were, of Dickinson's textual work. In the original scripted text, it is a face turned slightly away because Dickinson's work has other faces she wishes to turn to meet the faces that she meets. We encounter those other faces because Dickinson has played a game with the layout of her scripts. The game is simple: generate certain expectations and then short-circuit them. A poem like this seems so remarkable because so little has been done to produce such complex effects. Its power comes from its elegance and simplicity.

One moral of this story is that Dickinson's entire corpus needs to be re-examined closely at its primary material level. I close with two brief examples of some of the key issues involved.

The first example is J319, a poem Dickinson sent in her famous letter of 15 April 1862 to Higginson. He published the poem in his essay on Dickinson in the Oct. 1891 *Atlantic Monthly,* and again in the 1891 "Second Series" of Dickinson's *Poems.* None of these texts print the poem Dickinson wrote out for Higginson in her letter (see Illustration 3). Besides, Dickinson constructed another text of this work—it is the opening poem of fascicle 14 (see illustration 4).

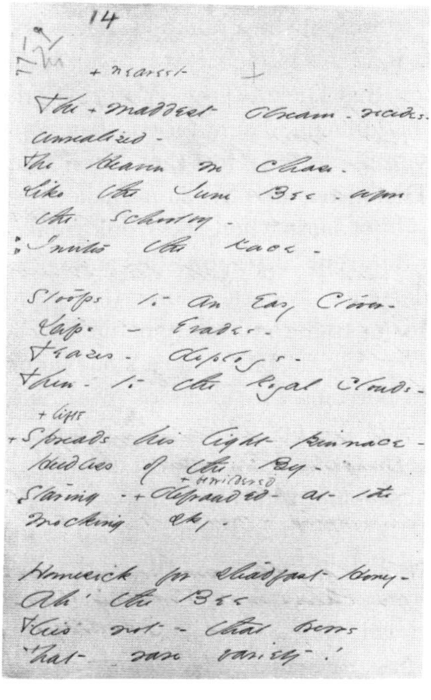

Illustration 3.

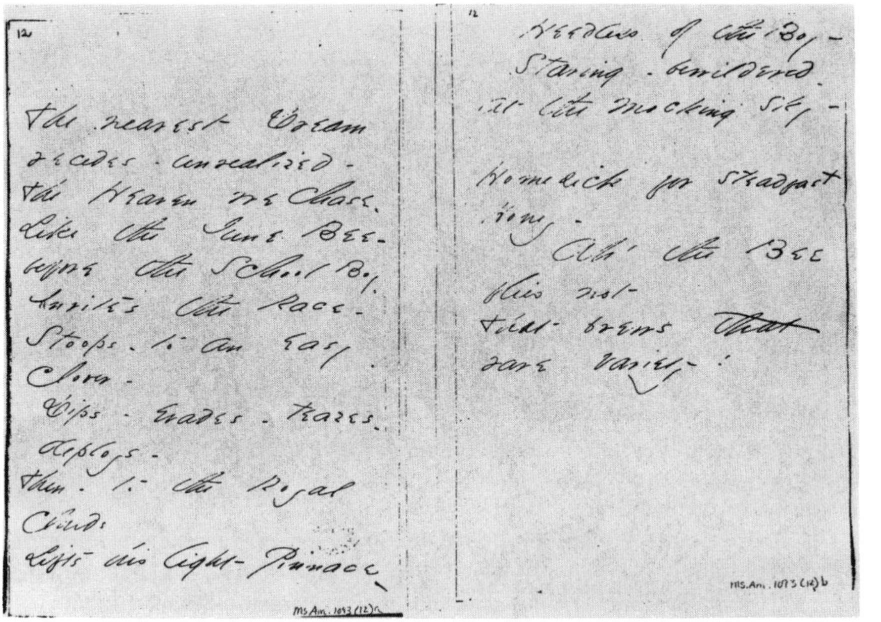
The nearest Dream
recedes - unrealized -
The Heaven we Chase,
Like the June Bee -
before the School Boy,
Invites the Race -
Stoops - to an easy
Clover -
Dips - evades - teases -
deploys -
Then - to the Royal
Clouds
Lifts his light - Pinnace
Heedless of the Boy -
Staring - bewildered -
at the mocking sky -
Homesick for steadfast
honey -
Ah! the Bee
flies not -
that brews That
rare variety - !

Illustration 4.

When Johnson came to edit the poems in 1955, this entire scene of transcription and publication was normalized. If we want to get a glimpse of Dickinson's actual writing, we have to look at the Franklin fascicle text of the poem Johnson numbered 319. Important as this fascicle text is, even it does not indicate the full range of textual freedoms that Dickinson was determined to have. As in so many other cases, Dickinson had imagined another construction for her work—the text she sent to Higginson with her letter, a text that differs markedly from the fascicle text. The fact is that Dickinson, like William Blake, regularly reimagined and reconstructed her texts—not least when she would make variant and particular copies of her poems for different correspondents and occasions.

These variations underscore my earlier point, that we must trace the structure of Dickinson's writing forms to her epistolary habits and conventions. The letter-form is absolutely central to Dickinson's poetry, since it encouraged her to seek an imaginative communion between the forms of prose and poetry. Poetical texts flow directly into (and out of) the epistolary text. Through the interplay of this new kind of textuality Dickinson brought a new birth of freedom to writing.

We find these generically anomalous texts throughout Dickinson's letters. Look at the letter to Samuel Bowles that contains the poem J691 ("Would you like Summer"; the letter is no. 229 in Johnson's edition). In this case (see illustration 5) the poem slips into the prose without any marginal signals that the textual rhythms are about to undergo a drastic shift. This is not a poem sent with a letter, or even *in* a letter; it is a poem that has grown up in a field of prose, like tares among the wheat.

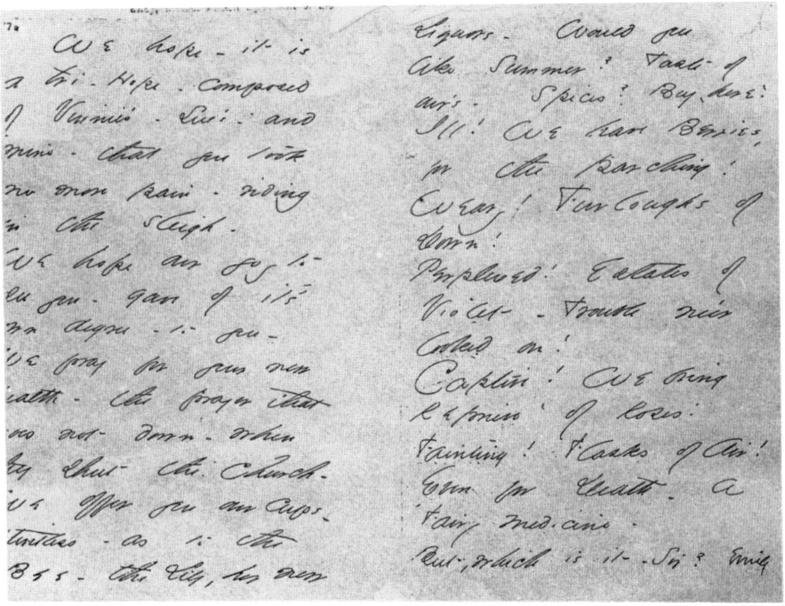
We hope - it is
a Tri - Hope. Composed
of Vinnie's - Sue's - and
mine - that you took
no more pain - riding
in the Sleigh.
We hope our joy to -
[illegible] you - gave of it's -
no degree - to you -
We pray for your new
health - the prayer that
goes not - down - when
they shut the Church -
We offer you our Cups -
Stintless - as to the
Bee - the Lily, her new
Liquors - Would you
like Summer? Taste of
ours. Spices? Buy, here!
Ill! We have Berries,
for the parching!
Weary! Furloughs of
Down!
Perplexed! Estates of
Violet - Trouble ne'er
looked on!
Captive! We bring
Reprieve of Roses!
Fainting! Flasks of Air!
Even for Death, a
Fairy medicine.
But, which is it - Sir? Emily

Illustration 5.

Johnson produced two texts of this "poem," one in the *Letters*, one in the *Poems*. Both misrepresent Dickinson's writing, misrepresent her *imagination.* Even the text of the letter normalizes what Dickinson actually wrote.

Johnson's editions of both the *Poems* and the *Letters* go astray, misrepresent Dickinson's writing, because they approach her work as if it aspired to a typographical existence. On the contrary, Dickinson's scripts cannot be read as if they were "printer's copy" or as if they were composed with an eye toward some state beyond their handcrafted textual condition. Her surviving manuscripts take themselves at face value, and they urge us to treat all her scriptural forms as potentially significant *at the aesthetic or expressive level.* Her poetry was not written *for* a print medium, even though it was written *in* an age of print. Indeed, her innovations work exactly because she manipulates the textual conventions of the age of print in which she lived, and against which she wrote. When we come to edit her work for bookish presentation, therefore, we must accomodate our typographical conventions to her work, and not the other way around.

Chronology of Important Dates

1828   Edward Dickinson of Amherst, Massachusetts, a Yale graduate and lawyer in his father's firm, marries Emily Norcross, daughter of a prosperous farmer from Monson, Massachusetts.

1829   Their son [William] Austin is born on April 16.

1830   Their daughter Emily [Elizabeth] Dickinson, the poet, is born on December 10 at 5 A.M.

1833   Lavinia [Norcross] Dickinson, Emily's sister and lifelong companion, is born on February 28.

1835   Emily and Austin attend Miss Nelson's primary school.

1837   Edward Dickinson begins a two-year term in the state legislature.

1838   Mrs. Dickinson takes Emily to the Congregational First Church of Christ. Emily attends reluctantly but with vigilant curiosity until about 1861. The Dickinsons move to a house on North Pleasant Street.

1840   Emily enters Amherst Academy in the Classics curriculum. Her studies include Latin, mathematics, and botany.

1844   Death of Emily's friend Sophia Holland. Grief-stricken, Emily is sent on a trip to Boston for recreation.

1847   Emily boards at Mary Lyon's Female Seminary, her studies including religion, Latin, Milton's *Paradise Lost* and Pope's *Essay on Man*, drawing, piano, and mathematics. She is one of 30 among 242 students who decline to profess themselves "saved" Christians.

1848   The Dickinsons withdraw her from Mary Lyon's because of delicate health.

1850   Emily sends a Valentine poem ("Awake ye muses nine" [*P*, 1]) to Elbridge Bowdoin and another poem with pasted illustrations to William Cowper Dickinson. Her circle of friends, male and female, now includes her future sister-in-law, Susan Huntington Gilbert.

1852   Dickinson's "Sic transit gloria mundi" (*P*, 3) appears in the *Springfield Daily Republican*, 20 February.

1853   Death of law clerk Benjamin Newton, whom she mourned as her first "tutor."

1855   Emily and Lavinia visit Washington, D.C. (where their father is serving in the House of Representatives) and Philadelphia (where Emily probably heard the sermons of the Reverend Charles Wadsworth).

          The Dickinsons move to the renovated Federal-style homestead on Main Street that will be the poet's home until her death.

1856   Austin Dickinson marries Susan Gilbert. They reside at the Evergreens villa, adjoining the Dickinson homestead. Still engaged in Amherst society, Emily wins second prize for rye and Indian bread at the Cattle Show. Samuel Bowles, editor of the *Springfield Daily Republican,* joins the Dickinson circle.

1858   Dickinson's years of greatest poetic productivity commence. She drafts her first letter to "Master" and begins assembling her poems into bound packets that her first editor, Mabel Loomis Todd, will call "fascicles." At Sue and Austin's, she spends sociable evenings in the company of guests such as Bowles and Kate Scott Anthon.

1860   The Reverend Charles Wadsworth visits Emily Dickinson.

1861   A crisis year of mysterious personal anguish. Dickinson composes two more "Master" letters and over 200 poems. "I taste a liquor never brewed" is published in the *Springfield Daily Republican,* 4 May.

               The Civil War begins on April 12. Ned Dickinson is born to Sue and Austin on 19 June.

1862   "Safe in their alabaster chambers" is published in the *Springfield Daily Republican* on 1 March. On 15 March, Charles Wadsworth accepts a ministry in San Francisco. On 9 April, Samuel Bowles departs for Europe. On 15 April, Dickinson writes her first letter to Thomas Wentworth Higginson asking for literary advice. She copies over 300 poems into the fascicles.

1864   Dickinson consults an eye specialist in Boston in February. From April to November, she stays with her Norcross cousins in Cambridge and undergoes treatment.

1865   She takes further treatment from April to October. End of the Civil War, in which Higginson is wounded.

1866   "A narrow fellow in the grass" is published on 14 February in the *Springfield Daily Republican,* Dickinson complaining that it was wrongly punctuated (See "Introduction"). She declines to visit Higginson in Boston, her reclusiveness becoming more habitual. The birth of a daughter, Martha, to Austin and Sue lessens the attention Sue is able to pay Emily and deepens Emily's need for other support.

1869   Dickinson writes Higginson that he has "saved [her] Life" but again refuses to visit him in Boston, saying that she no longer leaves her father's grounds.

1870   T. W. Higginson first visits Dickinson on 16 August. She has began to write fewer poems but maintains an extensive correspondence.

1874   Edward Dickinson dies on 16 June. Samuel Bowles, Dickinson's mainstay during her mourning, leaves for Europe.

1875   In June, Mrs. Dickinson is paralyzed. Dickinson helps to nurse her for seven years. Thomas Gilbert Dickinson is born to Sue and Austin on 1 August.

1876   Helen Hunt Jackson, poet and author of *Ramona,* visits Dickinson, urging her to publish.

1878   Samuel Bowles dies on 16 January.

Dickinson is courted by a friend of her father, Judge Otis Lord, with whom she engages in ardent correspondence but whom she refuses to marry.

"Success is counted sweetest" is published in *A Masque of Poets*.

1880   Charles Wadsworth pays her a second and final visit.

1881   Mabel Loomis Todd, wife of the Amherst College astronomer, and Emily Dickinson's future editor, is befriended by Austin and Sue.

1882   Dickinson's long relationship with Sue is strained to near rupture, we surmise by a few causes—among them Sue's caustic tongue, her rumored impatience with Emily's withdrawal and Emily's apparent approval of Austin's love affair with Mabel Todd (their trysts were conducted at Emily and Lavinia's home, and with the sisters' knowledge).

Charles Wadsworth dies on 1 April. Mrs. Dickinson dies on 14 November.

1883   Thomas Gilbert Dickinson dies on 5 October. Dickinson is prostrate with grief. Her letters offering consolation to Sue reestablish their never quite broken friendship.

1884   Otis Lord dies on 13 March. Dickinson collapses on 14 June from nervous strain.

1885   In November, Dickinson is bedridden with Bright's disease.

1886   Emily Dickinson dies around 6 P.M. on May 15 and is buried in the West Cemetery, Amherst, next to her parents.

1890   *Poems, First Series*, the texts "corrected" by Mabel Loomis Todd with T. W. Higginson, is published by Roberts Brothers, Boston.

1891   *Poems, Second Series*, is published.

1894   Publication of the *Letters*, edited by Mabel Loomis Todd.

1895   Death of Austin Dickinson.

1898   The Todds and Lavinia Dickinson go to court over a strip of land Austin promised to Mabel. In anger, Mabel abandons her work with the remaining Dickinson poems in her possession and the Dickinson corpus becomes permanently divided between Todd (Millicent Todd Bingham) and Dickinson (Martha Dickinson Bianchi) factions. Their daughters bring out rival editions of the poetry up until the 1940s, meddling with the texts.

1899   Death of Lavinia Dickinson.

1913   Death of Susan Dickinson.

1955   Publication of *The Poems of Emily Dickinson, Including Variant Readings Critically Compared with All Known Manuscripts*, edited by Thomas H. Johnson. The first scholarly text.

1958   Publication of *The Letters of Emily Dickinson*, edited by Johnson and Theodora Ward.

1971   28 August: the United States Postal Service issues an Emily Dickinson stamp, the second in its series "Famous American Authors."

1981   Publication of *The Manuscript Books of Emily Dickinson*, edited by R. W. Franklin.

Bibliography

Texts

Franklin, R. W., ed. *The Manuscript Books of Emily Dickinson*. 2 vols. Cambridge, Mass.: Harvard University Press, 1981.

Franklin, R. W., ed. *The Master Letters of Emily Dickinson*. Amherst, Mass.: Amherst College Press, 1986.

Franklin, R. W., ed. *The Poems of Emily Dickinson*. A variorum edition. Cambridge, Mass.: Harvard University Press, forthcoming.

Johnson, Thomas H., ed. *The Poems of Emily Dickinson*. 3 vols. Cambridge, Mass: Harvard University Press, 1955.

Johnson, Thomas H., and Ward, Theodora, eds. *The Letters of Emily Dickinson*. Cambridge, Mass.: Harvard University Press, 1958.

Biography

Bianchi, Martha Dickinson. *Emily Dickinson Face to Face: Unpublished Letters with Notes and Reminiscences*. Boston: Houghton Mifflin, 1932.

Bingham, Millicent Todd. *Ancestors' Brocades: The Literary Debut of Emily Dickinson*. New York: Harper & Brothers, 1945.

Johnson, Thomas H. *Emily Dickinson: An Interpretive Biography*. Cambridge, Mass.: Harvard University Press, 1955.

Leyda, Jay. *The Years and Hours of Emily Dickinson*. 2 vols. New Haven, Conn.: Yale University Press, 1960.

Longsworth, Polly. *The World of Emily Dickinson*. New York: W. W. Norton, 1990.

Sewall, Richard B. *The Life of Emily Dickinson*. New York: Farrar, Straus, and Giroux, 1974 and Cambridge, Mass.: Harvard University Press, 1994.

———. *The Lyman Letters: New Light on Emily Dickinson and Her Family*. Amherst, Mass.: University of Massachusetts Press, 1965.

Whicher, George F. *This Was a Poet, A Critical Biography of Emily Dickinson*. New York: Charles Scribner, 1938. Reprint ed. Hamden, Conn.: The Shoe String Press, 1980.

Wolff, Cynthia Griffin. *Emily Dickinson*. New York: Alfred A. Knopf, 1986.

Criticism

Note: Many works listed below include biographical interpretation.

Anderson, Charles R. *Emily Dickinson's Poetry: Stairway of Surprise.* New York: Holt, Rinehart & Winston, 1960.

Barker, Wendy. *Lunacy of Light: Emily Dickinson and the Experience of Metaphor.* Carbondale: Southern Illinois University Press, 1987.

Bennett, Paula. *Emily Dickinson: Woman Poet.* Iowa City: University of Iowa Press, 1991.

Blake, Caesar R., and Wells, Carlton F., eds. *The Recognition of Emily Dickinson.* Ann Arbor: University of Michigan Press, 1964.

Bloom, Harold, ed. *Emily Dickinson. Modern Critical Views.* New York: Chelsea House, 1985.

Buckingham, Willis J. *Emily Dickinson's Reception in the 1890s, A Documentary History.* Pittsburgh: University of Pittsburgh Press, 1989.

Cady, Edwin H., and Louis J. Budd, eds. *On Dickinson. The Best from* American Literature. Durham, N.C.: Duke University Press, 1990.

Cameron, Sharon. *Lyric Time: Dickinson and the Limits of Genre.* Baltimore: The Johns Hopkins University Press, 1979.

———. *Choosing Not Choosing. Dickinson's Fascicles.* Chicago: University of Chicago Press, 1992.

Capps, Jack L. *Emily Dickinson's Reading: 1836–1886.* Cambridge, Mass.: Harvard University Press, 1966.

Cody, John. *After Great Pain: The Inner Life of Emily Dickinson.* Cambridge, Mass.: Harvard University Press, 1971.

Dandurand, Karen. "Another Dickinson Poem Published in Her Lifetime," *American Literature* 54 (1982), 434–37.

———. "New Dickinson Civil War Publications," *American Literature* 56 (1984), 17–27.

Diehl, Joanne Feit. *Dickinson and the Romantic Imagination.* Princeton, N.J.: Princeton University Press, 1981.

Dobson, Joanne. *Dickinson and the Strategies of Reticence: The Woman Writer in Nineteenth Century America.* Bloomington: Indiana University Press, 1989.

———. " 'Compound Manner': Emily Dickinson and the Metaphysical Poets." In *On Dickinson.* Durham, N.C.: Duke University Press, 1990.

Eberwein, Jane Donahue. *Dickinson. Strategies of Limitation.* Amherst, Mass.: The University of Massachusetts Press, 1985.

Farr, Judith. "Emily Dickinson's 'Engulfing' Play: *Antony and Cleopatra*," *Tulsa Studies in Women's Literature* 9, no. 1 (Fall 1990), 231–50.

———. *The Passion of Emily Dickinson.* Cambridge, Mass.: Harvard University Press, 1992.

Ferlazzo, Paul J., ed. *Critical Essays on Emily Dickinson.* Boston: G.K. Hall and Co., 1984.

Franklin, R. W. *The Editing of Emily Dickinson: A Reconsideration.* Madison: University of Wisconsin Press, 1967.

———. "The Emily Dickinson Fascicles." *Studies in Bibliography* 36 (1983), 1–20.

Gelpi, Albert. *Emily Dickinson: The Mind of the Poet.* Cambridge, Mass.: Harvard University Press, 1966.

———. *The Tenth Muse.* Cambridge, Mass.: Harvard University Press, 1975.

Gilbert, Sandra M. and Susan Gubar. *The Madwoman in the Attic: The Woman Writer and the Nineteenth Century Literary Imagination.* New Haven, Conn.: Yale University Press, 1979.

Griffith, Clark. *The Long Shadow: Emily Dickinson's Tragic Poetry.* Princeton, N.J.: Princeton University Press, 1964.

Hagenbuchle, Roland. "Precision and Indeterminacy in Emily Dickinson's Poetry," *ESQ* 20, no. 2, (1974), 33–56.

Higgins, David. *Portrait of Emily Dickinson: The Poet and Her Prose.* New Brunswick, N.J.: Rutgers University Press, 1967.

Howe, Susan. *My Emily Dickinson.* Berkeley, Calif.: North Atlantic Books, 1985.

———. "Some Notes on Visual Intentionality in Emily Dickinson," *HOW(ever)* 3, no. 4 (1986), 11–13.

———. "These Flames and Generosities of the Heart: Emily Dickinson and the Illogic of Sumptuary Values," *Sulfur* 28 (Spring 1991), 134–55.

Juhasz, Suzanne. *"The Undiscovered Continent": Emily Dickinson and the Space of the Mind.* Bloomington: Indiana University Press, 1983.

———. Cristanne Miller, and Martha Nell Smith. *Comic Power in Emily Dickinson.* Austin: University of Texas Press, 1993.

———, ed. *Feminist Critics Read Emily Dickinson.* Bloomington: Indiana University Press, 1983.

Keller, Karl. *The Only Kangaroo among the Beauty: Emily Dickinson and America.* Baltimore: The Johns Hopkins University Press, 1979.

Lease, Benjamin. *Emily Dickinson's Readings of Men and Books.* New York: St. Martin's Press, 1990.

Lindberg-Seyersted, Brita. *The Voice of the Poet: Aspects of Style in the Poetry of Emily Dickinson.* Cambridge, Mass.: Harvard University Press, 1968.

Martin, Wendy. *An American Triptych: Anne Bradstreet, Emily Dickinson, Adrienne Rich.* Chapel Hill: University of North Carolina Press, 1984.

McGann, Jerome. *Black Riders. The Visible Language of Modernism.* "Introduction" (26–41). Princeton, N.J.: Princeton University Press, 1993.

McNeil, Helen. *Emily Dickinson.* New York: Pantheon-Virago, 1986.

Miller, Cristanne. *Emily Dickinson: A Poet's Grammar.* Cambridge, Mass.: Harvard University Press, 1987.

Monteiro, George, and Barton Levi St. Armand. "The Experienced Emblem: A Study of the Poetry of Emily Dickinson," *Prospects* 6 (1981), 186–280.

Mossberg, Barbara Antonina. *Emily Dickinson: When a Writer Is a Daughter.* Bloomington: Indiana University Press, 1983.

Mudge, Jean McClure. *Emily Dickinson and the Image of Home.* Amherst, Mass.: University of Massachusetts Press, 1975.

Patterson, Rebecca. *Emily Dickinson's Imagery,* ed. Margaret Freeman. Amherst: University of Massachusetts Press, 1979.

———. *The Riddle of Emily Dickinson.* Boston: Houghton Mifflin, 1951.

Paulin, Tom. "Emily Dickinson." In *Minotaur. Poetry and the Nation State.* Cambridge, Mass.: Harvard University Press, 1992.

Pollak, Vivian R. *Dickinson: The Anxiety of Gender.* Ithaca, N.Y.: Cornell University Press, 1984.

Porter, David T. *The Art of Emily Dickinson's Early Poetry.* Cambridge, Mass.: Harvard University Press, 1966.

———. *Dickinson: The Modern Idiom.* Cambridge, Mass.: Harvard University Press, 1981.

St. Armand, Barton Levi. *Emily Dickinson and Her Culture: The Soul's Society.* Cambridge: Cambridge University Press, 1984.

Sewall, Richard B., ed. *Emily Dickinson: A Collection of Critical Essays*. Englewood Cliffs, N.J.: Prentice-Hall, 1963.

Sherwood, William Robert. *Circumference and Circumstance: Stages in the Mind and Art of Emily Dickinson*. New York: Columbia University Press, 1968.

Shurr, William R., ed. *New Poems of Emily Dickinson*. Chapel Hill: University of North Carolina Press, 1993.

Small, Judy Jo. *Positive as Sound: Emily Dickinson's Rhyme*. Athens: University of Georgia Press, 1990.

Smith, Martha Nell. *Rowing in Eden: Rereading Emily Dickinson*. Austin: University of Texas Press, 1992.

Stonum, Gary Lee. *The Dickinson Sublime*. Madison: University of Wisconsin Press, 1993.

Weisbuch, Robert. *Emily Dickinson's Poetry*. Chicago: University of Chicago Press, 1975.

Wolosky, Shira. *Emily Dickinson: A Voice of War*. New Haven, Conn.: Yale University Press, 1984.

Journals

There are two journals devoted exclusively to Dickinson scholarship: *The Emily Dickinson Journal* (ISSN 1059-6879) and *Dickinson Studies* (ISSN 0164-1492). The *Bulletin* of the Emily Dickinson International Society (ISSN 1055-3932) is a source of current information about Dickinson scholarship and conferences.

Notes on Contributors

JOAN BURBICK is Professor of English and American Studies at Washington State University. She is the author of *Thoreau's Alternative History: Changing Perspectives on Nature, Culture and Language*, and *Healing the Republic: The Language of Health and Culture of Nationalism in Nineteenth-Century America*.

SHARON CAMERON has written *Lyric Time: Dickinson and the Limits of Genre*, *The Corporeal Self: Allegories of the Body in Melville and Hawthorne*, *Thinking in Henry James* and *Choosing not Choosing*. She is Professor of English at The Johns Hopkins University.

KAMILLA DENMAN is a Ph.D. candidate in English and American literature at Harvard University and has published articles on Christina Rossetti and Jean-Jacques Rousseau.

JANE DONAHUE EBERWEIN is Professor of English and Coordinator of American Studies at Oakland University. She is the author of *Dickinson: Strategies of Limitation*; the editor of *Early American Poetry: Bradstreet, Taylor, Dwight, Freneau, and Bryant*; and has published articles on poets from Anne Bradstreet to Robert Frost.

JUDITH FARR is Professor of English at Georgetown University. Her book *The Passion of Emily Dickinson* was cited as a Notable Book of 1992 by *The New York Times*. She has also published *The Life and Art of Elinor Wylie*; essays on Dickinson, D. H. Lawrence, the Elizabethan, Victorian and modern poets, and 19th- and 20th-century literature and painting; as well as her own poetry and fiction.

ANTHONY HECHT has written *The Hard Hours, The Venetian Vespers, The Transparent Man*, and other volumes of poetry for which he has received the Pulitzer Prize, the Bollingen Prize, the Prix de Rome, and many other honors. He is also author of two critical studies, *Obbligati* and *The Hidden Law, The Poetry of W. H. Auden*.

SANDRA M. GILBERT is Professor of English at the University of California, Davis. She is the author of several collections of verse including *Emily's Bread*. She is co-author with Susan Gubar of *The Madwoman in the Attic: The Woman Writer and the Nineteenth Century Literary Tradition*, *The Norton Anthology of Literature by Women*, and other books.

SUZANNE JUHASZ is Professor of English at the University of Colorado, Boulder, and editor of *The Emily Dickinson Journal*. Her books include *The Undiscovered Continent: Emily Dickinson and the Space of the Mind*, *Comic Power in Emily Dickinson* (with Cristanne Miller and Martha Nell Smith) and *Reading from the Heart: Women, Literature, and the Search for True Love*.

JEROME MCGANN is the John Stewart Bryan Professor of English at the University of Virginia. Among his works are *Black Riders, The Visible Language of Modernism* and *The New Oxford Book of Romantic Period Verse*. His major current project is *The Complete Writings and Pictures of Dante Gabriel Rossetti: A Hypermedia Research Archive*.

CRISTANNE MILLER is Professor of English at Pomona College and author of *Emily Dickinson: A Poet's Grammar* and co-author (with Suzanne Juhasz and Martha Nell Smith) of *Comic Power in Emily Dickinson*. Her forthcoming book is *Questions of Authority: The Example of Marianne Moore*.

DOROTHY HUFF OBERHAUS, Professor of English at Mercy College, Dobbs Ferry, New York, has written *Emily Dickinson's Fascicles: Method and Meaning*. She has published many articles on Dickinson and is now working on a second book about the fascicles.

VIVIAN R. POLLAK, author of *Dickinson: The Anxiety of Gender*, is Professor of English at the University of Washington and Adjunct Professor of Women's Studies. She has edited *A Poet's Parents: The Courtship Letters of Emily Norcross and Edward Dickinson* and *New Essays on Henry James's* Daisy Miller *and* The Turn of the Screw.

DAVID PORTER is Professor of English at the University of Massachusetts (Amherst). He has written *The Art of Emily Dickinson's Early Poetry, Emerson and Literary Change*, and *Dickinson, The Modern Idiom*.

RICHARD B. SEWALL, Professor of English Emeritus at Yale University, is author of *The Life of Emily Dickinson*, for which he won the National Book Award (1974), and of other publications including *The Lyman Letters* and *A Vision of Tragedy*.

JUDY JO SMALL is Associate Professor of English at North Carolina State University. She has written *Positive as Sound: Emily Dickinson's Rhyme* and *A Reader's Guide to the Short Stories of Sherwood Anderson*.

MARTHA NELL SMITH, who teaches at the University of Maryland, is the author of *Rowing in Eden: Rereading Emily Dickinson* and coauthor (with Suzanne Juhasz and Cristanne Miller) of *Comic Power in Emily Dickinson*. She and Ellen Louise Hart are co-editing *The Book of Susan and Emily Dickinson*, a volume of correspondence.

BARTON LEVI ST. ARMAND, Professor of English at Brown University, has written *Emily Dickinson and Her Culture* (1984) and numerous articles on Dickinson, Hawthorne, Emerson, and James, as well as two monographs on H. P. Lovecraft.

RICHARD WILBUR's volumes of poetry include *The Beautiful Changes, Things of This World*, and *New and Collected Poems*. He collaborated with Lillian Hellman on the comic opera *Candide*, and has translated Voltaire, Racine, and Moliere. His honors include the Pulitzer Prize for Poetry (twice), the Bollingen and Bollingen Translation prizes, and the National Book Award. *Responses* is a collection of his critical essays.